gp

De Lange Rak (the Long Reach),

a sailing course on the Hudson river named in 1609. The view is from *Kromme Elleboog* (Crooked Elbow), a point at the north end of the reach, looking south toward *Juffrouw's Hoeck* (the Madam's Point) on the west shore, beyond which and out of sight is *de Dans Kammer* (the Dance Chamber), a point at the south end of the reach.

DUTCH HOUSES

IN THE HUDSON VALLEY

BEFORE 1776

BY

HELEN WILKINSON REYNOLDS

✤

WITH AN INTRODUCTION BY

FRANKLIN D. ROOSEVELT

PHOTOGRAPHY BY

MARGARET DE M. BROWN

———

PREPARED UNDER THE AUSPICES OF

THE HOLLAND SOCIETY OF NEW YORK

Dover Publications, Inc., New York

THE HOLLAND SOCIETY
OF NEW YORK

Special Committee on

DUTCH HOUSES IN THE HUDSON VALLEY BEFORE 1776

FRANKLIN D. ROOSEVELT

CHAIRMAN

J. WILSON POUCHER, M. D.   WALTER L. SUYDAM

CORNELIUS G. VERMEULE   EDWARD DE WITT

DE WITT VAN BUSKIRK

Ex Officio

The Officers of the Holland Society of New York

JOHN E. VAN NOSTRAND, *President*

WALTER M. MESEROLE, *Secretary*

CHARLES M. DUTCHER, *Treasurer*

This Dover edition, first published in 1965, is an unabridged and unaltered republication of the work first published by Payson and Clarke, Ltd., for the Holland Society of New York in 1929. The map showing the Dutch Settlement of the Hudson River Valley, reproduced on pages 468-469 of this edition, is a reduced version of the large map which was folded and inserted in a pocket on the inside back cover of the original edition.

International Standard Book Number: 0-486-21469-9
Library of Congress Catalog Card Number: 65-26075

Manufactured in the United States of America
Dover Publications, Inc.
180 Varick Street
New York, N.Y. 10014

INTRODUCTION

T HE GENESIS of my interest in *Dutch Houses in the Hudson Valley before 1776* lies in the destruction of a delightful old house in Dutchess County, New York, when I was a small boy; for, many years later, in searching vainly for some photograph or drawing of that house, I came to realize that such dwellings of the colonial period in New York as had stood until the twentieth century were fast disappearing before the march of modern civilization and that soon most of them would be gone.

In giving some slight assistance to Miss Reynolds in the preparation of this book I have repeatedly been led to wish that the work on it might have been done fifty years ago and I am certain that in the passage of another fifty years even the record here presented would be impossible to secure. Such material as remains today has been carefully studied in behalf of this volume for the Holland Society and its friends, and many early houses which, hitherto, have never been described are now placed on record permanently.

That which has interested me in this survey even more than the collection of architectural data has been the information as to the manners and customs of the settlers of the valley of the Hudson which has been afforded by an examination of the houses the people lived in. We are prone to think of our forbears as living ideal lives of rural comfort in large houses of many rooms, with high ceilings and abundantly furnished, but one fact that stands out clearly in the text and in the illustrations of this book is that the mode of life of the first settlers of New Netherland and of their immediate descendants was extremely simple, a statement which is true not only of the smaller landowners but of many of the patentees of large grants. From high to low their lives were the lives of pioneers, lives of hardship, of privation and often of danger. Roads were few and rough, household belongings modest, and the dwelling that contained more than four rooms was an exception.

I have been impressed also by a thought that comes from consideration of the sites of these houses. In the choice of their locations the houses seem to represent a point of view on the part of their builders unlike that held in some other parts of the country, one with less of the community and village influence that is evident in

New England, and more of individual independence; for so often these houses of the Hudson valley are found in cosy places, back from the highway, down below a hill, far from a neighbor, snuggling as it were into a perfect landscape-setting and happy in their isolation.

In these days of good roads, of motors and, soon, of common travel by air, the valley of the Hudson river is becoming more and more accessible to the vast population of the cities. Localities which, a generation ago, were wholly agricultural sections, are today suburban, and thousands now flock to the country-side in summer where dozens went a few years since. It is my hope that *Dutch Houses in the Hudson Valley before 1776* will give to many the privilege of visiting what is left, architecturally, of our early civilization before it is too late. I hope too that through its pages its readers will be able to visualize more clearly the actual living conditions of the men and women who were the founders of the State of New York.

FRANKLIN D. ROOSEVELT.

HYDE PARK

DUTCHESS COUNTY

1928

CONTENTS

ILLUSTRATIONS

ILLUSTRATIONS

WESTCHESTER COUNTY

DUTCHESS COUNTY

ILLUSTRATIONS

WROUGHT-IRON WEATHER-VANE

FROM THE HOUSE OF

ARIAANTJE COEYMANS

IN EXPLANATION

A BOOK on pre-Revolutionary Dutch houses in the region of the Hudson river might reasonably be assumed by a prospective reader to be, primarily, a work on architecture, limited to houses built in a style peculiar to the Dutch and also limited to houses occupied only by families of Dutch descent. But those who turn these pages with that anticipation will find little or no discussion of technical architecture and it will soon appear that the standard for determining what should qualify a house to be classed as Dutch has been set up by circumstances as the product of particular conditions.

The key to an understanding of the point of view from which this volume has been prepared is the word archaeology, a term which covers many sciences and provides varied sources of information upon which to draw for a knowledge of how men lived at a certain place and time. Any building for man's habitation is essentially archaeological in value, whether built in the first century or the twentieth, and rightly to apprehend the significance of houses it is necessary to discard the popular notion that greater age confers superiority upon one house over another. Chronology is essential. Chronology is interesting. But chronology is a framework into which to fit facts, and facts are valuable for their meaning. Thus houses are significant in so far as they reveal the living conditions of a period and the capacity of the people who occupied them. They are a record of human society and of the peculiar genius of a given community.

It was therefore with the archaeological principle as a guide that the preparation of this book was undertaken and here, at the opening of the narrative, I would record the gratitude I feel to my colleague, Miss Margaret De Motte Brown, for obtaining for me with her camera not merely photographs of buildings but a record of an idea. That Miss Brown succeeded in registering the conception I had formed of the subject in hand was witnessed to when I showed advance proofs of her plates to an artist-friend, whose medium is the brush, and who, as she looked at the pictures, exclaimed spontaneously: " These houses are folklore! They are a song of the soil. They spring from the soil and they are an expression of the life of the people."

In former times an expression of the life of the people was a thing little reckoned with by historians. The study of history was the study of the apex of the social pyramid, and kings and kingdoms, campaigns and commanders filled the printed page. But kings and kingdoms, campaigns and commanders are effects, not causes. Causes lie deep down at the base of the pyramid, imbedded in the common life of all the people, and include such things as climate and topography; food-supplies; routes of travel and means of transportation; trade and economics; language and literature; religion and—yes—psychology, which is just human nature. The modern conception of society begins with the mass of humans and works up through the simpler aspects of their lives to the full flower of event and social development. At the present time history is not being written in large volumes, general in character. Students of history are chiefly concerned today with specialized research, by which method a single worker makes a single field his own and seeks out and records the facts it yields. To some historian yet to come is being left the task of gathering up the results of many particular studies and with that rich fruitage creating a comprehensive work. In this connection this monograph on houses in the Hudson valley is intended as a contribution to the fuller story of life beside the great river that some day will be written.

In these pages will be found mention of some houses which were occupied by persons whose names are well known and mention of some others where events of importance have taken place. But the persons and the events were not the primary reasons for recording the houses. The first object in preparing the book has been to learn what sort of house was built by the majority of Dutch families in the region of the Hudson river before 1776 and, by the establishment of that Dutch average, there has been afforded the by-product of the establishment of a general average; for the fact has been revealed that the people of the Hudson valley, of whatever European extraction: Dutch, English, French, Teutonic, Scandinavian,—all built alike.

This latter statement is based upon a literal field-survey. The territory examined consists of the portions of the original river-counties which were settled by Dutch families before 1776. Albany County, as at first outlined, included the present counties of Columbia, Rensselaer, Greene and Schenectady (set off from Albany in 1786, 1791, 1800 and 1809, respectively), and the area now represented by those five counties is treated in these pages as a unit. Ulster County is a second unit, West-chester a third, Dutchess a fourth. Omission is made of Orange because its settlement was preponderantly English and Scotch-Irish and Putnam is omitted because it held an overflow from New England; while Rockland County belongs to northern New Jersey in its topographical features, its family relationships and the style of architecture found in it.

For convenience, without thought of precedence, the four units outlined above,—Albany, Ulster, Westchester and Dutchess,—are presented in this volume in the order named. They are separated from each other by inherent differences but overlap in many similarities. Each makes its peculiar contribution to the subject-matter of the book, a contribution that must be studied on its merits and not in the spirit of local pride, which would place the record of one locality in competition with that of another.

The field-survey of the counties selected was made in 1925. It involved a thorough exploration of the interior of the several counties by motor and meant the

4

finding of old road-courses, back roads and by-roads, where changes of all sorts come slowly. It meant fording streams; sinking in the mud of obscure farm-lanes; approaching tentatively the farmer's dog (of unknown disposition); gaining the friendship of the farmer's wife and her permission to go over her house from cellar to attic; observing human nature; stumbling on life-stories, dramatic enough for any play or novel, and learning facts in the history and condition of the native element of the population. The motoring occasioned could not have been accomplished so exhaustively as it was had it not been for the cooperation of Mrs. Frank H. Van Houten of Beacon-on-Hudson and Miss May L. Reynolds and Mrs. George B. Waterman of Poughkeepsie, whose interest and whose cars made possible trips that a woman alone could not have taken. Hospitality accorded in outstanding measure was received from Mr. and Mrs. William Ten Broeck Mynderse of *Holland House*, Scotia, New York; from Mr. and Mrs. Edward W. Rankin of *Cherry Hill*, Albany; and at *Fair Lawn*, Greenbush Heights, the home of Mrs. J. Chester Chamberlain and her sisters, Mrs. Frank S. Fielder and Miss Alice Irwin.

In the course of the field-survey information accumulated regarding a large number of houses and it became a question which should be listed in this volume. The conclusion was reached that for a work produced under the auspices of the Holland Society the first requisite was to show where the forbears of the members of the society had lived and the rule for admission to the organization was taken as a general guide in the selection of material. Eligibility to membership in the Holland Society consists of descent in the male line from an ancestor who was a citizen of New Netherland before 1675,—a broad gauge, which covers the cosmopolitan population of the period of Dutch sovereignty. The final transfer of sovereignty from the Dutch to the English took place in 1674 by the Treaty of Westminster, up to which time immigration into the colony had been made up of representatives of all the more important races and nationalities of northern and central Europe, and it follows that the members of the Holland Society derive descent from a variety of sources. Under this definition of a Dutch house inclusion has been made of some houses belonging to families that come within the eligibility rule of the society but which were not Dutch in origin. Hence, in compiling a list of houses for record it became necessary to judge each house by itself and to decide in individual instances whether the item came within the scope of the work. The houses finally presented have been chosen as providing a general and a nearly accurate idea of what average domestic architecture was like along the Hudson before the Revolution.

Rightly to apprehend the spirit of the field-survey, as well as the results from it, it is necessary for the reader to love truth first of all. For truth it is that the average home of the seventeenth and eighteenth centuries was not luxurious according to present standards and it is a false pride that imputes now to ancestral residences a degree of elegance which existed only in exceptional cases. Much has been written

5

of manor-houses which will not bear analysis. Real manor-houses were few along the Hudson and not all of them were either large or handsome. Many houses loosely referred to in later years as manor-houses were actually not manor-houses at all and the incorrect use of the term has only served to expose arrogance or ignorance. Mansion is another word often inaccurately used. As legal phraseology in deeds it means the house in which the owner lives on his land. But to the layman it is apt to signify a large and handsome dwelling. In the latter sense there were a few note-worthy structures in the river-counties before the Revolution. The house of Frederick Van Cortlandt at Lower Yonkers; the Philipse house at Yonkers; *Clermont*, the home of the Livingstons in Columbia County; the Van Rensselaer manor-house of 1765 at Watervliet; *The Pastures*, Philip Schuyler's house at Albany; Hendrick Cuyler's house at *Greenen Bosch*;—these, all, might be called mansions but they bore to the average house of their day the relation that was borne in the nineteenth century by the French chateaus on Fifth Avenue to the comfortable, detached, one-family houses of the smaller cities and the country. Just as the chateaus in New York were American in the sense that they expressed the desire of American citizens for a handsome house, to be paid for handsomely by American money, so the Georgian English homes of the Hudson valley in the eighteenth century were imported architecture and ex-pressed the prosperity and sophistication attained in a generation several degrees removed from the pioneer.

The average house of the period before the Revolution was, however, more nearly the result of the actual time and place of its erection, and in the last analysis the severity of the winters in the Hudson valley and the forms of land-tenure that existed there were the influences that governed building. How far back the archi-tectural beginnings of the average house could be traced on the Continent or in England is a matter for an architectural expert to determine. The function of the field-survey has been to observe and record facts within a fixed territory and to specialists in various lines is left the task of correlating the results of the survey with other sets of facts.

Furthermore, the spirit of the survey has been that of the humanities, not of social discrimination. It requires but little reflection to realize that in the period under consideration the man of prominence in the community was subjected to the same conditions as his less wellknown neighbor in regard to heat and cold, water, light and transportation. Open fires served all, richer and poorer alike, until the stoves of the nineteenth century arrived. Storage of ice is a modern custom. Every house was dependent upon spring or well or rain-barrel for its supply of water and there were no pipes for the water to flow through. Candles were the brightest artificial light. The bad roads jolted distinguished persons as roughly as those of lesser station. Actual physical suffering resulted for all people, in all walks of life, from these causes. In the one matter of the misery that came in winter with only open log-fires to supply heat a vivid picture is drawn in *Grandmother Tyler's Book,* a volume of personal recollections lately published, which was written in New England but which affords for New Netherland an equally forceful first-hand description of the horrors endured from the cold.

Such differences as are found in the average houses of the period before the Revolution usually occur in dimension or finish. Some houses were a trifle longer or deeper than others. Some had either more wood trim or trim more elaborate in detail. But in selection of materials, method of construction and in floor-plan whole communities followed the same customs. As regards the size of houses it should be noted that houses were frequently added to, not only once but several times. This is more particularly true of the houses built of stone, as the masonry and the architectural style both lent themselves to a continuous expansion of the original unit on much the same principle as that of the sectional bookcase. It is true also that, while the eighteenth century saw structural additions made to houses, the nineteenth witnessed alterations of detail; interior partitions were inserted or removed, new porches and blinds were given the exterior and up-to-date hardware and window-glass were procured.

The additions and alterations made to dwellings frequently destroyed their typical and pictorial quality and careful analysis must be made in many instances to show what is now left of the seventeenth and eighteenth centuries. Two conspicuous examples of houses that are misleading are the Van Vechten house at Catskill (plate 53) and the Du Bois house at New Paltz (page 198). Across the front of the Van Vechten house are iron figures: 1 6 9 0, which were placed there in recent years. But while the foundations and the walls of the first story of the house may warrant the ascribed date, the walls of the second story bear a stone marked: 1 7 5 0, and the wood trim of the exterior is nineteenth century work. The Du Bois house bears iron figures: 1 7 0 5, but about 1835 the house was completely built over and, in this case also, only the foundation and the lower portion of the walls can be reckoned as from 1705. In outline and in proportion and in finish neither of these houses is characteristic of the date associated with it.

Beside a field-survey for ascertaining physical facts a survey by correspondence and by research in libraries has been made to secure data regarding the history of the houses selected for record. In correspondence I have been given cooperation by more persons than it would be possible to name. Without exception, a statement of the purpose of the request for information has evoked cordial response, and I only regret that limited space forbids my citing individually the many friends, old and new, to whom my gratitude goes out in proportion to their kindness. But, in particular, my thanks are offered in fullest measure to the archivist of the state of New York, Mr. A. J. F. van Laer. For all questions relating to official documents, to the colony of Rensselaerswyck and to the language and customs of the Dutch I have relied upon Mr. van Laer's rare erudition and always, unfailingly, he has stood ready to give me the benefit of his wide scholarship. Access to the library of the New York Historical Society, to the Thompson Memorial Library, Vassar College, and to the Adriance Memorial Library, Poughkeepsie, has been of untold assistance in the historical survey and to those institutions I acknowledge with appreciation the courtesies received from them.

Finally, to Mr. Franklin D. Roosevelt and to Dr. J. Wilson Poucher of the book-committee of the Holland Society I would say that the moral support and sympathetic interest they have extended to the preparation of this volume will always be recalled by me as one of my happiest experiences.

HELEN WILKINSON REYNOLDS.

POUGHKEEPSIE

NEW YORK

1928

DUTCH HOUSES
IN THE HUDSON VALLEY
BEFORE 1776

HOUSE OF ARIAANTJE
COEYMANS, AS BUILT
EARLY IN THE EIGH-
TEENTH CENTURY

DUTCH HOUSES

IN THE HUDSON VALLEY BEFORE 1776

Background

THE FIRST white men who visited the Hudson river, the adventurer-navigators, who were seeking a trade-route to the Orient, and the traders (seeking furs), who quickly followed the explorers, divided the river into sailing courses and gave names to the successive reaches. The Long Reach, known to the Dutch as *Lange Rak*, is a straight channel, ten miles in length, which extends from the vicinity of the present Hyde Park southward to New Hamburgh. At its northern end is a bend in the river, called in the seventeenth century *Kromme Elleboog* (Crooked Elbow) and at the southern end is a point on the west shore named *de Dans Kammer* (the Dance Chamber). Midway in the reach, on the west shore south of the bridge at Poughkeepsie, is *Juffrouw's Hoeck* (the Madam's Point). A picture of *de Lange Rak*, looking from the vicinity of *Kromme Elleboog* southward, past *Juffrouw's Hoeck* toward New Hamburgh, forms the frontispiece of this volume. The picture was given its place for the reason that a study of Dutch houses in the river-counties inevitably is based upon a knowledge of the river. The river! Beautiful, powerful, dominant and compelling; loved and admired and used and feared; the influence it exerts upon the affairs of those who live near it can hardly be over-emphasized.

Those first white men who ascended the river saw wooded shores along its whole length, such as the shores of the Long Reach recorded in the plate. Here and there the terraced slopes were cut by valleys, down which poured sparkling streams over rocky beds. At the mouths of the streams were the gathering places of the Indians. This was true of *de Noorman's Kil* (plate 1), where there was a native castle and which stream is reputed to be the original of the Vale of Tawasentha in *Hiawatha*. It was true of Stockport Creek in Columbia County, of the Wappingers in Dutchess, of the Croton in Westchester,—indeed of almost all the watercourses tributary to the Hudson.

Passing up and down the river in sailboats, the white men long feared the unknown dangers of the hinterland. The forests were uncut, penetrated only by the trails of the Indian, and land-travel was full of peril. So the newcomers held to the river and it was only little by little that permanent settlers ventured beyond the banks. Then, as the bolder ones pushed back from the water-front, the arable flats of the interior were found and occupied.

Among the tillable lands which were developed at an early date were those along Kinderhook Creek in Columbia County (plate 2) and similar meadows on Claverack Creek. In Ulster County *Bonte Koe* (Spotted Cow) was a typical plain and *Wagen Dal* on the Rondout a sheltered valley that was settled early (plates 3 and 4).

At the time that the valley of the Hudson was taken possession of by Europeans and permanently occupied by white men it contained wild life and natural products in great variety and abundance. If the settler, his livestock and his crops survived the depradations of wolves, panthers, bears, wild cats, foxes, polecats and poisonous snakes, food was ready at hand on the land, in the water and in the air. Deer filled the woods; fish of many kinds the waters; partridges were plenty; huge turkeys flew wild; geese, ducks and pigeons flew in flocks of thousands each, so that in their passing in the spring and fall migrations the sky was darkened by them. In the woods were edible nuts and the trees were heavily festooned with grapevines (bearing purple grapes and white). Maize, wheat, rye, barley and oats all were easily raised. Beans, peas, pumpkins, melons, hops, strawberries, apples, cherries, pears and peaches are referred to by the first arrivals as native to the region.

The People

Settlement of the wilderness was slow for many years. A trading post for fur-dealers on the site of Albany and another at the mouth of the Rondout, which were established in the first quarter of the seventeenth century, were followed by the building of Fort Orange, 1624; by the opening of the colony of Rensselaerswyck for settlement, 1630; and by the formal organization of the independent village of *Bever-wyck* (Albany) in 1652. *Wiltwyck* (Kingston) was founded in 1653. In 1662 Arent Van Curler and his associates obtained a charter for the free village of Schenectady, settlers made clearings in the woods near Coxsackie and *Nieuw Dorp* (Hurley) was begun. New Paltz dates from 1677. Along the Kinderhook and Claverack Creeks in Columbia County mention of *boers* (farmers) and their crops was made in 1680 and in 1680 farms were also taken up on the Catskill (near Leeds). Five white men were living on the site of Poughkeepsie in 1691 and before 1697 a handful of Dutch-men had organized a church at Sleepy Hollow.

As the movement toward general settlement, thus outlined, began to take form, the total population of New York, estimated in an official report in 1667, approximated 8,000 souls, a number which, at the close of the century, as shown by the census of 1698, had increased only to 18,067. Small as the population was in 1630—1700 for the occupation of so large and potentially valuable a territory, it prefigured the country of today as a meeting-place of races and nationalities. Arrivals from the Netherlands rubbed shoulders with Albert Andriesse Bradt from Frederikstadt in Norway, whose son, born on the voyage across the Atlantic, was given the Dutch name of Storm

Van der Zee. Bradt was known as *de Noorman* and the stream in Albany County on which he built a mill was *de Noorman's Kil* (the Northman's stream). A little south of *de Noorman's Kil* is "Vlauman's Kill", that is: the stream of *de Vlamingh* (the Fleming). Alexander Lindsay Glen, the Scotchman, was prominent at Schenectady. Thomas Chambers, English-born, was the first purchaser of land at *Wiltwyck*. Walloons were at New Paltz and Huguenot-French at New Rochelle. Hoffmans from Sweden, Schoonmakers from Hamburgh, Ten Broecks from Westphalia, Kierstedes from Prussia all multiplied in Ulster. These are but individual instances selected from a large assortment to illustrate the general truth that immigration into the Hudson valley was derived from many sources.

From the census of 1703 to that of 1771, immediately before the war of the Revolution, the number of the inhabitants of the river-counties rose from 11,680 to 168,007, the latter total being made up of 148,124 whites and 19,883 blacks. When it is considered that at the time of the Revolution the whole province held only as many people as some one lesser American city of today a perspective is gained as to what is represented by the houses of the people and a relative value is obtained for the illustrations contained in this volume.

Slaves

In the seventeenth and eighteenth centuries the white population of the river-counties was supplemented by a black minority and the story of the negro in the region of the Hudson is one yet to be adequately written. Trade in slaves began in the first years of New Netherland and continued until the Revolution and slavery, as an institution, had legal existence until 1827. Official documents of the middle of the seventeenth century contain many references to the importation of negroes from the West Indies and from Africa and South America to the slave market in New York City, whence they were distributed to farmers up the river. The documents in question emphasize that slave-labour was a necessity for the agricultural development of the colony but the reason thus stated was hardly more than a thin gloss over the fact that the shipping trade in general found the slave-trade in particular profitable, and local traditions do not support the contention that the negroes were indispensible or that they were used in rough work. According to the stories met with in going about among old families and old homes, the slaves were household and body-servants or, at most, were employed in the fields of the home-farm. They were quartered in the cellars and the attics of the masters' dwellings or in out-buildings near by and received practically no consideration in connection with provision for light and air (as viewed from the standard of modern hygiene), indeed if the sufferings of the masters were great from extremes of temperature those of the slaves were even worse. But the personal relations between the two races were kindly and, allowing for an occasional owner of irascible disposition and an occasional black of incorrigible tendencies, good will prevailed and often deep attachments. Such stories as those of Eype and Dina and Nanna, handed down in the Storm and Anthony and Van Voorhees families (pages 377, 389 and 395), are typical of the devotion of the negro house-servants to their owners. It was customary for the slaves to become members of their masters' church; a gallery in the church-building was reserved for their use and the ministers baptized and married and buried them. On the farms burial-ground for the slaves was often set aside and the location of some of those places is still remembered. The most cursory examination of eighteenth century wills reveals that masters frequently made provision for faithful servitors,—as, for example, when Abraham Schenck of Dutchess County ordered by will that aged Hannah (" who from her youth has deserved well of me and the family ") should have her freedom, her support, and care by a physician. The names borne by the slaves form material for a study of their own and their masters' range of taste, from the classical Jupiter and historic Caesar, the pretentious King and Prince, the Biblical Abraham and Isaac, to the domestic " Mom Dien ", which, perhaps, was a contraction of Mammy Dien. Later, the freed negroes took the former masters' family names as surnames. In actual numbers the slaves of the seventeenth century were a negligible group as, by 1698, after over half a century of importation, they totalled less than 2,200. Natural increase and further importation made the count grow more rapidly in the eighteenth century and from 6,171 in 1723 it rose to 19,883 in 1771. That was just before the outbreak of the Revolution, and the figures cited represent a substantial percentage of the population of the Province of New York for that year.

Land Titles

Land in the river-counties was held partly as manorial grants and partly as freeholds. There were nine manors, which were all created under English sovereignty. In Westchester County were: Fordham (1671), Pelham (1687), Philipseborough (1693), Morrisania (1697), Cortlandt (1697) and Scarsdale (1701); in Ulster: Fox Hall (1672); in Albany: Rensselaer (1685) and Livingston (1686). The manor of Rensselaer, dating from 1685, was equivalent in boundaries to the colony of Rensselaerswyck, which was begun in 1630 under Dutch auspices as a private enterprise in colonization, controlled by a patroon, and the patroon of the colony was transformed into the lord of the manor. The charters of the manors were issued under the English Crown; they vested the title to the land in the lord of the manor, entailed the title and conferred upon the lord the right to hold courts-leet and courts-baron within his own territory. Court-leet was a court of record and a criminal court, trying all cases from the smallest up to but not including treason. Court-baron redressed misdemeanors, punished offenses committed by tenants and debated and decided controversies.

The condition of the manors in 1700 was described by the Earl of Bellomont, Governor of New York, to the Lords of Trade in London in a report which shows that the development of manor-lands was slow because of the leasehold-system. Men of initiative were not satisfied, the governor said, to settle where they could not hope to own the land they cultivated, and the Province of New York was steadily losing possible citizens to the Jersies and Pennsylvania, where good freeholds could be had. On January 2, 1700—1701, the governor wrote: " Mr. Livingston has on his great grant of 16 miles long and 24 broad but 4 or 5 cottagers as I am told, men that live in vassalage under him and work for him and are too poor to be farmers, having not wherewithall to buy Cattle to stock a farm. Colonel Cortland has also on his great grants 4 or 5 of those poor families. Old Frederick Phillips is said to have about 20 families of those poor people that work for him on his grant."

Men on the manors, looking across invisible boundaries to the freeholders in adjacent counties, reacted against such items of social distinction as the canopied pew and straight benches, which were provided in church for the lord of the manor and his tenants, respectively. Mr. Edgar Mayhew Bacon in the *Chronicles of Tarry-town* draws a vivid picture of the scene in the Dutch church at Sleepy Hollow and the *History of Columbia County* records the violence of the emotion evoked in the congregation of the church at Claverack by the contrast between the elaborate dignity of the seat of the lord of the manor and the humble and uncomfortable arrangements made for lease-holders.

Thus the manors lagged in development. While the rents from them were, ultimately, a source of wealth to a few families that were socially prominent and many of whose members were able and distinguished citizens, the lands occupied under freeholds were preferred by men of ambition and energy who had their way to make and the farms and villages of the localities where titles in fee were obtainable built up more rapidly, on a more substantial economic basis and with a higher average of resultant prosperity than did the manors.

Title to land held in fee was taken under patents (which were merely confir-mations of title), issued by the Crown to the original purchasers. In the latter part of the seventeenth century there was great activity among speculators in real estate in buying large tracts of wild land. Groups of men who were possessed of capital bought enormous areas in the river-counties and sold farms as vigorously as the modern promoter develops new plots. Under Governor Fletcher there were scandals, occasioned by political graft, fraudulent grants and overlapping boundaries but the situation gradually cleared and, even at its worst, the lot of the smaller buyers, the actual homesteaders, was better on the land covered by the patents than that of the tenants on the manors. The men who owned their own homes eventually bred a race of substantial citizens, accustomed to some responsibility, who shared in the conduct of the public business of the province.

15

Due to the fact that accurate surveys were seldom made at the time that patents were issued, trouble frequently arose in connection with uncertain boundaries. And because settlers did not in all cases take up their farms as soon as their purchase was made squatters were often found occupying desirable parcels when the rightful owner arrived to take possession. The squatter of course had to give way; but for a time he was an element in the general situation.

Beside the squatter, who took up land he had not paid for, the shifting portion of the population included the rover, who was a woodsman by nature and subsisted by hunting and trapping. One of the most colorful personalities of the seventeenth century in the Hudson valley was Christopher Davis, English-born, known to the Dutch as *Kit Davidtsz*. Kit might well have served as the proto-type for *Rip Van Winkle*, for he hunted the woods, fished the streams, acted as interpreter between Indians and whites, drank heavily, engaged in numerous brawls, was in jail for contempt of court and wandered hither and yon throughout a romantic career in which he was both the tool and the despair of the authorities.

Dug-outs

Like all other pioneers the first arrivals in New Netherland were forced to provide shelter for themselves in the quickest and easiest way possible until the time should come when they would be able to build permanent dwellings. Contemporary evidence goes to show that in New Netherland dug-outs were the crudest form of habitation. The Reverend Jonas Michaelius, writing in 1628 at Manhattan Island, said: " They (the settlers) are therefore beginning to build new houses in place of the hovels and holes in which heretofore they huddled rather than dwelt." And in 1650 Cornelis Van Tienhoven, secretary of New Netherland, in an official report sent to The Hague, described in detail the holes in the ground which families used as temporary living quarters. Van Tienhoven said that men would " dig a square pit in the ground, cellar fashion, six or seven feet deep, as long and as broad as they think proper; case the earth all round the wall with timber, which they line with the bark of trees or something else to prevent the caving-in of the earth; floor this cellar with plank, and wainscot it overhead for a ceiling; raise a roof of spars clear up, and cover the spars with bark or green sods so that they can live dry and warm in these houses with their entire families for two, three or four years, it being understood that partitions are run through these cellars, which are adapted to the size of the family." Van Tienhoven recommended in his report that emigration from Europe should be made in winter in order to arrive in New Netherland in March or April so as to clear land, build cottages and plant garden vegetables, maize and beans that summer; he calculated that the next winter the settler could cut and clear timber, and in a second summer acquire cattle and build houses and barns. The report describes the first gardens planted as containing " all sorts of pot-herbs, principally parsnips, carrots and cabbages, which (it says) bring great plenty into the husbandman's dwelling. The maize can serve as bread for men and food for cattle. The hogs, after having picked up their food for some months in the woods, are crammed with corn in the fall; when fat they are killed and furnish a very hard and clean pork; a good article for the husbandman, who gradually and in time begins to purchase horses and cows with the produce of his grain and the increase of his hogs and, instead of a cellar as aforesaid, builds good farmhouses and barns."

Such were the conditions and the hardships encountered by the families which took up uncleared land in a new country to create homes for themselves and for unborn generations. But only in documents are the dug-outs learned of. Unfortunately, the survey of the river-counties failed to find any mention of them in the folk-lore of the native stock.

Log and Board Cabins

In the town and county histories that were published in the 1870's and 1880's there are occasional references to log houses as being the first form of dwelling erected in a neighborhood. Those volumes, while not always scholarly in quality, were prepared while the compilers had access to the reminiscences of elderly persons whose traditions were often derived from the early provincial period and the testimony they contain is of value from that point of view. Augustus Van Buren in: *Ulster County under the Dutch,* used however the scientific method of examining local public records for evidence as to what sort of houses were lived in at *Wiltwyck* (Kingston) from 1653 to 1664. As a result he was able to show that the dwellings there of that date were log or board cabins of one story, with a loft or garret. Sometimes a fire was built on the floor and an opening in the roof let out the smoke. Sometimes there was a wooden chimney. Finally, there were chimneys of stone or brick. Roofs were made of thatch until, in 1669, the parsonage was referred to as covered with tiles. It is thus safe to assume that the log or board house was a feature in the life of the pioneer but of so inherently perishable a nature that no standing example has of course been found.

Location of Houses

In the territory surveyed for this book the only groups of dwellings, existing in the seventeenth century, which by courtesy could be called villages were *Beverwyck* (Albany), 1652; *Wiltwyck* (Kingston), 1653; Schenectady, 1662; *Nieuw Dorp* (Hurley), 1662; and New Paltz, 1677. At Albany and at New Paltz some houses were built with the gable-end to the street, some with the front façade, as instanced by the Schaets, Schuyler, Bevier and Hasbrouck houses (plates: 32, 34, 58 and 75). At Schenectady the Bradt and Yates houses had their gables toward the walk (plates

14 and 56). In Hurley the houses faced the road (vignette, page 175; from a photograph made by Clarence J. Elting). Thus no general rule prevailed in village growth. On the farms houses stood in any and all locations. There is a widespread belief that the pioneers built to face the south but the survey disproves it, completely. The expediency of the time and place determined a site and position and, while making the survey, houses were found facing all points of the compass with no majority preference. Often no reason is apparent now for the choice of a spot for building. Then, again, shelter from the wind, under a hillside, would seem to have been the deciding factor. Sometimes access to water or to the highway may have led to a selection of location.

Building Materials

The conclusions drawn from observations made during the field-survey regarding the position of houses on village streets and in the open country apply to the houses built in the period following that of the dug-outs and the log and board cabins. Assuming the building of Fort Orange in 1624 and the opening of the colony of Rensselaerswyck in 1630 as marking a period from which to begin the study of dwellings north of Manhattan Island, it is evident that the settlers resorted to stone and brick as quickly as possible. In 1687 Governor Dongan made a report on the state of the Province of New York in which he said: " The principal towns within the government are New York, Albany and Kingston at Esopus. All the rest are country villages; the buildings in New York and Albany are generally of stone and brick. In the country the houses are mostly new built, having two or three rooms on a floor. The Dutch are great improvers of land." As has just been noted in connection with the location of houses, settlers spread out in Albany and Ulster counties in the period from 1662 to 1680 and for a while they must have lived in temporary structures. So the statement made by the governor in 1687 that in the country most of the houses were newly built is in accordance with other known facts.

Stone was probably made use of before brick inasmuch as it lay ready at hand, and brick had to be imported or manufactured. In the seventeenth century and for most of the eighteenth the use of stone was general in all the river-counties and examples of stone-construction are shown in this volume ranging in location from Albany County to Westchester and westward, on the Mohawk, in Schenectady County. In the earlier stone-structures the pieces of field-stone incorporated in the walls were untooled. They were laid one upon another just as they were taken from the ground in sizes portable by hand or as broken off from larger units and were held together by a filling of clay or mud that was mixed with chopped straw or horsehair. From the oyster-beds along the Atlantic coast shell-lime was soon obtained to add to the filling for the walls and, later, limestone-ridges in the Hudson valley were exploited, as for example at *Barnegat* (the " firehole ") in the town of Poughkeepsie, a place which earned its name in the eighteenth century from the flames flaring out of the many kilns in which limestone was calcined there.

The only documentary record of the expenses in erecting a typical stone house which, so far, has come to the knowledge of the writer is one which is preserved at the house near New Windsor, N. Y., that was occupied during the Revolution by General Knox as his headquarters. This house was owned by Thomas Ellison, who on February 1, 1754, entered into an agreement with a headmason, William Bull of Orange County, regarding the details of the work of construction. The contract provided that Ellison should furnish all materials and labourers and food and lodging for the workmen. Bull was to be responsible for the actual building, which was to be begun in April, 1754, and completed by September 1st according to stated specifications. Ellison was to pay Bull £ 60 for his services. From which particulars it appears that in the middle of the eighteenth century a man of some means procured a substantial house (still standing and in good condition), forty-four feet long, by thirty-six feet wide, which cost him £ 60 to build, plus labour and materials and food, and for the erection of which from four to five months time was allowed.

The use of stone in house-building declined toward the end of the eighteenth century in all the river-counties but Ulster, where it continued into the nineteenth; but a very little experience serves to enable an observer to distinguish between houses of stone built earlier and later. As time went on tooling increased and the stone houses ultimately consisted of blocks, carefully cut, smoothed and fitted. They also increased in height. Only rarely was a stone house built in two full stories before the Revolution. Very often the stone houses were added to and the seams in the walls are so easily seen that the story of the various stages by which a house reached its final form is obvious to the eye. One feature, common to all the stone houses, is the arched foundation-support (plate 5), which at first sight appears to be a cellar-fireplace, but which has no flue and is actually a structural item, designed to carry the weight of the gable-ends of the house, where usually a heavy chimney was placed.

While all the stone houses bear a general resemblance to each other there are some differences in detail. A very high roof of single slant was found at Rotterdam Junction, West Coxsackie, Kinderhook, Marbletown and New Paltz (plates: 42, 16, 51, 82, and 75), but no example of the same in Dutchess. Roofs built in a single slant at a moderate pitch are typical of Greene County and of Ulster and of Dutchess and Westchester. In Ulster the single slant was so universally used that the gambrel roofs of the Bruyn and Wynkoop houses (plates 63 and 104) are conspicuous for difference. The outline of the stone houses varied from square to oblong and from L-shaped to T-shaped structures and they were built so thoroughly that it is with much difficulty they are razed. They remain standing in comparatively large number but an unfortunately large proportion of them have been given wood trim, outside and in, which destroys their typical appearance. The illustrations contained in this volume are of houses as little changed as any the survey revealed.

In building the stone houses a custom prevailed of marking one stone of conveniently flat surface with the date of erection or the initials of the owner or builder. The markings are found on lintels, on cornerstones, at the line of the eaves and in the middle of the walls and wherever they are placed are almost invariably reliable. A painted inscription is one never to be trusted as it usually is the work of a recent resident imputing a supposed date. Large figures: 1 7 7 6, are also sometimes found and are obviously due to ill-directed enthusiasm of a late day. A typical lintel and cornerstone are shown in plates 6 and 7. The lintel, dated 1702, was marked for Baltus Barents Van Kleeck and Tryntje Van Kleeck, his wife, and the stone is now owned by Baltus Barentszen Van Kleeck of Poughkeepsie, who is in the seventh generation of descent from the original Baltus. The cornerstone bears the date: Ano 1713, and the initials are those of Pieter Viele, with the (later?) addition of those of his son, Myndert. The stone is in the custody of the Daughters of the American Revolution at Poughkeepsie.

A monotonous repetition is heard everywhere in the popular speech of the phrase: " old stone houses," the three words running together as one: " oldstonhouses," and it is a pity that the popular view-point is the one thereby expressed. By dropping the adjective: old, and thinking of " stone houses " as forming a chapter in the story of domestic architecture that is dignified and worthy of respect there is eliminated a tendency to regard the stone houses with a weak sentimentality. The stone houses are old by time-standards in the Hudson valley but the several types of houses, in successive periods, each have their own significance and the principle involved in studying them all is not so much whether they are old or new in relation to the present day but what message they bear from the men who built them. The message of the stone houses of the seventeenth and eighteenth centuries tells of durable material, conveniently procured under primitive conditions, which material was handled with little or no imagination or grace but with honesty and with a certain inherent propriety and suitability. The stone houses, however crude, are never vulgar and almost invariably fit their setting.

Within a few years after the opening of the colony of Rensselaerswyck the use of brick in house-building arose there and brick houses became characteristic of the village of *Beverwyck* (Albany) and of a wide radius of country around that center. In the territory now comprised in the counties of Albany, Columbia, Rensselaer, Greene and Schenectady three types of architecture are found among the houses built of brick and a discussion of the three types is offered in later pages under the head of: Albany County.

Brick in Ulster County was a negligible item until after 1800. The rear wall of the Ten Broeck house (plate 87) in Kingston is built of brick and brick was introduced incidentally in chimneys and gable-ends before the Revolution but a whole house of brick at New Paltz in 1786 was a notable innovation, as was also one at Guilford early in the nineteenth century, and brick continued subordinate in Ulster as a building material for many years.

Brick and stone in combination occurred in Dutchess in the middle of the eighteenth century, examples of such construction still remaining in the De Peyster, Verplanck and Du Bois houses (plates 115, 149, and page 339), which exhibit front and end walls of brick and rear walls of rough stone. Shortly before the Revolution the Evertson and Newcomb houses (page 342 and plate 129) were erected of brick throughout and brick has been in fairly general use in the county ever since.

One of the most widely spread traditions current among the native stock of the Hudson valley is that homesteads were built of brick brought from Holland. In the seventeenth century freight came from the Netherlands in small frail sailing-vessels and space in the ships was in demand for many articles to supply the daily needs of the pioneer on this side of the Atlantic. It is matter of record that some brick was brought over by the first ships as ballast but it is also matter of record that the patroon of Rensselaerswyck established brick-kilns in his colony soon after colonization began and ultimately brickmaking was a leading industry at Albany and at scattered points along the Hudson. The cost of the importation of brick, when freight charges were high, vessels few and voyages infrequent, was a consideration serious enough to lead the majority of citizens to construct their dwellings of bricks that were made near by and which were more easily moved to the site chosen to build on. Even then, carriage from the brickyard to interior farms was a laborious matter, whether over rough roads or by sloop on the river when loading and unloading occasioned much handling. It should also be remembered that there was keen competition in trade between the Dutch and the English in the seventeenth century and that after 1664, when England took over control of New Netherland, imports from Holland must have declined in volume.

To account for the tradition so frequently heard that a house consisted of brick brought from Holland there is a simple explanation. Under both Dutch and English laws there were standard measurements which the public manufacturer of brick had to use and the product of the yards was known in accordance with its size as either Holland brick or English brick. If a man built his house of " Holland brick " his descendants, a few years later, easily inferred that: " the brick came from Holland," and handed on a positive statement to that effect. In actual construction the bricks are found occasionally laid irregularly, without method; but as a rule they were placed either in Flemish bond or English bond. In Flemish bond one course consists of an alternation of stretchers and headers, while in English bond one row is laid in headers and the next in stretchers.

Dates were given to brick houses in three ways: in large iron figures, in inlaid

21

bricks of contrasting color and in incised marks on single bricks. Examples of the iron figures are noted in connection with the Schuyler house (1667), Wendell (1716), Beekman-Vanderheyden (1725), Van Alen (1737) and Muller (1767). Dates in inlaid bricks may be seen in the walls of the Brinckerhoff house (1738), Ten Broeck (1762), Verplanck (1768) and an unidentified house at Kinderhook of 1766. Incised bricks occur in the Van Bergen house (1729), Van Wie (1732), Bronck (1738), Gardenier (1753), Staats (1758), Conyn (1766) and at *Crailo* in 1762.

Frame houses of a permanent sort were not characteristic of Albany County as a whole before 1776. A few instances have been found but they date from the latter half of the eighteenth century and do not illustrate pioneer tendencies. In Ulster frame houses were almost unknown before the Revolution and became common there only in more recent years. And so it is only in Dutchess and Westchester that this survey registers a free use of wood. In Westchester the English stock established in the central and eastern portions of the county turned instinctively to timber and houses were also built of wood by the French at New Rochelle in the middle of the eighteenth century. But many a Dutch family, as well as families of other origins, were housed in frame dwellings in Dutchess and the frame houses are to be found in all parts of the county.

The method of construction followed in the earliest frame houses was to make a literal framework of lath, of the height desired and of a depth of perhaps twelve or eighteen inches, and to fill the interstices of the frame with the same mixture of mud or clay, held together by chopped straw or horsehair, that was put in the walls of stone houses. The outer side of such a wall of lath and mud was covered with plain boards or clapboards or shingles. Rough boards, sawed by hand, were presumably the first form of siding. Broad overlapping clapboards were a step beyond crude boards but were often hand-work, as were also the large shingles, such as the shingles on the house of Madam Brett (plate 111) and of Henry Livingston (plate 128). At Swartwoutville in Dutchess a house built by Jacobus Swartwout about 1760 is now in ruins and the gaping holes in its structure reveal the typical lath-framework and mud-filling of the frame house of the eighteenth century. A photograph of it (plate 8) provides an excellent record of this form of construction.

At a secondary stage of its development the house with walls of lath-framework is found with bricks filling the frame instead of mud and instances of brick filling are cited in connection with *Cherry Hill* and *Lithgow* and with the Storm-Adriance-Brinckerhoff house (plates: 50, 122 and 135).

Architectural Details

The field-survey of the several counties revealed that certain architectural details were peculiar to certain localities while others were widespread. The notched roof-line or stepped gable (Schaets, 1657; Wendell, 1716; plates: 32 and 55) was found only in the village of *Beverwyck* (Albany). The roof of extremely steep single pitch was characteristic primarily of Albany County; but two or three instances of it occurred in Ulster (see plates: 14, 15, 16, 17, 22, 24, 25, 32, 34, 40, 41, 42, 44, 47, 51, 54, 55, 56 for Albany, and 75 and 82 for Ulster). The broadly spread roof of single slant was common to all the river-counties from Coeymans Castle (page 71) near Albany to the Van Cortlandt manor-house on the lower Hudson. The gambrel roof (in which there are two slopes between ridge-pole and eaves, forming a pentagonal gable) was later than the roof of single slant but it is found throughout a large territory. Loosely approximated the period in which the gambrel was popular in the Hudson valley was the half-century between 1725 and 1775; but so early as 1705 the Salisbury house at Leeds was built with a gambrel and several examples of the type remain which date from after 1783. Excellent gambrels are to be seen at Cohoes, Kinderhook, Claverack and at scattered points in Dutchess. Of hipped roofs only a few examples have been found in the region of the Hudson. The hipped roof has four slopes, one from each of the four walls of the house, and rises from the eaves to a flat deck or a ridgepole. There is a hipped roof on part of the Glen-Sanders house at Scotia, on *The Pastures* at Albany, on the Cuyler house at Rensselaer, on the Van Cortlandt house in Van Cortlandt Park and there was one on the house of Henry Livingston at Poughkeepsie (which was razed in 1910).

In height the houses at *Beverwyck* (Albany) frequently rose to two stories and an attic; but in this respect they differed from the houses elsewhere surveyed. As has been noted already regarding stone houses, so was it true also of brick and frame dwellings, that the general rule before 1776 was to build a house only a story and a half high. Exceptions to the rule are found occasionally; but the rule holds good for the majority of instances.

A few floor-plans are found repeatedly. The earliest houses had but one or two rooms, as in the case of the Bronck and Van Antwerp homes (plates 16 and 42); but a little later there was a common plan that provided a hall through the center of the house with either one room or two each side of the hall. If there were two rooms on a side, one was usually larger than the other. By another arrangement a hall was not introduced and three rooms in a row, each with an outer door, constituted the first floor.

Windows were few in the primitive farmhouses (see plates 68 and 96), the omission of them being due perhaps partly to the cold winters and partly to economy. Chimneys are found both in the gable-ends and in the center of buildings. The hearth--side was the center of family-life, where warmth and sociability were had and where cooking was done. Beds were frequently placed next the chimney in the main living-room and were curtained off or closed in by doors. Grain was stored

23

in hogsheads in the attic and the granary door in the gable, under the peak of the roof, was a feature of many houses.

Houses of the seventeenth and eighteenth centuries were built when the local supply of wood was unlimited, a fact which is reflected in the great size of floor- and ceiling-beams and in the width of the floor-boards, all of which bear witness to the splendid forestation of the river valley at that period. In the Wynkoop-Lounsbery house at Stone Ridge, Ulster County, there is a bevelled panel on a chimney-breast of white pine in one piece, which measures forty-six inches by thirty-three; in the house of Abraham De Peyster at Beacon, Dutchess County, is one which measures forty-eight by thirty-seven; and there are other instances of fine old trees felled for use or ornament in house-building.

In the main, little attention was given at first to that which was merely decorative. Utility was the imperative consideration in a day of stern realities in living conditions. The most conspicuous external expression of the natural liking for decoration is the balustrade along the roof-line, which was found on a small number of houses. Balustrades survive on the Glen-Sanders house at Scotia; the Philipse manor-house at Yonkers; *The Pastures* at Albany; and the Verplanck-Van Wyck house in Dutchess; and old photographs of the Cuyler house at Rensselaer and of the house of Philip Van Rensselaer at Albany show the same detail.

Before 1776 the door which was typical was broad in proportion to height; was sometimes battened, sometimes panelled; was cut horizontally across the center and, in the stone houses, was set at the inner line of the thick walls, the depth of the wall forming a cased frame for the door. The beautiful and dignified carved doorways, of which so many may be seen in country homes (particularly in Dutchess, where wood was freely used), belong rather to the post-Revolutionary period, although one that is notable gives entrance to the Verplanck-Van Wyck house of 1768 on the Sprout Creek in Dutchess. In Ulster the verge board at the eaves often has a rounded end, as on the house of Andries De Witt, the Van Deusen and the Wynkoop-Lounsbery houses (plates: 71, 98 and 104), and in Albany County the handwrought iron pieces on the outer walls, which were strictly utilitarian in purpose (having been introduced to strengthen the general structure of the house), were unconsciously ornamental. The trefoils on the Yates house (plate 56) are good examples of a large number seen.

All the ironwork of the pre-Revolutionary houses is interesting, not only the wall-anchors but the hinges and locks on the doors, the fixtures for the fireplaces, the cooking utensils and farm implements. It was the period of iron. Brass came afterward. And all the many household necessities, hand-made in iron, were presumably the work of local blacksmiths. Strangely, however, there were just a few patterns in use and, how the smiths, far separated from each other in rural districts, could have wrought so consistently, one like another, can be explained only on the theory that the first workers had apprentices, who went out from the masters' shops, established elsewhere forges of their own and, in their turn, passed on the standardized patterns.

Of the trained masons and carpenters who worked on the early houses little is known. At Albany *The Pastures* was built in 1762 from professional architectural designs, imported from England, but the average house in the river-counties before the Revolution was the work either of the owners' own hands or of local tradesmen. The stone houses probably represent amateur construction more frequently than those of brick and frame and therefore they more frequently exhibit what may be called the felt line,—the line felt out instinctively, not planned and measured in advance; roofs especially show the felt line, the rippled ridgepoles and the slants and curves toward the ground at the rear being full of story and suggestion.

Brick houses probably required the services of a mason and after the pioneer period (when crude hand-hewn boards were used for siding and when there was no attempt at interior wood trim) a carpenter must have been needed for the frame houses. At Fishkill in Dutchess there is a house built soon after 1800 in which there are mantels and door-casings elaborately carved and the tradition there is that the carving was done by a travelling carpenter, who charged a dollar a day and his board for his work. This incident in the early nineteenth century could easily be the clue to a knowledge of how some things were done in the century preceding. As in the case of the blacksmiths, so perhaps it was with carpenters: a few standardized designs, introduced by the first workmen, were handed on to their apprentices, but the later carpenters developed a variety in the details of their work which the blacksmiths never attained to. The race of professional architects had, however, little representation in the Hudson valley until after the Revolution and, even then, houses were for many years built in the pre-war manner.

Outbuildings

Near to the main dwellings on the older farms were certain outbuildings, of which the more important were a barn, a smokehouse and a frame corn-crib. Such a barn as is standing now (plate 9) on the Verplanck-Van Wyck farm near the Sprout Creek in Dutchess was once to be seen in connection with almost all the homesteads. The Verplanck barn illustrates the breadth of the typical Dutch barn, carries typical iron hardware and shows the typical projection from the upper flooring. The smokehouses were small rectangular stone buildings, in which beef and pork were cured, and a number of examples of them and of the corn-cribs still survive. The well with a long sweep was also a feature on the farms, and one found at Rifton in Ulster is shown in plate 85.

Stone Walls

To the stone walls of the eighteenth century on the farms of the back country-side there clings as much that is colorful and storied in quality as to any survival of that period. The stone fences tell of the clearing of fields for a homestead, a labor performed by hand and at the cost of time, patience and wearied muscles; and which was carried on in stints, in the intervals of sowing, cultivating and reaping. The walls provided enclosure and protection for the home which a family—the social unit—was creating and they also emphasized individual property rights, for they served as indisputable boundary lines for fields and farms. Some of the first boundaries established are traceable in old neighborhoods by stone walls still standing, as on the Beekman Patent in Dutchess County. The patent (granted in 1703) was ultimately laid out in large lots among the heirs of the patentee and some of the stone walls that outlined those original lots are in existence, massive in construction, extending east and west in some length in the present town of Beekman. Manifestly, a stone wall represents a conservative in theories of sociology and economics!

Plantings

Assuming that the plantings which were first laid out in connection with a pioneer home were garden vegetables in a patch adjacent to the house and field vegetables and grain extended beyond on the farm, the next important item was an orchard. In early land-records orchards are frequently mentioned and with emphasis, as if much value was set upon them. Of flowers little is said in the seventeenth and eighteenth centuries. Perhaps the necessities of existence pressed too heavily upon the householder for the claim of mere beauty to be heeded at the same time as that of utility. In the *Memoirs of an American Lady* by Anne McVickar Grant of Scotland, which describes domestic life in and near Albany as Mrs. Grant knew it about 1755—1760, there is reference to the raising of flowers but whether there were flower-gardens throughout the river-counties at that period is a question. A few scattered indications tend to show that beds for flowers were, at a late day, laid out sometimes as borders for the vegetable gardens, the decorative being subordinated to the practical, but the premises are too few for generalized conclusions to be reliable.

In the course of the field-survey of the Hudson valley locust trees were found everywhere as intentional plantings. Grouped around houses and set out in rows on roadsides, they were certainly characteristic of the nineteenth century and, by reasonable inference, belonged also to the eighteenth. The inference is drawn from the age of many of the trees and from specific instances learned from local sources. At *Bethlehem House* (plate 29), built in Albany County about 1730, there are large locusts which according to family tradition were planted when the house was built. At *Lithgow* (plate 122) in Dutchess are locusts put out in 1813 which were the children of a parent-tree that is still standing (at the northeast corner of The Square in the town of North East, Dutchess County), and the latter came as a seedling from Long Island in a saddle-bag in the eighteenth century. Throughout Dutchess County among the representatives of the early families the statement is met with that the locust trees around this or that particular house "came from Long Island" and, as the exodus from Long Island to Dutchess was largest in the approximate period of 1735—1750, there can be little doubt that many of the locusts which are now to be seen in the county are either originals or offshoots from the same. The prevalence of the tree accounts for the frequency with which householders of the more sophisticated sort gave to their homesteads such names as: The Locusts, Locust Grove, Locust Lawn, etc., that are still heard in the interior neighborhoods, and the large number of the locusts, instead of making them commonplace, invests them with significance for the discerning observer. The tree planted methodically in a group, tells always of the site of a long established home and planted in rows beside the road indicates a route of travel opened by the first settlers in the locality. No one can know the story of the locust in the Hudson valley and understand its essentially domestic quality without realizing that sentiment allowably attaches to the tree.

An almost equal fondness might be formed for the lilac bush, which was second only to the locust tree in its association with homesteads. The lilac was planted by the doorstep and the porch, along the entrance-path and near the gate and fence. On the Du Bois farm in the town of Poughkeepsie (page 339) some fallen masonry is easily identifiable as the foundation of the first dwelling on the farm by the lilacs still flourishing beside it. A group of lilac bushes that is especially well known is the one which stands near the house built by General Schuyler at Schuylerville, the present bushes being supposed to be the original plantings of the eighteenth century and not slips from the parent-growth. In plate 31 is recorded a planting of lilacs and locusts in combination, bordering the driveway that leads to the house of Abraham Salisbury near Leeds, Greene County. It dates only from the 1830's; but the view of it is shown because the growth is particularly fine and because the use of the tree and of the shrub was so widespread as to be typical of the river-valley as a whole.

River and Road

Between 1630 (when the colony of Rensselaerswyck was opened for settlement) and 1700 the residents of the Hudson valley travelled almost entirely by water. The first homes in the vicinity of Fort Orange were on the low, flat shores that characterize the river near Albany, and the river was the route provided by nature for communication with Manhattan Island. In the middle of the century mills were standing on *de Noorman's Kil*, on *de Vlamingh's Kil* and at Coeymans; but in their case as with the shore-settlements outlet was on the river. When, in the third quarter of the seventeenth century, land was taken up on the higher levels in the interior (as at

Kinderhook, Claverack, Coxsackie, Catskill and Esopus), the *boers* wore wheel-tracks through the woods, east and west, between the farms and the river, with the one idea of reaching the waterfront to ship their produce. It was true, as Governor Dongan said in 1687, that " the Dutch (were) great improvers of land; " but they were not road-builders; they opened roads from the farms to the river but they were slow to begin through communication, northward and southward.

The Indian runner was the land-traveller of the seventeenth century and he followed two main trails, which he had established in the forest before the white man's arrival,—no one knows how long before. One trail ran from Manhattan Island northward on the east side of the Hudson. The other was the native route from Pennsylvania to Canada and it crossed Ulster through Ellenville and Accord in the Rondout valley, through Stone Ridge and the Esopus valley, passed on over the Catskill to West Coxsackie and so reached Albany. In 1670 there is documentary mention of a footpath between Kingston and Albany which, presumably, was the native's trail and government records of 1630—1700 are full of incidental references to the difficulties of a trip through the woods, on either side of the river (in summer because of foliage and in winter because of snow), and of the long intervals when communication by boat was also impossible because the river was frozen.

The statement is sometimes met with that a road was open on the east side of the Hudson from New York to Albany before 1700; but it must be taken with several grains of allowance; for there was at least one long stretch where the woods were unbroken then for wheel-traffic. In Dutchess County the known dates at which land on the river-bank was bought and cleared show that a wagon-road was not in use there at many points until after 1700. In the eighteenth century the *King's Highway* was an established feature on both sides of the river. In each case the road followed the course of the Indian trail; not in the literal sense that each foot of it was in the bed of the original path but in the general sense that it kept to the same valleys and water-courses, used the same fords and held to the approximate route and direction which the natives had found advantageous in relation to the topography of the region.

In the nineteenth century turnpikes were laid out and in the twentieth state roads and they, in turn, took up the main portions of the *King's Highway* just as the latter had taken up the trail. Here and there were deviations. One such occurred near Fishkill in Dutchess. The *King's Highway* passed over a high hill before entering the village of Fishkill from the north, while the state road now avoids the hill and runs into the village a little to the east of the early course. The view from the old road on the hilltop is one that was familiar to all travellers before and during the Revolution and plate 10 records the valley of the *Vis Kil* as seen from the vantage point the hill affords; the landscape is much the same now as when Dutch was spoken on the farms spread out across it.

In Columbia County the *King's Highway* passes through Claverack and the state road goes through Hudson; at Kinderhook the older road is east of the village and the newer one runs through the center of the town. The eighteenth century road in Greene County was inland, between Leeds and West Coxsackie, and the state road is near the river. Before the Revolution the *King's Highway* in Ulster ran from Accord to Stone Ridge on a course east of that of the modern road and only older residents in the vicinity recall that an obscure dirt road, now hard to find but marked by milestones, has a story of its own.

Halfway between New York and Albany on the east side of the river near Poughkeepsie is a spring which the Indians called: *uppuqui ipis ing* (the root of "Poughkeepsie"), but to which the Dutch settlers gave the name: *Rust Plaets* (Resting Place). And halfway between Ellenville and Kingston in Ulster is a ford, which also the Dutch designated: *Rust Plaets*, and which is still so called today. The two places were convenient in time and in distance to stop at and afforded water and they were undoubtedly halting places on the Indian trail that were taken over as such on the *King's Highway*.

Although the *King's Highway* was used in the eighteenth century it remained subordinate to travel by water, not only before the Revolution but after. Indeed it was not until the railroad was built in 1850 that the bulk of travel shifted from water to land. And it was not until the railroad or, perhaps, until the steamboat that there was much, if any, change in the appearance of the river-banks. The wooded terraces and unscarred shoreline which were gazed upon by the adventurer-navigators, the fur-traders and the first permanent settlers remained virtually the same until the industrial era. In 1680 Jasper Danckaerts, a traveller from the Low Countries, visited New York and kept a diary of his voyages on the Hudson. In 1769 Richard Smith of New Jersey and in 1774 Abraham Lott of New York also kept diaries of trips on the river and these all are in print. In the first quarter of the nineteenth century a diary (unpublished and in private ownership) was kept which tells explicitly of river-scenery and it is noteworthy that all four writers describe similar conditions, showing that few visible changes occurred along the banks of the Hudson between 1630 and 1830. The villages and most of the farmhouses were back from the river, out of sight from a boat, and almost the only buildings at the water-level were the occasional landing places, so that natural features remained unchanged. A landing consisted of a wooden dock, a storehouse and sometimes a dwelling (as in the case of the Farmers' Landing in Dutchess, plate 117), and the names: Kinderhook Landing, Claverack Landing (now Hudson), Esopus Landing, the Long Dock at *Kipsbergen*, the Upper and Lower Landings at Poughkeepsie, Fishkill Landing, all were once familiar and significant to many ears.

The landings were terminals for the early roads that led to the river, over which roads several generations of Dutch farmers carried grain and other crops to the storehouses on the docks for shipment by sloop. And not only grain passed over the interior county roads; large droves of cattle lumbered heavily over them in former years and sheep too were a frequent sight and it is to be supposed that those dirt roadbeds of the back country in the eighteenth century exhibited all degrees of mud and dust. In plate 11 is shown a bit of the road that crosses Dutchess County from northeast to southwest and which ends at the former Fishkill Landing (now Beacon). It was the route by which communication was maintained between New England and the South in the Revolution and the camera records a stretch between Brinckerhoff and Swartwoutville (a neighborhood settled by Dutch families) where from 1777 to 1783 the road was traversed continually by the officers of the Continental Army and by civil officials and where it echoed to the weary foot-treads of the Hessian soldiers, marching as prisoners from Massachusetts to Virginia.

Foot-travel for man as well as beast was common in the beginnings of things. Often the horse, with saddle and pillion, carried the head of a house and his wife and through the woods were bridle-paths, marked by blazed trees, which supplemented the so-called roads. Sleighs were in use early and were an especial convenience on the open stretches of thick ice on the river. There are traditions of travel by sleigh on the frozen river for pleasure trips as well as for trips of necessity and some of the pleasure-sleighing was by moonlight. But vehicles for mere pleasure were so few in the eighteenth century that a phaeton, belonging to Derick Brinckerhoff (page 331) of southern Dutchess, is said to have occasioned as much comment as did a tallyho on Fifth Avenue a hundred years later.

On the river the canoe of the Indian was omnipresent in the seventeenth century, while Europeans travelled between Manhattan Island and Fort Orange by sailing-vessels. The sloop for through trips north and south survived until the steamboat came and it carried both freight and passengers. Passengers took with them their own bedding and food; livestock were strapped fast before the mast; and the voyage was made without a time-schedule, subject to wind and tide. Ferries from one side of the river to the other were the result of the growth of communities and of the interrelations of the people in kinship and in business. Scows were used as ferries and also the periauger.

This bare outline serves to show that methods of transportation and means of communication were slow and uncomfortable before 1776, a fact which affected all phases of the life of the people, just as the developments in the last half-century, that have provided rapid transportation and almost instantaneous communication have wrought a social revolution and created conditions of an opposite extreme.

Traditions

In 1683 the Province of New York was laid out on the map into counties and those civil divisions of territory ultimately divided the people who lived in them into distinct groups. Each group was formed of families that intermarried and each group had its own trade affiliations and an arrangement by counties was adopted as a basis on which to present the houses illustrated in this volume as the houses, also, reflect the group principle.

From the immediate vicinity of Albany in the colony of Rensselaerswyck families migrated in the seventeenth century to Schenectady, Coxsackie, Coeymans, Catskill, Claverack and Kinderhook and also to Esopus and Poughkeepsie. The families that remained within the original limits of Albany County continued to look toward the village of Albany in matters of business and many marriages between their members created close kinship and near feeling. Ulster drew its first settlers not only from Rensselaerswyck but from New York, Harlem and Long Island and it became a unit in itself in family and trade relationships. The same thing was true of Dutchess and Westchester, where settlement was made by pioneers of various origins.

Between the people of the several counties communication was infrequent in ordinary circumstances. Individuals or families removed from one county to another and established new homes but after the removal had been accomplished they exchanged few visits with the relatives left in the place whence they had come. Such a separation of people into groups was the natural result of the lack of roads and the slow travel by water which has just been referred to in preceding pages. Except for trips by sloop for business errands or over bad roads on urgent calls (as for a doctor) people associated as a rule only with immediate neighbors.

It is therefore the more significant that there are a few traditions, still current among the families long resident in the Hudson valley, which are found throughout the whole region. One of the most prevalent tales carries the fort-idea. In almost all of the localities first settled there is to be heard the statement that a house was used as a fort, that people came to it for safety in Indian attacks and the visitor's attention is called to loopholes in the walls and to glass inserts in the doors. During the field-survey loopholes were found in a row at the line of the eaves and attic floor (in the house of Johannes G. Hardenbergh, plate 74); scattered irregularly in the walls (in the house of Francis Salisbury, plate 30); and placed in the gable-end (as in *Kost Verloren*, plate 26). In the Van Cortlandt manor-house (plate 109), *Crailo* and the Du Bois house (pages 113 and 198) there are genuine musketry openings in the walls, narrow at the outer ends and flaring at the inner, which are strikingly similar to each other. About the bull's-eyes in a door of the Van Aken house (plate 96) it is said that they were for observation in case of Indian raids. At Stone Ridge the bull's-eyes in a door between a hall and a room of the Wynkoop-Lounsbery house are believed to have been used by the owner for keeping watch over his slaves, who were visible to him while he was unseen by them. The oval glasses set diagonally in the handsome door of the Verplanck house of 1768 (plate 149) are considered to have been merely a source of light for an otherwise dark hall.

Three stories of the tomahawk of the Indian were found in the course of the survey which occur at separated points but which are similar in character. At Scotia, near Schenectady, the presence of a gash in the handrail of the main stairway of the Glen-Sanders house (plate 23) is explained as having been made by a tomahawk which was thrown by one Indian at another. A quarrel between the two men began out of doors and one Indian is said to have run from the other into the hall of the house to hide in the cupboard behind the door. The pursuer threw the tomahawk so that it just missed its aim and lodged in the banister. On Philip Schuyler's house in Albany, *The Pastures*, an attack by Tories and Indians was made in 1781 and the cut, still visible in the handrail of the broad stairway, marks the vigorous throw of a tomahawk, hurled upon Margaret Schuyler as she ran up stairs carrying her baby sister. The third story attaches to the Jansen house in Ulster County (page 209), where a Dutch door with a jagged cut is shown and where it is told that the door closed behind Colonel Johannes Jansen just as the tomahawk was thrown by one of an attacking party composed of Tories and Indians.

The tradition that the bricks used in building a house "came from Holland" is found in all the counties. But the few small ships in service on the Atlantic before 1664, when New Netherland was under Dutch sovereignty, could not have carried all the bricks claimed by the tradition. And after 1664, under English sovereignty and with plenty of bricks available of local manufacture, importation of brick from Holland became still less likely. The tradition is explainable, as has been stated previously, by the fact that bricks of different sizes were known as English brick and Holland brick.

In the kitchens of the early farmhouses the fireplace-openings were very large, so large that a back log for the fire was heavy and awkward for a man to handle, and on many an old farm the tradition has been passed down that it was a custom to have the back log drawn in from out of doors across the kitchen floor by a horse or an ox. Such a back log of large diameter and great length would sometimes last for a week.

Another tradition of general distribution is that a house was formerly a tavern. That taverns or inns existed in the pioneer period in rural districts in the sense that a hotel is now conducted is highly improbable. There was not enough travel to warrant the maintenance of a house solely for the entertainment of transient strangers. But that many farmers, in addition to carrying on their farms as their chief means of support, made a point of receiving passing guests as a secondary source of income is doubtless true. Such houses ultimately became well known and journeys were regulated in such a way as to reach them at hours convenient for obtaining meals or lodging. Hospitality was cordial in the day of lonely settlements and it is to be supposed that any householder would give shelter to those who came to his door in need of it; but when by tavern is meant a house that was a house devoted to public entertainment, which was in no sort a private home as well, then it must be understood that such an enterprise was a later, more modern development.

For those who were young in the nineteenth century the poem entitled: *A Visit from St. Nicholas*, of which the first line reads: " 'Twas the night before Christmas," is entwined with the dearest memories of childhood and to the Dutch element in the community the poem is of further interest for its form. It may be pertinent therefore to state to readers of Dutch descent that in the Dutch village of Claverack there is a tradition that *A Visit from St. Nicholas* was written there in the Hoogeboom house (plate 25); also that the descendants of Henry Livingston, Jr., are unanimous in the belief that their ancestor composed the poem in the house at Poughkeepsie which is described at page 354. At Claverack no name is offered for the writer of the poem but the tradition handed on from Poughkeepsie is so detailed that even a skeptical listener must be led to wonder what intriguing mystery in literary history lies hidden behind the much loved nursery lines.

With a portion of the public today the subject of the many places where Washington stayed over night on his travels is regarded as a threadbare joke. But in making the field-survey for this volume it was impossible not to be impressed with the fact that for the people of a former time a house which had been the scene of the entertainment of the Commander-in-Chief was invested with much interest and the tradition of his visit in a dwelling or in a village was long treasured by families and by communities. Mention of those visits is lifted from the plane of the ludicrous or trivial when made from the standpoint of a study of the houses. The simplicity of some of the dwellings where Washington cheerfully accepted hospitality on his many journeys is an illuminating side-light on the endurance, the determination and the self-sacrifice of the man who was the leader of the people in a crisis in their history.

One of the traditions of the Hudson valley which is most persistent is that of the British raid up the river in October, 1777, the story of which survives in many places. On October 12 a reconnoitering party (consisting of an armed schooner, two galleys and a small brig) went as far north of the Highlands as *Speck zyn kil* (plate 141), burned Matthew Van Keuren's mill and returned to its base to report the river clear. Then the real raid followed. In a letter written by Governor Clinton at New Windsor in Orange County at nine in the morning on October 15, 1777, the governor said that he had just been " informed by a light horseman that 20 sail of enemy's shipping (2 of them large vessels) are in the river below Butter Hill. Since writing above, enemy's fleet, consisting of 30 sail, have passed Newburgh with crowded sail and fair wind, are moving quick up the river and the front of them are already at the Dans Caamer. There are 8 large square-rigged vessels among them and all appear to have troops on board." This squadron was commanded by Captain Sir James Wallace and the troops it carried were under Major-General Sir

John Vaughan. As the ships passed up the river shots were fired on many houses, soldiers went ashore and burned buildings and at Kingston the whole village was destroyed. The raid is still talked of in old families and of the houses at which shots were aimed this volume lists (beside the Van Keuren) the Ten Broeck, Livingston and Van Voorhees homes in plates 88, 128 and 144 and the Du Bois and Stoutenburgh at pages 201 and 381.

Opposed to the tradition which is based upon fact in some form and which is inherently credible in some degree is the growth of rumor and the resultant statement as a fact of something that lacks foundation in truth. An instance of this occurs in the current tale that an underground passage connects the Dutch church at Sleepy Hollow with Philipse Castle on the Pocantico. The underground passage was conceived in the imagination of a writer, was put in a bit of published fiction and was quoted from that. The item passed from one to another until reference to its source and fictional character was dropped and the story became one of a passage actually in existence.

Survivals

The homes of the Hudson valley that are shown in this volume are occupied today in a variety of ways. There are many which long ago passed from the original owners and are lived in now in squalor by laboring aliens. Others are in the hands of newcomers but maintained with thrift and care. Some that are owned by native stock (either descendants of the first owner or a neighborhood family) exhibit one of the social problems of the region, that in which a pioneer family has been perpetuated but which has not progressed beyond the social development of the first members of it. In the interior there are still people who are today very like what their forbears were in the seventeenth or eighteenth centuries. Of houses built before 1776, which the survey of 1925 revealed as owned by the descendants of the builder and as maintained since erection on a rising scale of social standards, there are very few. Conspicuous instances of such survivals are the house of Philip Van Rensselaer in Albany and the Wynkoop homestead at Hurley, the homes of Madam Brett and Gulian Verplanck at Fishkill and the Van Cortlandt manor-house at Croton. The smallness of the number of the houses which can be recorded in this latter class is a significant commentary upon the movement of population and upon changes in domestic architecture. But even though people move about and the type of the average house changes, the survey as a whole induced a belief that there are pre-Revolutionary houses, standing now, which could be salvaged and, by intelligent restoration, be made into dwellings of taste and comfort which would be colored by the glow of romance that an historical background would provide.

PLATE 1

De Noorman's Kil (the Northman's Stream),

Albany County; a tributary of the Hudson, at the mouth of which the Indians had a castle and where Albert Andriesse Bradt, a Norwegian, built a mill. This valley is the reputed Vale of Tawasentha, described in *Hiawatha.*

35

PLATE 2

Meadows bordering Kinderhook Creek,

south and east of the village of Kinderhook. Typical of the low, well watered lands selected before 1700 by Dutch families at many points in the Hudson valley.

PLATE 3

The flat called Bonte Koe (Spotted Cow),

in Ulster County. A characteristic view of the Wallkill, near the Huguenot village of New Paltz, and with a suggestion in the background of the beetling crags of the Shawangunk range. The tower at Sky Top, Lake Mohonk, is outlined against the horizon.

37

PLATE 4

The valley of the Rondout,

Ulster County, at *Wagen Dal,* a locality settled by the Van Wagenen family before 1700. The stream here is narrow, the dale secluded. One of the homesteads of the Van Wagenens occupies the foreground.

PLATE 5

Arch-Support

Such arch-supports as this in the Van Kleeck-Hay house at Poughkeepsie are found in the cellars of almost all of the stone houses of the seventeenth and eighteenth centuries. They have no flues, are not fireplaces and were designed to bear the weight of end chimneys.

PLATE 6
Lintelstone,

house of Baltus Barents Van Kleeck, Poughkeepsie. Inscribed: 1702 BVK TVK. The initials stand for: Baltus Van Kleeck and Tryntje Van Kleeck.

PLATE 7

Cornerstone,

house of Pieter Viele, Poughkeepsie.   Inscribed: Ano * 1713 PV * MV.   The initials stand for Pieter Viele and (Myndert Viele?).

PLATE 8

House of Jacobus Swartwout,

Dutchess County, built about 1760. The plate shows the mud-filled framework of the walls, which was typical eighteenth century construction.

PLATE 9

Barn on the Verplanck-Van Wyck farm,

Dutchess County. The broad spread of the roof, low side walls, battened doors, iron strap-hinges and the overhang of the second story are all typical of the Dutch barns of the eighteenth century.

43

PLATE 10

The valley of the Vis Kil (Fish Stream),

Dutchess County. From a hilltop on the original course of the *King's Highway*, overlooking the village of Fishkill and the farms taken up by Dutch families under the title of the Rombout Patent.

PLATE 11

Road across southern Dutchess,

between Brinckerhoffville and Swartwoutville. Laid out by Dutch farmers early in the eighteenth century. During the Revolution it was the chief line of communication between New England and the South.

ALBANY COUNTY
Including COLUMBIA, RENSSELAER, GREENE and SCHENECTADY

EAST FRONT OF THE SCHUYLER HOUSE,
CALLED *THE FLATTS*,
AS IT WAS ABOUT 1870.

ALBANY COUNTY

INCLUDING COLUMBIA, RENSSELAER, GREENE AND SCHENECTADY

FROM 1614 to 1617 the United New Netherland Company of the Netherlands maintained a small fort, called Fort Nassau, at the head of navigation on the Hudson. The fort, which stood on the then Castle Island (since known as Van Rensselaer or Westerlo Island), was built in the interest of the fur-trade but had only a brief existence.

In 1623 the Dutch West India Company took possession of New Netherland and in the spring of 1624 sent from Europe a party of about thirty families of would-be settlers, most of whom were Walloons. Of this group, some eighteen families ascended the Hudson to the site of the present city of Albany; built a fort (where the steamboat square now is), which they named Fort Orange; built for themselves huts of bark (according to a statement made many years later by one of their number); but who very soon abandoned their settlement and removed to Manhattan. Only Fort Orange remained, occupied by a small garrison and by transient fur-traders.

Settled domestic life in Albany County really dates from the early 1630's. In 1630 the Colony of Rensselaerswyck was authorized as a private business enterprise in colonization and immediately thereafter Kiliaen Van Rensselaer of Amsterdam and his partners began to dispatch families and individuals to the colony, from whose arrival as permanent residents home-life began there.

As granted in 1630, Rensselaerswyck was a tract of wilderness, lying on both sides of the Hudson river and extending from Beeren Island (which is just below Coeymans, at the boundary line between Albany and Greene Counties) northward to the mouth of the Mohawk near Cohoes. It was twenty-two and a half miles long, north and south; forty-eight miles wide, east and west; and was divided in the center by the river. The first houses built by the colonists were placed on the low shores of the river near Fort Orange; north of the fort and opposite it at *Greenen Bosch;* a choice of location which proved unfortunate; for, when the river swelled in volume in the spring floods, serious losses frequently occurred.

A pen-picture of this small, weak community as it appeared in 1643, some ten years after it was founded, was drawn by Father Jogues, a Jesuit from Canada, who visited the place that year and who said in his account of it that it consisted of about one hundred people, living in twenty-five or thirty houses along the river. Father Jogues wrote that the people had saw-mills, with which they made boards out of the pine trees that abounded in the forest; that the houses were built of such boards and were thatched but had no mason-work except in the chimneys; and that the dwellings were near Fort Orange, the fort being a small structure of logs.

As time went on the number of houses near the fort increased to a total that, in the opinion of Peter Stuyvesant of Manhattan, impaired the military usefulness of the fort and a controversy arose between Stuyvesant as Director of New Netherland and Brant Van Slichtenhorst as Director of Rensselaerswyck, each of whom claimed jurisdiction. The dispute raged from 1648 to 1652 when Stuyvesant condemned the houses around the fort and laid out and organized a free village in the adjacent area, to which village the name *Beverwyck* was given. Also, with the establishment of the village, the beaver-trade (which had been controlled by the West India Company) was thrown open to citizens.

A fundamental difference was thus created between the village of *Beverwyck* and the colony of *Rensselaerswyck*. In the colony farms were occupied under leaseholds. In the village a house-lot could be acquired by a citizen and held in fee simple and it can hardly be questioned that the opportunity afforded in the village for men to own their own homes led to the improvement in house-building that began soon after the village was organized. If the assumption be correct that, up to 1652, the poor type of dwelling, seen by Father Jogues near Fort Orange in 1643, prevailed there and that the building of better houses began after 1652, then the parsonage that was built for Domine Schaets was one of the first substantial dwellings in *Beverwyck*. Erected in 1657 at a spot which became the northeast corner of State and Pearl Streets, the parsonage was a brick house, two and one-half stories high, which stood until 1832 and which in 1805 was recorded in an oil painting by James Eights. The painting, now owned by Mrs. William Gorham Rice of Albany, is reproduced in plate 32. Other dated instances of brick houses in the third quarter of the seventeenth century (1651—1675) are the house which was the birthplace of General Philip Schuyler, built in or before 1667 (plate 34); the house called *The Flatts*, built in 1668 by Richard Van Rensselaer (page 94); and the Van Rensselaer manor-house, built in 1668—1671 (plate 47).

The brick houses built in the village of *Beverwyck* and those built on the farms of *Rensselaerswyck* had in common the roof of steep single pitch, which was in general use from the day of the parsonage of 1657 to the middle of the next century (see: plates 15, 16, 17, 22, 32, 34, 40, 41, 42, 44, 47, 51, 54, 55). But while the brick houses in the village were in several instances two stories and a half in height, only houses a story and a half high have been found in the country (unless *Crailo* at *Greenen Bosch* were built originally as it now stands). Likewise, although the houses in the village were sometimes given a stepped or terraced gable, no such finish has been discovered elsewhere in Albany County. Why there should have been the difference between the houses in the village and those in the rural districts in regard to the height of the walls and the finish of the roof-lines, when in other respects

50

they closely resembled each other, is a question for which no answer has been learned. The survey revealed such a difference and can only record it without explanation.

In town and country many of the details of construction were standardized. The finial at the peak of each gable on the house built by Leendert Bronck in 1738 (plate 17) is also to be seen in prints of the early nineteenth century illustrating houses on the streets of Albany and it was presumably an early feature, generally introduced. Along the line of the roof, in the gable-ends of the brick houses, the bricks were often laid in a pattern of successive triangles (as shown in plates 15, 17, 40, 41, 56), a pattern called in Dutch *muizetanden* (mouse teeth). And the iron beam-anchors, that were used everywhere, may be seen more or less clearly in plates 14, 15, 16, 25, 38, 44, 47, 49, 54, 55 and 56. Dormer windows seem to have been an afterthought and not part of the houses as first built, except in the case of the Beekman house (plate 12) and of the house of Ariaantje Coeymans (vignette, page 9), which each exhibited conspicuous dormers with stepped roof-lines. The simpler dormers differ from each other to the extent that their roofs slope or are flat. Such sloping dormers as those of the Vanderheyden and Van Loon houses (plates 45 and 46) are of earlier date than those on the Staats, Van Antwerp-Mebie, Van Rensselaer, Van Vechten and Van Wie houses (plates 37, 42, 50, 53 and 54).

Brick houses were built with a gambrel roof at Catskill in 1729 (page 106); on the road below *Greenen Bosch* before and after the middle of the eighteenth century (see: plates 26, 37 and 49); on the site of Troy in the 1750's (plate 45); near Cohoes in the 1750's and 1760's (page 76 and plates 27 and 52); at Kinderhook in 1766 (page 83); and at Claverack in 1767 (plate 28). And brick houses with a roof of single slant, broadly spread as on the stone houses, were built by the Gardeniers and Van Alstynes in Columbia County in the 1750's and 1760's (pages 82, 83) as well as near Cohoes by the Lansings and Fondas before 1767 (page 76).

In the third quarter of the eighteenth century a trend toward Georgian English architecture showed itself in Albany County in the brick houses built by Philip Schuyler (*The Pastures*, 1762), Stephen Van Rensselaer (the manor-house, 1765), Hendrick Cuyler (*Vly House*, before 1767) and David Van Schaack in 1774 (pages 97, 112, 77 and 84); a trend that continued for some years to express itself in such houses as those of John Stephenson on State Street, Albany, 1780—1841 (a view of which is shown in Howell and Tenney's *History of Albany County* at page 667), and the built-over house of Christopher Yates in Schenectady of about 1785 (plate 57).

At very nearly the same time that the use of brick began in *Beverwyck* stone houses appeared on the farms. The stone house of Pieter Bronck of the 1660's (plate 16); of Barent Pieterse Coeymans of the 1670's (page 71); and that of Daniel Van Antwerp of approximately 1680 (plate 42) are three early examples. The roofs of the Bronck and Van Antwerp houses were of noticeably steep pitch, as was also that of the Van Schaack house of a later date at Kinderhook (plate 51), but nothing

51

has been found to show whether the Bronck and Van Antwerp roofs were typical or exceptional for the stone houses of 1650—1700 in Albany County. In the eighteenth century stone houses with roofs of a single slant but a broader spread were built at Coxsackie and Catskill, on Staats Island and at Claverack. A gambrel roof was given to the stone house of Francis Salisbury at Catskill in 1705 (plate 30) and gambrels occurred on the Van Loon house of 1724 (plate 46), on the Coeymans-Bronck house (page 75) and on the Staats house at the mouth of the Stockport Creek (page 99).

The house of Francis Salisbury was unusual for its date, not only in its roof but in the fact that it was two full stories in height. The house of Ariaantje Coeymans (plate 18), built about 1716, was also two stories high but the roof of the latter house was at first a steep single pitch and carried a stepped dormer (page 72) similar to the dormers on the Beekman-Vanderheyden house (plate 12). Indeed, if the house of Francis Salisbury were hailed in 1705 as notably large and handsome, as tradition says it was, it was crowded for first place when Ariaantje Coeymans built a few years later for the Coeymans house is the larger of the two and the original design was more elaborate than that of the Salisbury house. The Salisbury house is now in good repair, with many original features left, but the Coeymans house is in decay and almost past restoration.

Among the houses of Albany County those of brick and those of stone each include among their numbers one which is a conundrum, architecturally. The brick conundrum is *Crailo*, the Van Rensselaer house at *Greenen Bosch*, and the puzzle in stone is the Glen-Sanders house at Scotia. Neither of these two houses exhibits a pure architectural type. Each is the sum of a succession of additions and alterations but the problems they present need not be stated at this point as they are discussed on other pages (79, 113).

In connection with the farms laid out in the colony of Rensselaerswyck in the seventeenth century the first patroon, Kiliaen Van Rensselaer, instituted the custom of giving names to the separate holdings and a number of such farm-titles are still to be heard mentioned in the common speech of people familiar with old neighborhoods. Among the early names, still remembered, are: *Watervliet* (Water Course), *Crailo* (Crows' Woods), *de Vlackte* (the Flat), *Wolven Hoeck* (Wolves' Point), *Kost Verloren* (Money Thrown Away), *Hooge Bergh* (High Hill), *Domine's Hoeck* (Minister's Point), &c.

A visitor to America in 1749 was Peter Kalm, a Swede, who, during his travels, kept a diary that later was published.* On June 21, 1749, Kalm was in Albany and he wrote on that date of the dwellings there: " The houses in this town are very neat and partly built with stones, covered with shingles of the white pine. Some are slated with tiles from Holland because the clay of this neighborhood is

* Peter Kalm, *Travels into North America*, London, 1772, 2nd ed.

not reckoned fit for tiles. Most of the houses are built in the old way with the gable-end towards the street, a few excepted, which were lately built in the manner now used. A great number of houses were built like those of New Brunswick, which I have described; the gable-end being built towards the street of bricks and all other walls of planks."

Kalm's description affords a basis for the statement that in Albany in 1749 there were not only such houses of brick as the Schaets, 1657; Schuyler, 1667; Wendell, 1716; and Beekman, 1725; but two other types: one a stone structure, with shingled or tiled roof; and another, which was a combination of bricks and boards. His observations are borne out in part by items in the diary * of Richard Smith of Burlington, New Jersey, who passed through Albany in 1769 and recorded that the houses there then were built of brick or faced with brick and were covered with white pine shingles or, in a few instances, with red and black tiles. In Schenectady there is still standing, in perfect condition, a fine example (plate 56) of the type of house built with a brick gable to the street and planked side walls, which Kalm saw in Albany in 1749.

Schenectady, the only community in Albany County beside Albany which before 1700 can be considered as having amounted to a village, was founded in 1662 by Arent Van Curler. It was laid out as a free town, with streets on the plan of a checkerboard and, being on the frontier, was stockaded. But the stockade availed little in 1690 when, in an attack by French and Indians, fire and massacre very nearly wiped out the whole settlement. Permanent development in house-building at Schenectady dates therefore from after the losses of 1690 and data are few upon which to rest an opinion as to the type of dwelling built there in the years immediately succeeding those which were burned in that year. But the record of three houses of 1715—1730 (pages 64, 126) points to a probability that the streets of Schenectady presented a general resemblance to those of Albany. Richard Smith's journal of 1769 states that the village counted then some three-hundred dwellings, most of which were of wood, some of brick; that few buildings were contiguous; that some were " in the old Dutch taste "; and that there might have been " six or seven elegant mansions."

The custom of placing a house with its gable-end toward the street arose in the mediaeval walled cities of Europe as an economy of space. That it was not peculiar to the Netherlands is shown by the French proverb: " to have a gable on the street," meaning: to have a home of one's own. So the custom, transplanted to Albany and Schenectady, represented Europe, not merely the Low Countries; and the fact was fitting, inasmuch as the people who settled Albany County were of very generally distributed derivation. Only in part were they Low Dutch in origin and more and more as analysis is made of the first arrivals, is it demonstrated from what widely separated points of departure they came. This is the more interesting because of

* Francis W. Halsey, editor, *Four Great Rivers, Journal of Richard Smith*, 1769, Scribner's, 1906.

the strongly Dutch feeling that prevailed in Albany. The county was probably the most thoroughly Dutch in its characteristics of any portion of New Netherland but, as a matter of fact, it was actually an instance of social assimilation; for the Low Dutch culture of Albany County in general and of the city of Albany in particular completely absorbed all other elements in the community. The explanation for this may lie in the prosperity of the Dutch Republic at the time New Netherland was founded and in the adversities of its neighbors. Dutch rule was liberal, Dutch feeling was tolerant, Dutch commerce was flourishing and refugees, political and religious, and men of energy of small means flocked to the Netherlands for protection and for opportunity. In the first half of the seventeenth century Dutch cities and towns were filled with Walloons, French Protestants, English Pilgrims and representatives of almost all parts of northern and central Europe and of this motley throng large numbers moved on across the sea to the New Netherland, where still wider openings in life seemed to them to offer. Grateful for that which Dutch asylum had given them in their flight from their original hardships, they readily adopted the Dutch language and Dutch customs, made marriages in Dutch families and were succeeded by descendants who lost all knowledge of the fact that their ancestors were anything but Dutch. All of which is an illuminating illustration of the value to a nation of a broadly humanistic state policy, as opposed to legalism and compulsion, and the story supplies also a side light on the reaction of average men and women toward those who treat them well.

While the house built with its gable toward the street represents mediaeval Europe, the house with its front façade on the walk may be symbolic of America's wealth in land in the seventeenth and eighteenth centuries. Where it was unnecessary to conserve space men's natural instinct for expansion found expression and Kalm noted such a tendency as having begun some years before his visit to Albany in 1749. Perhaps the Beekman house (plate 12) of 1725 may be taken as an early instance of a house occupying a long street frontage.

Of the scenes in the streets of Albany in 1749, the customs of the people and their commercial affairs, Kalm's account furnishes a few details. It states that: " The gutters on the roofs reach almost to the middle of the street. This preserves the walls from being damaged by the rain; but is extremely disagreeable in rainy weather for the people in the streets, there being hardly any means of avoiding the water from the gutters. The street doors are generally in the middle of the houses, and on both sides are seats, on which during fair weather the people spend almost the whole day, especially on those which are in the shadow of the houses. In the evening these seats are covered with people of both sexes. *** The streets are broad, and some of them are paved; in some parts they are lined with trees. *** The streets upon the whole are pretty dirty because the people leave their cattle in them during the summer nights.*** Almost each house in Albany has its well, the water of which is applied to common use; but for tea, brewing and washing, they commonly take the water of the river Hudson, which flows close by the town. This water is generally quite muddy and very warm in summer; and on that account it is kept in cellars, in order that the slime may subside and that the water may cool a little."*** (The breakfast of the Albanians) " is tea, commonly without milk. About thirty or forty years ago tea was unknown to them, and they breakfasted either upon bread and butter or bread and milk. They never put sugar into the cup, but take a small bit of it into their mouths whilst they drink. Along with the tea they eat bread and butter, with slices of hung beef. Coffee is not usual here. They breakfast generally about seven. Their dinner is butter-milk and bread, to which they sometimes add sugar: then it is a delicious dish for them; or fresh milk and bread; or boiled or roasted flesh. They sometimes make use of butter-milk instead of fresh milk to boil a thin kind of porridge with, which tastes very sour but not disagreeable in hot weather. To each dinner they have a great salad, prepared with abundance of vinegar and very little or no oil. They frequently eat butter-milk, bread and salad, one mouthful after another. Their supper is generally bread and butter and milk and bread. They sometimes eat cheese at breakfast and at dinner; it is not in slices, but scraped or rasped so as to resemble coarse flour, which they pretend adds to the good taste of cheese. They commonly drink very small beer or pure water. The greater part of the merchants at Albany have extensive estates in the country and a great deal of wood. If their estates have a little brook they do not fail to erect a saw-mill upon it for sawing boards and planks, with which commodity many yachts go during the whole summer to New York, having scarce any other lading than boards."

Peter Kalm's description of Albany is tinctured by a prejudice he seems to have held against the place and people but it is supplemented by the writings of Anne McVickar Grant, another visitor there, to whom all was *couleur de rose*. Writing of Albany as she knew it in the decade from 1758 to 1768 and referring to the same points touched upon by Kalm, as quoted above, Mrs. Grant said: *

" The town in proportion to its population occupied a great space of ground. This city was in short a kind of semi-rural establishment; every house had its garden, well and a little green behind; before every door a tree was planted, rendered interesting by being coeval with some beloved member of the family; many of their trees were of a prodigious size and extraordinary beauty, but without regularity, every one planting the kind that best pleased him, or which he thought would afford the most agreeable shade to the open portico at his door."*** (The porticos were surrounded by seats and ascended by a few steps and) " it was in these that each domestic group was seated in summer evenings to enjoy the balmy twilight or the serenely clear moonlight. Each family had a cow, fed in a common pasture at the end of the town. In the evening the herd returned all together of their own accord, with their tinkling bells hung at their necks, along the wide and grassy street, to

* Anne McVickar Grant, *Memoirs of an American Lady*, London, 1808; Appleton, New York, 1846.

their wonted sheltering trees to be milked at their masters' doors. Nothing could be more pleasing to a simple and benevolent mind than to see thus at one view all the inhabitants of a town, which contained not one very rich or very poor, very knowing or very ignorant, very rude or very polished individual; to see all these children of nature enjoying in easy indolence or social intercourse 'the cool, the fragrant and the dusky hour,' clothed in the plainest habits and with minds as undisguised and artless. These primitive beings were dispersed in porches, grouped according to similarity of years and inclinations. At one door were young matrons, at another the elders of the people, at a third the youths and maidens, gayly chatting or singing together, while the children played round the trees or waited by the cows for the chief ingredient of their frugal supper, which they generally ate sitting on the steps in the open air."

The residents of Albany, according to Mrs. Grant, " were exceedingly social and visited each other very frequently besides the regular assembling together in their porches every fine evening. Of the more substantial luxuries of the table they knew little, and of the formal and ceremonious parts of good breeding still less." (They were shy and cold at first toward strangers. Dinner was served very early and was plain and unceremonious.) " Tea here was a perfect regale, being served up with various sorts of cakes unknown to us, cold pastry and great quantities of sweetmeats and preserved fruits, and plates of hickory and other nuts, ready cracked. In all manner of confectionery and pastry these people excelled; and having fruit in great plenty, which cost them nothing, and getting sugar home at an easy rate in return for their exports to the West Indies, the quantities of these articles used in families, otherwise plain and frugal, was astonishing."*** (Supper was substantial, though plain.) " You had either game or poultry, roasted, and always shellfish in the season; also fruit in abundance. All this with much neatness but no form.*** The girls, from the example of their mothers, rather than any compulsion, very early became notably industrious, being constantly employed in knitting stockings and making clothes for the family and slaves; they even made all the boys' clothes. This was the more necessary as all articles of clothing were extremely dear. Though all the necessaries of life and some luxuries abounded, money as yet was a scarce commodity."*** (It was the practise to) " cut down trees and carry them to an adjoining saw-mill, where in a very short time they made great quantities of planks, staves, &c., which is usually styled lumber, for the West India market. And when a shipload of their flour, lumber and salted provisions accumulated, they freighted a vessel and went out to the West Indies with it.*** When its cargo was discharged in the West Indies it took in a lading of wine, rum, sugar, coffee, chocolate and all other West India productions."

" Every one in town or country," said Mrs. Grant, " had a garden; but all the more hardy plants grew in the field in rows amidst the hills, as they were called, of Indian corn. These lofty plants sheltered them from the sun, while the same hoeing served for both; there cabbages, potatoes and other esculent roots, with variety of gourds, grew to a great size and were of an excellent quality. Kidney-beans, asparagus, celery, great variety of salads and sweet herbs, cucumbers, &c., were only admitted into the garden, into which no foot of man intruded after it was dug in spring. Here were no trees; those grew in the orchard in high perfection. Strawberries and many high-flavored wild fruits of the shrub kind abounded so much in the woods that they did not think of cultivating them in their gardens, which were extremely neat but small and not by any means calculated for walking in. I think I yet see, what I have so often beheld both in town and country, a respectable mistress of a family, going out to her garden in an April morning with her great calash, her little painted basket of seeds, and her rake over her shoulder, to her garden labors. These were by no means merely figurative. 'From morn till noon, from noon till dewy eve,' a woman in very easy circumstances and abundantly gentle in form and manners would sow and plant and rake incessantly. These fair gardeners were also great florists; their emulation and solicitude in this pleasing employment did indeed produce 'flowers worthy of Paradise.' Though not set in 'curious knots,' they were arranged in beds, the varieties of each kind by themselves; this, if not varied and elegant, was at least rich and gay. To the Schuylers this description did not apply; they had gardens, and their gardens were laid out in the European manner.''

Anne McVickar Grant, the writer of the recollections just quoted, was born in Scotland in 1755 and died there in 1838. She was the child of Captain Duncan McVickar of the English army, who in 1757 was ordered with his regiment to the Province of New York and who in 1758 was followed to America by his wife and daughter. The latter was then three years old and she remained with her parents in the vicinity of Albany until she was thirteen, returning to Scotland with her father and mother about 1768. While at Albany the little girl became a pet in the household of Mrs. Philip Schuyler (born 1701, died 1782), who was known in her own day as " Madam " and as " Aunt." Madam Schuyler lived on the estate called *The Flatts* (plate 33), where Anne McVickar was her guest for a long time, and the child formed a deep attachment for Madam and for Madam's home. In after years Mrs. Grant, the former Anne McVickar, wrote and published her recollections of Albany and in honor of her early friend entitled the volume: *Memoirs of an American Lady*. The book is written from the viewpoint of a person of mature mind and as Mrs. Grant was but a child when at Albany it must be assumed that many statements in it are based upon what her parents observed and later commented upon to her. But even so, with due allowance for a margin of inaccuracy, the volume affords a record of domestic life at Albany about 1758—1768 which is of definite value. By supplying details of the life of the Schuylers at *The Flatts* it provides not only a knowlege of

57

that particular household but a gauge by which to measure the ways of other homes in Albany County at that same time. Manners and customs at *The Flatts* were the maximum of elegance and of comfort in that vicinity at the date of Mrs. Grant's sojourn there and to form a general idea of the standard of living where the standard was the highest within a given area makes it possible to estimate gradations in detail in smaller houses and among people of lesser wealth. The following excerpts from Mrs. Grant's book provide a vivid picture of the home-life and surroundings of people who were the leaders of their community in the third quarter of the eighteenth century.

The family residence of Colonel Philip Schuyler (born 1696, died 1758) "was at the Flats, a fertile and beautiful plain on the banks of the river. He possessed about two miles on a stretch of that rich and level champaign. This possession was bounded on the east by the river Hudson, whose high banks overhung the stream and its pebbly strand, and were both adorned and defended by elms (larger than ever I have seen in any other place) decked with natural festoons of wild grapes, which abound along the banks of this noble stream.*** As you came along by the north end of the town (Albany), where the Patroon had his seat, you afterwards passed by the enclosures of the citizens where they planted their corn, and arrived at the Flats, Colonel Schuyler's possession. On the right you saw the river in all its beauty, there above a mile broad.*** Opposite to the grounds lay an island, above a mile in length, and about a quarter in breadth, which also belonged to the colonel.*** At the end of the island, which was exactly opposite to the family mansion, a long sandbank extended; on this was a very valuable fishing-place, of which a considerable profit might be made. In summer, when the water was low, this narrow stripe (for such it was) came in sight and furnished an amusing spectacle; for the bald or white-headed eagle (a large picturesque bird, very frequent in this country), the ospray, the heron and the curlew used to stand in great numbers in a long row, like a military arrangement, for a whole summer day, fishing for perch and a kind of fresh-water herring which abounded there. At the same season a variety of wild ducks, which bred on the shores of the island (among which was a small white diver of an elegant form), led forth their young to try their first excursion.

"Be it known that the house I had so much delight in recollecting had no pretension to grandeur and very little to elegance. It was a large brick house of two or rather three stories (for there were excellent attics), besides a sunk story, finished with exactest neatness. The lower floor had two spacious rooms, with large light closets; on the first there were three rooms and in the upper one four. Through the middle of the house was a very wide passage, with opposite front and back doors which in summer admitted a stream of air peculiarly grateful to the languid senses. It was furnished with chairs and pictures like a summer parlor. Here the family usually sat in hot weather, when there were no ceremonious strangers.

58

" Valuable furniture (though perhaps not very well chosen or assorted) was the favorite luxury of these people, and in all the houses I remember,—except those of the brothers, who were every way more liberal,—the mirrors, the paintings, the china, but above all the state-bed were considered as the family Teraphim, secretly worshipped, and only exhibited on very rare occasions. But in Colonel Schuyler's family the rooms were merely shut up to keep the flies, which in that country are an absolute nuisance, from spoiling the furniture. Another motive was that they might be pleasantly cool when opened for company.

" This house had also two appendages, common to all those belonging to persons in easy circumstances there. One was a large portico at the door, with a few steps leading up to it and floored like a room; it was open at the sides and had seats all round. Above was either a slight wooden roof, painted like an awning, or a covering of lattice-work, over which a transplanted wild vine spread its luxuriant leaves and numerous clusters.***

" At the back of the large house was a smaller and lower one, so joined to it as to make the form of a cross. There, one or two lower and smaller rooms below and the same number above afforded a refuge to the family during the rigors of winter, when the spacious summer-rooms would have been intolerably cold and the smoke of prodigious wood-fires would have sullied the elegantly clean furniture. Here, too, was a sunk story, where the kitchen was immediately below the eating-parlor and increased the general warmth of the house. In summer the negroes inhabited slight outer kitchens in which food was dressed for the family. Those who wrought in the fields often had their simple dinner cooked without and ate it under the shade of a great tree.

" One room, I should have said, in the greater house only was opened for the reception of company; all the rest were bed-chambers for their accomodation; the domestic friends of the family occupying neat little bedrooms in the attics or in the winterhouse. This house contained no drawing-room; that was an unheard of luxury; the winter-rooms had carpets; the lobby had oilcloth painted in lozenges to imitate blue and white marble. The best bedroom was hung with family portraits, some of which were admirably executed; and in the eating-room, which, by the by, was rarely used for that purpose, were some fine scripture-paintings.***

" The house fronted the river, on the brink of which, under shades of elm and sycamore, ran the great road towards Saragota, Stillwater and the northern lakes; a little simple avenue of morella cherry-trees, enclosed with a white rail, led to the road and river, not three-hundred yards distant. Adjoining to this, on the south side, was an enclosure, subdivided into three parts, of which the first was a small hay-field, opposite the south end of the house; the next, not so long, a garden; and the third, by far the largest, an orchard. These were surrounded by simple deal fences.***

" Adjoining to the orchard was the most spacious barn I ever beheld, which

59

I shall describe for the benefit of such of my readers as have never seen a building constructed on a plan so comprehensive. This barn, which, as will hereafter appear, answered many beneficial purposes besides those usually allotted for such edifices, was of a vast size, at least a hundred feet long and sixty wide. The roof rose to a very great height in the midst and sloped down till it came within ten feet of the ground, when the walls commenced; which, like the whole of this vast fabric, were formed of wood. It was raised three feet from the ground by beams resting on stone; and on these beams was laid, in the middle of the building, a very massive oak floor. Before the door was a large sill, sloping downwards, of the same materials. A breadth of about twelve feet on each side of this capacious building was divided off for cattle; on one side ran a manger at the above-mentioned distance from the wall, the whole length of the building, with a rack above it; on the other were stalls for the other cattle, running also the whole length of the building. The cattle and horses stood with their hinder parts to the wall and their heads towards the thrashing floor. There was a prodigious large box or open chest in one side, built up for holding the corn after it was thrashed; and the roof, which was very lofty and spacious, was supported by large cross-beams. From one to the other of these was stretched a great number of long poles, so as to form a sort of open loft, on which the whole rich crop was laid up. The floor of those parts of the barn which answered the purposes of a stable and cow-house was made of thick slab deals, laid loosely over the supporting beams. In the front of this vast edifice there were prodigious folding doors and two others that opened behind.*** When speaking of the doors I should have mentioned that they were made in the gable-ends; those in the back equally large to correspond with those in the front; while on each side of the great doors were smaller ones for the cattle and horses to enter. Whenever the corn or hay was reaped or cut, a wagon loaded with hay, for instance, was driven into the midst of this great barn. From the top of the wagon the hay was forked up into the loft of the barn, and then the unloaded wagon drove in rustic state out of the great door at the other end.***

" Colonel Schuyler's barn was by far the largest I have ever seen; but all of them in that country were constructed on the same plan, furnished with the same accommodation and presented the same cheering aspect. The orchard, as I formerly mentioned, was on the south side of the barn; on the north, a little farther back towards the wood, which formed a dark screen behind this smiling prospect, there was an enclosure in which the remains of the deceased members of the family were deposited.***

" There certainly never were people who received so much company, made so respectable a figure in life and always kept so large a family about them with so little tumult or bustle or, indeed, at so moderate an expense. What their income was I cannot say; but am sure it could not have been what we should think adequate to the good they did and the hospitality and beneficence which they practised; for the rents of lands were then of so little value that, though they possessed a considerable estate in another part of the country, only very moderate profits could result from it; but, indeed, from the simplicity of dress, &c., it was easier; though in that respect, too, they preserved a kind of dignity and went beyond others in the materials though not the form of their apparel. Yet their principal expense was a most plentiful and well ordered table, quite in the English style, which was a kind of innovation.*** They always breakfasted early and dined two hours later than the primitive inhabitants, who always took that meal at twelve.*** With regard to the plenty, one might almost call it luxury, of their table it was supplied from a variety of sources that rendered it less expensive than could be imagined. Indians were constantly bringing the smaller game and, in winter and spring, loads of venison. Little money passed from one hand to another in the country; but there was constantly a kindly commerce of presents. The people of New York and Rhode Island, several of whom were wont to pass a part of the summer with the colonel's family, were loaded with all the productions of the farm and river. When they went home they again never failed at the season to send a large supply of oysters and all other shellfish, which at New York abounded; besides great quantities of tropical fruit, which from the short run between Jamaica and New York were there almost as plenty and as cheap as in their native soil. Their farm yielded them abundantly all that, in general, agriculture can supply. The negroes, whose business lay frequently in the woods, never willingly went there without a gun and rarely came back empty handed. Presents of wine, then a very usual thing to send to friends to whom you wished to show a mark of gratitude, came very often. As there were no duties paid for the entrance of any commodity there wine, rum and sugar were cheaper than can easily be imagined, and in cider they abounded."

HOUSES in ALBANY COUNTY

Beekman-Vanderheyden House

Formerly at Albany, New York

PLATE 12

In 1725 Johannes Beekman built a house on the west side of North Pearl Street, Albany (on the lot where the Albany Savings Bank now stands), which remained standing until 1833 and was occupied by the builder until his death in 1756. Johannes Beekman was succeeded in the house by his daughters, who lived in it until the period of the Revolution when, in 1778, they sold it to Jacob Vanderheyden. The new owner rented the house to tenants for some years (during part of which time an academy was conducted in it) and then, in 1797, he moved into it himself and continued to make it his home until he died in 1820. The occupation of the house by Jacob Vanderheyden from 1797 to 1820 gave it the name of *Vanderheyden Palace*, by which it is generally mentioned. The house was made more or less famous by Washington Irving, who in his visits to Albany in the first quarter of the nineteenth century admired its picturesque quality and used it as the prototype for the residence of *Heer Antony Vanderheyden* in *Bracebridge Hall*.

The Beekman-Vanderheyden house was an oblong structure of brick, with a roof of single slant and two stepped dormers toward the street. It had a frontage of fifty feet and was twenty feet in depth, with a hall and two rooms on the ground floor. In its latter years the interior was modernized to some extent but the massive ceiling beams and the early wainscoting were unaltered. On the gable-end the date of erection, 1725, appeared in iron figures. Iron wall-anchors occurred at intervals. The bricks over the windows were laid in ornamental design. On each dormer was a weather-vane, one a cock and the other a running horse. The horse was acquired by Irving and taken to his home, *Sunnyside*, at Irvington-on-the-Hudson, where he is said to have incorporated in his remodelled dwelling architectural features copied from the *Vanderheyden Palace*.

For purposes of architectural study the Beekman-Vanderheyden house should be compared with the house of Ariaantje Coeymans (plate 18), built about 1716 at Coeymans, New York. Two pictures of the *Palace* survive. The first is in the painting done in 1805 by James Eights and reproduced in plate 32, where it occurs in the middle distance behind a poplar tree. The second is a woodcut, which was published in 1850 in Munsell's *Annals of Albany* (1 : 278), seventeen years after the house had been torn down. The woodcut must have been derived from a sketch or a print but whether the original drawing were made directly from the house or based on the artist's memory there is no way now to learn. In essentials the painting of 1805 and the woodcut of 1850 are well agreed, the only important difference being in the representation of the front entrance.

The accompanying plate was made from a photograph of the woodcut, taken by the late Colonel Augustus Pruyn of Albany and obtained through the kindness of his daughter, Miss Margaret Ten Eyck Pruyn.

Bogardus-Ten Broeck House
Formerly at Albany, New York
PLATE 13

In 1806 James Eights, the artist, painted a view of the north side of State Street, Albany, which is shown in plate 13. The painting was photographed by the late Colonel Augustus Pruyn and through the courtesy of Miss Margaret Ten Eyck Pruyn reproduction is here made from a print of her father's negative. The sketch begins at the left with the house of Domine Schaets and follows State Street to a point east of James Street. The small house on the corner of James Street was the house owned by Anneke Jans. Architecturally, the view of this house may be of minor value. Sentimentally, the home of the woman whose name is so widely known is of interest. Anneke Jans was born in Holland about 1600 and died in Albany (*Beverwyck*) March 19, 1663. Her first husband, Roeloff Jansen, came out to Rensselaerswyck about 1630 as steward for the patroon and she accompanied him. About 1634 they removed from Rensselaerswyck and Roeloff Jansen died soon after (perhaps in Brazil). His name is perpetuated by the stream, *Roeloff Jansen's Kil*, in Columbia County. In 1638 his widow married the Reverend Everardus Bogardus. After the latter's death in 1647, Anneke Jans returned to *Beverwyck*, owned this house and there died. Her heirs sold the house to Major Dirck Wessels Ten Broeck, the founder of a well known family and the brother of Wessel Wesselse Ten Broeck, whose house at Kingston is shown in plate 87.

House of Captain Arent Bradt
Formerly at 7, State street, Schenectady, New York
PLATE 14

Albert Andriesse Bradt and Arent Andriesse Bradt, brothers, were among the early settlers at Rensselaerswyck. They were Norwegians. Albert established himself a few miles south of Albany on a stream, where he built a mill. He was known as " de Noorman " and the stream today is still the *Norman's Kil*. Arent removed from the colony to the independent town of Schenectady, of which he was one of the patentees in 1662. He died soon after the charter was granted and title to his lands was confirmed to his widow, Catelyntje DeVos Bradt. Her home-lot in Schenectady, on the north side of State street near Washington, passed to her son, Andries Arent Bradt (killed in the Indian massacre of 1690). He, by his wife Margreta Van Slyke, had a son Arent, who was born about 1680, married 1704 to Jannetje Vrooman, and died in 1767. This last Arent Bradt built about 1715 on the home-lot of his grandmother on State Street a brick house, which stood until about 1900, and which was a good example of the houses built in the seventeenth and early eighteenth centuries, gable-end to the street and with roof of high pitch.

Although the Bradts came from Norway they so merged themselves with their Dutch neighbors as to be regarded as wholly Dutch themselves. Arent Bradt, who built and occupied the house illustrated, prospered as a brewer, was long a trustee of Schenectady and represented that place in the provincial assembly. His son, Captain Andries Bradt, who succeeded to the brick house, was the father of Jannetje Bradt, born 1743, who married Christopher Yates and lived in the house shown in plate 57.

House of Arent Bradt
Schenectady, New York

West of the city of Schenectady is the municipal pumping station on the south bank of the Mohawk river. Near the station Schermerhorn Road runs south from the river-road and below the junction on the right is the house of Arent Bradt, now owned by the heirs of Simon Schermerhorn. Local histories give 1730 (or 1736) as the year of the erection of the house and there is no occasion to question the approximate accuracy of the statement. The builder was a grandson of the Arent Bradt who was a patentee of Schenectady in 1662 and a cousin of Arent whose house is shown in plate 14. His wife, Catrina Mebie (born 1691, died 1773), was a daughter of Jan Pieterse Mebie and lived before her marriage in the house of her father (plate 42) near Rotterdam Junction.

Arent Bradt's house is built of brick, with a high-pitched roof. But modern doors, windows, blinds and porch alter its general appearance. A picture of it may be found in Weller's: *Tales of Old Dorp* and Greene's: *Old Mohawk Turnpike*. The roof of this house belongs in a class with the roofs of the Bradt, Bries, Bronck, Douw, Van Alen, Vandenbergh, Van Rensselaer and Van Wie houses (plates: 14, 15, 16, 22, 41, 44, 47 and 54).

House of Hendrick Bries
Town of East Greenbush, Albany County, New York
PLATE 15

About three miles south of the city of Rensselaer on the river-road to Castleton stands one of the best surviving examples of a house with a Dutch roof of steep pitch.

The house is entered on the map that was made of Van Rensselaer Manor in 1767 as the dwelling of the "Widow Bries" (this family name having been variously spelled in early days and having finally evolved into the current form of Breese). The widow is assumed to have been Wyntje Van Vechten, who married in 1726 Hendrick Bries. He (baptized in Albany in 1697) settled in young manhood on a *bouwerij* on the low land near Papsknee Creek on the east side of the Hudson and is supposed to have built the house shown in plate 15. The house passed from Hendrick's widow to his son, Anthony (born 1734, died 1810), and then to the latter's son, John (born 1774), whose heirs, in 1836, sold it to Matthew Van Benschoten Schryver. In recent years the place came into the possession of Mrs. George S. Finkle (Cathaline Staats), whose grandmother, Catharine Breese, daughter of John (above), was married in the house in 1817 to Joachim Staats. Mrs. Finkle does not know the date of the erection of the house but has been told that the roof of the present front porch is built across a marked brick. Mrs. Matthew Van Benschoten Schryver, who lived in the house many years, told a life-long resident of the river road that: " the house was built in 1722, before George Washington was born ", a saying that has the flavor of folklore but which may have been based on the inscription over the front door. Attached to this house is the familiar traditional story of the back log for the kitchen fireplace, so large it had to be hauled in from outside. In this case oxen are said to have been used for the work. Often a horse is mentioned. There is also an anecdote about an attack by an Indian upon one of the Bries family after a quarrel between the two.

The brick walls of the Breese homestead are laid in Flemish bond with a border along the line of the gable in triangular groupings. There are fine iron beam-anchors in trefoil pattern. In the central hall is an early staircase. Originally, there was one larger and one smaller room on each side of the hall but the partitions have been removed, making one room on either side. The woodwork in the hall is recent and inferior but in the south room the original ceiling-beams remain, black with age and resting on bracket-supports.

House of Pieter Bronck
West Coxsackie, Greene County, New York
PLATE 16

The name Bronck is best known to the present generation from its association with the section of New York City called " the Bronx ", a tract purchased from the Indians in 1641 by Jonas Bronck. Jonas Bronck was a Dane, a man of means, who came to New Amsterdam in 1639, bringing with him his family, servants and personal property. He built a house (stone, covered with tiles), which he called *Emmaus*, on a site near the Harlem River station of the New York, New Haven and Hartford Railroad, but died in 1643. His widow, Antonia Slaghboom, a Dutch woman, soon married Arent Van Curler, a relative of the patroon of Rensselaerswyck and, in 1662, the founder of Schenectady. In June, 1643, Van Curler wrote to the patroon: " I am at present betrothed to the widow of Mr. Jonas Bronck.*** She is a good house-keeper, as I hope your honor shall learn from others."

The good housekeeper, Antonia, had a son, Pieter Bronck, who, when grown, conducted a brewery in *Beverwyck*. In November, 1661, Pieter mortgaged his brewhouse for 2272 Carolus guilders and two months later, on January 13, 1662, spent his ready money in buying from the Indians a tract of land in the wilderness south of *Beverwyck*. The deed provided that he should go to live upon the land in May, 1662. On August 5, 1662, Pieter made an advantageous sale of his real estate in *Beverwyck* (his dwelling, brewery, millhouse, horse-stable and a second house and lot) and on the same day paid off the mortgage he had given the year before. He thus is known to have retired to his new *bouwerij* in the spring of 1662. In 1665 his " farm of cleared land " was formally measured and found to comprise 176 morgens, 110 rods (a little over 352 acres) but his activities on it lasted less than seven years for, in January, 1669, the deacons' account-book of the Albany Dutch church received the entry: " 2 skipples of wheat (10 g.) from the widow of Pieter Bronck for the pall."

Inasmuch as Pieter Bronck bought his *bouwerij* in 1662 and died in 1669 and between those dates cleared his land, he must in those years have had some sort of a dwelling. By tradition in the Bronck family the stone house standing on the farm and owned in 1925 by Pieter's descendant, Leonard Bronck Lampman of New York City, was built by Pieter himself. Pieter's son, Jan Bronck (born 1652, died 1742), inherited the farm and from him the property passed in the male line for four generations to Leonard Bronck (born 1797, died 1872), the grandfather of the present owner.

The house is about two miles south of the village of West Coxsackie on a dirt road that once was the *King's Highway* and which approximates the Indian trail to Canada. It stands on an open arable plain, with a ridge west of it, and in Pieter Bronck's day was a lonely pioneer outpost as it is some distance back from the river and water transportation served for only part of the journey to it. Approach by land must have been by blazed trail or bridle-path.

Two additions were made to the Bronck homestead, one in 1738 (which is really a separate building and is treated as such in connection with plate 17) and one in 1792, which is attached to the first house. The stone house shown in plate 16 is well and solidly built, its roof of steep slant being its significant feature architec-turally. Originally it consisted of two rooms, one above the other; a chimney in the west wall and a door, opening northward. A strip taken off the north side of the lower room now forms a hall, leading to the extension at the west. A separate covered passage runs between the stone and brick houses. Family needs presumably occasioned the western extension, when an elderly couple and a younger man and

67

wife lived on the farm at the same time. In the north wall of the west wing is a stone marked:

```
J B   (E) B   1792
  L B     C B
```

the initials being those of Jan Bronck (1723—1794) and his wife, Elsie Van Buren; and of Leonard Bronck (1752—1828) and his wife, Catryntje Vandenbergh. By the addition made at the west in 1792 there was gained a hall (opening on the Dutch *stoep*, shown in the plate) and a parlor (having a fireplace and a panelled wall); also a half-story above. For general similarity the house of Pieter Bronck should be compared with the Van Antwerp—Mebie house, plate 42.

The owners and occupants of the Bronck *bouwerij* have been: Pieter Bronck (married Hilletje Tyssinck; died 1669); Jan Bronck (born 1652; married Commertje Leendertse Conyn; died 1742); Leendert Bronck (married 1717 Anna De Wandelaer); Jan L. Bronck (born 1723; married 1747 Elsie Van Buren; died 1794); Leonard Bronck (born 1652; married Catryntje Vandenbergh; died 1828); Leonard Bronck (born 1797; married Maria Ely; died 1872); Adelaide Bronck (born 1837; married 1871 the Reverend Lewis Lampman; died 1904); Leonard Bronck Lampman.

House of Leendert Bronck
West Coxsackie, Greene County, New York
PLATE 17.

The second dwelling on the Bronck farm at West Coxsackie was always known in the family as " the New House," the north wall of the house bearing the date: Ano 1738. The house is built of brick, laid in English bond, and is one and one-half stories in height, with an attic under the peaked roof. Along the eaves the bricks are laid in a pattern of successive triangles, the gable-ends are stayed with iron wall-anchors and there is a granary door at either end of the attic. The one chimney rises in the center, between two rooms. The room to the south on the first floor has a recess for a bed. Overhead the ceiling-beams are unenclosed. Each room has a door to the east, opening on a porch which is unique in design, there being an enclosed square platform before each door, and a bridge, or passage, on a higher level, connecting the two platforms. The doors are divided horizontally and carry excellent eighteenth century hardware. This house should be compared with the Douw, Van Alen, Vandenbergh, Van Rensselaer and Van Wie houses (plates 22, 41, 44, 47, 54).

Houses in or near Catskill, New York
House of David Abeel

In the vicinity of Catskill there are a few eighteenth century houses still standing, of which it is not possible to include pictures here, but of which mention is made as a matter of record. One is the house of David Abeel, the scene of a Tory and Indian raid in the Revolution, and from which David Abeel was carried a prisoner to Canada. It is now owned by Mrs. Overbaugh and is in an obscure lane off the Rip Van Winkle Trail between Catskill and Palenville. For this and other houses reference may be had to *Historic Catskill* and *The Catskill of the Yesterdays* by J. V. V. Vedder, and also to C. G. Hine's: *Annual for 1906.*

House of Cornelius and Huybartus DuBois

The house at 281, West Main Street, Catskill, now owned by Mrs. William Palmatier, is an ell in shape and consists of two units: a rear wing, built in 1762 by Cornelius DuBois and his brother, Huybartus (offshoots of the DuBois family of New Paltz), and a front portion, dating from about 1800. The Du Bois house is of stone and is marked in its south wall:

HD (?)

LDB—BDB—GDB

1762—CDB—S(ep?) 2

It consists of two rooms and a hall, with an enclosed staircase (to a half-story), and has large ceiling-beams and excellent wrought iron hardware. To a student of houses of the early Republic the front portion of Mrs. Palmatier's dwelling is commended as a particularly fine example of work of that period. In floor-plan it consists of a hall between two rooms. The ceilings are very high. In the north room is a carved mantel. In the south room a mantel and chimney-breast are puttied in elaborate Adam festoons. The front door has a fine half-circle light above it and lights at either side. The curving stairway is long and graceful and has a mahogany handrail.

Houses in or near Claverack, Columbia County, New York

House of John Bay

Toward the west end of the village of Claverack on the south side of the street is a frame house, two stories high, with a gambrel roof. It is believed that the house was built soon after the Revolution by John Bay, who practised law in Columbia County for many years. In its architecture the house is of the late eighteenth century, its two full stories and frame construction differentiating it from the brick houses of a story and a half with gambrel roof which were built before the war; but the wood trim it contains is in the style of the middle of the century. The panelled side walls and wainscoting, stairway and ceiling-beams are all admirable. In 1925 the house was owned by the Rev. Henry DuBois Mulford, D. D.

Esselstyn House

Eastward from the village of Claverack, off the state road but on the course of the *King's Highway*, is the Esselstyn homestead. The land has been held in the male line of the family for seven generations and is typical of the choice of farm-sites made by the first Dutch settlers, being broad, arable meadows, well watered. The house now standing is in part an eighteenth century structure; originally a frame house of one and one-half stories, it has been raised to two stories and an attic and wings have been added to it. Inside, partitions have been removed and the first floor-plan has disappeared. But the place is full of tradition, is occupied with sentiment and care and among surviving homesteads it is one of the most enjoyable to visit. The present owner is Everett J. Esselstyn.

House of Stephen Miller

A frame house, built about 1790 by Stephen Miller (of the Mulder-Muller family of Columbia County), stands a little to the east of Claverack on the south side of the main road. It was owned in 1925 by Mrs. Jacob Southard Van Wyck (widow of a great-grandson of the builder), since deceased. Erected shortly after the close of the Revolution the house is in the pre-war style, except for the small windows at the line of the eaves. It is a story and a half in height, has a gambrel roof, and much of its original wood trim remains. There are especially handsome Dutch doors at the front and rear of the hall, which runs through the center of the house between two main rooms.

Van Deusen House

Under the shadow of Becraft Mountain, on the dirt road that parallels the west side of Claverack Creek, is a house credited to the Van Deusen family. It is on the west side of the road, immediately north of the bridge which crosses the creek at this point. The Van Deusens settled early on the flats along Claverack Creek and must have had several houses in the vicinity. This surviving example of the homes of the family (which is now owned by Mr. William Hiscox) is in two parts, a main unit of brick and a wing of stone. The brick house is one and one-half stories high with a roof of steep pitch and in the wall are portholes and iron beam-anchors. The house contains two rooms, an enclosed stairway, two chimneys, exposed ceiling-beams (with bracket supports) and each room has an outer doorway. The stone wing is a one-room structure, its Dutch door having original hardware. In its west wall is a Dutch oven. A frame addition of recent date has been made to the south front of the brick unit. This house of the Van Deusens is built on a small scale but in plan and detail is typical of its period. An exact date for it cannot be given. By tradition, iron figures: 1 7 4 2, were once affixed to the east wall.

Van Hoesen House

On the land of the Knickerbocker Cement Company east of the city of Hudson might be seen, in 1925, the ruin of a stone house. It stands (if not lately torn down) north of the concrete road to Claverack and south of the Boston and Albany Railroad. From over the front door of the house the marked lintel was removed some time since and placed in the office of the Cement Company. The stone is chipped but a portion of the cutting remains which, apparently, was intended for a monogram or combined form of letters representing: Ano Nor 1729 V H (Anno, November, 1729, Van Hoesen), which inscription links the house with the Van Hoesen family. Jan Franz Van Hoesen purchased from the Indians in 1667 a tract including the site of the present city of Hudson; his patent extended from Stockport Creek, southward along the Hudson river to Kishna's Kil at South Bay and ran east to Claverack Creek. He died about 1703 and the mark on the lintel can be attributed to a son or a grandson of his. In its day the house was one of the rectangular, slant-roof dwellings common in 1729, built of rough stones and finished with severely plain wood trim.

Van Ness House

North of Claverack Dutch church and on the same side of the road (the former *King's Highway*) is a stone house, built by William Van Ness in the middle of the eighteenth century, which is, however, so altered and added to as to have lost its original appearance entirely. It was one of the usual rectangular stone dwellings of two or three rooms, with a very large chimney in the south wall. About 1800 the building was doubled in length by an addition toward the south, and a long porch was built across the front. The ends of the house are now clapboarded and the front cemented. The present owner is Peter Mesick.

Coeymans Castle

Formerly at Coeymans, New York

Barent Pieterse Coeymans came out from Holland to Rensselaerswyck as a mere lad and, in 1639, was engaged by the patroon to work in the colony under the mill-wright as the latter's *jonghen* (boy). He continued in the grist- and saw-mills of the patroon for some eighteen years, during which he must have been thrifty for from 1657 to 1673 he leased mills and operated them himself. In 1673 he bought of the Indians a large tract of land south of Albany, with water-power, and soon after established himself on the site of the village of Coeymans, where he built a dwelling and mills.

The validity of Barent Pieterse' title to his purchase from the Indians was contested in the courts by the patroon of Rensaelaerswyck (who claimed the land

71

as part of his domain) and litigation dragged along until 1706 when a compromise was reached. Barent Pieterse remained in possession and in 1714 the Crown confirmed the title by patent to his son. Barent Pieterse died between 1706 and 1714. The house he built was inherited and occupied by his descendants but finally passed out of the family and was torn down in 1833.

A sketch of Coeymans Castle in Munsell's *Albany Collections* was made for or by Mr. Munsell from information furnished by old residents of Coeymans. In 1925 Miss Charlotte Amelia Houghtaling of Coeymans (a descendant of Barent Pieterse) told the writer that her mother, who went to school in " the Castle ", had said that the sketch was substantially accurate. The measurements quoted for the building were taken from the foundations after the house was pulled down.

Coeymans Castle faced the river from the corner of Westerlo and First Streets. It was fifty feet long and thirty feet deep (with a rear wing thirty by twenty feet) and was built of stone. The thick walls were one and one-half stories in height and the gable-ends filled with brick. The roof was a single slant and on the front slope was a large triangular dormer. In the center of the first floor was a Dutch door, with two windows either side of it. There were two windows in the gable-end, two circular portholes in the gable and one in the dormer. At either end of the house was a chimney. The land on which the house stood having been purchased in 1673 Barent Pieterse Coeymans presumably built a dwelling about that time. It is possible that the small rear wing preceded the larger house in front of it. The roof and dormer of the main portion should be compared with those of the Beekman-Vanderheyden house (plate 12) and with the dormer on the house of Ariaantje Coeymans (vignette, page 9; notes, plate 18).

Romance attaches to Barent Pieterse Coeymans, whose story belongs with those of the builders of modern American fortunes, differing from the latter only in degree, not in kind. Nothing is known of his background in Holland. He arrived in New Netherland penniless, when very young, and died well-to-do at a great age, his success being of his own unaided creation. The name Coeymans has vanished from Albany County but many persons with the blood of Barent Pieterse in their veins are to be found among the Ten Eyck, Bronck, Houghtaling and other Dutch families.

House of Ariaantje Coeymans

Coeymans, New York

PLATE 18

Barent Pieterse Coeymans of Coeymans Castle (page 71) died between 1706 and 1714 and in 1716 his heirs effected a division of his estate. Of his children one was a daughter, Ariaantje (born 1672), and her life-story is one of the dramas of the Hudson valley. A few facts, only, constitute her known biography. But, as the mariner charts a submerged ledge by the few upthrusts of rock-tips, so the few facts preserved in connection with Ariaantje Coeymans indicate romance and tragedy. When her father died Ariaantje was a woman in middle life, unmarried, and it is to be supposed that she had lived a repressed existence in the home of her aged father, longing for the things of a larger, fuller life; for immediately after she received her share of the estate of Barent Pieterse she reacted, psychologically, in a marked way: she built a house, noteworthy for size and elegance; had her portrait painted life-size, in oil; and married. Ariaantje Coeymans came into her patrimony in 1716 when she was forty-four years old. She built her house between 1716 and 1723, in which latter year (when she was fifty-one) her wedding took place under the new roof. She married David Verplanck, twenty-three years her junior, and the marriage was not happy. Her portrait shows Ariaantje to have been tall and angular, her face one with no claim to beauty, but her great frame arrayed in the most elegant of gowns and in her hand a rose, uplifted. What a revelation of the inner history of a woman's life two centuries ago is made when these significant items are placed in sequence to each other! They disclose to us a mature and obscure spinster, eager for elegance and beauty and affection, and reaching out for all three but doomed to ultimate disappointment. Ariaantje's house still stands; her portrait is treasured; but she, herself, died in 1743 in her handsome house, a lonely figure.

The house built by Ariaantje Coeymans is on the north side of Coeymans Creek near the junction of the creek with the Hudson. It was inherited from her in the line of her niece, Anna Margaretta Coeymans (born 1725), who married Andries Ten Eyck, and title to it remained in the Ten Eyck family until comparatively recent years. The present owners are the Messrs. A. R. and T. M. Briggs of Coeymans, who rent the building to several Italian families. Mention of the house and of the Ten Eycks was made in 1774 by Abraham Lott, treasurer of the Province of New York, in his journal of a voyage up the Hudson in that year. The portrait of Ariaantje, which for over a century hung in the main hall of her house, is now owned by her kinswoman, Miss Gertrude Watson of Onala Farm, Pittsfield, Massachusetts, and a woodcut of the portrait is included in Munsell's *Albany Collections*.

In the eighteenth century an oil painting (vignette, page 9) was made of the house of Ariaantje Coeymans which, in the nineteenth, was inherited from the Ten Eycks by Miss Charlotte Amelia Houghtaling of Coeymans, New York, and she, in 1926, presented it to the Holland Society. While faded in color and crude in execution, the picture is a valuable record of the architectural design in which the house was built about 1716. The structure was one of two full stories and a high front basement and had a steeply pitched roof of single slant, with a large stepped dormer on the east front. The high steps that led to the front door approached the porch-platform from the side. The stepped dormer was surmounted by an iron weather-vane (vignette, page 1) in the shape of a deer, running at full speed, which vane is now

73

the valued property of the Holland Society. It has a counterpart in the iron horse which Washington Irving salvaged from the *Vanderheyden Palace* (plate 12) and removed to *Sunnyside.*

In floor-plan the house of Ariaantje Coeymans has been little changed. A hall runs through the center of each of the two main stories, with two rooms at each side. The east door of the first hall opens on a high flight of steps; the west door (a survival of the eighteenth century) is on the ground-level. Tiles are known to have faced the fireplaces but they have all been removed by souvenir-hunters. Beside the chimney and under the windows in the northeast room on the first floor some early panelling remains. The main staircase has the narrow tread and steep rise of an early type.

At an unknown date but undoubtedly before 1800 the original roof and stepped dormer were removed by the Ten Eycks and the present badly proportioned gambrel substituted. Also the original front steps were then replaced by another flight and a porch with flat hood characteristic of the second half of the eighteenth century. A photograph (plate 18) is shown here through the courtesy of Mrs. S. H. Niles of Coeymans, which records the appearance of the house about 1870 when it was still a family home. The building is now in a state of rapidly increasing decay and soon there will be little but stone walls left to tell of the enthusiasm and the enterprise with which a woman once pursued a quest for beauty and a larger life.

Ariaantje Coeymans' house is noteworthy for its positive architectural features and for its distinct importance in comparison with other contemporary dwellings. About 1704 *Crailo* (page 113) was an excellent house of brick. There is a tradition of the comparative elegance that characterized the house of Francis Salisbury (plate 30), built in 1705 at Leeds. The Glen-Sanders house (plate 23) at Scotia was enlarged to great size in 1713. Literary glamour invests the Beekman-Vanderheyden house (plate 12), built in 1725 at Albany. But among these houses of the first quarter of the eighteenth century that of Ariaantje Coeymans was really the most remarkable. It exceeded any one of the others in size; the roof, dormer and porch were the most distinctively Dutch and correct in design and the finishings were equal if not superior to those of the other, better known, dwellings. As an architectural item of real significance in its own day the house of Ariaantje Coeymans is entitled to be rescued from oblivion and put in its proper perspective.

Coeymans-Bronck house

Coeymans, New York

PLATE 19

In the division of the lands of Barent Pieterse Coeymans in 1716 Pieter Coeymans, his son (or grandson?), received an allotment at the mouth and along the course of *Haane Craai Kil* (Crowing Rooster Creek), a stream entering the Hudson about half a mile south of the center of the village of Coeymans. Near this stream and north of it stands a house, owned and occupied by Mrs. S. H. Niles, that was built in the eighteenth century, either by Pieter Coeymans or by his heirs.

Pieter Coeymans (who married his first wife in 1713) is understood by his descendants to have occupied Coeymans Castle in the village and a map of 1767 shows his widow, Charlotte, living there at that date. He died in 1744, leaving five daughters, who inherited his real estate and who married into the Witbeck, Van Allen, Barclay, Ten Eyck and Bronck families. His will, made in 1736, was not proved until 1765 and not until 1770 was a formal partition made of his land. By that partition his daughter, Charlotte Amelia (born 1727, married about 1745—1750 to Jan Jonas Bronck), received the property now owned by Mrs. Niles.

It is open to proof whether the house now standing were built by Pieter Coeymans before his death in 1744 or whether it was erected by his daughter and her husband. In either case there can be no question that it is a structure of the mid-eighteenth century. The house is built of stone and the roof has a double pitch, similar to that of the roof of the house of Jan Van Loon, built in 1724 at Athens (plate 46). Modern window-glass, west door and stairs and a kitchen wing of late date replace original details. The door at the west of the central hall is on the level of the ground but at the main entrance to the east, where the ground is lower, an eighteenth century door and *stoep* are happily preserved, as shown in the accompanying plate. A hall of unusual width runs through the center of the house, with a larger front room on either side at the east and a smaller one at the west. In the northeast parlor the north wall and chimney-breast are handsomely panelled and in the southeast room there is a carved wood mantel above a fireplace opening of great size. The whole house is given meticulous care by the owner and the woodwork is in exceptionally fine preservation.

From 1673 to 1842 the land on which this house stands was in the possession of Barent Pieterse Coeymans and of his descendants. Since 1842 it has been held by the Niles family.

Houses in or near Cohoes, New York

The modern industrial city of Cohoes at the mouth of the Mohawk river was preceded in the eighteenth century by an agricultural community, established by Dutch families who removed from Albany, Half Moon and Niscayuna. Farms were taken up under the patroon of Rensselaerswyck in the area south of the Mohawk and west of the Hudson between 1725 and 1750, although development was slow until after the Revolution. A few of the houses built by the families that first came to the neighborhood are still standing. They are probably homes of the second

75

generation, representing prosperity and permanent residence. They all date prior to 1767, in which year they are shown on a map of the manor of Rensselaer. Architecturally, they are characteristic of the style followed by the Dutch of that vicinity in 1750—1765. They are similar to each other in floor-plans and finishings, the chief variation being in the roofs, some of which are gambrels and some slants. Four typical houses, all within a short distance of each other on the upper road from Albany to Cohoes, are here listed and grateful acknowledgement is made of the cordial and generous assistance given to the preparation of the list by the City Historian of Cohoes, Hugh P. Graham, and the City Comptroller, Miss Grace Reavy.

House of Douw Fonda (1)

Owned in 1767 by Douw Fonda. Owned in 1925 by Peter La Mora. Built of brick, in English bond. One and one-half stories. Gambrel roof. Central hall and two rooms. Altered in details.

House of Douw Fonda (2)

Owned in 1767 by Douw Fonda. Owned in 1925 by the Simmons estate. Built of brick, in English bond. One and one-half stories. Gambrel roof. Central hall and two rooms. Eighteenth century iron brackets for gutters. Iron wall-anchors in trefoil design. Old window-glass, twenty-four panes to a window.

House of Jan L. Fonda

Owned in 1767 by Jan L. Fonda. Owned in 1925 by Michael Murphy. Built of brick, in English bond. One and one-half stories. Slant roof. Central hall and two rooms. Many eighteenth century details, among them: front porch, Dutch door, iron hardware, window-glass, panelled shutters, portholes in gables, a shallow cornice over the fireplace, bevelled chimney-breast, panelled cupboards. Occupies a commanding location on west side of road, overlooking extensive view. Is in fair repair and, as a colonial survival, could be restored.

House of Frans Lansing

Owned in 1767 by Frans Lansing. Owned in 1925 by Clinton Fonda. Built of brick, in English bond. One and one-half stories. Slant roof. Central hall and two rooms. Modern windows, blinds, porch, etc.

House of Henry Lansing

See PLATE 27

Conyn-Van Rensselaer House
Town of Claverack, Columbia County, New York

PLATE 20

A house associated with the Conyns and Van Rensselaers stands a little east of Humphreysville in Columbia County. It consists of two architectural units, which present the familiar story of a smaller, temporary dwelling, built first and followed by a larger, permanent home as convenience permitted. In this instance a stone house of crude workmanship forms the rear wing of a well-built house of brick, two stories in height, with a gambrel roof.

The Dutch family of Conyn was founded at *Beverwyck* about 1655 by Leendert Philipse Conyn, whose descendant, Casper Leendertse Conyn, moved down to Claverack early in the eighteenth century, dying in 1727. The stone wing of this house was perhaps built by a son of Casper Leendertse and the brick house by the third generation. In one gable-end of the brick house is a tile, marked: K K 1766; and in the other a tile, marked: L K 1766, the initials supposedly representing father and son or husband and wife. The letters: K K are equivalent to Kasper Konyn, C and K being interchangeable at the time.

Ultimately, this property passed from Kasper Konyn to his daughter (or granddaughter), Cornelia, who married in 1800 Jeremiah H. Van Rensselaer (son of Henry I. Van Rensselaer). The house remained in the family of Jeremiah and Cornelia Van Rensselaer until 1884. It is now owned by Cornelius H. Evans of Hudson, New York.

To the exterior of the brick house alterations have been made that give it the appearance of a house of recent date. A fretted cornice, the front porch, the window-glass and shutters are all nineteenth century details and under each of the marked tiles in the gables a modern hand has painted in large figures: 1 7 6 6.

Inside, this house retains some of the atmosphere of its first estate. There is some original woodwork and the relation of floor-space to ceiling-height is such as to impart a livable, domestic quality. There is an early staircase (with wainscoted side) in the central hall. The property has long been known as *Locust Dale*, from trees in front of the house, said to have been planted in 1765.

House of Hendrick Cuyler
Formerly at 40, Riverside Avenue, Rensselaer, New York

PLATE 21

The earliest record found of the house of Hendrick Cuyler is in 1767, when it was entered upon the map of the manor of Rensselaer that was made that year. Then, in 1769, the diary of a traveller, Richard Smith of New Jersey (published under the title: *Four Great Rivers*), states in the course of the description of the writer's voyage up the Hudson that: " Henry Cuyler's Brick House on the East side about a mile below the Town " (Albany) " looks well." The house was also mentioned in 1774 in the *Journal of a Voyage to Albany*, kept by Abraham Lott, treasurer of the Province of New York, who, on June 26 and July 6, 1774, was entertained by Hendrick Cuyler in his house: " situated on the east bank of the river, about a mile and a half from the city of Albany."

Hendrick Cuyler's house stood on land which was leased from the lord of the manor of Rensselaer, a lease that is variously described as having been for ninety-nine years or for four lives. At the expiration of the lease the land reverted to the Van Rensselaer family, members of which occupied the house in the nineteenth century. In 1926 the building was razed in connection with the creation of port facilities for the city of Albany.

Vly House (House by the Marsh), as Hendrick Cuyler's dwelling was best known, stood at the southern end of the city of Rensselaer, with only the old road (now Riverside Avenue) separating it from the Hudson and when it was built it was a country-seat, with an open view in all directions. Architecturally, *Vly House* was a conspicuous instance of the trend toward Georgian English that prevailed at the time of its erection. Built of brick in two full stories, the first and second floors each had a central hall with two rooms on either side. The halls were wide, the rooms large and the ceilings high. Across the center of the first floor hall was an arch. The staircase, with its two landings, rose at the rear of the hall, a long, broad, courtly flight. The woodwork throughout the house was noteworthy and closely resembled that of *The Pastures*, Philip Schuyler's house in Albany. In the front rooms on the main floor pink tiles faced the fireplace openings. In the northwest room, second floor, the tiles were decorated with flowers and birds in blue and green and yellow, while in the northeast bedroom the design on the tiles was a bunch of grapes in blue on white. All these interior decorations were saved by the last owner, Miss Katherine Van Rensselaer Arnold of Albany, when the house was torn down.

The photograph of *Vly House*, shown in plate 21, taken a long time ago, was obtained through the courtesy of C. G. Van Rensselaer of Schenectady and is shown in preference to a picture of recent date because it records the balustrade that once surrounded the roof and which afterward disappeared. Miss Katherine Van Rensselaer, who owned and occupied *Vly House* for many years and who was beloved by all who knew her, appears in the old photograph, standing beside the tree.

House of Petrus Douw
Formerly at Wolven Hoeck, Rensselaer County, New York
PLATE 22

In 1715 Kiliaen Van Rensselaer, lord of the manor of Rensselaer, conveyed to his brother, Hendrick Van Rensselaer, a piece of land on the east shore of the Hudson, opposite Albany, called *Wolven Hoeck* (Wolves' Point). The conveyance describes the property as bounded north by land of Hendrick Van Rensselaer and south by land of Melgert Abrahamse and as running east from the river one mile. Two years later (1717) Hendrick Van Rensselaer's daughter, Anna, married Petrus Jonas Douw (born 1692, died 1775) and this young couple were soon established on the *bouwerij* with the pointed river-frontage, where the wolves were numerous.

The house at *Wolven Hoeck*, occupied by Petrus and Anna Douw, was built (tradition says) in 1724 and it was torn down 1835—'40, shortly before which removal an oil-painting was made of it. A reproduction of the painting is included here through the courtesy of Charles G. Douw of Scotia, New York. The traditional date of 1724 is credible when the house is compared with others of that approximate period (as, for example: the Bries house, 1722; Van Wie, 1732; Bronck, 1738). It was a story and a half in height and had a roof of steep, single pitch; end chimneys; portholes in the gable; board shutters; and a central hall. At the rear was a wing (with a gambrel roof?).

The house of Petrus Douw stood close to the Hudson on the river-road, only a short south distance of *Crailo*, the home of Mrs. Douw's father. A house of the nineteenth century now occupies the site but the handsome trees of an early date still grace the roadway.

Glen-Sanders House

1, Riverside Avenue, Scotia, New York

PLATE 23

At the northern end of the Western Gateway Bridge that crosses the Mohawk river between Schenectady and Scotia stands the Glen-Sanders house, owned and occupied by Mrs. Charles P. Sanders. Alexander Lindsay Glen, a Scot, was one of the first settlers on the banks of the Mohawk, his property on the north side of the river opposite Schenectady being called by him: Scotia. He himself was known among his Dutch neighbors as " Sander Leendertse Glen; " his descendants married into Dutch families, spoke Dutch and were a part of the local Dutch community. Sander Leendertse Glen built a dwelling for himself on the flat at the river's level at Scotia, perhaps in the 1660's, a dwelling that was ultimately wrecked by a flood. By tradition, some of the materials used in it were salvaged and then utilized in the construction of another house on the bluff that overlooks the original site on the flat.

Because the date: 1 7 1 3, appears in iron figures on the east façade of the house now standing on the bluff it has been assumed that the whole house belongs to that year. But an examination of the structural features of the house reveals facts that suggest that the west end was built first and the east part later. The west end is a unit in itself, a rectangle of stone, consisting of a hall and two (or three) original rooms. The ceilings are low and the staircase in the hall has the steep rise and narrow tread of an early colonial type. The east end of the house, also built of stone (both portions being stuccoed), is on a higher floor-level, with ceilings of unusual height. The wall between the two parts is of stone, very thick, as if it had been the outer wall of the west unit. It is understood in the Sanders family that the groundfloor of the east end was originally one oblong room of great size, the description of it suggesting the Long Room of an eighteenth century inn. The floor-space is now divided into two rooms with a hall between, the hall having an entrance-door at the east. Incidental details in windows, partitions, period woodwork, etc., go to support the family tradition that the division of the large room was an afterthought.

Photographs of the Glen-Sanders house have usually been taken from the east and southeast, showing the square effect of the east and south walls. For example, see: *The Ten Broeck Genealogy*, page 120; *The Historic Mohawk*, page 50; *The Old Mohawk Turnpike*, page 68. The accompanying plate is from a photograph (reproduced through the courtesy of Mrs. William Ten Broeck Mynderse of Scotia, N. Y.) which was taken about 1870 from the northwest and which bears upon the theory that the house consists of two architectural units.

According to such an hypothesis, the west unit was a house of one and a half (or two and a half) stories, against the east wall of which was built in 1713 a large, oblong unit two stories high. The front wall of the first house was then squared to agree with the addition and the eastern and southern parts became an ell-shaped structure of two stories. The wooden extension to the west that shows in the photograph, was removed some years since.

The main entrance to the house is on the south side and is marked by a frame porch of primitive design, unlike any discovered elsewhere. The roof of the porch slopes and the three boarded sides have openings that can be closed at will by board shutters, which are hung to slide up and down not to swing on hinges.

If it be true that the westerly unit was built before 1713 the time of its erection can only be conjectural. No date is found for the freshet which flooded the first house on the flat. The building of a house on the bluff (which occurred after the freshet) may have been before 1685, when Sander Leendertse Glen died, well on in years, or after his death, when he had been succeeded by his son, John Alexander Glen. John A. Glen (who married Deborah Wendell) is said by his descendants to have been the builder of the part marked 1713. His son, Jacob Glen (born 1691, died 1762), married in 1717 Sarah Wendell and inherited the house. Jacob Glen's only child, Deborah (born 1721, died 1786), married in 1739 Johannes Sanders and the house has come down in the possession of their descendants to the present day. Several marriages between the Sanders of Scotia and the Ten Broecks of Roeloff Jansen's Kil (plate 38) have since 1799 made intimate relationships between the occupants of the two houses.

Many original features of the interior of the house at Scotia are unaltered. Much of value in furniture, china, plate and portraits still remains, as passed down through the generations, while men prominent in public life have been guests within the old walls and stories of the Indians and of the colonists cling to the house. Altogether the Glen-Sanders homestead is one of the most important and interesting colonial houses now left standing.

House of Abraham Glen

14, Mohawk Avenue, Scotia, New York

PLATE 24

The house of Abraham Glen stands near the northern end of the Western Gateway Bridge that spans the Mohawk river between the city of Schenectady and its suburb, the village of Scotia. The village corporation is the present owner of the property. By tradition a stone house first stood on the land. Then the structure shown in plate 24 was added. Later the stone unit was taken down and still more recently a wing was added to the second unit. The second portion has lost much of its original appearance by the substitution of slatted blinds and modern window-glass and porches for eighteenth century details. The photograph, reproduced in plate 24 through the courtesy of DeLancey W. Watkins of Schenectady, was taken many years ago and shows the characteristic architectural feature of the steeply pitched Dutch roof.

Abraham Glen (born 1694, married in 1724 to Marretje Teller) is said by tradition to have built the present house about 1730. The walls are of brick, clap-boarded. The original floor-plan (now changed) apparently consisted of two rooms, a narrow hall (along the side of one room) and between the two rooms a space, taken up partly by a steep stairway and partly by a bed-recess. It is allowable to suggest that the clapboards may not have been included as the house was first built and that the brick walls were then open to view; in which case this house should be classed with the house of Arent Bradt on Schermerhorn Road, west of Schenectady, a brick dwelling of about the same size and type and date.

Hoogeboom House

Formerly at Claverack, Columbia County, New York

PLATE 25

The erection of the house shown in plate 25 is ascribed to Jeremias Hoogeboom (born 1711, died 1784) who, in his young manhood, became a resident of Claverack. He was a grandson of Bartholomeus Pieterse Hoogeboom of Albany, skipper of a sloop on the Hudson, whose name is often found in seventeenth century documents.

Through his second wife, Annatje Van Hoesen, Jeremias Hoogeboom came into possession of a large amount of land near Claverack, his wife being one of the heirs under the Van Hoesen Patent, that covered the site of the city of Hudson. Jeremias was the father of Stephen Hoogeboom (born 1744, died 1814), who was lieutenant-colonel of an Albany County regiment in the Revolution. Colonel Hoogeboom's daughter, Catherine (born 1768, died 1805) married in 1790 Samuel B. Webb and they and their descendants long occupied the house.

An exact date for the building of the Hoogeboom house is lacking. "About 1760" is the time at which it is usually put; but it represents a style more common in 1740 and 1750 than in 1760, when the gambrel roof was popular and the roof of sharp peak had begun to disappear in Albany County. The house stood on the south side of a dirt road that forks to the southwest from the state road at a point a little west of the village of Claverack. It was burned in 1890 and the view of it here shown is reproduced from a photograph obtained through the courtesy of Miss Bertha F. Webb of Hudson, N. Y.

The homestead of the Hoogeboom family is rendered of peculiar interest because of the fact that a tradition in Claverack of persistent circulation is that in this house was written the poem: *A Visit from St. Nicholas*. The tradition at Claverack must, however, be compared with a similar tradition that attaches to the house at Poughkeepsie of Henry Livingston, Jr. (page 354).

Houses in or near Kinderhook, Columbia County, New York

A number of dwellings still standing in or near Kinderhook of undoubtedly early date have unfortunately been so built around and upon and are so altered in a variety of ways that their pictorial value as illustrations of the architecture of the pre-Revolutionary period is destroyed. The history of these houses is presented in *The History of Kinderhook* by the Reverend E. A. Collier. A few still retain some colonial features and of those the following instances are listed.

Gardenier House

On the west side of the state road between Valatie and Chatham is a house built by the Gardenier family, now owned by Mrs. Egan. It is built of yellow brick and is marked on the east front: A G 1753 and T G 1753. Apparently about 1800 the roof (a single slant) was raised a few feet and small second story windows cut.

Schermerhorn-Pruyn-Beekman House

The house of the Misses Beekman on the main street of the village of Kinderhook is said to have been sold by Cornelius Schermerhorn in 1736 to Arent Pruyn, whose descendants owned it until 1856. Since 1878 it has been in the Beekman family.

Apparently it was a typical brick house of 1736 (oblong; peaked roof; one and one-half stories; a hall and two rooms; brick walls laid in English bond), but in the nineteenth century it was raised to two stories, partly clapboarded and the porch and windows modernized. The house contains an original bed-closet, resembling a wardrobe.

Unidentified House

On William Street, Kinderhook, is a house built of brick in English bond, with the date—1766— laid in contrasting bricks in the east gable. The roof is a gambrel; the floor-plan a central hall with one larger and one smaller room at either side; and the rooms contain some good panelling. The builder is unidentified. The present owners, the Misses Mills, have repaired and restored the house.

Van Alen House (supposed)

Elmhurst, the residence in Kinderhook of James A. Reynolds, is a mid-nineteenth century house, having at the rear a wing of unknown but early date, which is ascribed to the Van Alen family. The wing is a brick unit of two rooms. It is entered from the south by a vestibule, which has an outer and an inner door and a window on either side. A similar vestibule on the north side of the wing forms a passage, connecting the wing with the main house. The doors and windows of the two vestibules are conspicuously unlike anything found elsewhere. The doors are nearly eight feet in height, about three feet wide and are battened vertically. The windows are tall and narrow, with leaded, diamond-shaped panes. Both the doors and the windows are ecclesiastical in character rather than domestic and it is not unreasonable to suggest that they once formed part of the Dutch church of Kinderhook, built about 1717 and torn down about 1813, which stood on ground which now is included in the lawn at *Elmhurst.* To the owner of *Elmhurst,* Mr. Reynolds, grateful acknowledgements are made for many courtesies extended in the collection of material for this book.

House of Abraham I. Van Alstyne

West of the covered bridge at Chatham Center stands a house, built before 1767 by Colonel Abraham I. Van Alstyne (born 1738, died 1808), who rendered notable service in the Revolution. The present owner is Mrs. K. V. V. Williams. The house is built of brick, laid in Flemish bond; the roof is a single slant; and while the walls are but one and one-half stories the ceilings of the first story are of unusual height. The attic was used as a granary (there is a granary door in each gable) and in the cellar are two kitchens, one for the family and one for the slaves. The family occupied the main floor, of which the plan (now altered) seems to have been originally three front rooms and three smaller rear rooms.

House of David Van Schaack

On the west side of the main street of Kinderhook is the house, built in 1774 by David Van Schaack (son of Cornelis Van Schaack, whose house is shown in plate 51), which was known to many in past years as the home of Mrs. Aaron J. Vanderpoel and which is now held in the estate of Mrs. Vanderpoel's daughter, the late Mrs. Waldo Newcomer. In July, 1774, Abraham Lott, treasurer of the Province of New York, passed through Kinderhook and in his diary of his journey noted that: " Mr. David Van Schaack has built him a house like a castle near the town. It is built of brick, two stories high, four rooms on a floor and a large hall through the middle of it, and is built in a very elegant Taste." Mr. Lott's mention of " elegant Taste " has reference to the finish of the interior of the house. The original carved woodwork has been carefully preserved and it is of much dignity. The hall and rooms are large in area and in height, the mantels handsome in design and a broad graceful staircase, rising in three banks of steps with two landings, fills the west end of the hall. In the nineteenth century wings were added to the north and the south of the main part of the house and a piazza built across the front and these have destroyed the eighteenth century appearance of the exterior. Much of interest attaches to this house in connection with the character and prominence of those who have occupied it or who have been entertained in it.

The *Bouwerij* called *Kost Verloren*
Town of East Greenbush, Rensselaer County, New York
PLATE 26

In 1708—1709 Kiliaen Van Rensselaer, the fourth patroon of Rensselaerswyck, gave to Melgert Abrahamse Van Deusen a perpetual lease for the *bouwerij* " heretofore called by the name of *Kost Verloren*, with the house, barn," &c., the *bouwerij* being described in the lease as situated on the east side of the Hudson near the north end of Papsknee Island.

Evidently the patroon had had his difficulties with this bit of property for *Kost Verloren* (literally " cost lost ") is equivalent to " money-thrown-away " and tells its own tale as a name for the farm, a tale still further indicated by the accounts of Rensselaerswyck, which record Melgert Abrahamse as in debt to the patroon in 1678 for three years rent for *Kost Verloren*. However, better times must have followed for *Kost Verloren* remained in the possession and occupation of Melgert Abrahamse and his descendants for five generations and for one hundred and seventeen years. From 1825 to 1830 it was owned by James C. Norton and from 1830 to 1925 by William Teller, his brother—Jacob Van Benschoten Teller—and the latter's heirs. Among the title papers to the farm, held by the heirs of Jacob V. B. Teller, is the original lease given by Kiliaen Van Rensselaer in 1708—1709.

84

On this old farm stands a house which has been known for nearly a century as the Teller farmhouse, having been occupied by the farmers employed by the Teller family. Prior to 1825 the owners of the house lived in it themselves. Whether this house is the one mentioned in the lease granted to Melgert Abrahamse Van Deusen in 1708—1709 it is impossible to say. The land on which it stands was conveyed by Melgert Abrahamse in 1733 to Jannetje Van Deusen (his sister?), widow of Thomas Jans Witbeck; passed from her to her son, Abraham Witbeck, by whose will in 1786 it went to his daughter (Jannetje, wife of James Cole) for life and then to her son, Abraham Cole. If the house now standing were built before the perpetual lease it was probably erected by the patroon himself. But it has a gambrel roof and that makes so early a date as 1708 improbable for it. Its small size and primitive character put it well back in the eighteenth century and, as the widowed Mrs. Witbeck was doubtless seeking a home in 1733 (rather than planning to build), it is reasonable to ascribe the erection of the house to Melgert Abrahamse Van Deusen between 1708 and 1733, probably not so very long before he sold it to his kinswoman.

The Teller farmhouse stands south of the city of Rensselaer on the west side of the river-road to Castleton. Almost grazing its west wall are the tracks of the New York Central and Hudson River Railroad, the railroad and the highway crossing each other in the form of an X immediately north of the house. The house is built of brick, one and one-half stories in height, with gambrel roof; it has portholes in the gable; iron hooks at beam-ends; and modern door and shutters. The central hall lies between two rooms, each having a chimney. In the north room the chimney-breast is panelled and the fireplace opening is surrounded with a primitive facing of wood. On either side of the north chimney are panelled cupboards. The south wall of the south room is also completely panelled, from floor to ceiling.

In 1925 the farm was purchased by John G. Amerongen, a recent immigrant from Holland.

House of Henry Lansing
Cohoes, New York
PLATE 27

The house shown in plate 27 is in Cohoes on South Saratoga Street (i. e. the Troy road), which runs parallel with the canal. The house is now owned by the Mohawk Paper Mill Company and is no longer habitable. The photograph reproduced here and taken some years ago before the house fell into decay was obtained through the courtesy of Hugh P. Graham, City Historian of Cohoes. The name of Henry Lansing is associated with the house as that of its builder and the date of erection is locally given as about 1750. The house was a home and not a tavern but because of its location on the main highway from Albany to Canada this house, like *The Flatts* and the Van Schaick house (plates 33 and 52) on the same road, sheltered many an occasional traveller. It is built of brick in English bond and a hall and two rooms constituted the ground floor. The ceiling-beams were open to view; shallow cornices were over the fireplaces; bevelled panels over the cornices; and at either side of the north chimney were panelled cupboards; all of which are visible in the ruins. The house is now a shell of roof and walls, the flooring having in large part given way. Its structural lines should be compared with those of *Kost Verloren* and the Muller, Schuyler, Staats, Vanderheyden and Van Rensselaer-Genêt houses (plates 26, 28, 33, 37, 45, 49).

The Manor-House of Livingston Manor
Formerly in Columbia County, New York

Robert Livingston, the first lord of Livingston Manor, was a Scotchman and in many ways he and his descendants manifested their attachment to the land of his birth. But Robert Livingston married at Albany a Dutch wife (Alida Schuyler, widow of the Reverend Nicholas Van Rensselaer); many of the members of his large family also became allied with the Dutch by marriage; and a survey of pre-Revolutionary Dutch houses in the Hudson valley which failed to report upon houses occupied in that period by the Livingstons could easily be criticized as incomplete.

The manor of Livingston (which lay within the borders of the present Columbia County) was held by three lords: Robert Livingston, born 1654, died 1728; Philip Livingston, born 1686, died 1749; and Robert Livingston, born 1708, died 1790. In 1699 the first lord built a manor-house at the mouth of *Roeloff Jansen's Kil* on a site near the present station called Linlithgow on the New York Central and Hudson River Railroad. The house was standing in 1798 but early in the nineteenth century was either torn down or burned. The surprising fact is that very few traditions have been handed down about it. It is known to have been built of stone. An account of it published long ago in a New York City newspaper (signed: C. B. T.) says it was a long low dwelling, with heavy roof, oaken doors and deep window embrasures; that a hall ran through the center and was hung with arms, antlers, bearskins, &c.; that to the right and left of the hall were rooms furnished with an approach to elegance; and that in the rear the hall opened into a wing with kitchen and servants' quarters. How accurate this description is no one now can say with certainty but it depicts a house in a type of architecture characteristic of 1699 and may be accepted cautiously as being an approach to the probable truth.

This long low stone house with the thick walls was the home of the first lord. The second lord maintained a handsome establishment on Broad street, New York City, and a residence in Albany as well and the manor-house served him more perhaps as a summer dwelling; that he did regard it as his real home is evident however because, when he died in New York City, his body was brought to the family vault

86

at Linlithgow (where the church now stands) and elaborate funeral ceremonies were conducted at the manor-house.

The third lord inherited the manor-house in 1749 and, under the entail, the fourth lord would have been his son, Peter R. (born 1737, died 1794); but the Revolution broke the entail and, as the third lord lived until 1790 and his great estate was divided at his death between a number of heirs, Peter R. Livingston received only a small part of the property which would have been his as a whole.

In the expectation of becoming in the course of nature the fourth lord of the manor Peter R. Livingston began to build for himself a handsome house, three miles and a half south of the manor-house. That was just before the War of the Revolution began or during its early stages. The walls of the new house (built of brick on a large ground-area) had reached the height of one story and a great stairway had been placed in the main hall when hostilities halted construction. Then, at the conclusion of the war, the entail was broken and Peter R. Livingston, facing his changed fortunes, put a makeshift roof on the walls of one story and retired in deep disappointment to this peculiar dwelling, to which the name: *The Hermitage* was given. *The Hermitage* still stands, out of sight from the county-road at the end of a long winding by-road. It is no longer owned by the Livingston family and is occupied by laboring tenants but it is a landmark and it bears witness to one of the dramatic stories of the days that tried men's souls.

The fact that Peter R. Livingston had the desire to build a handsome house coincides with the theory that the manor-house of 1699 was a typical stone house of that date and was not large enough or elegant enough to accord with the standard of living which the lords of the manor held to in New York City in the middle of the eighteenth century. That brick was the material chosen by Peter R. Livingston for a new manor-house reflects the fashion of his generation in Columbia and Dutchess Counties.

Beside *The Hermitage* there are now left in Columbia County two other houses built by the Livingstons before 1776: *Clermont* and *Teviotdale*. Of *Clermont* there is such wide knowledge and so much has been written of its history that it is only necessary to refer the reader to the following well prepared descriptions of it: an article by Joseph Livingston Delafield in the *Annual Report for 1911* of the American Scenic and Historic Preservation Society; the volume entitled: *Livingstons of Livingston Manor* by Edwin Brockholst Livingston, privately printed 1910 by the Knickerbocker Press; and *A Biographical History of Clermont* by Thomas Streatfield Clarkson, published 1869 by subscription. The large landed estate called *Clermont* was bequeathed at his death in 1728 by the first lord of the manor to his younger son, Robert Livingston (born 1688, died 1775). The latter, soon after coming into possession of his great inheritance, built a stone house close to the shore of the Hudson at a point a half-mile north of the present boundary line between Columbia and Dutchess Counties. The house stood until 1777 when it was burned by the British in their raid up the river that year. Rebuilt at once (in 1778?) the main portion of the present house (to which north and south wings were added in the nineteenth century) is understood to reproduce the lines of the original building, which thus must have been a square structure, two stories in height with a hipped roof, large in all its measurements and which was a genuine mansion (in the popular sense of the word) as compared with the average house of 1730—1777. The walls are now covered with stucco, ruled to imitate ashlar, which was a fashionable finish in the early nineteenth century. To this great stone dwelling Robert Livingston of the third generation (born 1718, died 1775) brought in 1742 his bride, Margaret Beekman, daughter of Colonel Henry Beekman of Rhinebeck (whose house is shown in plate 125), and it was as his widow that Margaret Beekman Livingston rebuilt *Clermont* after the fire of 1777. The house called *Clermont* is one of the few pre-Revolutionary homes left in the Hudson valley which is still occupied by descendants of the first owners and it still is (as it always has been) one of the most beautiful places along the river.

The other one of the remaining Livingston homes of the pre-war era, *Teviotdale*, belonged to Walter Livingston (born 1740, died 1797), third son of the third lord of the manor, who married in 1769 Cornelia Schuyler and whose handsome house was inherited by his daughter, Harriet, who married in 1808 Robert Fulton. *Teviotdale* could easily have been copied in design from *Clermont* although its measurements may be somewhat less. It is of rough stone; is nearly square; and in height is two stories with a hipped roof. It long ago passed out of the Livingston family and now, badly out of repair, is used by a farmer as a storage place for hay. It stands about a mile south and east of Linlithgow church on a county-road.

A mile and a half north of the site of the manor-house of 1699 is a house called *Oak Hill*, built about 1790—1800 by John Livingston (born 1750, died 1822), the fifth son of the third lord of the manor. It stands on a height that rises directly from the river and is still owned in the Livingston family. The ceilings in this house are very high and an anecdote is told to the effect that when the dwelling was in course of erection his relatives exclaimed to the owner: " John, you will freeze! " This little item is one of much significance in connection with the story of architecture in the Hudson valley; for it is direct evidence for the truth of the theory that climatic conditions account for the fact that very few large houses were built in this region in the time when open fires of wood were the sole source of heat in the bitterly cold winters.

House of Cornelius C. Muller
Claverack, Columbia County, New York
PLATE 28

The numerous and prominent Miller family of Columbia County, New York, derives origin from Cornelis Stephense Mulder of Nykerk, Gelderland, an early arrival at *Beverwyck*, some of whose descendants migrated to Claverack. The name evolved from Mulder through Muller to Miller and members of the family spoke Low Dutch among themselves until about 1870. One of this family, Cornelius C. Muller, built in 1767 a brick house (plate 28) which stands in the village of Claverack on the south side of the main street. In the nineteenth century the house passed to Jeremiah Race (whose first wife was a Muller) and from him to his widow (his second wife), who later married Anthony Van Rensselaer. Mr. and Mrs. Anthony van Rensselaer were hosts in this house for a long time to the Reverend A. P. Van Gieson, pastor, first of the Dutch church at Claverack and later of the Dutch church at Poughkeepsie, and endeared to several generations of members of the Reformed Communion.

Across the front of the house of Cornelius C. Muller are the iron figures: 1 7 6 7, a date which quarrels with the painfully recent door, porch and window shutters. The present dormers (on old lines) replace earlier windows. Architecturally, the significance of the house as it now is lies in its being a well preserved example of the brick-work of the 1760's and of the gambrel roof then popular. It bears some resemblance to the Lansing, Schuyler, Staats, Vanderheyden and Van Rensselaer houses (plates: 27, 33, 37, 45, 49). The interior has been altered by the present owner, Roscoe Williams, and retains few of its original features.

During the Revolution the Muller house was the scene of local activities. Prisoners were confined in the cellar and on June 20, 1780, a court martial was held in the house for the trial of delinquents of the militia regiment commanded by Colonel Robert Van Rensselaer.

House of Rensselaer Nicoll

Town of Bethlehem, Albany County, New York

PLATE 29

Anna Van Rensselaer (born 1665), daughter of Jeremias Van Rensselaer (the director of Rensselaerswyck), married in 1686 her first cousin, Kiliaen Van Rensselaer, the third patroon of the colony. The latter died in 1687 and his widow married for her second husband William Nicoll, a great-nephew of Colonel Richard Nicoll, the first governor of New York after the transfer of sovereignty from the Dutch to the English. William and Anna (Van Rensselaer) Nicoll had a son, Rensselaer Nicoll (born 1707, died 1776), who inherited from his mother's brother, Kiliaen Van Rensselaer (fourth patroon), an estate of thirteen hundred acres called *Bethlehem*, situated eight miles south of Albany on the west bank of the Hudson. In 1736 Rensselaer Nicoll married Elizabeth Salisbury of Catskill (whose father's house is shown in plate 30) and for his bride he built a house which still stands (although much enlarged and altered) near the shore of the Hudson at the mouth of " *de Vlauman's Kil* " (that is: the *kil* of *Pieter de Vlamingh* or Peter the Fleming). The house, which has always been called *Bethlehem House*, is owned by the heirs of the estate of Robert H. Moore (Mrs. James Hunter and Joshua Babcock of Albany) and is occupied by tenants. Approach to the house is by a lane that has an obscure beginning on the east side of the state road, immediately south of the bridge over the *Vlauman's Kil* and north of the hamlet of Cedar Hill.

Bethlehem House consists of four parts: the first, built about 1736; an addition, built to the south in 1795; an addition west of the second part, made in 1812; and an addition west of the first portion, made in 1820. A gambrel roof covers the first and second parts. The house is built of brick, laid in English bond, and the walls are thick. By tradition, the bricks of the first part were manufactured on the estate. Beams and flooring are said to have been prepared in a mill which the then patroon had established on the falls on the *Vlauman's Kil* early in the seventeenth century, the *kil* forming the northern boundary of *Bethlehem*. The woodwork of *Bethlehem House* is noticeably plain on the first floor. On the bedroom floor there is some simple panelling in the middle and north rooms. At the front of the house, toward the river, the present porch (of about 1875) was preceded by a covered *stoep* with side seats as shown in plate 29, reproduced from an old photograph obtained through the courtesy of Howard Sill of Baltimore, Md. Large locust trees around the house are believed to have been planted when the first part of the house was new.

No tradition has come down among the descendants of Rensselaer Nicoll that the house he built in 1736 was a structure one and one-half stories high, with roof of single slant. But in the east wall of the present house is a horizontal band of stone-masonry, dividing the bricks of the north half of the house between the first and second stories; and on the north gable-end there is a band of similar width and location made of bricks and projecting from the surface of the wall. Also in the north gable is a faint diagonal line or seam in the brick-work of the second story. Observing these structural features in the light of the knowledge that in 1736 the customary architectural type was still that of *Watervliet* (plate 47) and of the Bries, Bronck, Douw, Van Alen and Van Wie houses (plates 15, 17, 22, 41, 54), the belief is irresistible that the dwelling of Rensselaer Nicoll conformed to the fashion of that time and was later both raised and lengthened into the large house it now is. The horizontal band of masonry on the exterior of the northern half of the house finds something of a counterpart in the ornamental band on the remodelled house of Christopher Yates (plate 57).

Possession of *Bethlehem House* was had by one family-line from 1736 to 1875. From Rensselaer Nicoll it passed to his son, Francis (who married his second cousin, Margaret Van Rensselaer, in the house at Claverack shown in plate 48); from Francis Nicoll to his daughter, Elizabeth, who married Captain Richard Sill and whose wedding in 1785 brought to *Bethlehem House* Alexander Hamilton, Aaron Burr and others of that day who were well known. In the nineteenth century the descendants of Captain and Mrs. Sill owned and occupied the place.

An article in the *New York Genealogical and Biographical Record* for January, 1925, written by Dunkin H. Sill on the subject of the slave, Caesar, who lived at *Bethlehem* and reached the age of one-hundred and fifteen years, affords also detailed information about the place. The owners were people of means and leisure. They entertained lavishly and made annual rounds of visits up and down the river. Hence the traditions of the home are numerous and colorful. Architecturally *Bethlehem House* is a growth, not a type, and it was lived in in a manner somewhat out of the ordinary, so the place was more or less individual and the interest attached to it is peculiarly its own.

House of Francis Salisbury
Leeds, Greene County, New York
PLATE 30

At the time it was built the house shown in plate 30 was heralded as the handsomest house between Albany and New York City. The tradition of its contemporary reputation has been handed down with some definiteness and the experience gained in making the survey of the Hudson valley for material upon which to base this book tends to confirm the tradition. Built in 1705 by Francis Salisbury, in what was then the extreme southern portion of Albany County on the west side of the Hudson, no house has been learned of in any other part of the river valley which was standing in 1705, two full stories in height, with a gambrel roof, unless the houses built by Frederick Philipse at Yonkers and Sleepy Hollow were equally large. There is no certainty, however, as to the original height of the Philipse houses and it is unsafe to use them for purposes of comparison. With the stone houses there is always the possibility that alterations have been made and in this case it might be that the walls were at first only a story and a half high. But in appearance they do not so indicate and one is disposed to accept the tradition that an exceptionally elegant house was actually built here at an unusually early date.

The founder of the Salisbury family was Captain Sylvester Salisbury, an officer of the British troops that took over New Netherland from the Dutch. Sylvester Salisbury married a Dutch wife and by successive Dutch marriages his descendants became completely merged in the Dutch social life of the Province of New York. Captain Salisbury acquired large property interests in the province, one of his investments being the purchase in 1677 of many thousands acres along the Catskill. Soon after the purchase was made a portion of the tract was leased to Andreas and Hendrick Whitbeck for ten years, it being agreed that the lessees instead of paying rent should build a dwelling (twenty-two and a half feet square, with cellar and shingled roof) and a barn and should plant an orchard of two-hundred fruit trees. The decade of the lease was approximately 1680—1690.

Sylvester Salisbury died in 1680, soon after he bought this extensive estate. His son, Francis, married in 1693 Maria Van Gaasbeck of Kingston, whose father, Domine Laurentius Van Gaasbeck (a graduate of the University of Leyden, 1674), was pastor of the Kingston Dutch church 1678—1680 and whose step-father, Wessel Wesselse Ten Broeck, was the builder of the house in Kingston, shown in plate 87. Francis and Maria Salisbury settled on the Catskill estate and they, in 1705, built the house so widely known in its own day.

The house is an L in shape, the base of the L facing east and consisting of a hall between two rooms. At the rear is a kitchen-wing. Entering at the front by a nineteenth century porch, through a fine eighteenth century door, the stairway rises before the visitor at the left in the rear corner of the hall. The first bank of steps is open to view, the second is boxed in. Ceiling-beams in the hall and in the north front room are massive, unenclosed and in color tobacco brown. In the north wall of the north room is a fireplace, simply faced, and flanked on either side by panelled cupboards. In the kitchen the north wall has panelled cupboards and at the west is a chimney with large fireplace opening. It is not improbable that the kitchen-wing is the dwelling built by the Whitbecks in the 1680's and that the house of Francis Salisbury was erected across its gable-end. At numerous, irregular intervals the walls of the main house are pierced with loopholes. Most of the windows are of modern glass. There is a frame lean-to at the northwest corner and a recent porch at the southwest corner. Across the front of the house, close to the eaves, are the figures: 1 7 0 5, in wrought iron and, below, on a level with the roof of the front porch the letters: F S M S, appear in iron. Figures and letters all measure over a foot, each, in height. The initials stand, of course, for Francis Salisbury and Maria Salisbury.

The Salisbury house is on the north side of the Mohican Trail of the motorist (the ancient country turnpike), a short distance west of the bridge that spans the Catskill at the village of Leeds. Title to the property remained in the name of Salisbury until 1831, when conveyance was made to James Van Deusen, step-son of Abraham Salisbury (the latter having married, in 1799, Rachel Elting, widow of Cornelius Van Deusen). Dr. Claudius Van Deusen (son of James) inherited the house, dying unmarried in 1907. Thus for one-hundred and fifty-four years, 1677—1831, the land was owned by the Salisburys and for seventy-six years, 1831—1907, by the Van Deusens. The house is now the property of the Messrs. W. J. and H. S. Tiffany.

House of Abraham Salisbury
Leeds, Greene County, New York
PLATE 31

Abraham Salisbury (born 1699, died 1756—1757), a son of Francis Salisbury whose house is shown in plate 30, married in 1730 his first cousin, Rachel Ten

92

Broeck (daughter of Wessel and Jacomyntje Van Gaasbeck Ten Broeck of Kingston), who in 1743 inherited a one-fifth interest in the Ten Broeck house shown in plate 87. For this couple, at the time of their marriage, Francis Salisbury built a dwelling a little west of his own and on the same road. The house of 1730 still stands but it was enlarged in 1823 from a height of one and one-half stories to two stories and an attic. It is built of stone and the first floor consists of a hall with two large rooms on either side. In the outer east wall is a stone near the first story windows marked:

1 7
Built by
3 F S o

Above, near the peak of the roof are the figures:

1 8
2 3

while in the west gable, high up, are the initials:

A S
R S

which stand for Abraham Salisbury (born 1753, died 1825) and Rachel (Elting) Salisbury, his wife. In the interior one wall in the northeast living room is covered with handsome panelling that probably goes back to the earliest years of the house. But the carved door-casings and beautiful front doorway and porch belong undoubtedly to 1823, when the house was remodelled. The roof of 1823 extends beyond the walls of the house in the same manner as do the roofs on the houses of Madam Brett (plate 111) and David Johnstone (plate 122).

The unique feature of this property is the avenue between the house and the highway. It is not long, but is so laid out as to simulate length. A stone wall outlines each side of the drive and on the outer side of each wall is a planting, first of a row of lilac bushes and then of a row of locust trees. The avenue and the planting are believed to date to the 1830's. A picture of the avenue is shown rather than one of the house because the latter has lost the appearance characteristic of the eighteenth century and the avenue, although a creation of the nineteenth, is so beautiful an adjunct to this homestead. The avenue is conspicuously superior to any other landscape work found in connection with the old estates in the Hudson valley.

Abraham Salisbury, for whom the house of 1730 was built, is supposed to have occupied the house until he died. The best information obtainable is to the effect that Abraham's brother, William Salisbury (born 1714, died 1801), succeeded him in the house, while Abraham's direct heirs took up their residence in the Salisbury house of 1705 (plate 30). The house of 1730 is linked with the house of Barent

Staats (plate 36) by the fact that Barent Staats's daughter, Eunice, lived in it as the wife of William Salisbury and by the further fact that three sons of William and Eunice Salisbury went to the Staats family for their wives. General William Salisbury (born 1801, died 1883), a grandson of William and Eunice (Staats) Salisbury, was the last of the name to own the house. The present owner is G. Y. Clement of Philadelphia.

House of Domine Gideon Schaets

Formerly at Albany, New York

PLATE 32

The Reverend Gideon Schaets came from the Netherlands in 1652 to serve as pastor of the Dutch church at Fort Orange. In 1657 a pulpit and bell for the church were imported from Holland and with them came bricks, woodwork, tiles and ornamental irons for a house for the domine (Munsell: *Annals of Albany,* 1: 287—288). The house then built stood until 1832, when it was torn down. The site is now the northeast corner of State and Pearl Streets, Albany. Frequently the dwelling is spoken of as the Lydius house, having been occupied by Balthazar Lydius for many years prior to his death in 1815. In 1805 a painting was made of this corner by the artist, James Eights. The painting is now owned by Mrs. William Gorham Rice of Albany and the plate here shown is from a photograph of the painting taken by the late Colonel Augustus Pruyn and reproduced through the courtesy of his daughter, Miss Margaret Ten Eyck Pruyn of Albany.

The house of Domine Schaets illustrates well the mid-seventeenth century brick house at Albany, with stepped gable and the gable-end of the house toward the street.

The Schuyler House called *The Flatts*

Troy Road, south of Watervliet, New York

PLATE 33

The property known as *The Flatts,* owned now by Mrs. Richard Schuyler of Ballston Spa, New York, was purchased in 1672 by Philip Pieterse Schuyler and thus has a record of two-hundred and fifty-three years of possession by one family. The low land which gives the *bouwerij* its name is a continuation northward of the strip of river-frontage on which the Van Rensselaer manor-house (plate 47) stood. *The King's Highway* originally ran close to the shore of the Hudson with these houses fronting upon it, whereas the present road from Albany to Troy, that replaces *the King's Highway,* lies back from the river parallel with the Delaware and Hudson Canal. At the southern boundary line of the city of Watervliet a bridge crosses the canal to a long avenue leading eastward on the flat to the rear of the house.

Called in Dutch *de Vlackte* (and in obsolete English: *the Flatts*) this *bouwerij* was part of the colony of Rensselaerswyck and the house on it was leased in 1648 to Arent Van Curler for six years,—that is, until 1654. Van Curler may have continued to occupy *de Vlackte* until 1662; but in that year he removed to Schenectady and in 1668 Jeremias Van Rensselaer, director of the colony, wrote a letter in which he stated: " On the Flats the house has settled or caved in, it will have to be totally restored and I can get no tenant for it."

Other correspondence of Jeremias Van Rensselaer's shows that the house on the flat was taken over about 1668 by Richard Van Rensselaer, who repaired it and occupied it until he went to Holland in 1670 or 1671. In 1671 Jeremias described in detail the unfavorable condition of the farms of the colony,—houses were in decay, there were few tenants, other tenants were not to be had and the writer wished the whole estate could be sold. However, in 1672 Philip Pieterse Schuyler purchased *de Vlackte* and in 1689 title to the *bouwerij* was confirmed to his widow, Margareta Schuyler, by a deed recorded at Albany, which also recites Richard Van Rensselaer's use of the place.

From Philip Pieterse and Margaretta (Van Slichtenhorst) Schuyler *The Flatts* passed to their son, Pieter Philipse (born 1657, died 1724), and then to their grandson, Colonel Philip Pieterse Schuyler (born 1696, died 1758). The latter married his first cousin, Margaretta Schuyler (of Johannes, of Philip Pieterse), who is the central figure in the volume entitled: *Memoirs of an American Lady*, written by Mrs. Anne McVickar Grant of Scotland and published in London in 1808. Dying in 1758 without children, Colonel Philip Pieterse Schuyler left the life-use of *The Flatts* to his widow, after whose death the property passed to the colonel's nephew (in the line of his brother, Peter Schuyler), through whose descendants in direct male line it has come to the present owner.

Shortly after Colonel Schuyler's death (supposedly in the summer of 1759) the house on *The Flatts* took fire and the roof and interior were destroyed. Mrs. Grant in the *Memoirs* draws a graphic picture of the scene of the fire. The " American Lady " was seated out of doors one warm summer day in the driveway, lined with cherry trees, that led to the house. General John Bradstreet (commander of the British troops stationed at Albany) came riding down *the King's Highway* to call on Madam. He saw smoke issuing from the house and gave the alarm. Madam retained her composure and from her chair under the cherry trees directed the work of rescue. The dwelling had consisted of a larger unit, facing east, and a smaller one extending to the west and the brick walls of these two parts withstood the fire to a great extent. " Madam ", or " Aunt Schuyler ", (as the colonel's widow was addressed by her contemporaries) rebuilt the wing between the summer and winter of the year of the fire, with the aid of soldiers detailed by General Bradstreet. Somewhat later the walls of the main unit were evened off and carried up and the present dwelling finished. As it now stands, the house at *The Flatts* has a gambrel roof, which dates undoubtedly to the reconstruction after the fire and which reflects the architectural fashion current at that time. The main house of 1668—1759 must be assumed to have had a slanting roof-line, like the wing and similar to the roof of the Van Rensselaer manor-house (plate 47), the slant or peak being characteristic of its period and ante-dating the introduction of the gambrel.

The floor-plan of the front part of the rebuilt house has a central hall, with one larger and one smaller room on either side. The ceilings are low. The doorways are unusually wide and the doorcasings have arched tops. Little of the early appearance of the interior now remains. The front door, a massive one, divided horizontally and equipped with large iron bolt and hinges, is the best survival of the eighteenth century finishings of the house. At the front entrance a recent veranda has succeeded a simple porch (the latter was put on record in a photograph of about 1870) and over the veranda is a modern bay-window.

The view of the house shown in plate 33 is from a photograph made by the late Colonel Augustus Pruyn of Albany (reproduced through the courtesy of his daughter, Miss Margaret Ten Eyck Pruyn) and shows the rear of the house. While an excellent picture of the front (vignette page 47), taken fifty or sixty years ago, is owned by Henry Sage Dermott of Albany, the rear has been selected for illustration here because it can be dated as rebuilt by " the American Lady " immediately after the fire. Seams in the brickwork suggest that Madam Schuyler enlarged the wing to the north and south on the groundfloor. The main portion of the house, with the gambrel roof, is in general similar to the Van Rensselaer-Genêt house in the town of East Greenbush, Rensselaer County, the front of which is shown in plate 49.

The Homes of Philip Schuyler

Three houses are associated with the name of Philip Schuyler, patriot of the Revolution. The first, the one in which he was born, is no longer standing but in its day it was an example of the type of dwelling that the Dutch residents of *Beverwyck* (Albany) built in the seventeenth century. The other two, which were built by General Schuyler himself, were not Dutch in architecture and can be considered as Dutch houses only in the sense that they were occupied by a man of Dutch descent. Philip Schuyler was however so essentially a product of the Dutch racial strain and the Dutch social culture of the Hudson valley that all three of the houses he lived in are listed below.

Birthplace of Philip Schuyler
Formerly on State Street, Albany, New York
PLATE 34

Regarding the title to the land at the southeast corner of State and South Pearl Streets, Albany, and regarding the houses which originally were built upon that site more or less has been written and published in past years. The first printed references to the property contained certain errors which were perpetuated in following accounts and the confusion occasioned thereby prompted the archivist of the state of New York, A. J. F. van Laer, to make a careful investigation of all the evidence and to submit a report of his findings in the Year Book of the Dutch Settlers Society for 1926. Without quoting in detail the data contained in Mr. van Laer's article it may be briefly stated here that the land in question was granted in 1653 to Abram Staats, who in 1664 conveyed it to Philip Pietersen Schuyler (by contract of sale?). Schuyler soon built upon the lot the tall narrow structure, shown in plate 34, and on April 27, 1667, he received from Staats a deed, confirming the initial transaction, in which document mention is made of the house that he had already erected. Against the west wall of this dwelling a second house was next built, supposedly in 1667, and an inscription in iron: Anno 1667, ultimately extended under the eaves across the front of the twin buildings.

Of the two houses, the first (built before 1667) was the birthplace in 1733 of Philip Schuyler. It remained in the Schuyler family until 1777, when Stephen J. Schuyler sold it to Henry Staats, and it stood until 1887, when it was razed. The sepia drawing of it, shown in plate 34, is reproduced from: *Random Recollections of Albany*, published 1866 by G. A. Worth. A photograph of the house in its last years when the first floor had been made into shops occurs at page seven of *Albany's Historic Street*, published by the National Savings Bank of the City of Albany in 1918, and a print from another slightly different negative of about the same period is presented at page seventy of Reynolds's: *Albany Chronicles*.

The second of the two houses stood until 1798, when it was torn down to permit the widening of South Pearl Street. It was the residence of Captain Johannes Schuyler, born 1668, died 1747, and from him was inherited by his daughter Margaretta, wife of Colonel Philip Schuyler of *The Flatts* (plate 33), who is known as "the American Lady" and who made it her town residence until her death in 1783. In the years immediately preceding its destruction the house was called the Lewis tavern.

House of Philip Schuyler: The Pastures

Albany, New York

In 1762 Philip Schuyler built at Albany a large brick dwelling in Georgian English style which still stands. It is now owned by the State of New York and preserved as a memorial to Schuyler and his times. When erected, the house stood in a conspicuously isolated location, south of the village of Albany and in plain view from the Hudson. It is on a steep hillside, that slopes toward the river, and it was named *The Pastures* because of the open ground all about it, an area which now is closely built up with small modern houses. A monograph on *The Pastures* by Miss Georgina Schuyler was published in 1911 by the DeVinne Press; an article upon the house appears in the *Report of the American Scenic and Historic Preservation Society* for 1912; and printed descriptive matter and picture post-cards are obtainable by application to the custodian.

House of Philip Schuyler

Schuylerville, New York

At Schuylerville, town of Saratoga, Saratoga County, New York, is a house built by Philip Schuyler about 1777—1783. In that vicinity a large tract of land was acquired at an early date by Philip Johannes Schuyler of Albany, who built mills on the Fish Creek and, near the mills, a dwelling for himself. During an attack made in the neighborhood by the Indians in 1745 Philip Johannes Schuyler was killed and his house burned and from then until the peace of 1763 between France and England Schuylerville was the scene of border alarms which prevented its development by permanent settlers. Philip Johannes Schuyler willed his property there to two of his nephews, one of whom, Philip, the future general, was in 1745 but twelve years old.

Philip Schuyler married in 1755 " sweet Kitty Van Rensselaer " (born at *Klaver Rak*, plate 48; brought up at *Crailo*, page 113), and they, after the peace of 1763, built a house and new mills where Schuylerville now is. But a second time war and fire did their devastating work. The new home was seized and occupied in 1777 by General Burgoyne and then burned by him just before the battle of Saratoga.

The house now standing was erected by General Schuyler to replace the one Burgoyne destroyed. One tradition says that immediately after the battle Philip Schuyler hired a large number of men from the victorious American army and, in seventeen days, rushed the construction of a house to completion. Another statement is that he rebuilt just after the peace of 1783. The present house, now the home of Charles A. Marshall, is said to reproduce the architecture of the house of 1763—1777, which may be true, either wholly or in part. It is a frame building, wider than deep and two stories in height; the floor of the front veranda is on the level of the ground and pillars rise from it to the line of the eaves in southern fashion (see: illustration, page 324, *Albany Chronicles* by Cuyler Reynolds). The property remained in the Schuyler family and was used as a summer home until 1837, when it was sold to George Strover and is now owned by his descendants. Near the house is a famous group of lilac bushes, which are believed to have been planted before the Revolution.

Staats House
Stockport Creek, Columbia County, New York

PLATE 35

The Stockport station of the New York Central and Hudson River Railroad stands in the angle formed by the confluence of Stockport Creek with the Hudson. Immediately east of the station, facing south on the creek, is a Staats homestead, the exact age of which is not known. The land it occupies is part of a tract bounded south by the creek and west by the Hudson that was acquired in the seventeenth century by Major Abram Staats (or Staes).

Abram Staats came out to New Netherland in 1642 as surgeon for the West India Company and practised his profession six years. He bought real estate in *Beverwyck* (Albany) and lived a long time on State Street where the Albany County Savings Bank now stands. Also, he owned a sloop, the *Claverack*, plying between *Beverwyck* and New Amsterdam, and traded in furs with the Indians. The Indians often gathered in large numbers at the mouth of Stockport Creek and so, in 1654, Major Abram bought from the natives two hundred acres bordering on the north shore of the stream (an acreage which in 1685 he increased to a total of six hundred). On this land he built a house, in which he installed a farmer. Unfortunately, in July, 1664, a report was sent from Fort Orange to Director Stuyvesant of depredations made on the upper Hudson by marauding Indians in which the following statement occurs: " The tidings are also certain that the Indians burnt last Friday the dwelling house on one Mr. Abraham Staets' *bouwerij*, with the farmer; his wife and negro are not to be found up to this date. Mr. Abraham's wife's people have sent a canoe thither today." And two letters written by Jeremias van Rensselaer (one on July 17th, the other on July 26th, 1664) refer to this fire in the following words: The Indians " burned Mr. Abraham Staets' house in the Klaaver Rack. The farmer was found in the burned house, his wife and a boy are still missing." " Thereafter they set fire to the house of Mr. Abraham Staets in Klaver rack. Jantie, from Katskill, who lived there with his wife and a boy, was found burned in the house."

The house now standing on the site near the Stockport station may represent the foundation of the house burned in 1664. It might conceivably represent the walls of the seventeenth century house, assuming that that house was built of stone and that only the roof and interior were destroyed by the fire. But more probably the present walls date to the period of a son or grandson of Major Abram. He had four sons. One (Samuel) settled in New-York City. One (Jacob) lived in Albany and left no descendants. One (Jochem) settled on *Hooghe Bergh*, a *bouwerij* on the shore of the Hudson eighteen miles north of Stockport Creek. The fourth son, Abraham Staets, is mentioned as " of Claverack " (the name applying along the shore of the Hudson in the *Klaver Rak*). Until modern times the stream before the door of the house at Stockport station was known as *Major Abraham's Creek,* and in 1752 a map made by Charles Clinton shows the house on this site as occupied by Samuel Staats.

The present house consists of two units, one of stone (shown in plate 35) and the other a wing of brick to the west. The wing is a story and a half in height, with a gambrel roof. It is clearly the product of the middle of the eighteenth century and may be likened to the house of Gerret Staats (plate 37), although smaller. Its existence as an addition to the stone portion pushes the latter back a number of years earlier for erection. A description of this house written in 1878 (*History of Columbia County*, published by Everts and Ensign) refers to the stone portion as having at that time a gambrel roof, similar to the roof on the brick wing. If that statement can be relied upon, it indicates that the stone house belongs in a class with the house of Jan Van Loon, built at Athens in 1724 (plate 46). When visited in behalf of this book access to the interior of the Staats house was not obtained and it is impossible to say whether its primitive details still remain. Loss of the original roof and porch, window-glass and shutters, leaves the exterior with but a brief architectural story to tell but the story of the land the house stands upon is a long one.

The present owners of the property are the Messrs. Harry and Joseph Hoes.

House of Barent Staats
Staats' Island, Rensselaer County, New York
PLATE 36

Between Rensselaer and Castleton the shore of the Hudson is low and wet. Papsknee Creek and its tributaries wind about, creating marshes or wet meadows, and Papsknee Island lies along the shore, almost indistinguishable from the main land. The Staats house is situated on the southern end of Papsknee Island (referred to there as " Staats' Island "), five miles south of Rensselaer, and is approached from the river-road, westerly across the marshes.

A *bouwerij* called *Hooghe Bergh* (High Hill) was acquired here by Jochem Staats (born 1654, died 1712), son of Major Abram Staats (plate 35), the name of *Hooghe Bergh* being possibly a derisive reference to a knoll on the island on top of which is a family burial-ground. In a quit-claim deed, passed in 1765 between some of Jochem Staats's descendants, the recital of title to *Hooghe Bergh* states the ownership of it by him but does not give the date of his purchase. Jochem's eldest son, Barent (born 1680, died 1752), inherited the *bouwerij*. He married in 1701 Neltje Vandenbergh. Their son, Joachim (born 1717), married in 1739 Elizabeth, daughter of Nicholas Schuyler, and succeeded to the property at Barent's death. The place is now owned by Philip Schuyler Staats of Rensselaer, a descendant of Barent and Elizabeth Schuyler Staats.

The quit-claim deed, referred to above, does not state who owned *Hooghe Bergh* before Jochem Staats. There is a deed on record at Albany, dated September 7, 1696, whereby Kiliaen Van Rensselaer conveyed to Samuel Staats of New York City a farm on the east side of the Hudson and delivered it into the possession of Samuel Staats upon the island called *Paepsknoy*, with all houses, etc. If this latter farm were one and the same as *Hooghe Bergh* it may be assumed that Samuel Staats conveyed it to his brother, Jochem, who thus would have become a settler on Papsknee Island after 1696 and before 1712, when he died.

The house now standing on *Hooghe Bergh* (plate 36) may have been built before 1696. It may have been built by Jochem Staats between 1696 and 1712. That it is an unusually old house is a tradition current in its vicinity. But in the center of the south front, close to the eaves, is a tooled stone, smoothly set and obviously inserted after the house was built, which bears the inscription:

B S—N S
1(7)22
I S—E S
16(??)

Unquestionably, the initials stand for: Barent Staats and Neeltje Staats; Joachim Staats and Elizabeth Staats; and so the letters must of necessity have been cut after the second couple were married, that is: after 1739. In the second line the second figure is difficult to read. In the fourth line the figures are painted in red, not cut, and are manifestly a late addition to the inscription and hence unreliable.

Balancing tradition and the marked stone with each other, the evidence tends toward the probability that the house was built by Barent Staats in 1722 and, architecturally, the house itself is supporting evidence for that conclusion. It is built of rough field stones, with a recent frame wing to the west and brick wing to the north. The gable end is filled with brick. The roof is a single slant, broadly spread and quite unlike the steep Dutch roofs common near Albany before 1700; it is a companion to the roof on the Van Buren house of (approximately) 1730, farther north on the river-road, which also was a wide, single slant. The Staats house is built on ground that slopes from north to south, entrance being had from the southern ground level. On the first floor is a hall between two rooms; the west room is wainscoted and has deep window openings, a simple mantel and a cupboard in the chimney-corner. The porches and window-blinds are modern.

House of Gerret Staats
Staats' Island, Rensselaer County, New York
PLATE 37

North of the house of Barent Staats (plate 36) is a knoll, on the top of which is the ancient burial ground of the Staats family. North of the knoll on lower ground is the house of Gerret Staats, son of Barent and brother of Joachim Staats. Gerret was born in 1722, grew up in the house of his father, married (about 1747) Deborah Beekman and founded a new home. South of the west door the wall of his house is marked:

S

G D

1758

The house of Gerret Staats, built of brick laid in English bond and having a gambrel roof, is similar to the Van Rensselaer-Genêt house (plate 49) but is on a smaller scale. It is occupied by Polish tenants and access to the interior was not obtained in visiting it. There is one room on the north of the central hall and on the south are supposedly two. The house stands close to the shore of the Hudson and large old trees near it are noteworthy.

The Ten Broeck Bouwerij

Roeloff Jansen's Kil, Columbia County, New York

PLATE 38

Through the southern portion of Columbia County winds a stream known as *Roeloff Jansen's Kil.* Roeloff Jansen was assistant *bouwmeester* for the patroon of Rensselaerswyck in the first years of the colony but it has been his fate to belong to the group of men who are remembered by posterity as their wives' husbands. In this case the wife was the famous Anneke Jans, whose first husband Roeloff Jansen was. To account for the association of his name with this stream tradition tells that in a severe winter of the 1630's Roeloff Jansen's boat became wedged in the ice and he was obliged to stay with the neighboring Indians and await a spring thaw before he could return up the river to *Beverwyck.*

Along the course of *Roeloff Jansen's Kil,* in the present towns of Clermont and Livingston, lies the land taken up as a *bouwerij* in 1694 by Major Dirck Wesselse Ten Broeck of Albany (born 1638, died 1717), who in 1663 had purchased the house in the then *Beverwyck* that Anneke Jans died in (plate 13). Major Ten Broeck built a house on his *bouwerij* and is said to have lived in it the last years of his life. Partly by inheritance and partly by buying out other heirs his grandson, another Dirck Wesselse, son of Samuel Ten Broeck and Maria Van Rensselaer, acquired the sole title to the *bouwerij* and in 1762 built the house shown in plate 38, which remained in the possession of his descendants until very lately.

As *Roeloff Jansen's Kil* crosses the Ten Broeck *bouwerij* it takes a course between high banks and then through meadow flats. The house stands on the first rise of ground on the west side of the stream, the fertile meadows spread before it and behind it a high hill, crowned by the family burial ground. It is built of brick laid in English bond and is two and one-half stories high, with a gambrel roof. A covered Dutch *stoep* at the front was replaced about 1865 by the present veranda. In each gable are two circular portholes, about a foot in diameter. The north gable carries an ornamental design in the bricks: three graduated diamonds, one above another, outlined by black headers. Across the front of the house white headers form the figures: 1 7 6 2.

The interior of the house consisted originally of a hall between two rooms on each floor. Panelling remains over the fireplace in the south room on the first floor; across the north wall of the north upper room; and in the south upper room; in which last is also an iron fireback, marked: 1763. In the north room on the first floor is an ornamental arch on either side of the chimney. Blue and white tiles faced the fireplace opening in the north parlor, prior to the present mottled marble.

It is an unsettled question whether a wing at the rear of the brick house was an addition after 1762 or whether the brick house was built in front of a smaller and older dwelling. The latter theory is more in accordance with observations made elsewhere in the Hudson valley and, in altering the wing, the present owner, Theodore Gaty, found old panelling cut on the reverse side with a variety of marks, one of which was the date: January, 1735/6. Family opinion, however, tends to hold that the wing followed the main house and that panelling from a previous house was utilized in it. The wing has of late been completely altered and it is not now possible to make a comparison between the workmanship of its construction and that of the main house.

Between the Ten Broeck house on *Roeloff Jansen's Kil* and the Glen-Sanders house (plate 23) at Scotia are close ties, formed by several marriages between members of the families that occupied the two homes. Architecturally, the house of Dirck Ten Broeck of 1762 belongs in a group with the Conyn-Van Rensselaer house of 1766 (plate 20); the house of Jacob Evertson, 1763 (page 342); and the house of Sarah Tobias Newcomb 1777—1780 (plate 129).

House of Samuel Ten Broeck

Town of Livingston, Columbia County, New York

PLATE 39

About a mile, as the crow flies, southeast of the house of Dirck Wesselse Ten Broeck (plate 38) is the house of Dirck's brother, Samuel Ten Broeck (born 1745, died 1841). Samuel, who married in 1768 Emitje Van Alstyne, was major of militia in the Revolution. He became general of militia after the war and served in the assembly. About 1773 he built the dwelling shown in plate 39 but after a few years sold it to Henry Livingston, who called it *Callender House*. It is now owned by Mrs. Charles Coons.

This house stands on a part of the original Ten Broeck *bouwerij* but is on the east side of *Roeloff Jansen's Kil* and is reached by the road that runs south from Manorton. It is built of brick and is one and one-half stories high, with a gambrel roof. The approximate date of its erection is learned from an iron fireback, once in the house (now owned by William Ten Broeck Mynderse of Scotia), marked:

1773

E

STB

the initials standing for Samuel and Emitje Ten Broeck.

Surrounding the house is a grove of trees—chiefly locusts— of great size and age, which form a beautiful setting for the dignified dwelling. The house is yellow and, like the Van Schaick house, Cohoes (plate 52), is an unforgettable picture if seen in the midst of its trees on a summer day, when color, light and shade combine to produce a lovely whole.

Unidentified House
Formerly at Albany, New York
PLATE 40

Among the photographs made by the late Augustus Pruyn of Albany, New York, is one of an oil painting of a house which, through the courtesy of Miss Margaret Ten Eyck Pruyn of Albany, is presented here as plate 40. As some uncertainty exists as to when or by whom the house was built or with what family name it was chiefly associated it is listed merely as an unidentified item but its inclusion is justified by the typical quality of the dwelling. The painting recorded one of the steep-roofed structures of early Albany, two stories in height, with a rear wing. Along the line of the roof in the gable-end the bricks are laid in the triangular pattern which the Dutch called: *muizetanden* (mouse-teeth), and they are also set in ornamental arrangement over the large windows in the gable-end. In the front façade the window-openings are irregularly placed and are filled with diamond-shaped panes of glass. The tall and narrow shape of the windows is similar to that of windows that still remain in the house of John Brinckerhoff in Dutchess County (page 333). The house has but one chimney and the flue must have been double, rising at either side of the granary door that, apparently, led into the attic.

Van Alen House
Kinderhook, Columbia County, New York
PLATE 41

The Van Alen house stands east of the village of Kinderhook on the former Albany Post Road and is owned and occupied by Mrs. William Herrick (Maria

Van Alen), whose title to the property has been handed down through several successive generations of the Van Alen family. The builder of the house was either Adam Van Alen (born 1703, died 1784) or his father, Johannes. One of the two erected a dwelling that consisted of two rooms, each with a chimney, and an open attic over both; to which structure was added later to the north a hall (with enclosed stairs) and one room with another chimney. In the roof the seam created by the addition is visible in the plate. The brick walls of the house are laid in English bond and in the south gable are affixed iron figures: 1737. External details of the house are now of recent date. An early front door, inset, with two rows of small panes of glass above it, has been replaced by a later door and modern porch. The dormers on the east front are also modern. Inside, two bed-recesses have been taken out of the part of the house built in 1737 but the ceiling beams are still open to view and are dark brown in color from age. Architecturally, the Van Alen house of 1737 should be compared with the Bries house, 1722 (plate 15); Douw, 1724 (plate 22); Van Wie, 1732 (plate 54); and Bronck, 1738 (plate 17).

This homestead at Kinderhook is linked with literature and romance by the imagination and the pen of Washington Irving, whose acquaintance with it was made during his visits near by in the home of his friends, the Van Ness family. The Van Ness house, enlarged, was afterwards the residence of Martin Van Buren, ex-President of the United States, and is well known under the name: *Lindenwald*. In the *Legend of Sleepy Hollow* Irving's description of a Dutch colonial farmhouse is understood to be based upon the Van Alen house and a certain pretty Van Alen daughter is said to have been the prototype for his heroine, *Catrina Van Tassel*.

Van Antwerp-Mebie House

Rotterdam Junction, Schenectady County, New York

PLATE 42

In 1670 Daniel Janse Van Antwerp bought land about eight miles west of Schenectady on the third flat on the south side of the Mohawk river, for which he obtained a patent in 1680, and on which he built a house. The property was sold by Van Antwerp in 1706 to Jan Pieterse Mebie, who (with his wife, Anna Pieterse Van Borsboom) occupied it and whose descendants,—Mrs. Harry B. Franchere and her sister, Miss Mabel A. Scrafford, of Rotterdam Junction, New York,—now own it.

The Van Antwerp-Mebie house stands close to the south bank of the Mohawk on the river-road, a fraction of a mile east of the bridge that crosses the Mohawk near Rotterdam Junction. It is built of stone, one and one-half stories high. The west gable is clapboarded. At the east end are a modern lean-to and two windows with modern glass and shutters. The house faces south and consists of two rooms, each having a chimney. In the east room the opening of the fireplace is wide and has a primitive facing of wood. An enclosed stairway (steep as a ladder) leads from one corner of the room to an attic story, where in late years room-partitions were built. From the east room to the lean-to is an early Dutch door. A door that was originally in the south wall of the west room has been made into a window.

Southwest of the house is a small building, probably of brick throughout, but clapboarded on the west and north, which (by local tradition) was a dwelling for slaves. It consists of a basement, with a fireplace, and one room on the main floor, from which enclosed stairs lead to one room above. The Dutch door carries early wrought iron hinges and latch.

The distinctive architectural feature of the Van Antwerp-Mebie house is the steep pitch of the roof but the building as a whole affords an excellent idea of a Dutch pioneer home of the last quarter of the seventeenth century. The roof of this house should be compared with the roofs of the Bronck, Van Schaack, Hasbrouck and Pawling houses (plates: 16, 51, 75, 82).

Van Bergen-Vedder Farm
Leeds, Greene County, New York
PLATE 43

Crossing the Catskill by the bridge at the village of Leeds to the open flat west of the stream and turning south from the Mohican Trail into a farm-road close to the bridge, a motorist can easily find the way to the homestead-farm of the Van Bergens and the Vedders. The farm was purchased in 1680 by Marte Gerretse Van Bergen of Albany, who built a stone house and smoke-house and a barn on a rise of ground beyond rolling meadows and leased the property to tenants. When Garret Van Bergen, eldest son of Marte, was grown he came down from Albany to occupy his father's lands on the Catskill, where he built for himself in 1729 a brick house, placing his slaves in the stone tenant-house of 1680. The latter has now been torn down but the smoke-house of the same period still stands and much of the structure of the present barn is believed to date to the seventeenth century.

The house built by Garret Van Bergen in 1729 was of brick laid in English bond; the roof was a gambrel, covered with red tiles; the entrance was through a Dutch *stoep* and double Dutch door; and the windows held leaded, diamond-shaped panes. In the nineteenth century the walls were raised from one and one-half to two full stories; a roof of single slant was put on and a modern porch and door substituted for the originals. But in the east gable may still be read:

Ano 1729

July 4

M G V B

and over the north door occurs:

Ano 1729

Capt June 28

G V B A V B

The interior of the house has lost its primitive character, except as to floor-plan. On the right of the central hall are two rooms; on the left one parlor, which was the room kept closed for weddings and funerals. In the living-room to the right of the hall the fireplace of the eighteenth century was faced with tiles, while a four-poster bed (with a trundle-bed beneath it) once filled the space at one side of the chimney. The older children slept in the dim half-story above and in *Historic Catskill* Mrs. Jessie V. V. Vedder draws a vivid picture of a slave using a brass warming-pan, filled with red-hot embers to heat the homespun woolen sheets on winter nights, at a time when wolves came from the mountain to howl around the sheep-pens and when the cries of panther and wildcat could be heard near by. That was a time when the produce of this remote farm was carried over a road that was hardly more than a rough wheel-track to the landing on the Hudson for shipment to market by water.

In 1774 the Van Bergens sold this farm to Arent Vedder, whose descendant, Henry Vedder, now owns and occupies it. Thus but two family names are associated with it,—Van Bergen from 1680 to 1774 and Vedder from 1774 to the present.

In its appearance now the house built by Garret Van Bergen in 1729 is not pictorial for the purposes of this book, as its eighteenth century features have been removed or modified. But in plate 43 the fertile meadows of the old farm are shown, with the house above them, on a natural terrace, in order to illustrate the topographical features of the land taken up for settlement in 1680.

Van Buren-Van Rensselaer House

Formerly in the Town of East Greenbush, Rensselaer County, New York

Willem Cornelis Van Buren, born 1706, married about 1730 Teuntie Vanden-bergh. He died in 1752 and was buried at Papsknee (the locality on the east side of the Hudson, opposite Albany, watered by Papsknee Creek), leaving his widow, Teuntie, with a large family of minor children. The map of Rensselaer Manor made in 1767 shows the house of Teuntie Van Buren about three miles south of *Crailo* on the river-road to Schodack. The house stood (with some alterations or additions) until recent years, when it burned down and was followed by a frame house on the same site.

The Van Buren homestead was built of brick, with a roof of single slant, and the floor-plan was, as so often, that of a central hall with a room, or rooms, on either side. The date of erection may be assumed as approximating that of the marriage of Willem and Teuntie. Their son, Cornelis Van Buren, born 1736, who married in 1758 Maicke Hun, succeeded them in the occupation of the house and he, in turn, was followed by his daughter, Elsie Van Buren, born 1759, died 1844, who married in 1780 Colonel Nicholas Van Rensselaer.

Nicholas Van Rensselaer (born 1754, died 1848) grew up in the Van Rensselaer house (plate 49) on the river-road which was but a short distance south of the Van Buren home. He lived to be ninety-four and in his kindly, mellow old age was affectionately known among his kindred as " Uncle Nicky ", while from his long residence there the Van Buren house came to be called " Uncle Nicky's house." In 1834 a visit was made at this house by the Reverend Maunsell Van Rensselaer (then a lad) who in 1888 wrote a description of the house and of the elderly Dutch relatives living in it, who were still in 1834 speaking Dutch. The manuscript refers to the sacred best parlor on the right of the main entrance, kept scrupulously closed except for weddings, christenings and funerals. It speaks also of the ancient spinster, named Annie Aunitje, who formed part of the household, and who was always found knitting. The place, said the Reverend Mr. Van Rensselaer, " was a country bouwerij, inhabited by quaint and old-fashioned people, who were very kind and hospitable. Everything about it was of the past generation and delightfully antiquated and simple. My uncle was eighty years old and a hale, hearty old man, with a very sweet and kindly face and a very quiet and cordial manner."

On the hill that rises behind the site of the Van Buren—Van Rensselaer house may still be seen the family burial-ground.

House of Gerret Vandenbergh
Town of Bethlehem, Albany County, New York
PLATE 44

On the east side of the state road, immediately south of the bridge at Glenmont, Albany County, between the road and the river is a house of the eighteenth century. It stands on land that was part of a tract called: *Domine's Hoeck*, which was leased in 1696 by Kiliaen Van Rensselaer to Marte Gerretse Van Bergen. On the map of the manor of Rensselaer made in 1767 the house is shown as Gerret Vandenbergh's. In 1796 Gerret Vandenbergh conveyed it to Thomas Spencer. Philip Wendell of Albany bought the property in 1800 and it is still owned by his descendants, represented by William S. Dyer, attorney, Albany, New York. An excellent map of *Domine's Hoeck* farm, made in 1790, is on file in Mr. Dyer's office.

The house at Glenmont is built of bricks (obviously of early manufacture), laid in English bond. It consists of two rooms, with a hall between; has a steep roof-line and iron wall-anchors in trefoil design. The porch and interior woodwork are recent.

Comparison of this house should be made with: the Bries, Bronck, Douw, Van Alen, Van Wie, and Yates houses (plates 15, 17, 22, 41, 54, 56).

House of Matthias Vanderheyden

Formerly at Troy, New York

PLATE 45

In 1707 Dirck Vanderheyden of Albany bought the land on which the city of Troy now stands. The *Poesten Kil* (Cowherd's Stream) watered his farm, which became known as *Poesten Bouwerij*. He secured ferry privileges on the Hudson and prospered. In 1731 he divided his *bouwerij* into three parts for his three sons, the southerly portion falling to his son, Matthias. Matthias Vanderheyden erected in 1752 a brick house in the style of architecture then prevalent in that vicinity,—a house of one and one-half stories, with a gambrel roof. The accompanying plate is from a wood engraving, obtained through the courtesy of the late James H. Potts, sometime editor of the Troy *Times*. The house stood until comparatively lately on the east side of River Street, at Division, but much altered and a photograph of it taken before its original features disappeared and before it had gone into decay could not be found.

A house built on the river road in 1756 by Jacob Vanderheyden is now incorporated in the Seton Home for Girls at Troy and has completely lost its identity but a woodcut of it shows it to have resembled closely the house of his brother, Matthias. The latter was nearly square in its proportions and had dormer windows, while the house of Jacob was much longer than broad and had a lean-to but no dormers.

Van Loon House

Athens, New York

PLATE 46

The house shown in plate 46 stands on the east side of the principal street of the village of Athens, New York, near the north end of the village. In the front wall near the ground at the south end of the house is a stone marked in monograms: (?) V L Anno 1724 Ap 2 (?). Erection of the house is ascribed to Jan Van Loon, one of a family from Luyck, Holland, which in the late seventeenth century bought land in the vicinity of Athens and founded a settlement known as Loonenburgh. The house is now owned by Mrs. Alice Goetschius of Athens and rented to Italian laborers. When visited, it was closed and access to the interior not to be had but, by report, it still contains at least an early mantel. A photograph of the marked stone occurs at page thirty-two of C. G. Hine's: *Annual* (1906). In general outline the gable-end of the Van Loon house is similar to that of the Coeymans-Bronck house (plate 19) at Coeymans, New York.

Three Van Rensselaer Houses:
Watervliet, Crailo and Klaver Rak

Three houses identified with the Van Rensselaer family,—*Watervliet, Crailo* and *Klaver Rak,*—are so closely connected each with the other by reason of their common historical setting that they are presented here as a group, before discussing them separately in detail.

The background against which the three houses stand out is the story of the title to the colony of Rensselaerswyck and the business management of the property. Rensselaerswyck, that vast estate (twenty-two and a half miles north and south, forty-eight miles east and west), lying on both sides of the Hudson river above and below Albany was purchased by a group of men in Holland, one of whom was Kiliaen Van Rensselaer, and the descendants of Kiliaen Van Rensselaer eventually bought out all other interests. Kiliaen Van Rensselaer became the first patroon of the colony, a title that was inherited from him under the law of primogeniture, although his heirs all held his land in common. The first and second patroons lived in Holland and the business of Rensselaerswyck was carried on from 1630 to 1685 by a succession of agents or directors, who resided in the colony as the patroon's representatives.

The third patroon, Kiliaen Van Rensselaer (born about 1658, died 1687), came to the colony about 1685, in which year a patent was issued under Governor Dongan whereby the colony of Rensselaerswyck was created a manor under English law and the lordship vested in the third patroon. The latter was succeeded as fourth patroon and as second lord of the manor by his cousin, another Kiliaen Van Rensselaer (born 1663, died 1720). The fourth patroon in 1695 made a settlement with his relatives in Holland by which he released all his interests overseas and received in return the entire estate in America. His title to the latter was confirmed by Queen Anne in 1704.

During the time that the colony of Rensselaerswyck was under a director, a house was built near Fort Orange which was occupied by Jeremias Van Rensselaer (the director). This house was swept away by a freshet in 1666 and was followed in 1668—1669 by the one shown in plate 47 and known as *Watervliet*. *Watervliet* stood until 1839 and is more particularly described below.

On the east side of the Hudson opposite the city of Albany is a locality that in the first days of the colony of Rensselaerswyck was called *Greenen Bosch* (Pine Forest), and which later bore the name Greenbush (a corruption of the original). At *Greenen Bosch* from 1642 to 1649 lived the Reverend Johannes Megapolensis, a Dutch *domine* sent over to the colony by the non-resident first patroon. The patroon owned an estate southeast of Amsterdam in Holland, called *Crailo* (Crows' Woods), and in the *Greenen Bosch* on the Hudson a farm was soon laid out which by 1661 had

110

received the name of *Crailo*. A letter written by Jeremias Van Rensselaer in 1668 refers to: " a convenient dwelling-house " on *Crailo*. From 1675 to 1678 this farm was occupied by the Reverend Nicholas Van Rensselaer (then director), after whose death it was in the possession of his widow and her second husband, Robert Livingston, who rented it to a tenant.

In 1685, by a formal agreement, *Crailo* reverted to the Van Rensselaer family in Holland and then in 1695, by the settlement above mentioned in that year, it became the property of the fourth patroon, Kiliaen Van Rensselaer. When the latter received in 1704 from the English Crown confirmation of title to his great landed estate he made provision for his younger brother, Hendrick Van Rensselaer (born 1667, died 1740), by giving him the *Greenen Bosch* (inclusive of *Crailo*) and also a tract called *Klaver Rak* in what is now Columbia County, New York.

The tract called *Klaver Rak* (Clover Reach) and now known as Claverack took its name from a sailing course on the Hudson. It consisted of several purchases from the Indians that were made by the director of Rensselaerswyck and for which confirmation of title was obtained in 1681. The title was held in common by the members of the Van Rensselaer family until 1695, when by the agreement then made it became vested solely in the fourth patroon. He, in 1704, presented *Klaver Rak* to his brother.

From this brief statement it is clear that in the seventeenth century *Watervliet* became the residence of the heads of the colony of Rensselaerswyck; that *Crailo* was a farm occupied by a succession of tenants until in 1704 it became a permanent home for the cadet branch of the Van Rensselaer family; and that *Klaver Rak* was a remote tract, little heard of until made over in 1704 to Hendrick Van Rensselaer.

Watervliet

Formerly on the Troy Road, Albany County, New York

PLATE 47

North of the city of Albany there is low flat land, lying between a ridge to the west and the Hudson to the east and threaded by several small streams that run down from the ridge to the river. On this low land, near the Patroon's Creek and about fifteen-hundred paces north of the limits of *Beverwyck* (Albany), stood the first Van Rensselaer manor-house, the place being called *Watervliet*, in seventeenth century letters,—a name and a locality not to be confused with the present city of Watervliet somewhat farther north on the same road.

The Van Rensselaer manuscripts (letters, accounts, etc.) are now undergoing translation from the Dutch by the Archivist of the state of New York, A. J. F. van Laer, who has kindly supplied from those unpublished papers contemporary evidence for the statement that the house of Jeremias Van Rensselaer, director of the colony, was carried away by a freshet on April 8, 1666, and that in June, 1668, Jeremias declared himself as busy building a house near " the fifth creek." He then wrote to his brother that for a year and a half he had been living in the house of Jan Bastiaensen van Gutsenhoven, deceased, and had just rented the house of Willem Teller. For the house of Willem Teller Jeremias Van Rensselaer paid rent from May, 1668, to May 1671; but in January, 1669—1670, he dated letters from *Watervliet* (the house shown in plate 47) and was presumably living there then.

Watervliet served as a residence for the patroons of Rensselaerswyck until 1765, approximately a century, although during that period the patroons may also have maintained a house in town, as did the Schuylers of *The Flatts*. In 1765 the then patroon built a large brick house in Georgian English architecture that stood until the late nineteenth century, when it was moved to Williamstown, Massachusetts, for use as a chapterhouse at Williams College. Meanwhile the house of 1668—1669 is said to have been occupied by the business agents of the patroons from 1765 until the death of the last patroon in 1839, at which time it was torn down to allow the road near it to be widened. The agent in 1839 was Casparus L. Pruyn and shortly before the house was razed a pencil sketch of it was made by Major Francis Pruyn. The late Colonel Augustus Pruyn photographed the sketch and through the courtesy of his daughter, Miss Margaret Ten Eyck Pruyn of Albany, the accompanying plate has been made from a print from his negative.

Jeremias Van Rensselaer's house of 1668—1669 was built of brick on a stone foundation and had a small wooden lean-to. It was longer than broad in its proportions and one and one-half stories in height; the roof had a steep slant and carried (in 1839) small dormers; the location of the three chimneys along the ridge-pole indicates a floor-plan that consisted of three rooms, each with a chimney and with the front door opening into the middle room. In the north gable a granary door, with iron hook above it, suggests attic space. The trefoil iron wall-anchors, battened shutters with strap-hinges, small window-panes and low porch, with side seats, are all the customary finishings of the houses of New Netherland in the seventeenth century.

That the house of the director of Rensselaerswyck was a dwelling that did not differ in size or elegance from the average house of the better class in the colony in 1668 may have been due to the fact that at the time it was built the colony was not prosperous financially. In 1663 the Esopus war had interfered with the beaver-trade; then came the surrender to the English in 1664, followed by a bad freshet in 1666 (that carried away many houses and barns), which events were accompanied by a period of bad crops. In 1672 *Crailo*, the Van Rensselaer estate near Amsterdam in Holland, was devastated by a French invasion and so all things combined to make ready money scarce for the proprietors of the colony.

The sketch of *Watervliet* is valuable, architecturally, as affording an excellent record of the type of house that was built, on the average, in the vicinity of Albany in the second half of the seventeenth century. The name: *Watervliet*, given to the house (meaning literally " water course "), may be attributable to the location of the estate on the Patroon's Creek. It is interesting to remember however that at the time the name was chosen one of the elegant country homes of Holland was so designated. The Coymans family, owners of a great banking-house in Amsterdam, had a magnificent seat called *Watervliet* between Haarlem and Beverwijk (in the tulip-country) and Jeremias Van Rensselaer could easily have had the same in mind when he christened the house on the Troy Road.

Crailo

Rensselaer, New York

At 10, Riverside Avenue, Rensselaer, New York, is a large brick house, owned by the State of New York and commonly called " Fort Crailo." The date of the erection of this house has been the subject of discussion. In the cellar, built into the foundations, are two stones, one of which is marked: K V R 1642 Anno Domini; and the other: apolensis; and the inscriptions have given rise to the belief on the part of some that the house was built in 1642 by the first patroon of Rensselaerswyck for Domine Johannes Megapolensis, who lived at *Greenen Bosch* from 1642 to 1649. But sober consideration of the house points out that the building as it now stands quite obviously represents construction at several different dates and that the obscure location of the marked stones suggests that they were taken from an original place and put where they now are, in other words that materials from some other house were used in the foundation of the present one.

Crailo consists of two parts: a main portion, which is a parallelogram that faces west and is two stories in height, and a wing at the rear to the north and east which, also, is two stories high. The roof on both parts of the house is a gambrel in shape; but its architectural proportions are not good: it does not fit the house well. The disproportion arises in the great height and shallow depth of the main house; for the houses of the eighteenth century which were built with gambrels were usually one and one-half stories high and deeper in relation to their height than is *Crailo*. These observations lead to the hypothesis that the present roof is not the one that originally covered *Crailo*. If that assumption is correct, the original roof must have been one of those of steep, single pitch, such as was common in Albany and in Rensselaerswyck from the middle of the seventeenth century to the middle of the eighteenth. Support of this theory is perhaps supplied by what appears to be a suture in the brickwork of the east wall of the wing. A faint line there, in the form of an inverted V, occurs where the roof-slope would have been had the wing been built originally one and one-half stories in height. Interior details of the wing (materials, construction, trim) show it to have been built at a later date than the main house and a second deduction is therefore that to a first and main house, having a roof of one steep pitch, there was added a rear wing, one and one-half stories high, with roof of single slant, which addition was subsequently raised to two stories and covered with a gambrel.

The question that next arises is whether the main house were built at first in two full stories. To the layman no seams are visible in the brickwork to indicate that the walls were ever raised in height. But if *Crailo* were built in two stories it was a departure from custom among the brick houses in the colony of Rensselaerswyck. The survey made for this volume revealed that, while two-story houses of brick were common in the village of Albany, no such houses were found in the country. The brick houses in the rural districts were all similar in general plan to *Watervliet* (plate 47). Among the stone houses of Rensselaerswyck the Salisbury of 1705, the Glen of 1713 and the Coeymans of c. 1716 (plates 30, 23, 18) were of two stories but they were noteworthy exceptions and such *Crailo* must also have been if it is the same now as when erected.

Determination of the dates at which the two parts of *Crailo* were built is another problem and one which cannot be settled certainly. As was stated on a preceding page, a letter written in 1668 refers to " a convenient dwelling-house " then standing on the farm called *Crailo*. In January, 1669—1670, the director of the colony of Rensselaerswyck was living in a new manor-house, called *Watervliet*, across the river from *Crailo* on the west side. *Watervliet* was a house a story and a half in height, and it is difficult to think that a house for the head of the colony would have been erected in 1669 which was smaller and inferior to a house on the farm called *Crailo*, which latter house and farm were rented to a succession of tenants up to 1704.

The development of *Crailo* as an important family-center dates from 1704, when the farm of that name at *Greenen Bosch* was presented by the then patroon to his younger brother, Hendrick Van Rensselaer, who made *Crailo* his permanent residence from 1704 until his death in 1740. This known fact affords a basis for the theory that in entering upon his property Hendrick Van Rensselaer built a large house in the style of the more pretentious houses in Albany, that is: a house two full stories in height covered by a very steep roof; and that either he or his son, Johannes Van Rensselaer (born 1708, died 1783), later added a low rear wing. To Johannes Van Rensselaer could then be credited the raising of the rear wing and the placing of a gambrel roof on both parts of the house, the gambrel being in very general popular use in the lifetime of Johannes Van Rensselaer. On the northwall of the rear addition, east of a door, is a brick marked: I V R, the initials of Johannes Van Rensselaer; and west of the same door, partly covered by a later door-casing, is another inscription of which all that is uncovered reads: Rensselaer, 1762. The date 1762 could well stand for the time when the gambrel roof was given to the house. This theory is offered, however, as merely tentative and is subject to proof or to discard in the light of possible future information.

The floor-plan of the main part of *Crailo* is the typical one of two rooms with a hall between; the first and second floors being alike and the house containing just the four rooms and two halls. The addition at the rear consists of a hall (running north and south at the back of part of the main house) and one large room. The two parts of the house form an ell as a whole. About 1800 Johannes Van Rensselaer's grandson, John Jeremias, who had inherited *Crailo*, did over the finishings of the interior of the main house and nothing remains there of primitive details except two funnel-shaped holes in the west wall, designed for the defense of the house by musketry, and which perhaps are the occasion for the popular use of the word 'fort' in connection with *Crailo*. Similarly constructed openings are to be seen in the Van Cortlandt manor-house at Croton and in the DuBois house at New Paltz, in which instances also tradition insists upon the early use of the buildings as "forts."

In general it must be said of *Crailo* that it has lost its original and typical architectural character and has become, like so many old homes, a register of social evolution. It was lived in by people of wealth, who occupied it with the greatest luxury of their period, and it was a center of social influence. So much has been written of the hospitality extended at *Crailo* to persons of prominence and importance that it would be gratuitous to touch again upon that side of its history. Also well known is the tradition that the lines of *Yankee Doodle* were composed here. That was in 1758. General Abercrombie, his staff and troops, on the way to Ticonderoga to battle with Montcalm, halted in the vicinity of *Crailo*. A young officer, it is said, was seated on the curb of the well near the house, saw the raw recruits coming in from the farms in motley garments and in his amusement at their appearance dashed off the famous doggerel.

For a carefully considered and documented statement of the history of *Crailo* the reader is referred to a pamphlet written by A. J. F. van Laer, archivist of the state of New York, and published in 1924 by the State Department of Education; and a thorough analysis of the structure of the building (with plan and photographs), written by Edward Hagaman Hall, appeared in the *Twenty-First Annual Report* (*1916*) of the American Scenic and Historic Preservation Society.

Klaver Rak
Claverack, Columbia County, New York
PLATE 48

In the village of Claverack, New York, stands the house (plate 48) known in past years as the manor-house of the lower Van Rensselaer manor, which lower manor was the great tract of *Klaver Rak*, presented in 1704 by the fourth patroon of Rensselaerswyck to his brother, Hendrick Van Rensselaer. There is a tradition in Claverack that the house was built by Hendrick Van Rensselaer about 1685 but as Hendrick was then a lad of eighteen and as he acquired his title to *Klaver Rak* in 1704 the tradition can hardly be accurate so far as he is concerned.

The house as it now stands consists of an original architectural unit, plus additions and alterations, and the date of the earliest portion can only be conjectural. From the *Journal of Jasper Danckaerts*, which records a visit at *Klaver Rak* in 1680, it is certain that there were a few Dutch farmers then living near Claverack Creek and the fact that the original part of the manor-house was a dwelling of two rooms, similar to the Bronck and Van Antwerp-Mebie houses (plates 16 and 42), makes it possible that it was one of the primitive seventeenth century structures of *Klaver Rak*. It is not certainly known whether the walls of that part are of stone or brickor mud-filled. If they are brick-filled the early date claimed for the house is less probable.

By a second tradition current at Claverack, the first couple to occupy the house were Samuel Ten Broeck (born 1680, died 1756) and his wife, Maria, daughter of Hendrick Van Rensselaer of *Crailo*, who were married in 1712. If this means that the Ten Broecks were the first members of the Van Rensselaer family who lived in the house the story is credible for it simply indicates that Hendrick Van Rensselaer made this provision for his daughter's comfort when she married.

During the eighteenth century the actual occupation of the lower manor-house seems to have shifted from one to another of the descendants of Hendrick Van Rensselaer of *Crailo*, as convenience dictated. For most of the nineteenth century the Mesick family owned and occupied the house and the present owner, A. M. Barnard, is a descendant of both the Van Rensselaers and the Mesicks. The house is now an L in shape, the base of the L, facing south, being the oldest portion. At an unknown date an addition was built to the northeast, forming a wing. Later the angle thus created was partly built in and the walls of the wing were raised and covered by a flat roof. The long roof-line in front was occasioned by the erection of the south porch. The two porches, the clapboards, panelled shutters and window-panes of the front and of the lower story of the wing all suggest the early nineteenth century but to date accurately these and other changes in the house would be difficult. The lower manor-house at Claverack is a growth and belongs to no recognized type of architecture. Architecturally, it therefore has little significance but it is full of significance when allowed to tell its own story. That story involves the truth, often blinked by the lover of romance, that in the eighteenth century most of the people of the Hudson valley lived in dwellings of a simple sort. Prominent this lower manor-house was because of the position in the community of those who lived in it. Its social history is well known. But structurally the dwelling was without claim to special distinction and that very fact is illuminating. Exceptions to the rule of course there were. Some few houses before the Revolution stand out as unusually elaborate in design and finish. But aside from those few there was an average in house-building that was peculiar to all classes, the house of the man of greater wealth and social prominence being but little better than that of the man of modest means.

Van Rensselaer-Genêt House

Town of East Greenbush, Rensselaer County, New York

PLATE 49

About four miles south of the city of Rensselaer the river-road to Castleton is joined by a side-road. East of the river-road and north of the side-road stands the house shown in plate 49. Little has heretofore been known of its history but a careful search of many sources of information makes it possible to present a brief outline of its ownership. For lack of space a discussion of the authorities for these newly assembled facts is omitted.

In 1716 Kiliaen Van Rensselaer, patroon of Rensselaerswyck, deeded to his brother, Hendrick, lands southward from *Crailo*. Hendrick Van Rensselaer had a son, Kiliaen (born 1717, died 1781), who entered upon the occupation of the said lands. In 1742 Kiliaen married Ariaantje Schuyler (daughter of Nicholas and Elsie Wendell Schuyler) and the house under consideration was presumably built for his bride. He and his wife were the parents of four sons, who became men of high reputation. In the period of the Revolution the father and his three older sons served with distinction in the war. Of the four sons: Colonel Henry K. Van Rensselaer (born 1744, died 1816) succeeded his father in the house; Colonel Philip Van Rensselaer (born 1747, died 1798) went out from the home and built *Cherry Hill* on the opposite side of the river (plate 50); Colonel Nicholas Van Rensselaer (born 1754, died 1848) moved up the road to the homestead of his wife, Elsie Van Buren (page 108); while the fourth son, Kiliaen K., settled in Albany. Family ties also link the house shown in plate 49 with the house of Barent Staats (plate 36) as Kiliaen Van Rensselaer and Joachim Staats married sisters, the daughters of Nicholas Schuyler.

Colonel Henry K. Van Rensselaer (1744—1816) married in 1764 Alida Bradt and at a subsequent date, not known, his father, Colonel Kiliaen, is supposed to have left him in possession of the house on the river-road and to have removed to a new house on the high ground east of the first one. In the first house (plate 49) was born in 1774 Colonel Henry K. Van Rensselaer's son, Solomon Van Rensselaer, whose name later became associated with *Cherry Hill* across the Hudson (plate 50).

At an unrecorded date the property on the river-road was purchased by George Clinton, who soon sold it to his son-in-law, Citizen Genêt. It is now owned by Citizen Genêt's descendant, Miss Marie L. Getty of New York City, from whose title-papers several of the foregoing facts have been gleaned. Citizen Genêt bought the place in 1802. A letter, written by him to his wife (Cornelia Clinton) on September 9, 1802, from Albany says in reference to it: " The estate is situated five miles below Albany on the other side of the river. It contains about six-hundred acres, three-hundred of which are woodland and the rest mowing and tillable land. The house

117

(is) Holland Ganacht * but lately repaired; the Barn is good; the other outbuildings are wanted; but with some improvement it can be made a comfortable residence until we build on the Hill, which commands an elegant and extensive prospect. General Killian Van Rensselaer, who lived there **, had built on that spot a handsome frame house, which he had removed to his wife's property." The Citizen and his wife lived in the old house for several years and then moved into a new house (called *Prospect Hill*) on the ridge to the east. *Prospect Hill* has since been burned.

The house on the river-road is built of brick and has a gambrel roof. In the north gable, high in the wall, are two portholes; in the south gable iron wall-anchors; the porch, window-glass and shutters belong to the nineteenth century. The woodwork of the interior is very plain and probably not original. South of the central hall is one room in front to the west, with two smaller ones back of it. North of the hall are two rooms.

The Van Rensselaer-Genêt house should be studied in connection with: *Kost Verloren*, and the Lansing, Schuyler, Staats, Van Bergen and Vanderheyden houses (plates: 26, 27, 33, 37, 43, 45).

House of Philip Van Rensselaer, called Cherry Hill

South Pearl street, Albany, New York

PLATE 50

The Van Rensselaer homestead, which stands just within the southern boundary of the city of Albany, is one of the few well-cared-for survivals of the eighteenth century now remaining in the Hudson valley. The house is built on the ridge of high land which runs north and south for some distance, paralleling South Pearl Street, Albany, and is not far from *The Pastures*, which was built on the same ridge by Philip Schuyler in 1762. Its commanding position gives it an extended open view of the river and opposite hills but it is now an oasis of culture and refinement, emerging with undiminished (indeed with enhanced) dignity from the scene of modern industrialism surrounding it.

This house, called *Cherry Hill*, was built by Philip Van Rensselaer (born 1747, died 1798), a son of Colonel Kiliaen and Ariaantje Schuyler Van Rensselaer (of the house shown in plate 49). His family Bible records that his marriage to Maria Sanders took place February 24, 1768, at the home of her grandfather, Peter Schuyler (who lived in a house next south of the Schuyler house called *The Flatts*), and tradition adds that he built *Cherry Hill* for his bride. The year 1768 has always therefore been accepted as the date of erection of the house.

Philip Van Rensselaer's daughter, Arriet, married her cousin, Solomon Van

---

* Word obscure. Possibly *gemaeckt* (made) or a corrupt form of *genoech* (enough).
** i. e. on the Hill.

Rensselaer (the son of her father's brother), who was born in the house in the town of East Greenbush shown in plate 49. After the death of Philip Van Rensselaer, his son-in-law bought *Cherry Hill*. Solomon Van Rensselaer was one of the prominent men of Albany in his own day, and his half-century of occupancy of *Cherry Hill* has invested the old home with traditions of interest. His public career began before he was eighteen, when he entered military service under General Anthony Wayne. He was seriously wounded in the battle of the Miami, was in the campaign on the Niagara frontier and at the battle of Queenstown received six balls in his body which he carried till he died. He held office as adjutant-general of the state of New York, was postmaster of Albany, member of the Congress and a delegate to the national convention of 1839. In 1824 General Van Rensselaer was host to LaFayette during the latter's visit to Albany, a visit which was a gala occasion at *Cherry Hill*. From Solomon Van Rensselaer *Cherry Hill* passed to his daughter, Mrs. Peter Edmond Elmendorf, and then to his wife's greatniece, Mrs. Edward W. Rankin, who now owns it.

Built of brick-filled framework, clapboarded, *Cherry Hill* is two full stories in height and, placed on sloping ground, has a large front basement. The gambrel roof was at first surmounted by a balustrade, which is to be seen in a photograph taken in the second half of the nineteenth century, but which has since then been removed. The plan of the main floor is a central hall with one larger and one smaller room on either side of it. The rear door opens on the level of the ground, while the front is reached by a long flight of steps. The ceilings are high and the rooms of generous floor-space. An original mantel of carved wood remains in the dining-room (southwest corner) and in the guest chamber on the second floor but mid-nineteenth century marble mantels now replace those of carved wood which were in the two parlors and large upper bedroom. The fireplace openings were outlined in the beginning with pink and blue tiles.

At the rear of the main hall rises a staircase (in three banks of steps, with two landings) but a partition now divides the hall into two parts. On the second floor the hall has been reduced by a partition that creates a bedroom over the front entrance. Much eighteenth century hardware is still to be seen at *Cherry Hill*, especially in the capacious basement where there are large and fine examples of wrought iron hinges and latches of Dutch design.

Having been in the possession of one family-connection for nearly one-hundred and sixty years, *Cherry Hill* contains accumulated effects in furniture, portraits, silver, china and documents which create a whole condition now rarely found. Each generation has preserved heirlooms and at the same time kept pace with the progress of its own period. The cradle, marked: V R 1740, is under the eaves in the brimming attic; chairs of Dutch pattern, inherited by Philip Van Rensselaer's bride of 1768 from her forbears of the Sanders family, surround the dining-table; but electric bulbs illumine the frosted shades of astral lamps. *Cherry Hill* is filled with a spirit

119

truly Dutch in hospitality and domesticity and it is notable in the small group of houses in the Hudson valley which since the pre-Revolutionary period have been maintained continuously on a high social plane.

House of Cornelis Van Schaack
Formerly at Kinderhook, Columbia County, New York
PLATE 51

" On 22d (October, 1777) *** came to a plain between hills, borough of Kinderhook (about seventy straggling houses). The most prominent house in the village belonged to a man named Van Schaaken. It was built of stone and three stories high." Such is the mention of the Van Schaack homestead at Kinderhook found in: *Letters of Brunswick and Hessian Soldiers*, translated by W. L. Stone. The house thus referred to stood east of the present Reformed Church building on a bluff abutting the old course of the Kinderhook Creek and overlooking the meadow shown in plate 2. The builder of the house, Cornelis Van Schaack (born 1705, died 1784), married in 1728 Lydia Van Dyck (daughter of Hendrick Van Dyck, chirurgeon, of Albany). He owned a sloop on the Hudson, traded in furs, acquired land and probably built his house at Kinderhook at the time of his marriage or soon after.

The house of Cornelis Van Schaack stood until the middle of the nineteenth century when it was razed for the reason that the creek overflowed, washed out the bank and undermined the foundation of the house. Early in the nineteenth century a sketch of the house was made which is now owned by Augustus Wynkoop of New York City and reproduced here through his courtesy. As it includes the Reformed church that was built in 1813 it may be assigned tentatively to 1815—1825. The sketch shows a lawn east of the dwelling, sloping to the creek, the laying out of which is interesting as an example of the planting of the time. A gambrel-roofed addition to the stone house is also included in the sketch and for a similar combination of two distinctly different structural units a comparison should be made with the two Bronck houses, plates: 16 and 17. The steeply pitched roof of the stone house of Cornelis Van Schaack reflects the houses of early Albany and might also be compared with the roofs of the Bronck, Van Antwerp-Mebie, Hasbrouck and Pawling houses (plates: 16, 42, 75, 82).

Cornelis and Lydia (Van Dyck) Van Schaack brought up in the house with the steep roof a family of several sons and daughters and their granddaughter, Maria Van Schaack, who married Jacobus I. Roosevelt (1759—1840) of New York City, was the ancestress of Theodore Roosevelt, who served the nation as its Chief Executive. Of Cornelis Van Schaack's sons, Henry (1733—1823), David (born 1736), and Pieter (1747—1832) were men of distinguished ability, who had high reputations as lawyers. They were loyalists during the Revolution and Pieter was exiled to England in the years of the great struggle. Returning after the peace, his former

120

associates, Jay, Benson, Morris and other leaders, all resumed their personal friendship with him, which speaks for the estimate his contemporaries placed upon his moral and intellectual worth. Pieter Van Schaack built the house at Kinderhook now known as the Harder property but which has been completely modernized in appearance. His brother, David, built a house referred to on another page of this volume. Henry Van Schaack removed to Massachusetts after the Revolution but returned to Kinderhook in the late years of his life.

From Cornelis Van Schaack the homestead at Kinderhook passed to his daughter, Jannetje, wife of Peter Silvester (1734—1808), one of the leading members of the bar in Albany County and in whose office Martin Van Buren was a student. While resident in this house Peter Silvester was a deputy to the Provincial Congresses of 1775 and 1776, a regent of the state university and a member of Congress. Anna Maria Silvester, who married Augustus Wynkoop, inherited the house from her parents and in the nineteenth century the homestead was known as the Wynkoop house. A modern dwelling now occupies the site.

Van Schaick House
Van Schaick Island, Cohoes, New York
PLATE 52

In 1664 Captain Goosen Gerritse Van Schaick and Philip Pieterse Schuyler of Albany bought a tract of land north of Cohoes, called from its contour *de Halve Maen* and the patent for which became known commonly as the Van Schaick or Half Moon patent. Included in the patent was an island in the Hudson at the mouth of the Mohawk which took the name of Van Schaick's Island. It continued in the possession of the Van Schaick family from the time of Captain Goosen Gerritse until the middle of the nineteenth century. On the island a house was built in the eighteenth century that is still standing.

From Captain Goosen Gerritse Van Schaick the property descended to Wessel Van Schaick (1712—1782/3) and he it was undoubtedly who built the house, prior to 1767, in which year it was entered on a map of the manor of Rensselaer. Masten's *History of Cohoes* gives 1762 as the date of erection but with no proof for the statement. It has been claimed by some that the house goes back to the 1730's but the fact that it is a handsome house, larger and better finished than houses were wont to be before 1750 and more of a house than a young man newly-married would indulge in, tips the scale of probability to a date later than Wessel Van Schaick's marriage in 1743 and earlier than the map of 1767, in other words to the period of 1750—1765.

The Van Schaick house is built of brick and—unlike the tale customarily heard, which tells of importation from Holland—the tradition here is that the bricks used for the house were made hard by on the Van Schaick place. One and one-half stories high, the building is topped with a gambrel roof. The house rests upon a foundation that rises four feet above the level of the ground and it gives the impression of greater height than the average house of its day in the same architectural design. In floor-plan it illustrates the usual central hall (which runs from east to west) but a feature of the floor-plan not usual is the fact that the one larger and one smaller room on either side of the hall alternate. That is: a larger and a smaller room are at either side toward the east and a larger and a smaller behind at the west. The front door is a good survival of the eighteenth century but the front porch dates from 1875. In the south gable there was originally a granary door with a wrought iron bracket and hook above it. The iron fixtures remain but the door has been partly bricked up and a small window made of it.

In the eighteenth century the *King's Highway* from Albany northward ran close to the west side of the Hudson for some distance. Passing *Watervliet* (plate 47) and *The Flatts* (plate 33) and the house of Henry Lansing (plate 27) it presently reached and passed over Van Schaick Island. The road was the route taken by the troops in the French and Indian wars and in the war of the Revolution. In the latter, the house on Van Schaick Island was the headquarters of the officers of the northern army from June to October, 1777, and large numbers of soldiers encamped on the island near the headquarters. As the headquarters of the officers, the house was visited by the leading men of the day in military and political affairs and it was the scene of the surrender of the command of the northern army by Philip Schuyler to Horatio Gates. Through Schuyler's influence John Gerritse Van Schaick (son of Wessel Van Schaick), then a young man of twenty-nine and who inherited the house at his father's death, loaned General Gates ten-thousand dollars in gold for military expenses, receiving in exchange continental notes of credit that were never redeemed.

The Van Schaick house stands upon a bit of flat land at the base of a bluff and faces the Hudson, with the replica of the *Half Moon* beached immediately in front of it. Its brick walls are yellow and it is surrounded by well-kept grass and handsome locusts and lilacs. When the sunshine filters through the green foliage with a play of light and shadow on the yellow house a memorable picture is made. The owner, Karl Ohman, gives the place every care and is doing a public service by his preservation of a landmark so important.

For a general similarity of structure and of setting comparison should be made between the Van Schaick house and the house of Samuel Ten Broeck (plate 39).

Van Vechten House
Snake Road, Catskill, New York
PLATE 53

West of the village of Catskill a dirt road branches south from the Mohican Trail and runs down hill into the valley of the Catskill. At the foot of the hill a small monument commemorates the fording place at that point on the Indian trail to Canada (later the *King's Highway*) and a stone's throw east of the monument is the Van Vechten homestead.

In 1660 the low lands lying along the Catskill near the ford were leased by a man named Van Bremen who agreed in his lease to build a stone house thereon. Then in 1681 the property was purchased by Dirck Teunisse Van Vechten and it is now owned by the heirs of the late Van Wyck Van Vechten of New York City, having remained in the direct Van Vechten line since 1681, except for the years 1835—1872.

By tradition, the house built by Van Bremen on the flat by the creek was swept away by high water and whether the present house, on higher ground, represents a second foundation dug by him is not known. Members of the Van Vechten family, men born in the house that is now standing and who lived to be over ninety, handed down a definite statement that the Van Vechten dwelling was built in 1690. So positive was this belief in the family that the late Van Wyck Van Vechten, who bought back the house in 1872, had iron figures—1 6 9 0—affixed to the north wall. The will of Dirck Teunisse Van Vechten, dated April 4, 1687, enjoined his widow to keep his house in good repair, an injunction which may refer to a previous structure or to the lower portion of the present one. Dirck Teunisse lived until 1702 and may have rebuilt or enlarged in 1690.

The house as it now is is an accumulation of alterations and additions and it is well nigh impossible to determine what it originally was. An old woodcut pictures it as facing south, one and one-half stories, one chimney, one door to the south and to the east a small one-story wing. The main part has since been raised to two stories and an attic. On the north side the second story windows are close to the line of the eaves, lacking normal wall-space between, while the verge-boards, shutters and north door are nineteenth century woodwork. The line of the roof of the wing overlaps the sill of a gable window, showing successive changes there. In the middle of the north wall, under the iron figures, is a stone marked: P V V 1750, which must commemorate some one of the many changes in structure. In the interior, doors from the main part into the wing were once outer doors and suggest that the wing was an afterthought. Early bed-recesses, one on either side of the chimney, still remain. Much detail of the life of the occupants of the house in the colonial period is on record. In the writings of Jessie V. V. Vedder, Greene County Historian, —*The Catskill of the Yesterdays, Historic Catskill*—a colorful story is to be read of the slaves of the Van Vechtens (Caesar and Dinah, who slept in the kitchen; Tom, Jupiter, Claes, Hans and Dick, who occupied the attic in the wing); of the shoemaker and the tailoress who made annual visits; of the room for spinning and weaving; and much more that re-creates the Dutch family life of the Hudson valley in the eighteenth century. Acknowledgement is made here to Mrs. Vedder for much valuable assistance in the researches made for this book in the vicinity of Catskill.

Teunis Van Vechten (born 1742, died 1785) married Judith Ten Broeck (a daughter of Jacob Ten Broeck and Elizabeth Wynkoop of Kingston) and by so doing related the Van Vechten homestead to the Ten Broeck houses of Kingston (plates: 87, 88, 89), the Wynkoop house of Hurley (plate 103) and also to the Salisbury houses at Catskill (plates: 30 and 31), to which Maria Van Gaasbeck and Rachel Ten Broeck of Kingston went as young wives.

House of Hendrick Van Wie
Town of Bethlehem, Albany County, New York
PLATE 54

About four miles south of the city of Albany on the west shore of the Hudson is a locality which in 1643 received the name: *Paerde Hoeck* (Horses' Point), and from the Court Minutes of Rensselaerswyck the state archivist, Mr. van Laer, salvaged an item which explains the peculiar designation. According to Quiryn Cornelisz, who appeared in court on March 4, 1649, it happened " that in the fore part of the year 1643, as the wedding guests were going over the ice to the wedding of the daughter of" Cornelis Hendricksen Van Nes, who had a farm at *Bethlehem*, "a mare of the said Cryn and a stallion of van der Donck were drowned near the *swarte* or *paerde hoeck*, and that he, Cryn, is under the impression that van der Donck received therefor from the wedding guests one-hundred and fifty guilders."

At *Paerde Hoeck* settlement was made by members of the Van Wie family so early as 1675 and there, in 1732, Hendrick Van Wie built a brick house, still standing (plate 54), and now owned by the Knickerbocker Ice Company. Hendrick Van Wie (born 1703, married 1732) was a son of Gerret and Annatje (Conyn) Van Wie and a grandson of Hendrick Gerritse Van Wie (Wye, Wey, Verwey), who was of *Beverwyck* in 1654. The rear or west wall of the house is marked: H V W 1732, and the house appears on the map of the manor of Rensselaer made in 1767 and upon a map of *Paerde Hoeck* dated 1789 which is among the Van Rensselaer manuscripts (now undergoing translation by Mr. van Laer).

The main portion of the house of Hendrick Van Wie faces east and stands on ground that slopes from north to south. The slope of the ground occasioned a basement and also high steps up to the front door (as at the house of Ariaantje Coeymans, plate 18). Built of brick, the main structure has portholes and a granary door in the north gable. In both gables are iron beam-anchors in the shape of a *fleur-de-lis*. A wing of stone at the rear may have been the original dwelling, antedating the house of 1732. Neighborhood tradition tells of a stone building for slaves' quarters, which formerly stood near by. Occupation in recent years by tenants of the laboring class has altered the house in many details.

Comparison of the Van Wie house should be made with *Watervliet* and with the Bries, Bronck, Douw and Van Alen houses (plates 47, 15, 16, 22, 41).

House of Harmanus Wendell
98, State Street, Albany, New York
PLATE 55

The house of Harmanus Wendell was built in Albany in 1716 and torn down in 1841. It stood on the south side of State Street, the second house west of the corner of Pearl, and was a good example of the Dutch houses which had their stepped gables toward the street. Near the peak of the gable were the iron figures: 1 7 1 6; at the line of the eaves the letters: H W; and at several places on the wall trefoil beam-anchors of iron. The wrought iron-work was highly characteristic of the period. A woodcut of this house appears in Munsell's: *Annals of Albany*, 1: 280, based apparently upon a sketch. The accompanying plate is reproduced from a photograph made of the woodcut by the late Colonel Augustus Pruyn of Albany and obtained for use here through the courtesy of Colonel Pruyn's daughter, Miss Margaret Ten Eyck Pruyn.

Harmanus Wendell, who built and occupied this house, was a fur-trader and apparently had his shop on the first floor of his dwelling. He was a son of Hieronomus and Ariaantje Visscher Wendell; a grandson of Evert Jansen Wendell (founder of the family); married Anna Glen (daughter of Jacob Sanderse Glen of Scotia); and died in 1731.

Houses at West Coxsackie, Greene County, New York

Toward the west end of the village of West Coxsackie, New York, north of the state road, are several stone houses of the middle of the eighteenth century. The one nearest the village belonged to the Broncks but its primitive finishings have all disappeared. Behind it in an open field is a crude stone dwelling, square and similar to the early houses of Ulster County, which also is attributed to the Broncks. Further west on the road is the house of Petrus Van Bergen (now used by the owner of the Good Luck Dairy), across the south front of which are the iron letters: P V B, while on the north wall the date: 1 7 6 4 is affixed in iron. In the kitchen of this house is some panelling, dark with age, but most of the original features of the house are gone. A picture of the house, taken in 1906 (C. G. Hine: *Annual*, page 18), shows a front porch of a design much earlier than that of the present one. This house is two full stories in height and in that respect is noteworthy for its period (1764). Beyond it, across the creek to the north, is a stone house, built in 1754 by Anthony Van Bergen, who was colonel of a local regiment in the war of the Revolution. Still farther west, on the dirt road that crosses the open flat beyond West Coxsackie, were once four homesteads of the Vandenbergh family. Good views of them made in 1906 occur in C. G. Hine's *Annual* for that year.

House of Abraham Yates
109, Union Street, Schenectady, New York
PLATE 56

The house now standing at 109, Union Street, Schenectady, is known as the house of Abraham Yates, who was born in 1724 and who married in 1749 Sara Mebie. It is owned by Mrs. Nettie Van der Bogart Lansing, a descendant of the Yates family, and according to local tradition was erected about 1730. If the tradition is correct the house could not have been built by Abraham Yates, who was then but six years old. Apparently the original house consisted of two rooms and a hall, a unit which has been added to several times. The brick gable-end, flush with the street and characteristic of Dutch village construction, appears to be unaltered (except as to window-glass, shutters and door). The bricks are laid in English bond and are yellow. Clapboards cover the side walls. In 1749 Peter Kalm noted in his journal that many houses in Albany were built with gable of brick toward the street and with planked side walls. His description fits the Yates house, which thus may be studied as an illustration of a type common to Albany and Schenectady about 1750.

House of Christopher Yates
26, Front Street, Schenectady, New York
PLATE 57

The dwelling shown in plate 57 is standing but completely altered in general appearance. Front Street, Schenectady, was opened about 1705 and the land on which this house stands was sold in 1731 by David Ketelhuyn to Joseph Yates. The beams in the cellar of the house indicate that the original structure was one with a narrow end to the street, the street façade having been extended westward at a later date. Undoubtedly the house at first was similar to the Bradt and Yates houses, shown in plates 14 and 56. The widening and squaring of the street-front, and the alteration of the roof of single slant into a modified gambrel is said to have taken place about 1785 and to have been copied from Sir William Johnson's house at Fort Johnson, seventeen miles west of Schenectady. However accurate the tradition may be, the remodelled house is an instance of the liking, shown in the second half of the eighteenth century near Albany, for the general lines of the Georgian English style and, from that point of view, it should be considered as the result of the movement that produced the Van Rensselaer manor-house of 1765 on the Troy Road above Albany; *The Pastures* (Philip Schuyler's house) in 1762; and *Vly House* (Hendrick Cuyler's), plate 31. The doorway should be compared with that of *Vly House*. As remodelled, the hall through the center of Christopher Yates's

126

house was panelled, as was also the chimney-breast of the northeast room, where the fireplace opening was outlined in blue and white tiles.

Joseph Yates of Leeds, England, came to the Province of New York about 1665. He settled at Albany, married Hubertje Marselis Van Bommel and was the father of Christoffel Yates of Albany (1684—1754). Christoffel married Catelyntje Winne and their son, Joseph, removed to Schenectady, married in 1730 Eva Fonda and bought in 1731 the above-described property on Front Street. The property passed from Joseph Yates to his son, Christopher (1737—1785), a colonel in the war of the Revolution and a leading citizen of Schenectady. Christopher Yates married in 1761 Jannetje Bradt (whose father's house is shown in plate 14) and their son, Joseph C. Yates, Justice of the Supreme Court of New York 1808—1823 and Governor of the State of New York 1823—1824, was born at 26, Front Street, in 1768 before the house was enlarged.

The picture of the house, reproduced here through the courtesy of DeLancey W. Watkins of Schenectady, was taken about 1870 with Mrs. John Reade Stuyvesant (Mary Austin Yates) standing in the doorway and her daughter, Katherine Livingston Stuyvesant, on the steps. The house remained in the Yates family until 1889, when it was sold to the present owner, A. P. Walton, who rebuilt the exterior. While the first Yates in this country was an Englishman, the family he founded is a conspicuous instance of racial absorption, so entirely did it become part of its Dutch environment.

PLATE 12

Beekman-Vanderheyden House, Albany,

built in 1725 by Johannes Beekman. Torn down in 1833. Known in the nineteenth century as " the Vander-heyden Palace." Used by Washington Irving in his novel: *Bracebridge Hall,* as the proto type for the residence of *Heer Antony Vanderheyden.* The plate was made from a photograph taken by the late Augustus Pruyn of Albany.

PLATE 13

The north side of State Street,

Albany; from North Pearl Street, eastward, in 1806. From a painting by James Eights. At the left on the corner of North Pearl is the house of Domine Schaets, built in 1657. At the right on the corner of James Street is a small house in which Anneke Jans, the widow of Domine Everardus Bogardus, died in 1663, and which later was owned by Dirck Wesselse Ten Broeck. The plate was made from a photograph taken by the late Augustus Pruyn of Albany.

130

PLATE 14

House of Captain Arendt Bradt,

Schenectady, N. Y. Built about 1715. Torn down about 1900. Illustrates the Dutch custom of placing the gable-end of the house toward the street. Carries wrought iron beam-anchors in trefoil design. The plate was made from a photograph obtained through the courtesy of DeLancey W. Watkins of Schenectady, N. Y.

131

PLATE 15

House of Hendrick Bries,

Rensselaer County, New York. Built (1722?). One of the best surviving examples of the Dutch roofs of steep pitch. Bricks laid in triangles along roof-lines. Handsome iron beam-anchors.

PLATE 16

House of Pieter Bronck.

The stone house in the foreground, built (1662—1669) by Pieter Bronck at West Coxsackie, affords an excellent illustration of the roof of steep single pitch characteristic of Dutch construction in Albany County in the seventeenth century. The portholes, casement-windows and iron beam-anchors are all fine examples. The hooded porch on the addition that was made in 1792 should be compared with the hoods and porches shown in plates 18, 19, 69, 144 and 150.

PLATE 17

House of Leendert Bronck,

built 1738. A good surviving example of the type of house built of brick by the Dutch in Albany County in the late seventeenth and early eighteenth centuries.

PLATE 18

House of Ariaantje Coeymans.

Built about 1716 with roof of steep single pitch and with a stepped dormer, similar to the dormers shown in plate 12 (see vignette, page 9). An exceptionally handsome house at the time of its erection. Altered later (1783—1800?), when a gambrel roof and new front entrance were given it as recorded in plate 18. Plate 18 was made from a photograph (taken about 1870) obtained through the courtesy of Mrs. S. H. Niles of Coeymans, New York. The porch-hood is similar to the hoods shown in plates 16, 19, 69, 144 and 150. The hood, the platform and the high steps, here shown in combination, suggest what the entrances to the Van Wie, Van Cortlandt and De Peyster houses (plates 54, 109, 115) may have been like in the eighteenth century.

135

PLATE 19

East porch and door of the Coeymans-Bronck house

Coeymans, New York. The door is an unaltered example of a Dutch door (divided horizontally) of the eighteenth century, with original hardware and handcarved tracery for the overhead light. The porch and the hood above it are in standard designs of the eighteenth century, similar to those shown in plates 16, 18, 69, 144 and 150.

PLATE 20

The Conyn-Van Rensselaer house

in Columbia County consists of a primitive rear wing of stone, of unknown date, and a main front portion of brick, erected in 1766. Modern trim destroys the period character of the exterior. The plate illustrates the manner in which earlier and later structures were combined to form one dwelling.

137

PLATE 21

House built near Greenen Bosch

by Hendrick Cuyler before 1767. Torn down 1926. Known as *Vly House* (House by the Marsh). Owned and occupied in the nineteenth century by Miss Katherine Van Rensselaer. In elegance of interior finish second only to: *The Pastures*, the house of Philip Schuyler at Albany. The plate was made from a photograph obtained through the courtesy of C. G. Van Rensselaer of Schenectady, New York.

138

PLATE 22

House of Petrus Douw.

Front portion built about 1724 in a style typical of Dutch construction in brick in Albany County at that date. Rear wing with gambrel roof presumably an addition before 1800. House torn down about 1835—1840. It stood on *Wolven Hoeck* (Wolves' Point) on the east shore of the Hudson, opposite Albany. The plate was made from a photograph (of a painting) obtained through the courtesy of Charles G. Douw of Scotia, New York.

PLATE 23

Rear view of the Glen-Sanders house about 1870 from the northwest.

The central portion was built first at unknown date. In 1713 the eastern end was added. The frame wing at the west was of the nineteenth century and has been removed. The southern front of the first and second parts and the eastern side elevation are rectangular walls, two stories in height. The plate was made from a photograph obtained through the courtesy of Mrs. William Ten Broeck Mynderse of Scotia, New York.

PLATE 24

House of Abraham Glen,

Scotia, New York. It affords an illustration of the sharp peak which the Dutch gave to the roofs of their houses in Albany County in the eighteenth century. The plate was made from a photograph obtained through the courtesy of DeLancey W. Watkins of Schenectady, New York.

PLATE 25

Hoogeboom House.

Built at Claverack, New York, about 1760. Burned 1890. A late instance of a type of brick house commonly built in Albany County in the first half of the eighteenth century. The plate was made from a photograph obtained through the courtesy of Miss Bertha F. Webb of Hudson, New York.

PLATE 26

The bouwerij called Kost Verloren

(the farm called Money-Thrown-Away). Home of a leaseholding tenant on Rensselaer Manor in the eighteenth century. The structural lines are the same (but on a reduced scale) as those of the Staats and Van Rensselaer houses in the immediate vicinity (plates 37 and 49).

PLATE 27

House of Henry Lansing.

One of a number of dwellings built of brick with gambrel roofs about 1750—1760 near Cohoes. Similar to the houses shown in plates 26, 28, 33, 37, 45, 49. The plate was made from a photograph obtained through the courtesy of Hugh P. Graham of Cohoes, New York.

PLATE 28

House of Cornelius C. Muller,

Claverack, New York. Bears across the front iron figures: 1 7 6 7. Although its trim is modern the house is important as a dated example of work in brick and in the use of the gambrel roof. In design it resembles the houses shown in plates 26, 27, 33, 37, 45, 49.

PLATE 29

House of Rensselaer Nicoll,

Albany County, about 1870 from the southeast. The north end of the east front was built about 1736 and was raised and lengthened and given a gambrel roof about 1795. As it now stands, the house illustrates post-Revolutionary architecture; but it has a background rich in family traditions of the eighteenth century. The plate was made from a photograph obtained through the courtesy of Howard Sill of Baltimore, Maryland.

146

PLATE 30

House of Francis Salisbury,

Leeds, New York, built in 1705 and reputed when built to be an unusually handsome dwelling. For size and elegance the house should be compared with the Glen-Sanders house of 1713 and the house of Ariaantje Coeymans of about 1716 (plates 23 and 18 and vignette, page 9).

PLATE 31

House of Abraham Salisbury,

Leeds, New York, erected 1730, enlarged 1823.   The entrance-drive is bordered by a remarkable planting of locusts and lilacs, a tree and shrub particularly associated with domestic life in the Hudson valley.

148

PLATE 32

House of Domine Schaets,

formerly at the northeast corner of State and Pearl Streets, Albany, as recorded in 1805 in an oil painting by James Eights. The painting is now owned by Mrs. William Gorham Rice of Albany. The house erected in 1657 was torn down in 1832. Its walls of two stories and a half, roof of steep pitch, notched roof-line and decorative brickwork over door and windows were all characteristic of Dutch construction at Albany in the seventeenth century. The plate was made from a photograph taken by the late Augustus Pruyn of Albany.

PLATE 33

The Schuyler house called The Flatts.

Built about 1668, partly burned 1759, rebuilt after the fire. The portion of the rear wing having roof of steep pitch is known to be a reproduction of the original wing. The gambrel roof on the main house dates from after the fire. The original house was undoubtedly covered by a roof similar to that shown in plate 47. The gambrel should be compared with those shown in plates 26, 27, 28, 37, 45, 49. Plate 33 was made from a photograph taken by the late Augustus Pruyn of Albany, New York.

PLATE 34

House in which Philip Schuyler was born.

Built 1667, torn down 1887. Stood at southeast corner of State and Pearl Streets, Albany. Characteristic of Dutch dwellings in Albany in the second half of the seventeenth century. Illustrates typical height, width and roof-line. Faced the street, instead of presenting gable-end as did the house of Domine Schaets (plate 32) on opposite corner. The plate was made from a sepia drawing in an extra-illustrated copy of Worth's: *Random Recollections of Albany*, in the Library of the State of New York.

PLATE 35

Staats House on Stockport Creek,

Columbia County. Date of erection uncertain, but assumed as approximately 1725. A recent mansard roof replaces a gambrel, covered with red tiles. Porch and shutters are of the nineteenth century.

PLATE 36

House of Barent Staats,

Staats Island, Rensselaer County. The stone walls are of 1722. Porch and shutters of the nineteenth century. House owned and occupied by the Staats family in direct male line from its erection to the present day.

PLATE 37

House of Gerret Staats,

Staats Island, Rensselaer County. Erected in 1758. A good example of the brick houses with gambrel roofs which the Dutch built in Albany County in the eighteenth century.

PLATE 38

House of Dirck Wesselse Ten Broeck

on Roeloff Jansen's Kil, Columbia County. The date: 1 7 6 2, across the front, is inlaid in white bricks. Not-withstanding a modern porch and new covering for the roof, the house illustrates in general style a trend in building that was evident in the third quarter of the eighteenth century.

PLATE 39

House of Samuel Ten Broeck

near Roeloff Jansen's Kil, Columbia County. Typical in design of the 1760's and 1770's. Compare with the Van Schaick house, plate 52.

156

PLATE 40

Unidentified house,

characteristic of the village of Albany in the second half of the seventeenth century. The plate was made from a photograph of an oil painting taken by the late Augustus Pruyn of Albany.

157

PLATE 41

Van Alen House,

near Kinderhook in Columbia County. Iron figures: 1 7 3 7, are affixed to this gable-end between the upper and lower windows, but did not photograph clearly. The house is built on lines similar to those of the Bronck, Douw and Van Wie houses (plates 17, 22 and 54).

PLATE 42

Van Antwerp-Mebie House,

Rotterdam Junction, Schenectady County. Built before 1700. The steep pitch of the roof is the important feature of the house, architecturally. Tradition says that slaves were housed in the small building at the left, the door of which structure is an unaltered primitive item.

PLATE 43

Van Bergen-Vedder Farm.

The plate shows the farm of the Van Bergens (1680—1774) and Vedders (1774—1927) at Leeds, Greene County. On the farm in 1729 was built a house still standing. The house is at the base of the foothills of the Catskills and occupies a natural terrace that overlooks rolling meadows.

PLATE 44

House of Gerret Vandenbergh at Domine's Hoeck,

Albany County. One of the brick dwellings of which there were many in Albany County about 1725—1750.

PLATE 45

House of Matthias Vanderheyden,

formerly at Troy, New York. Built 1752. Characteristic in its lines of architecture in Albany County in the middle of the eighteenth century. The plate was made from a woodcut obtained through the courtesy of James Potts of Troy.

PLATE 46

Van Loon House,

Athens, New York. Built in 1724. One of the earliest dated gambrels in Albany County. The gambrel was usually given to houses of brick, and instances of its combination with stone are infrequent.

PLATE 47

House called Watervliet.

Built by Jeremias Van Rensselaer, 1669, on the Troy road north of Albany. Torn down about 1839. It was the residence of the successive directors and patroons of Rensselaerswyck and of the lords of Rensselaer manor from 1669 to 1765. Sketched by Francis Pruyn of Albany just before being razed. Important as a standard with which to compare other dwellings in Albany County for the approximate period of 1670—1750. The plate was made from a photograph of Francis Pruyn's sketch taken by the late Augustus Pruyn of Albany.

PLATE 48

Van Rensselaer House at Claverack (Klaver Rak),

Columbia County. Often referred to as 'the lower manor house'. Built in several parts and of no established type of architecture. Significant structurally as an illustration of haphazard growth. Has a long social history.

PLATE 49

House of Kiliaen and Ariaantje (Schuyler) Van Rensselaer,

Rensselaer County. Supposedly built about 1742. Similar to the Schuyler house called *The Flatts* (plate 33). In height and roof typical of mid-eighteenth century construction in Albany County. Porch, shutters and windows all modern. The house was owned for a time by George Clinton, who sold it in 1802 to his son-in-law, Citizen Genêt.

PLATE 50

House of Philip Van Rensselaer

(called *Cherry Hill*), South Pearl Street, Albany. Built 1768. Still owned and occupied by the descendants of Philip Van Rensselaer. An early instance of frame construction in Albany County. Noteworthy for the size of the rooms and height of the ceilings in the era of open fires and also for walls of two full stories. The gambrel roof was in accordance with the fashion of the mid-eighteenth century.

PLATE 51

House of Cornelis Van Schaack,

formerly at Kinderhook, Columbia County. The stone portion, with roof of steep pitch, was presumably built in the second quarter of the eighteenth century and reflected the type of house found in the village of Albany. It was unlike the houses usually built on the farms. The wing with gambrel roof was probably added before 1800. Both were torn down in the middle of the nineteenth century. The plate was made from a sketch owned by Augustus Wynkoop of New York and photographed by his courtesy.

PLATE 52

Van Schaick House,

Van Schaick Island, Cohoes, New York. A fine example, well preserved, of the story and a half house with gambrel roof that was popular in the quarter century prior to the Revolution. It should be compared with the Ten Broeck house (plate 39) in Columbia County.

PLATE 53

Van Vechten House,

near Catskill, New York. The walls are old, the wood trim more recent. It is a house to which clings much of tradition and sentiment, due to ownership by one family for many generations.

PLATE 54

House of Hendrick Van Wie,

Albany County. Built 1732. Despite a state of decay and the loss of some original details, the house is an admirable illustration in structure and plan of the type of architecture that was commonly seen on the farms of Albany County at the time of its erection.

PLATE 55

House of Harmanus Wendell,

Albany, New York. Built 1716. Torn down 1841. It stood on the south side of State Street with its gable-end
to the walk. In continental fashion the main front room was the shop of the owner, whose living quarters were
behind and above the same. The plate was made from a photograph of a sketch taken by the late Augustus
Pruyn of Albany.

172

PLATE 56

House of Abraham Yates

at 109, Union Street, Schenectady. Built in a style characteristic of 1730—1750, with brick gable-end on the street, clapboarded side walls, bricks in triangle pattern at roof-line and handsome iron beam-anchors. The doorway, porch, blinds and window-glass are of the nineteenth century. The plate was made from a photograph obtained through the courtesy of DeLancey W. Watkins of Schenectady, N. Y.

PLATE 57

House of Christopher Yates

at 26, Front Street, Schenectady, as it was about 1870. The east (right) end was built (about 1731?) with the gable to the street (see plate 56). About 1785 the house was extended along the street and raised to two full stories in height, with a gambrel roof. (For similar structural alterations see the house of Rensselaer Nicoll, plate 29). Comparison of the door-frame of the Yates house should be made with that of *Vly House*, plate 21. The plate was made from a photograph obtained through the courtesy of DeLancey W. Watkins of Schenectady, N. Y.

ULSTER COUNTY

NORTH SIDE OF HURLEY STREET

IN 1906

ULSTER COUNTY

WHEN the United New Netherland Company built Fort Nassau on the upper Hudson (1614—1617) it also established a trading post midway between Albany and New York on the west side of the river at the mouth of the Rondout Creek. That post or fort on the Rondout was the first occupation by white men of land within the limits of the present county of Ulster but it served merely as an introduction to the neighborhood as it was used only by traders and contributed nothing toward permanent settlement. House-building and home-making date in Ulster from the middle of the seventeenth century.

In 1652 there arose in the colony of Rensselaerswyck a dispute between three or four settlers on the one hand and the patroon's representative on the other regarding land and boundaries, as a result of which the men who were dissatisfied left the colony and made purchases of home-sites farther down the river on the west side at a locality known in a general way as Esopus, where they could obtain freeholds and avoid the restrictions of the leasehold system, by which tenure alone farms were to be had in Rensselaerswyck.

The high plateau which is occupied now by the city of Kingston was the site chosen for settlement by the first arrivals at Esopus and there they and others who soon joined them built a village to which the name *Wiltwyck* was given. During the decade from 1653 to 1663 the people at *Wiltwyck* lived in houses built of logs or boards and in *Ulster County under the Dutch* by Augustus Van Buren may be found a detailed description of the living conditions in the village in those first years of its existence. While it is possible that between 1653 and 1663 an occasional house was built of stone, the researches of Mr. Van Buren seem to show that wood was chiefly used then and that it was not until after 1664 (when transfer of sovereignty over New Netherland was made by the Dutch to the English) that the people of Esopus began to build in any number the rectangular stone structures, one and one-half stories high, with roof of single slant, which now are so familiar a sight in all parts of Ulster.

The outstanding aspect of the architectural history of Ulster County is summed up in the word uniformity. Stone was the material that was used throughout the county, not only in the period of the pioneer (1665—1775) but after the Revolution and in the nineteenth century and the same general type of house was repeated over and over, varying but little here and there in detail. So pronounced was this observed uniformity and so long was uniformity characteristic of Ulster that it excites comment in the first place and, in the second, demands an explanation. Why should it have been that for so many years houses in the county were built of stone to the exclusion of wood or brick (which were both available) and why should it have been that they were built in a style that was practically the same all over the county, throughout a long period of time? In Albany County no such sameness in architecture occurred. In Dutchess there was a wide diversity in material and plan in house-building. Westchester also contained variety. It was in Ulster alone that uniformity prevailed and the fact provokes enquiry and an endeavor to ascertain what causes produced such an effect.

While the uniform architecture of Ulster County may have been induced by several inter-acting causes, one agency which, beyond question, had a predominant influence was the topography of the region. Ulster consists of a succession of mountain-ranges, parallel with each other, and running north and south. Between the hills lie the valleys and the hills and valleys rise and fall like waves across the width of the county. Threading the valleys are streams, some of great length and volume, and the first settlers laid out their farms on the banks of the water-courses. Thus small groups formed in the valleys but were separated one from another by the mountains, which were almost impassable barriers. Roads grew up naturally along the line of least resistance, which was northward and southward in the valleys; to go east or west the traveller had either to cross a stream or to labor through a difficult pass between the hills. While the survey of Ulster was being made in behalf of this book, an elderly resident of one of the valleys was heard to say that he had not been to the house of a certain relative across the creek for forty years because of the inconvenience of getting over the stream. As the crow flies the two men lived about two miles apart but the ford or bridge was some distance from each and thus two kinsmen had not met for nearly half a century. If such a thing could occur in recent times it is obvious that in the time of the first settlers visits between neighbors must have been infrequent.

To the limitations that topography placed upon travel, or ease of movement, and hence upon social contacts, is to be ascribed much of the conservatism that marked Ulster County and which was manifested in many ways, one form of it being the standardized house of stone. Such a house was built at Kingston by early arrivals there and then by those who moved back from Kingston into the valleys and such a house continued to be built because in the fastnesses of the valleys new ideas were slow to penetrate and still more slow to be adopted. What had been good enough for his grandfather, a man thought good enough for himself.

Second only to the effect of topography upon the architecture of Ulster was the influence of the fact that families remained for generations upon one farm or in one locality and transmitted from one generation to another the established ways of the community. Between 1652 and 1700 there was a stream of immigration into Ulster, when settlers arrived in numbers to take up freeholds under good title. They came from the colony of Rensselaerswyck, from Manhattan Island and from Long Island and had their origins in all parts of northern Europe. But that trend spent itself and was not followed by any other movement into the county so pronounced. On the contrary, in the eighteenth century many men went out from Ulster carrying with them and making well known elsewhere the family names identified with the founders of the county, so that the population did not maintain a proportionate rate of increase.

The mixed elements that formed the original group of settlers soon became a harmonious whole, one in the use of Dutch as the common language and one in Dutch feeling, a condition which was largely contributed to by the ministrations of the Reformed Dutch Church, into which communion all families were gathered and held in close association with each other under the guidance of Dutch pastors. Even at New Paltz, where at first a French church was organized, a Dutch church ultimately succeeded the French and survived.

When the physical map of Ulster County is studied in connection with the story of the people and their homes it is seen that the Esopus Creek follows a course which forms a letter V; that by the junction of the Wallkill with the Rondout the letter Y (stem toward the north) is created and that a subordinate Y (also reversed) results from the confluence of the Shawangunk with the Wallkill. The point of the V, made by the Esopus, is in Marbletown and, at the point, the stream turns northward between two mountain-ridges and is bordered by meadow-flats that are famous for their rich productive soil. The stretch of valley from Stone Ridge to Hurley is as mellow and lovely a sight on a summer's day as could be imagined and one who once has seen it in all its brilliant green of level field and hillside forest, with the white spire of Hurley church shining skyward against the blue of the distant Catskills and with golden sunlight flooding all, has a mental picture to be treasured. It was into this beauty-spot that the first out-push from the primary settlement at Kingston was made in the 1660's when *Nieuw Dorp* (Hurley) was established; and the village of Marbletown followed soon after 1670. In 1677 land on the Wallkill was secured by a group of Huguenots, who obtained the New Paltz Patent, and there again homes were placed on the lower ground near the stream and it was not until after the Revolution that the uplands were cleared. The valley in which New Paltz lies differs from the Esopus valley in that the ranges which enclose it are marked by outcroppings of grey rock which impart a severity to the appearance of the hills. But the severity of the rocks was a harmonious background for the Huguenots. They, in their Puritanism and moral austerity, had a fit setting in the mountains, at whose base they planted and developed a unique community. Before 1700 settlers were at Rochester on the banks of the Rondout and, early in the eighteenth century, they had reached Napanoch and Wawarsing. But in the Rondout valley difference occurs again in natural features. Where the valley of the Esopus is intimate and where the hills along the Wallkill are rugged, the valley of the Rondout between Kerhonkson and Leuren Kill spreads out widely and was literally a broad western frontier up to the Revolution. The people who lived in it knew all the terrors of Indian attacks and of Tory raids and many stories of violence of all sorts are told by their descendants at the present day.

When the British raided Kingston in 1777, the roofs and the wood trim of the houses there were burned but the stone walls stood and the dwellings soon were made habitable again. The wood trim which is now to be seen in Kingston is largely nineteenth century work and it destroys the typical appearance of the houses for the pictorial purposes of such a work as this. At Hurley, too, the hand of the destroyer has wrought heavily. The one short street which constitutes the village and which for long was famous as an unspoiled survival of the eighteenth century has lost from the southern side almost all of its early houses of stone and on the northern side the houses have been added to and altered to such an extent that little of their original character is left. New Paltz is fortunate in having three houses that have escaped change almost entirely but, on the whole, the survey of Ulster revealed that a greater number of pure examples of pre-Revolutionary architecture are now to be found in the interior of the county on the farms than in the communities that have been closely built up.

Of all the counties bordering the Hudson river Ulster has known the most of frontier hardships. Indian warfare at *Wiltwyck* 1659—1663; the burning of *Nieuw Dorp* (Hurley) in 1663; the captivity of the prisoners taken by the Indians in 1663 to New Fort on the Shawangunk; Indian attacks and Tory forays in the Rondout valley; and the British raid upon Kingston in 1777;—all these form a story of violence and resultant suffering that outweighs anything in the record of the other counties. And the memory of the events is indelibly stamped upon the minds of the inhabitants. Ulster is essentially aware of herself and of her own history, a self-realization that is directly traceable to the conservatism which has been referred to above. There are today more people in Ulster than in any other section of the Hudson valley who are living right where their forbears lived for successive generations, who are rooted to the soil and who are perpetuating the manners and customs of a former period.

A remarkable illustration of this self-realization occurred at New Paltz recently, when in an historical pageant the main events in the lives of the Huguenot settlers were presented by a caste which, almost throughout, was made up of descendants of the characters impersonated. Even the negroes who participated were said to be sprung from the slaves of the eighteenth century.

Ulster County thus makes a distinctive and individual contribution to the composite modern culture of the region of the Hudson. Because of her topographical features, her hills and valleys; because of the comparative lack of roads between her frontage on the Hudson and her settlements in the valleys; and because of the cessation of any considerable immigration into the county and the occurence of some emigration out of it, her people have been led to preserve much of the spirit of the past which has vanished from neighboring counties, and they form today a marked survival of native stock, living under native conditions. As a symbol, therefore, of Ulster conservatism and Ulster survivals, the stone houses that have sheltered so large a proportion of her population for so long a time should be studied and recorded.

HOUSES in ULSTER COUNTY

Bevier-Elting House

New Paltz, New York

PLATE 58

In 1699 Louis Bevier bought a home-lot at New Paltz on which before his death in 1720 he is believed to have built the earliest portion of the house shown in plate 58. He was succeeded in his house by his son, Samuel Bevier (born 1680, died 1759), and about 1765 the property was sold to the Eltings, in which family it still is owned.

The house is oblong east and west (the accompanying plate showing the west gable) and was built certainly in two and, perhaps, in three sections. In the center is one room with an attic above and a cellar and sub-cellar below. This section was undoubtedly the work of Louis Bevier soon after 1699. East of it is a section added in 1735 (the date, cut in the chimney, being visible until late years). Whether the west end was built at the same time as the center is another question. It contains one room, in which is a fireplace and also a boxed-in staircase to the half-story above. The room was used by the Eltings as a store for many years. While the doorway leading into this room from Huguenot Street is a delightful survival of the eighteenth century (and to be observed in comparison with the doorways shown in plates 60, 95 and 105) it does not look as if of the period of Louis Bevier (1699—1720), and it would seem more probable that Samuel Bevier, who had a large and growing family, added the west as well as the east end of the house. On the north side of the house a flagged walk is covered with a roof supported by a row of columns. Hand-workmanship and eighteenth century designs and materials are found throughout the house, which is a primitive item of real interest and capable of a restoration both artistic and comfortable.

House of Abraham Bevier

Town of Wawarsing, Ulster County, New York

In 1705 Louis Bevier, first of the name in Ulster, whose house in New Paltz is discussed above, bought land in the valley of the Rondout where the village of Napanoch later grew up. On that purchase he established his sons: Jean (born 1676, died before 1764) and Abraham (born 1678, died 1774). The name of Abraham Bevier was attached by tradition to a stone house at Napanoch that burned down in late years, and there is no reason to question the truth of the tradition for the

183

dwelling was of crude workmanship, typical of the first quarter of the eighteenth century on the outskirts of civilization. It possessed but one chimney and lacked windows almost entirely, if one may judge from the two sides of it shown in a photograph at page forty of: *The Bevier Family.* A better picture occurs at page eighty-one of: *The Old Mine Road* by C. G. Hine but the latter view adds no facts as to plan or finish. The house was built in two parts, an original section of one room, attic and chimney dating to the first years of the owner's settlement in Wawarsing and a second unit, added later, of equal size. According to local tradition a stockade was maintained around the house in its first years and the building was used not only as a home but as a place of refuge during Indian forays.

House of Coenradt Bevier

Napanoch, Ulster County, New York

PLATE 59

The house shown in plate 59 is still standing at Napanoch, Ulster County, although uninhabitable. It is called Coenradt Bevier's house and Coenradt (born 1758, died 1836—'38), a grandson of Abraham Bevier (page 183), did live in it at some time. But who built the first of its several, successive parts is a point open to determination. At first sight this house would seem to be a hopeless and unimportant ruin. As a matter of fact it is an epitome of life in the Rondout valley from the first settlement to the present time. It tells eloquently the story of the small beginnings made by some pioneer in the wilderness; of an addition, built in days when some prosperity had been achieved; of a doubling in size by 1800—1810, that marked economic recovery after the war of the Revolution; of a large house, comfortably occupied in the nineteenth century by native stock, possessed of traditions and a standard of living; and finally of a pitiful wreck, abandoned by the fast vanishing native population in the period of the incoming alien and of the cheap, frame dwelling, equipped with modern conveniences.

The oldest portion of the house of Coenradt Bevier is at the southwest corner, at the left of plate 59. The masonry shows it to have been a low, square structure, one room and attic, with a chimney. In the south wall may be seen a cellar-way; also the original entrance-door (Dutch, with handsome strap-hinges), leading into the room that still retains its heavy, overhead beams. East of this kitchen is a large parlor and north of the kitchen is a hall which has an outer, west door and an inner, east door into the parlor. In the east wall of the parlor there is an excellent Dutch door with iron hardware. The hall may be presumed to have been a part of the southwest room and to have been set off by a partition when the east room was built. Desire for a hall and the introduction of simple, decorative wood-trim around the fireplace of the east room mark the progress attained in the middle of the eighteenth

184

century. In the nineteenth century there was a porch at the west door of the hall which had side seats and a flat roof but which has now disappeared.

Two large rooms (with chimney between) were the second addition. They extend across the north end of the kitchen and parlor and probably their erection was the occasion when the roof over the whole house was raised; for the walls of the two south rooms bear evidence in horizontal seams in the stone-work of having been carried up some three feet to meet the broad, squat spread of the roof that covers this really large house.

No better example of the hap-hazard method followed in Ulster in the building of stone houses could be found than this ruin and, in its doors, windows and interior detail, it provides a genuine archaeological record of the social life of two centuries.

Bevier House

Town of Wawarsing, Ulster County, New York

Following the state road from Ellenville, Ulster County, a mile and a half southwest to *Leuren Kil*, a right turn is made up a side-road to a point where the road-bed is close to the edge of the *kil* and a footbridge crosses the stream. On the opposite side is a stone house of the eighteenth century, the erection and early occupation of which are ascribed to the Bevier family and in connection with which stories of the Indian are still current. The house is built on sloping ground and a long flight of steps leads to the door in the center of the front. The interior may be assumed to have consisted originally of two rooms, with a hall between them, a half-story attic above, a front basement-room and a chimney at either end of the house, the assumption being based upon the visitor's hasty observation of the exterior. Like an ant-hill the house and hillside swarmed with the lowest life of the Ghetto and it was tragic to see a once pleasant farmstead in a condition of such indescribable filth and decay that hasty flight from its vicinity was a first thought. The house is listed here as an example of a pre-Revolutionary dwelling built all at one time (as contrasted with the sectional growth of the house shown in plate 59) and a good photograph of it, made in 1908 (before its evil fate fell upon it) is at page ninety-eight of: *The Old Mine Road* by C. G. Hine.

House of Cornelis Lamberts Brink

Town of Saugerties, Ulster County, New York

PLATES 60 and 61

In 1688 Cornelis Lamberts Brink bought a tract of land in Ulster County, bounded south by the Platte Kill and east by the Esopus. On the low flat land on the north bank of the Platte Kill he built a dwelling, supposed to have been of logs. Thirteen years later he built a second house, of stone, on the higher ground above the flats, and over the entrance marked a stone: C L M B 1701, for himself and his wife (Marritje Egbertse Brink). At a subsequent date, not known, an addition was made at the north to the house of 1701, by which the original square structure, one and one-half stories high, was doubled in length. Plate 60, made from an old photograph, shows the seam in the wall where the addition was put on. In late years the present owner of the house, Mrs. Fremont Davis (whose father was a descendant in the direct male line from Cornelis Lamberts Brink), tore down the second stone part and replaced it with a frame house. The part built in 1701 and containing the marked stone still remains and exhibits a detail which is unique, so far as the survey made for this book determined. At the southwest angle of the walls rough stones project at intervals (plate 61) and tradition in the Brink family explains them as steps by which to reach the roof quickly for observation in times of alarm over Indian forays.* Small as this house is, tradition also relates that one winter night, when the Indians made trouble in the neighborhood of Ashokan, fourteen families took refuge in it. Fourteen families, occupying one room and a half-story attic in a Hudson-valley winter, present a picture of pioneer hardship hardly to be outdone. Tenure of land by one family from 1688 to the present is also noteworthy in this day of frequent change.

Brink House

Town of Saugerties, Ulster County, New York

In the southern part of the town of Saugerties, on a tract of land between the Esopus and the Platte Kill which was purchased in 1688 by Cornelis Lamberts Brink, one of Cornelis Lamberts' descendants, (Henry?) Brink, built in 1743 a stone house on the west side of *the King's Highway* which is owned now by the estate of Howard Finger and occupied by H. Clinton Finger. The house is back from the road, half hidden by a brick dwelling of recent date, and a short distance north of it is the family burial-ground of the Brinks. Built in two parts, the older end of the house contains a marked stone in the east front that reads: H B 1743. To the north is an undated addition. The interior of the first portion has undergone some changes but apparently consisted originally of four rooms, two larger in front and two smaller in the rear. Some simple panelling remains in one room and the doors and window-casings are early hand-wrought trim. The dormers on this house are much like those of the Osterhoudt and Ten Broeck houses in Ulster and the Brett, Brinckerhoff and Verplanck houses in Dutchess (plates: 81, 87, 111, 114, 148).

---

* In 1925 an American in France observed an ancient house with projecting stones (as in plate 61) and was told by the French stone-mason at work on the building that for centuries such a form of construction had been used in France as a means of locking two walls securely.

House of Jacobus Bruyn
Town of Wawarsing, Ulster County, New York
PLATE 62

Jacobus Bruyn, the Norwegian, who founded in Ulster County a numerous family, fixed his home before 1700 on the Shawangunk Kill at the eastern base of the Shawangunk range of hills. In after years some of his descendants migrated across the mountains to their western base in the valley of the Rondout. There, in 1781, another Jacobus Bruyn was living in the house shown in plate 62 when the house was sacked by Tories and Indians in a raid on Wawarsing.

The house stands midway between Kerhonkson and Wawarsing on the south side of the state road, some distance back from the road at the end of a lane. The present owner, Arthur Gary, bought the farm recently from the Hoornbeck family, who had owned it for much of the nineteenth century and who, in their turn, had purchased from the Bruyns. It is not known who built the house or when but in general character it is somewhat suggestive of the Hoornbeck homestead at Pine Bush (page 207), which is supposed to belong to the period of the 1760's. When compared with the Bevier house (plate 59), it is seen to be less crude in workmanship than that, which fact removes it from the day of the pioneers in this region and confirms the belief that it is construction of the second or third generation in the occupation of Wawarsing.

The lovely curve in the line of the roof of the Bruyn house is illustrated in plate 62 as an instance of the instinctive feeling possessed by the local workmen of the colonial period. It was more or less common in Ulster for the rear wall of a house to rise but a few feet from the ground in eighteenth century building. But in such cases the roof usually slanted from ridge-pole to eaves in a single direct pitch. The curved line of the Bruyn roof is the only one of its kind found in this survey and its individuality makes it interesting. The independence of the early builder, his disregard for exact measurements, is often met with,—notably in sinuous ridge-poles, windows of irregular size and location, &c.,—but it is to be remarked that, however erratic he may have been, he never offended good taste and usually imparted (albeit with naïve unconsciousness) an artistic quality to his creation, that is absent from the houses of the twentieth century, built in wholesale numbers, by stereotyped plans, without hint of imagination.

House of Jacobus S. Bruyn
Kingston, New York
PLATE 63

On Crown Street, Kingston, at the corner of North Front, is the shell of a once handsome house. It is noteworthy as a residence because occupied by Colonel

Jacobus S. Bruyn, a prominent citizen of Kingston in the period of the Revolution, and noteworthy architecturally because it exhibits one of the few gambrel roofs to be found in Ulster County. The roof must date however from after the Revolution, inasmuch as the house was partly burned on October 16, 1777, and was rebuilt by Colonel Bruyn after the peace of 1783. In 1926, after an adjoining building had been torn down, it was possible to see that the original stone house of Colonel Bruyn, with roof of single slant, had been extended northward about two feet by a brick addition and raised into a gambrel roof by bricks at the north and east and by stone at the west and south. The building is now converted into stores on the ground floor and tenements above.

Jacobus Severyn Bruyn, born 1751 (a descendant of Jacobus Bruyn, the Norwegian who settled in Ulster in the second half of the seventeenth century), graduated from Princeton just as the war of the Revolution began. He went to the front in command of a company of Ulster militia that he had equipped at his own expense and was soon promoted to a lieutenant-colonelcy. At the fall of Fort Montgomery in 1777 he was captured and was a prisoner until the end of the war, when he returned to Kingston, married Blandina Elmendorf and established a home in the house on Crown Street that was known for its culture and hospitality.

Bruyn House
Wallkill, Ulster County, New York
PLATE 64

In Ulster County there were so few departures in the eighteenth century from the structural type of a stone rectangle, with a roof of single pitch, that instances of such are conspicuous. The accompanying view (plate 64) is therefore shown of a house in the village of Wallkill which is of frame construction and has a gambrel roof. The house is now owned and occupied by Miss Ella Phinney and J. H. Phinney, whose mother, Catherine Bruyn (born 1838), wife of Dr. L. B. Phinney, was descended from the builder. An iron fireback in the house, marked: S B 1766, is supposed to record the name of Severyn Bruyn and the date of erection.

It may be true that Severyn Bruyn built this house in 1766 but there are certain facts which, when considered, leave the matter open to proof. The house is built on two levels. On the lower level is an old stone basement, above which conceivably a stone house could once have risen. The front and rear verandas are approximately 1800 in design and so also is the carved fan-light over the front door. These details suggest that the house belongs in the period of 1790—1810 and that it superseded a stone house to which the fireback had belonged. The owners however date the dwelling from 1766 and only study of evidence of all kinds could settle the point. Even with the uncertainty outlined above concerning it, the house is an interesting exception to the architectural rule in Ulster and as such is recorded here.

Decker House

Town of Shawangunk, Ulster County, New York

PLATE 65

One of the most delightful of the eighteenth century houses in Ulster is the homestead of the Decker family, a mile south of Bruynswick in the town of Shawangunk. Cornelius Decker married in 1695 Elsie Ten Broeck (daughter of Wessel Wesselse Ten Broeck, whose house at Kingston is shown in plate 87) and they at an unrecorded date after their marriage removed from Kingston to what was in their day an undeveloped, inaccessible region in the center of Ulster County on the west side of the Shawangunk Kill. At the point where they settled the *kil* follows a winding course, in a direction generally northeast, between low banks and with meadows on either side of it that form an arable tract. This alluvial plain was an Indian maize-field and a place of gathering for the aborigine and the Decker homestead shown in plate 65 is close to the Shawangunk and looks across the stream, southward, to the field where Captain Kregier's expediton of 1663 surprised the Indians, whose white captives were being held in New Fort on the plateau east of the field.

According to tradition a log house was built by Cornelius and Elsie Decker, which was followed by a stone house erected by their son Johannes. From Johannes Decker, born 1696 (who married in 1720 Cornelia Wynkoop and secondly in 1726 Marytie Jansen), the property passed to Cornelis Decker (born 1731? died 1812); Johannes C. Decker (born 1767); John DePuy Decker (born 1799, died 1881). The heirs of John DePuy Decker sold in 1910 and in 1925 the place was purchased by Edward B. Edwards of New York City with the intention of repairing and restoring the house in harmony with its eighteenth century character.

Three additions have been made to the house originally built on this site: one to the west; then one to the north; and finally one to the east; so that the dwelling is now a T in shape, the long, low front (across which runs a nineteenth century veranda) being the crossbar of the T and the north wing forming the standard of the letter. The oldest part is the unit in the center of the front, which contains two rooms and a crooked staircase by which to reach an upper half-story. The latest portion (at the east end) has a stone marked with the figures 1 7 8 7 and some initials hard to decipher. This part is more sophisticated in plan and proportion and finish than the earlier units and thus registers the improvement made in living conditions in the eighteenth century. In the north wing the masonry is crude and in later years at least the slaves of the Decker family had quarters in it. A large Dutch oven in the west wall of the kitchen is just visible in the plate.

Tradition in the Decker family dwells upon the kindly relations between the members of the family and their black servitors and records the instance of one old

189

mammy, housekeeper for a bride of 1827, who refused to accept freedom under the state act of 1827. Another story illustrates the difficulties pioneers have to meet. Baptism was desired for an infant Decker and the nearest domine was at Kingston. The parents started to ride to Kingston with the baby and one of their blacks. It was midwinter and as they drove across the frozen Rondout at *Rosendaal* the ice broke and the father and the horses were drowned but the mother and the child were thrown out on the ice and rescued by the slave.

As a primitive structure the Decker house has suffered few changes and the fact that its new owner will give it sympathetic and understanding treatment is one that is cause for congratulation. Many landmarks are now going to decay which intelligence and judicious expenditure would transform into desirable modern homes.

Decker House
Town of Shawangunk, Ulster County, New York
PLATE 66

The house shown in plate 66 is a homestead of the Decker family. It belongs in the class of pioneer dwellings and is rigidly plain in finish but it is possessed of character and is an admirable example of a type. It was built in two parts,—first a small structure, nearly square, with primitive windows irregularly placed; then to the east of that a long, low addition. The seam in the masonry between the two parts is visible in the photograph as is also a difference in the workmanship. The earlier west end is undated. Over the door in the eastern portion is the inscription:

D

W G 1776

for William and Garret Decker, and the present owner, T. A. Terwilliger is a descendant, through his mother, from this Decker line. The house stands in the hamlet of Dwaar Kill, just south of the bridge over the tiny watercourse from which the place takes its name. The Dutch word: *dwaars* means athwart or across and this stream flows across a low flat area into the Shawangunk Kill.

House of Jacobus DePuy
Town of Rochester, Ulster County, New York
PLATE 67

At Accord in the town of Rochester, Ulster County, two roads converge and form a V-shaped junction. One of the two is an old highway, which runs southward from High Falls parallel with the west side of the Rondout Creek. It is said to be the route followed by the stage-coaches that plied between Kingston and Ellenville a century ago. The other is the modern state road from Stone Ridge to Accord. Between these two roads and parrallel with them is a third, that follows the top of the ridge that lies west of the Rondout. The third or middle road was *the King's Highway* of the eighteenth century and out-dates the other two but is now almost forgotten. It runs into the state road half a mile north of the point of the V, above described, and on it is an ancient milestone just east of the state road.

In the wide opening of the angle of the V, formed by the roads, there stands on *Peter's Kil* a homestead of the DePuy family. Nicholas DePuy of Artois, who migrated to New Netherland, had a son, Moses (born 1657), who took up a large tract of land in this vicinity when the locality first opened for settlement. Jacobus DePuy (1703—1757), ninth child of Moses DePuy and Maria Wynkoop, his wife, married in 1725 Sarah Schoonmaker and on a farm carved out of his father's many acres built a house. The property passed (through one or two intervening links) to his granddaughter, Catherine Jansen DePuy (1793—1884), the twelfth child of Joseph DePuy (1749—1831), who was the thirteenth child of the builder of the house. Miss Catherine Jansen DePuy, who lived to be ninety-one, and her sister, Miss Helena, long owned the homestead and occupied it together. After the death of " Miss Katie ", as she was called in the neighborhood, title to the property passed to her niece, Mrs. Lucas E. Schoonmaker of Stone Ridge. Then for thirty years the house was closed. Finally it was regretfully sold. The owner now is a Russian Jew, named Sandak, and when the photograph (plate 67) was made of the house the camera was surrounded by a throng of youthful summer-boarders from the east side of New York City. All of which is a bit of modern history, sad to those of native stock but full of meaning to be faced and understood.

The DePuy house is long and low and the first floor is close to the ground along the front. The front faces northwest and is pierced with windows that are irregular in size, shape and location,—a peculiarity noticeable in structures of an early date. A recent frame porch has destroyed the pictorial character of the front and the plate records the northeast gable and the lean-to across the back, which are unaltered although in decay. The windows of the lean-to, with drop-shelf shutters for milk-pans, are good survivals that tell a story of early domestic customs and the entry to the cellar is probably just as it was built. Such shutters and hardware as are left in the gable are originals. Beyond the lean-to a Dutch door, with good strap-hinges, opens into the south end of the house, where the overhead beams are still visible. The date of erection of the house can only be approximated as after Jacobus DePuy's marriage in 1725 and before his death in 1757 but it was probably soon after 1725.

In late years the floor-plan of the DePuy house has undergone alteration but in the time of " Miss Katie " there was a central hall from west to east, a large parlor to the north of the hall and another south of it. At the south end of the house

191

was a bedroom and in the upper half-story two bedrooms and an attic. In the basement there was a kitchen and a bedroom for slaves and the slaves had also quarters of their own in a separate outbuilding. The rear extension shown in the plate bears unmistakeable evidence of having been a typical lean-to of the eighteenth century but, in the nineteenth, the Misses DePuy kept it in perfect repair and used it as a summer dining-room. In their day the homestead was a storehouse of furniture, china and clothing, accumulated in the course of one-hundred and fifty years, and it was the pride of the two elderly ladies who lived in it to maintain the house and furnishings unchanged.

DePuy-DeWitt House

Town of Wawarsing, Ulster County, New York

PLATE 68

The accompanying plate is made from a photograph taken in 1906 by Clarence J. Elting of Highland, New York, and is reproduced through his courtesy in order to show the DePuy-DeWitt house in the town of Wawarsing before certain alterations were made to it. The house stands on the southeast side of the state road from Kingston to Ellenville, in a neighborhood called Soccanissing which is immediately north of the village of Wawarsing.

Nicholas DePuy of Artois, who arrived in New Amsterdam in 1662, was the father of Moses DePuy (born 1657), who married in 1680 Maria Wynkoop and settled in the town of Rochester, Ulster County. Moses DePuy's son, Jacobus, built the house shown in plate 67. His son, Cornelius (born 1688) and grandson, Moses C. DePuy (born 1719) removed from Rochester to Wawarsing in the middle of the eighteenth century and built this house at Soccanissing, or at least the earliest portion of it for the house consists of three sections. Moses C. DePuy's daughter, Elsie (born 1758), married in 1776 Tjerck DeWitt and the house passed into the name of DeWitt through her and her descendants.

As witnessed to by the camera the DePuy house was a typical frontier dwelling of the Rondout valley. It was one of the houses raided in 1781 and stories of Indians and of use as a " fort " cling to it. The masonry is crude (the rough stones being held together by a mixture of mud and straw) and the small number of windows and doors affords an indication of the absence of light and air which was one of the hardships of the pioneer. In this respect the DePuy house and the Van Aken (plate 96) are alike. Two seams in the north wall are shown in the picture from which it may be deduced that the east end of the house was built first, then a small addition to the west and then a second, somewhat larger than the first one. Inside there have been changes in partitions and the original floor-plan is difficult to identify. There is primitive woodwork in the east room (now a kitchen); an early Dutch door on the south side, covered by a recent frame shed; and some eighteenth century iron hardware on interior doors.

The present owner of the house is Mrs. Ida M. Snyder of Wawarsing, a descendant of the De Witts, and the occupant is Aldrich Munro, manager of the farm of the Napanoch Reformatory.

De Witt House
Kingston, New York
PLATE 69

The De Witt house shown in plate 69 stands just within the northwest angle formed by the boundary lines of Kingston corporation. The road from Kingston to the village of Hurley runs through the city to the northwest and then turns sharply to the southwest. At the sharp turn is the entrance to the lane that leads across the De Witt farm to the house. The house as it now stands is a growth and what the date of its beginning may have been is not certainly known. The oldest portion may go back to 1670.

Tjerck Claessen De Witt emigrated from Grootholdt in Zunderlandt to New Netherland in 1657 and bought a house in *Beverwyck*. In 1660 he exchanged his house for land at *Wiltwyck*, possession of the land to be given him on May 1, 1661. He was actually living at *Wiltwyck* in 1663 for in that year his daughter, Tjaatje (later the wife of Mattys Mattysen Van Keuren), was carried away captive by the Indians.

In January, 1669—'70, Governor Lovelace issued a permit to Tjerck Claessen De Witt which authorized the latter to: " erect a house and barne with convenient outhouses for his cattle upon his own land at Esopus, lying betwixt Hurley and Kingston;" for which land the permit recites that De Witt had formerly had a grant from Colonel Nicoll and " in confidence whereof" (that is: in confidence of receiving the permit) De Witt " hath provided all materials ready for the same." The permit also stated that for De Witt to build as planned would not be " prejudicial to the towns adjacent but rather in tyme (might) prove a benefit and relief to such as (should) travail that way." It is evident from the permit that occupation by the De Witts of the farm on the road from Kingston to Hurley dates from 1670. And apparently Tjerck Claessen acted at once upon the permission to build for in 1672 the governor gave him a deed (equivalent to a confirmation of title) which covered: " a parcel of bush land, together with a house, lot, orchard and calves' pasture, lying near Kingston in Esopus."

Tjerck Claessen De Witt died in 1700, leaving a will by which he gave to his wife (Barbara Andriessen) life-use of his property. After her death (which occurred in 1714) two of his sons were directed to hold his estate in trust for appraisal, following which it was to be divided equally between his six sons and six daughters.

193

Andries De Witt, oldest son of Tjerck and Barbara, is said by tradition to have been given by his father land in Marbletown on which he lived for a short time but from which he returned to Kingston (perhaps at his father's death in 1700?). He married in 1682 Jannetje Egbertson and he met a sudden death in 1710 when he was crushed under two beams that fell upon him. An old record says: " Captain Andries De Witt departed this life in a sorrowful way, through the breaking of two sleepers; he was pressed down and very much bruised; he spoke a few words and died." Captain DeWitt was buried in the northwest corner of the yard of the Dutch church at Kingston, where the stone at his grave was lately to be seen, marked: A D W 22 Dy Iuly 1710. It is supposed that Andries De Witt bought out the interests of his brothers and sisters for he succeeded his father on the farm between Kingston and Hurley.

Immediately after the accident to Captain Andries DeWitt his eldest son, Tjerck, on September 28, 1710, made a formal division of his estate. By the division, Tjerck himself was to receive: " the land and buildings in Kingston corporation devised by (his) grandfather to (his) father." Tjerck De Witt (born 1683, died 1762) occupied the farm on Hurley avenue, Kingston, and left behind him there an iron fireback, marked: T D W 1749; and an inscription on a beam in a barn: T D W 1758. A later Tjerck who lived in the house dated a barn: T D W 1796; and put a brass knocker on a door, inscribed: T D W 1799. The house remained in the possession of the De Witt family until 1875 when it was sold to John C. Suydam. The present owner is Mrs. Gertrude Suydam Smith and for twenty years John H. Beatty has been the lessee.

Of the five sons (beside Andries) of the original Tjerck Claessen De Witt: Jan and Jacob removed from Kingston to the town of Rochester, Ulster County; Lucas died early and his sons went to the present town of Saugerties; Peek settled in Dutchess County; but of Tjerck, Jr., nothing is known after the mention made of him in his father's will.

Captain Andries De Witt's son, Tjerck, who inherited the homestead on Hurley Avenue, married in 1708 Anna Pawling and by so doing tied the De Witt house (plate 69) to the Pawling homestead (plate 82), which stands four miles to the south on the same road. Tjerck and Anna (Pawling) De Witt had a son, Petrus (born 1722), who went from his parents' home to Staatsburgh, Dutchess County, and whose son, John De Witt, built the house in the town of Clinton, Dutchess County, shown in plate 116.

The accompanying illustration gives the east front of the De Witt house, Hurley avenue, with noteworthy sycamore trees before it. The barn of 1758 is just out of sight to the north. A few feet from the southwest corner of the house there was formerly a small stone building, torn down in 1904, in which at that time an iron fireback was found, buried under the fireplace. The fireback has been affixed to the south end of the outer west wall of the present house. It bears the marks quoted above.

In the south wall of the De Witt house a vertical seam in the masonry indicates that that end of the structure was built in two parts. Immediately south of the hood over the east doorway is another vertical seam and at that point a thick stone wall runs through the dwelling from east to west, which in the beginning was the outer wall of the first two parts. All to the north of this division-line is an addition which more than doubled the size of the house. Some early beams and wood trim remain inside the house but changes have been made by taking out certain partitions and putting others in.

The small size of each of the two units that form the south end of the house gives ground for the belief that one or the other was the dwelling built by Tjerck Claessen De Witt in 1670. Perhaps the second unit was being added by Captain Andries in 1710 when the beams fell upon him. Or perhaps it was built by Andries' son, Tjerck, later in the eighteenth century when prosperity was increasing.

The second and larger addition suggests in appearance that it dates from about 1799 when the brass knocker was placed upon a new east door. In 1799 the farm was occupied by Andries De Witt (born 1728, died 1806); he was a son of Tjerck and grandson of Captain Andries and married Rachel Du Bois. Andries and Rachel (Du Bois) De Witt and their two sons, Tjerck and Isaac, who long lived with them on the farm, imparted to the place in the early nineteenth century a reputation for efficient farming and for being a home of much comfort and quiet content.

House of Johannes De Witt

Town of Rosendale, Ulster County, New York

PLATE 70

Johannes De Witt (born 1701), fourth son of Captain Andries De Witt, married in 1724 Mary Brodhead and went out from the farm on the road between Kingston and Hurley (plate 69) to make a home for himself on the Green Kill. At a point on the *kil* about a mile west of where the stream enters the Rondout Creek he built his house (plate 70), in the wall of which a stone, marked: 1736, was visible until covered in 1924 by a coat of whitewash.

The house built by Johannes De Witt consisted of two large rooms with a hall between and an open half-story attic above. It faced south and at an unknown date, but one undoubtedly in the eighteenth century, an addition of two long and narrow rooms was made across the rear. In the nineteenth century the present roof and dormer and porch were put on and window-glass and shutters changed. The stone walls of the house are thick and make deep window-openings. There is an early stairway in the hall (with two landings), and the door from the hall to the kitchen is pierced with bull's eyes. Until lately there was a carved corner-cupboard in the southeast room. In the attic in 1925 was still preserved a painted signboard, exhibiting a crocodile in the center between the word: *Crocodile* (above) and: *G. De Witt's Inn* (below), the sign being a reminder of the period when the road past the house was the stage-route between Kingston and Ellenville.

From Johannes De Witt this house was inherited in direct male line through: Charles De Witt (born 1727; married 1754 Blandina Du Bois; died 1787); Gerret De Witt (born 1762; married 1786 Catherine Ten Eyck; died 1846); Richard Ten Eyck De Witt; Charles Richard De Witt; to Richard Ten Eyck De Witt, the owner in 1925.

Charles De Witt (1727—1787), son of the builder of the house, was in public life at the time of the Revolution and one of the most prominent men in Ulster County. He was colonel of a regiment of militia and served in the Provincial Congress, the state Assembly and in the state Constitutional Convention. At this home on the Green Kill he established a mill that was a landmark until succeeded in 1849 by a new mill-building, erected by his grandson (Richard Ten Eyck De Witt).

In the accompanying plate one of the eighteenth century outbuildings of the farm (probably a smoke-house) appears at the right; west of the house (behind the camera) are very old barns.

De Witt House

Town of Saugerties, Ulster County, New York

On the road at the base of the ridge in the town of Saugerties called Mt. Marian and three-quarters of a mile north of the hamlet that bears the name of the ridge is a De Witt homestead which has remained in the De Witt family from its erection early in the eighteenth century down to the present owner, Mrs. Catherine De Witt Louther.

Tjerck Claessen De Witt of Kingston (plate 69) had a son, Lucas, who died in 1704 leaving a son, Lucas, Jr., born 1703, who married in 1729 Catherine Roosa and is believed to have built the stone house in which Mrs. Louther now lives. The house was occupied at the time of the Revolution by Captain John L. De Witt (born 1734) and his son, Abraham, who also was in military service, and they are both buried on the farm. By tradition the dwelling was surrounded during the Revolution by a stockade of pine posts and used as a neighborhood refuge. The original appearance of the house has been done away with by frame extensions, porches, dormers, etc., which leave nothing of the eighteenth century that is pictorial.

House of Andries De Witt

Town of Marbletown, Ulster County, New York

PLATE 71

Andries De Witt (born 1728, died 1813), a son of Johannes De Witt of the house on the Green Kill (plate 70) and a grandson of Andries De Witt of the farm

196

on the Kingston-Hurley road (plate 69), married (in 1753?) Blandina Ten Eyck and removed (presumably around the time of his marriage) to a farm on the west side of the Esopus Creek, three and a half miles south of the bridge that now spans the Esopus at the village of Hurley.

From the bridge at Hurley a cross-road leads west over a fertile flat to the mountain-ridge that parallels the Esopus on its western side. Close to the base of the ridge the Mountain Road runs north and south, a lovely bit, known to but few beside the dwellers on it and practically never traversed by the summer-motorist. In the day of Andries De Witt, when roads at the best were very bad, the location of his farm was more inaccessible than today (when, if the route is known, the farm is easy to reach), and it is not hard to understand why it was selected in 1779 as a storage-place for military supplies. In June, 1779, rations for six-hundred men for a month (hard bread and salt provision) were concentrated at this house and on August 3, following, it was stated that the guard over the magazine consisted of two sergeants and twenty-eight privates.

By tradition, this farm in Marbletown was given by Tjerck Claessen De Witt (deceased 1700) to his son, Captain Andries (1657—1710). It is difficult to believe that any part of the house now standing was built by Andries De Witt of the second generation. His unproved occupation of the land was short, if it occured, and at a date when the locality was so far in the wilderness from the small settlements at Hurley and Kingston that any building enterprise would have been of a crude and transient character. By 1753 when Andries De Witt of the fourth generation married and settled on the land, there were at least two other houses on the Mountain Road (the Wynkoop, plate 103; and the Ten Eyck, plate 90), and the richness of the soil where he laid out his homestead fully explains his choice of a location. His large, productive acreage passed to his son, John A. De Witt (born 1756, died 1836), who served in the Revolution, and it remained in the possession of his descendants until recent years. The owner in 1925 was the Honorable John G. Van Etten of Kingston.

The De Witt house on the Mountain Road was built in three parts; first the middle section, then the south and lastly the north end. The first part contained two rooms, two chimneys, a door to the west and a half-story attic. The second portion added one large room to the south, with a chimney, and like the first part had an entrance-door on the west side. Finally, in 1800 (according to a marked stone in the east wall), the present kitchen was built at the north. Probably at the same time that the kitchen was put on, some changes were made in the interior and the porch on the east side of the house (plate 71) built. Pink and blue tiles, known to have faced the fireplaces, have all disappeared and there are other evidences of the occupation of the house by tenants in late years. Panelled shutters, good verge-boards, inset doorways and some distinctive iron hardware still bear witness to the eighteenth century as integral parts of a house that was long a much-loved home.

Deyo House

Town of New Paltz, Ulster County, New York

PLATE 72

Among the early settlers in New Paltz the custom prevailed of naming particular farms and fields, one instance of which occurs on the Wallkill, north of the village of New Paltz, where the arable meadows along the stream have been known so long as *Bonte Koe* (Spotted Cow) that all knowledge of why the name was applied there is lost.

At *Bonte Koe* Hendericus Deyo (born 1690), son of Pierre and grandson of Christian (the pioneer of the family in Ulster), settled after his marriage in 1715 to Margaret Van Bommel. He was succeeded on his farm by his son, Benjamin Deyo, and either Hendericus or Benjamin was the builder of the house shown in plate 72. Since 1903 the house has lost a stone wing to the east and a frame one to the west, which appear in a photograph at page 272 of LeFevre's *History of New Paltz;* but the accompanying plate records the location of this early farmhouse on the bank of the winding stream, the course of which is outlined by aged willows. The property remained in the Deyo family until nearly 1900.

Du Bois House

New Paltz, New York

On the west side of Huguenot Street in the village of New Paltz is a picturesque house that is usually referred to as the DuBois fort or the DuBois house of 1705. But if the observer is interested in the study of architecture that is typical of the period before 1776 the house is a pitfall for the unwary inasmuch as its beauty is the beauty of the 1830's and not of the eighteenth century. Iron figures: 1 7 0 5 on the east gable help to mislead the visitor and it is necessary to make it clearly understood that the house built in 1705 by Daniel DuBois (born 1684, died 1755), was one and one-half stories in height and was raised to two stories and an attic about 1835 by Daniel DuBois (born 1795, died 1852), a great-grandson of the first Daniel. The stone walls of the first story, in which are cut large loopholes for musketry, date undoubtedly to 1705 if not to an earlier year. As in the case of the Van Cortlandt manor-house at Croton, there is a vague tradition attached to the DuBois house that it was originally a flat-roofed stone refuge or fort and the story could be true.

Across the south front of the house are two artistically effective verandas, an upper and a lower, which were among the alterations made in the nineteenth century. Most of the woodwork and hardware of the interior belong also to that period. The march of progress is further witnessed to here by the removal of open fireplaces and the substitution of small bricked chimneys, having holes for stove-pipes. A
198

window with leaded panes at the west end of the upper veranda in the wall of the wing is a lone survival of the eighteenth century.

Du Bois-Kierstede House

Saugerties, New York

PLATE 73

In the village of Saugerties, New York, on the north side of the Main Street, stands the Du Bois-Kierstede house (plate 73), one of the most attractive homesteads in Ulster County. West of the front porch in the south wall of the house are two marked stones; one inscription reads: I P den 6 Juni 1727; and the other: s W 1727. Whether the initials refer to the masons who laid the walls or to an owner now forgotten does not appear. The first owner of the house of whom there is local knowledge was Hezekiah Du Bois (born 1701, died 1767), who was a son of Matthew Du Bois of Poughkeepsie and a grandson of Louis Du Bois, patentee of New Paltz. From New Paltz Hezekiah Du Bois removed in early manhood to the sparsely settled neighborhood near the mouth of the Esopus Creek, where now is the flourishing village of Saugerties. There he either built or bought this house, which was inherited by his son, David (born 1737). The latter sold it in 1773 to Dr. Christopher Kierstede (born 1736, died 1791), a descendant of Dr. Hans Kierstede of New Amsterdam who married a daughter of Roeloff Jansen and Anneke Jans. From Dr. Christopher Kierstede the house passed to his son, John (born 1786, died 1862), and grandson, John, Jr. It is now owned by his descendant, Mrs. P. J. Ehrgott of Brooklyn, N. Y., by whom it is maintained as nearly as possible in original condition.

Dr. Christopher Kierstede's second wife, whom he married in 1773, was Leah Du Bois of New Paltz, a cousin of David Du Bois of Saugerties from whom Dr. Kierstede made his purchase of the house. Leah Du Bois's cousins, Cornelius and Huybartus, were the builders of a house at Catskill, elsewhere described; David Du Bois's grandfather, Matthew, owned a farm referred to in connection with the homes of Dutchess County; all members of the Kierstede family are descended from Anneke Jans, whose house in Albany is shown in plate 13. So, by family relationships, the house in Saugerties is associated with a number of other known dwellings in the Hudson valley.

The Du Bois-Kierstede house consists of the part marked 1727; a kitchen wing on a lower level to the east; and a modern extension to the north. The main portion contains three rooms, the center one of which serves as a hall with an enclosed staircase to the half-story above. An original front door of Dutch design swings on iron strap-hinges and there is some other excellent early hardware in the house. In the southwest corner of the west room is a bed-recess; over the front door is a window, half-oval in shape, of early workmanship, but hardly as old as the house.

The kitchen fireplace is an original, equipped with iron household utensils. The front porch is nineteenth century. A noteworthy planting of locust trees imparts additional dignity to the exterior and provides a setting of much beauty.

House of Coenradt Elmendorf

Kingston, New York

The house on the southeast corner of Maiden Lane and Fair Street in the city of Kingston, now owned by Mrs. Charles W. Deyo, should be cited as one of the houses in Kingston which can be dated accurately and for which a record of title, showing ownership and occupation, has been worked out.

In 1688 the land on which the house stands was purchased by the widow of Jacobus Elmendorf (Grietje Aertse Van Wagenen) and was inherited from her by her son, Coenradt Elmendorf (born 1693). Coenradt Elmendorf married for his second wife in 1704 Blandina Kierstede (daughter of Dr. Roeloff and Eycke Roosa Kierstede) and they, in 1725, built the house now standing, as is attested by a stone in the west gable, inscribed: K E D 1725 B E D. The next owner was their son, Coenradt, Jr. (born 1710), who married in 1734 Sarah Du Bois and was the occupant of the house in 1777 when the British burned Kingston. From the immediate heirs of Coenradt Elmendorf, Jr., the title passed to relatives named Louw, the widow and family of the Reverend Peter Louw of the Reformed Dutch Church occupying it in the first quarter of the nineteenth century. The Louws sold in 1825 to Madam Rose Hardy, whose son-in-law, Judge Van Buren, lived in the house many years. General Daniel T. Van Buren conveyed it in 1890 to the present owner.

Genealogically, the Elmendorf house belongs in a group with the homes of the Van Wagenens (plate 100); Kierstedes (plate 73); Bruyns (plate 63); Van Burens (plate 97) and other inter-related families. One granddaughter of Coenradt and Blandina Elmendorf (Blandina Du Bois) married Charles De Witt of the Green Kill (plate 70); another (Blandina Ten Eyck) married Andries De Witt of the Mountain Road (plate 71); and a grandson (Matthew Ten Eyck) built the house shown in plate 90. The ramifications of cousinship could be carried on at length.

As regards the architecture of the Elmendorf house, nothing pictorial of the eighteenth century remains. The house is high in proportion to its breadth and in that respect so unlike the average house of 1725 that it gives rise to the question whether the roof were not raised and the walls carried up when it was rebuilt after the fire of 1777. The wood trim is of the nineteenth century.

Much is in print regarding the use of the house from October 11 to 15, 1777, as the meeting-place of the sessions of the Council of Safety of the State of New York, which information is easily accessible and is omitted from these pages, where the architectural and personal facts are of prior concern.

Frame Houses

In the course of the survey of Ulster County, made in behalf of this work, there were found but three houses of frame construction which were believed to ante-date the Revolution. The use of stone for house-building continued in Ulster until after 1800 and not until the nineteenth century was wood employed in the county to any general extent. One of the three frame dwellings, reputed to have been built before 1776, is the Bruyn house (plate 64) at Wallkill but (as is elsewhere herein explained) the shadow of a doubt falls across the date claimed for it and so, perhaps, like the nursery rhyme of the ten little Indians of descending scale, the three frame houses become two frame houses.

A frame house in Ulster pointed out as of pre-Revolutionary erection and not reasonably to be doubted as such is at Nescatack (now Libertyville), three miles southwest of New Paltz on the Wallkill. LeFevre's *History of New Paltz* contains a picture of this house and ascribes the building of it to Captain Louis J. Du Bois. It differs architecturally from the eighteenth century type, common to all Ulster, only in materials, being a story and a half in height, with a roof of single pitch and the first story containing one file of rooms.

The third house on this list is at Marlborough and was the home of Lewis Du Bois (born 1728, died 1802), who served in the Revolution as colonel of the Fifth Regiment, Continental Line. Colonel Lewis Du Bois of Marlborough and Captain Louis J. Du Bois of Nescatack were first cousins and it is a coincidence, unexplained but worthy of note, that the two men so closely related should have departed from the architectural tradition of the county and have adopted frame construction at about the same time. An exact date is not reliably provided for either house but the one at Marlborough can be approximated at 1763, more or less, because in 1763 Lewis Du Bois took title to the land on which it stands and he may have been already in possession and occupation of the farm. The house is now the home of John Rust, thanks to whose good care a place with Revolutionary associations is being preserved for another generation. A cannon-ball, fired by Vaughan's raiders in 1777, fell short of the house (which was a good target for the ships coming up the river) and is now in Mr. Rust's keeping.

Architecturally, the chief importance of the house of Colonel Du Bois lies in the fact, as outlined above, that although built before the Revolution it was not built of stone. The walls are of frame, brick-filled and clapboarded. In design it was apparently originally, like the house at Nescatack, true to the standard type of the time. Unfortunately it was altered subsequently and its true character destroyed. Minor changes were a porch and dormers and windows and window-shutters, all of the nineteenth century, but the major item was a new roof, of peculiar and individual design, which cannot be called a true gambrel or true hip in its lines. There can be little doubt that it is early nineteenth century work and, as Colonel Du Bois died in 1802, the alterations may reasonably be attributed to his son, who inherited the property. In the southwest parlor of this house there is elaborate wood-trim of the eighteenth century and in the kitchen the original crane and fixtures are still in the large fireplace.

House of Johannes G. Hardenbergh
Town of Wawarsing, Ulster County, New York
PLATE 74

Following the state road for a mile southwest from the village of Kerhonkson, Ulster County, a point is reached where the Rondout Creek (which the road parallels) makes a pronounced bend. At the bend is the house built in 1762 by Johannes G. Hardenbergh (born 1731, died 1812). The house sits flatly on a plateau, a little back from a bluff that descends precipitously to the Rondout, and it looks southward to the meadow-flats on the opposite side of the stream.

Johannes G. Hardenbergh, the builder of the house, was a son of Gerardus and grandson of Johannes Hardenbergh (who married Catherine Rutsen), which parentage made him nephew and cousin, respectively, to Colonel Johannes Hardenbergh and the Reverend Jacob Rutsen Hardenbergh, who lived in the Rutsen-Hardenbergh house (plate 83) at *Roosendaal*. He erected his house in the Rondout valley when the neighborhood was a frontier region and built so substantially that his dwelling has only in late years suffered decay and that more from disuse than from wear. The house is now owned by Charles Osborne, who occupies a large frame dwelling close to the state road and reserves the stone house for the storage of farm goods.

The Hardenbergh house consists of three rooms, each room having a door and a chimney. Over the easterly door is a lintelstone, recording clearly the date: 1762; but erosion has blurred the remainder of the inscription, made up of letters and standing it is supposed for the syllables in the names of Colonel Hardenbergh and of his wife, Cornelia Du Bois. In the kitchen at the west end of the house a steep, enclosed stairway leads to an open attic that extends over the three rooms and from which several portholes look out from between the floor-level and the southern eaves-line. In the east wall of the attic is a large granary-door.

The room at the east end of the first floor is panelled above and on either side of the fireplace in wood that is a dark green in color from age, not paint. In the middle room there is some panelling next the chimney of secondary importance.

From the architectural standpoint this house should be compared with the unidentified house below High Falls (plate 93), which it resembles in floor-plan and size. It is also akin to the unidentified house in the town of Rochester, shown in plate 95, except that the latter contained originally two rooms, not three.

It is an illuminating side-light on domestic life in Ulster in the third quarter of the eighteenth century to know that the builder of such a house as this was a leading citizen. The outstanding chapter in Colonel Hardenbergh's career is the story of his care of the public records in the Revolution. As the British ships sailed up the Hudson in October, 1777, the Council of Safety of the State of New York, in session at Kingston in the house of Coenradt Elmendorf (page 200), ordered on October 12 that removal to a place of safety should be made of all monies and property of the state, the papers of the council and the public records of New York City and of Ulster County. As a committee to effect such removal, the council appointed Hendrickus Hoornbeck, Johannes G. Hardenbergh and Comfort Sands and accordingly the books and papers, filling ten wagons, were transported from Kingston to the house of Colonel Hardenbergh, twenty-five miles inland to the southwest on the Rondout Creek. The Rondout valley was then safely distant from the scene of alarm and action but later it was ravaged by Tories and Indians and blood flowed freely. The Hardenbergh house was one of the points of attack and is said to have been sacked in August, 1781.

House of Jean Hasbrouck

New Paltz, New York

PLATE 75

The house in the village of New Paltz, Ulster County, which was purchased in 1899 by the Huguenot Patriotic, Historical and Monumental Society and which is maintained by the society as the Memorial House, was built by Jean Hasbrouck, a native of Calais and patentee of New Paltz. One marked stone in the east wall records the date of erection: 1712, and another the initials of the builder: I H. The house was inherited from Jean Hasbrouck by his son, Jacob (born 1688, died 1761); by Jacob's son, Jacob, Jr. (born 1728, died 1806); by the latter's son, Josiah (born 1755, died 1821); by Josiah's son, Levi (born 1791, died 1861); and until about 1808 was occupied by this direct male line. For the greater portion of the nineteenth century it was rented to tenants but the title remained vested in the descendants of the builder and to the members of this family the present generation owes a debt of gratitude for their deliberate preservation, unchanged, of the original features of the homestead.

Architecturally the house of Jean Hasbrouck is a variant of the type that prevails in Ulster. It should be compared with the Bronck and Van Antwerp-Mebie houses of Albany County and perhaps also with the Pawling house (plates 16, 42, 82). The high, steep roof-line is the important structural feature and the fact that the interior has suffered few alterations makes the house valuable as source-material for a knowledge of eighteenth century details. There is little in the finish of the house which cannot be duplicated elsewhere but in many of the dwellings of the same period, that now survive, nineteenth century " improvements " elbow the eighteenth century items and a harmonious whole (such as the Hasbrouck house still is) is lost.

The Memorial House is open to the public for inspection and descriptions of it are already in print so it is unnecessary here to give details, except to say that the plan of the first floor is the one, so often found, of a central hall with two rooms at each side. In the attic are two or three small finished rooms and above the open floor-space is a framework or flooring that may be what the Dutch called a *vliering*. In the Hasbrouck attic grain was stored in hogsheads, according to primitive custom, until within recent memory. The cellar of this house is paved, partly with brick and partly with stone, a better finish than is often found in the older houses. But this whole structure represents good materials and honest workmanship; handwork is in evidence throughout and, while the trim is severely plain, it is substantial and in good condition. Jacob Hasbrouck, Jr., third owner of the house, major of Ulster militia in the Revolution, was in 1765 one of the three wealthiest men in the town of New Paltz. His son, Colonel Josiah Hasbrouck, was a member of the Assembly of the State of New York and of the Congress of the United States and was a man of large property. The inference is clear that something of the Puritan spirit of the Huguenot and an individual, family aversion to change combined to preserve this house just as it was first built and so to have made of it a landmark that is educational for later generations.

House of Abraham Hasbrouck
New Paltz, New York

Not far from the house of Jean Hasbrouck at New Paltz (plate 75), on the opposite side of Huguenot Street, is a dwelling part of which is believed to have been built by Jean's brother, Abraham Hasbrouck, who, like Jean, was a native of Calais and patentee of New Paltz and who died in 1717.

The long low house on the east side of the street, now owned by I. E. Evers, is in three structural parts, of which the south end is the earliest. That section consists of two rooms, a half-story and a large cellar, in which latter are evidences of a former kitchen-fireplace. North of this unit and now in the center of the house, is a unit containing one room on the main floor. In the room there is a recess for a bed and at the chimney the beams witness that the present small bricked flue (adapted to the period of stoves) was preceded by a hooded hearth. The third portion of the house, forming the present north end, has a primitive flagged cellar with a large fireplace and on the main floor are two rooms. The thick partition walls in the house bear testimony to having been outer walls originally and the masonry, woodwork and hardware throughout are manifestly of the eighteenth century.

Abraham Hasbrouck's son, Daniel (born 1692, died 1759), succeeded him in the home and their descendants retained the property until recent years. Comparatively little was done to the house in the nineteenth century to alter or add to it and it is good source-material for the study of eighteenth century designs and work.

House of Jonathan Hasbrouck

Newburgh, New York

PLATE 76

Under the name of Washington's Headquarters a certain landmark at Newburgh, N. Y., is widely known to the general public but by comparatively few is it now recalled as the house of Jonathan Hasbrouck. As headquarters for the Commander-in Chief of the Continental Army it served for a year and four months (April, 1782,— August, 1783) but for ninety-nine years (1750—1849) it was occupied by Jonathan Hasbrouck and his descendants and so, assuming all the interest attached to it through its connection with the events and scenes of the Revolution, it is to its domestic aspect that space in these pages must be given. To illustrate this homely point of view a copy is shown (plate 76) of an oil painting from the brush of Robert W. Weir, who from 1832 to 1874 was professor of drawing at the United States Military Academy, West Point, New York. The painting is now owned by Silas Wodell of Millbrook, New York, and is reproduced through his courtesy. At the present time the Hasbrouck house is an historical monument, open to the public; and park-benches, cannon, piled-up cannon-balls and signs mark it as such. On the other hand Professor Weir's picture caught the spirit of the original rural character of the place and preserved a record of its matchless location on the Hudson and the painting is therefore more suited to the purposes of this volume than a modern photograph would be. A steel engraving of the oil painting, made by the artist-engraver, James Smillie, was published in 1834 in *The New York Mirror*. The domestic appearance of the Hasbrouck house (with a cornfield and rail-fence west of it) is also perpetuated in a woodcut, published in 1841 in Barber and Howe's *Historical Collections of the State of New York*.

In 1751 Jonathan Hasbrouck (born 1722, died 1780), son of Joseph Hasbrouck of Guilford, Ulster County, married Tryntje, daughter of Cornelius Du Bois, and took his bride to a house at Newburgh (then in Ulster County) on a farm that he had purchased in 1747. Some years later he and his wife doubled the size of the house on the farm and it is of some interest to note that at the time when they were enjoying their enlarged and improved home near relatives were occupying other prominent dwellings in Ulster. Jonathan Hasbrouck's cousin, Major Jacob Hasbrouck (whose wife, Janitie, was a sister of Jonathan's wife) was in the house of Jean Hasbrouck (plate 75) at New Paltz; his cousin, Daniel, was living in New Paltz in a house still standing on Huguenot Street (page 204); his brother, Benjamin, was established at

205

Wallkill in a house that is now a conspicuous portion of the dwelling of Mrs. E. L. Borden; and Mrs. Hasbrouck's sister, Rachel, was the wife of Lewis Du Bois, whose house at Marlborough is listed on page 201.

The house of Jonathan Hasbrouck at Newburgh, as it now stands, is a rectangle, longer to the north and south and divided into two files of rooms, one file facing east and the other west. According to the best evidence, the large room on the southeast corner is the part first erected. It is believed to have been built at an early unknown date and to have been on the farm when Jonathan Hasbrouck bought the property. To this one-room structure, of primitive materials and workmanship, Jonathan Hasbrouck added two more large rooms so that the three made an oblong dwelling, one room in depth. The northerly room of the three is subdivided by a north-and-south partition into two small bedchambers. In the middle room an enclosed stairway leads to an attic and also in the middle room is a very large fireplace. Originally there was a hood over the hearth of the same character as that in the middle room of the house of Abraham Hasbrouck at New Paltz (page 204). In the outer wall, over the door which opens eastward from the middle room is a stone inscribed: HB A D 1750, which imparts a bit of romance to this portion of the house inasmuch as it so evidently was built by Jonathan Hasbrouck in preparation for his marriage the following year.

Reference is often made with amusement or with surprise to the fact that the middle east room of this house has many doors but only one window. Such comment arises from an unthinking assumption that the house was built all at one time. But when it is recalled that the room was an addition to an earlier unit; that the subdivision of the north room into two bed-chambers (each having a door) may have been an after thought; and that the whole west side of the house was built in 1770 (necessitating connecting doors); it is understood for what it is: an evolution. And as an evolution it is a good example of the way in which many houses in Ulster grew into their ultimate form.

The west side of the house contains three rooms and a hall. At the north end is a parlor, with panelling across the east wall and the chimney-breast. Next south of the parlor a hall, with an open staircase, and beyond the hall two more rooms. The wood trim in the parlor and the introduction of a hall and unenclosed stairway indicate a definite increase in material prosperity and also a progression in manner of living beyond the simple customs witnessed to by the east half of the house. Fortunately this bit of social development is accurately dated by the inscription: HB A D 1770, at the west doorway. The west or formal entrance to the house is one of the inset doors, with a row of small panes of glass above it, such as is found (with some variation of detail) in the eighteenth century houses.

Hoffman House

Kingston, New York

On North Front Street at the corner of Green in the city of Kingston stands a house identified with the Hoffman family for about two-hundred years. Martinus Hoffman, a Swede, came to New Netherland about 1657. He settled ultimately at Kingston, as did also his wife's brother, Tjerck Claessen De Witt (plate 69). Martinus and Emmerentie De Witt Hoffman had a son, Nicholas Hoffman (born c. 1680, died 1750), who married in 1704 Jannetje Crêspel, whose father, Antoine Crêspel of Hurley was a Huguenot from Artois. On November 5, 1707, Antoine Crêspel deeded to his daughter, Jannetje Hoffman, a house and lot in Kingston, described as: " a corner house on the west of Kingstowne, bounded north and west by the street, east by the house of Everardus Bogardus and south by the house of Jellis La Grangie." The following day (November 6, 1707) Crêspel made his will (proved June 10, 1708) in which he stated that he had conveyed to his daughter, Mrs. Hoffman, by deed, a house and lot that he had bought from Jan Gacherie and confirmed the gift. When Nicholas Hoffman made his will (February 12, 1749) he directed that after his wife's death the property given to her should pass to their son, Anthony Hoffman (born 1711, died 1784). Thus the house on the corner, sold by Jan Gacherie to Antoine Crêspel and by him deeded to Jannetje Crêspel Hoffman, was inherited by the latter's son, Anthony, and by his descendants in the male line until after 1900. Recently the Salvation Army has occupied the old dwelling.

It is not to be supposed that the house was built in the form in which it now appears. In 1707, when presented to Mrs. Hoffman by her father, it was undoubtedly the usual dwelling of the time of small ground area and one and one-half stories in height. In 1777, when Kingston was burned, the house lost its roof and interior wood trim and was later rebuilt. At present the masonry is covered with paint and it is difficult to see the walls but an old photograph shows seams in the stonework which indicate additions and changes. Vertical seams in the north front point to extensions at the east and west ends and a horizontal seam in the west gable must have been occasioned by the raising of the roof.

Hoornbeck House

Town of Rochester, Ulster County, New York

Between Accord and Kerhonkson, on the southeast side of the state road that follows the Rondout Creek, in a locality known as Pine Bush, a Hoornbeck homestead stands all by itself in the fields at the end of the farm lane that leads in from the highway. A beam in the barn is inscribed: A HM 1766, and the date may indicate the approximate period when the house was built. The present owner, Morris

Myers, has raised the roof and put on large dormers, alterations that have destroyed the pictorial quality of the house as eighteenth century architecture but a good photograph of it (showing the original dormers, of long sloping lines) occurs in C. G. Hine's: *Old Mine Road* (1908).

The Hoornbeck house was built in two parts, an addition of one room being made at an early date to the first portion. The original house contained a hall, running through from east to west, with a Dutch door at each end; south of the hall two rooms, north of it one. The stairs in the northeast corner of the hall were a crooked, enclosed flight. The door from the hall to the north room still contains a large peep-hole. On its outer side the east front door is panelled and carries brass hardware; on the inner side there are iron strap-hinges. In the south parlor the chimney breast is panelled in pine, painted white, and a shallow cornice frames the opening of the fireplace. On either side of the chimney are panelled cupboards of cherry, stained, and having brass handles on the doors. In this parlor are also exposed ceiling-beams, beaded. The north room contains a large fireplace, known to have been faced formerly with tiles. There is now a shallow mantel-shelf (not as early as the house) and panelled chimney-breast. West of the chimney is a panelled cupboard and east of it a carved corner-cupboard. Next to the corner-cupboard a large original door, that was first an outer door, leads to the kitchen, which is the one-room addition noted above.

The use of brass hardware in this house suggests that the wood trim was introduced after the close of the Revolution but, although the panelling may not be colonial in workmanship, it is in the general style of the earlier period. The present owners are proud of their house as a colonial survival and give it good care. The house stands in the path of the raids made in the Rondout valley during the Revolution by Tories and Indians and is said to have suffered its share in the attacks made.

House of Thomas Jansen

Town of Shawangunk, Ulster County, New York

PLATE 77

A mile and a half west of Dwaar Kill in the town of Shawangunk is the Jansen homestead shown in plate 77. The photograph of the house was made on a spring day when a misty rain and the fruit blossoms, the sky and the whitewashed stone house were merged in varying degrees of soft grey with white and formed an unforgettable picture.

The house stands alone on a by-road on open rolling ground at the base of the Shawangunk range and its erection is ascribed to Thomas Jansen in 1727. The date is reported as cut in the wall but filled in with recent whitewash, which same fate befell the marked stone in the house of Johannes De Witt at the Green Kill (plate 70).

In shape the Jansen house is an ell, facing east. The interior of the wing has been made into a modern kitchen and has lost the primitive features it may once have had. The front porch and dormers are recent. But the large room at the south end of the main house is unchanged. It contains overhead beams, good hardware and panelled cupboards and is wainscoted. Across the central hall are two rooms, plainly finished.

Thomas Jansen belonged to the family founded by Mattys Jansen van Keulen, who died at Esopus before 1663, leaving two sons. Of the two sons, the descendants of Jan took the surname: Jansen; those of Mattys have been known as: Van Keuren. The house of Thomas Jansen, here shown, is owned at present by Mrs. Aldret Jansen but the owner is a recent purchaser and not to be confused, genealogically, with the branch of the family to which the builder belonged.

House of Johannes Jansen

Town of Sawangunk, Ulster County, New York

West of Rutsenville in the town of Shawangunk, Ulster County, stands a house generally known in the neighborhood as the house of Colonel Johannes Jansen and as the scene of a violent attack by four Indians and one Tory during the Revolution. Johannes Jansen, the reputed builder, born in 1725 and an early settler in Shawangunk was a great-grandson of Mattys Jansen van Keulen of Esopus, through the latter's son, Jan, whose descendants bore the patronymic: Jansen. He was a colonel of militia in the war of the Revolution and his prominence among the Whigs led to the raid upon his dwelling in September, 1780. As the story goes, he was pursued by the raiders, one of whom threw a tomahawk after him just as he crossed the threshold of the house, so that the tomahawk lodged in the door as he closed it behind him. An ancient door with a deep gash in it, saw-tooth in shape, is stored in the present house near Rutsenville. This is one of three alleged tomahawk marks found during the survey made for this work, the other two being at Scotia and Albany, in the Glen-Sanders and the Schuyler houses, respectively.

In appearance, outside and in, the main portion of the Jansen house suggests the style of 1800—1820 rather than that of the period before the Revolution. It is two full stories in height; the ceilings are high, the rooms large; and the windows, shutters, doors, porch, etc., all belong to the nineteenth century. The supposition forces itself that the small wing at the west was the home of Colonel Johannes and that his nephew, General John Jansen (born 1771), who succeeded to the property, built the more pretentious dwelling. The present owner is Mrs. Cora Christian.

Krom House
Town of Rochester, Ulster County, New York
PLATE 78

In a territory newly opened for settlement the water-supply is an important consideration in the life of the pioneer and on remote farms in the Hudson valley in the colonial period a rain-barrel was a familiar institution. The rain-barrel shown in plate 78 was found in the interior of Ulster County on a farm inherited by the present owner, Herman Rosenkrans, from his mother, Helena Krom, wife of John Rosenkrans, and which several generations of the Krom family had owned and occupied. As the photograph shows, the house is an almost unaltered example of an early farmhouse, with characteristic low rear wall and with a granary-door in the gable.

House of Abraham Le Fevre
Town of Gardiner, Ulster County, New York
PLATE 79

Simon Le Fevre, one of the patentees of New Paltz and the ancestor of the Le Fevre family of Ulster County, built a stone house on the west side of Huguenot Street, village of New Paltz, some time after 1677 (the date of the patent) and before his death, which occurred about 1690. The house remained in the possession of his descendants until 1839, when it was torn down and the stone in it used in the foundation of the present brick church of the Dutch Reformed congregation at New Paltz which stands on the lot immediately south of the site of the house.

Meanwhile, Simon Le Fevre's grandson, Abraham (born 1716), married Maria Bevier of New Paltz and about 1742 removed to a farm four miles southwest of the village. There he built the house shown in plate 79. The house is in a locality that was known in the eighteenth century as Kettleborough but which is now called Forest Glen. It was inherited by Abraham Le Fevre's son, Philip, whose daughter, Maria, married Abraham Van Orden, and it is now a tenant-house on the Van Orden farm.

House of Pieter Cornelise Louw
Kingston, New York
PLATE 80

The house of Pieter Cornelise Louw affords an illustration of the fact that a search of title is one of the most reliable sources for information about early dwellings and is a source that has only just begun to be drawn upon by students. The house shown in plate 80 is commonly called the Bogardus house but a record of the title to it, established by Frank D. Lowe of Albany in 1922, reveals that the dwelling belonged originally to Pieter Cornelise Louw. Louw owned the land the house stands upon in partnership with Pieter Jacobsen, who died in 1665.

In 1668 Pieter Cornelise Louw married Matthew Blanchan's daughter, Elizabeth, and at some time before his death Pieter built a stone house near the northwest corner of the stockade at Kingston and not far from the Groat Kill. Pieter Louw's will (dated 1690, proved March 4, 1707—8) left one-half of his estate to his widow and one-half to their children. The youngest child came of age in 1710 and in that year four of the children bought from their mother: "that certain house, millhouse, mill, mill-dam, barn, etc., and land on the south side of the Groat Kill, as the same formerly did belong unto Pieter Cornelise Louw, deceased." Three of the four purchasers next sold to Benjamin Smeedes, the husband of their sister, Madeleine, who held the remaining fourth interest.

The property remained in the Smeedes family until 1783 and in 1777 the house was partly burned by the British. From 1783 to 1816 it was owned by Benjamin Bogardus and by his widow, Rachel. Since 1816 there has been a succession of brief tenures. The present owner is Clarence Clark and the lane past the house, leading to a one-time fording place, bears the name of Frog Alley.

The house in Frog Alley consists of two units, a seam in the south wall revealing the original eastern portion and the westerly addition. The first house was tiny, one room above another, built on sloping ground. Inside, the thickness of the early stone-work is visible in the west wall of the first house, which now forms the partition between the original and the addition. The earlier part of the Louw house should be noted as an instance of a pioneer home and as early masonry. The reference to it in the deed of 1710 places it in the lifetime of Pieter Cornelise Louw (deceased 1707—8) and the fact that he married in 1668 and must soon have been obliged to provide shelter for a wife and growing family is presumptive evidence that his house was built well before 1700. The small size of the first unit is significant as an illustration of the living conditions of an early settler.

Whether the addition to the west was made by Pieter Cornelise Louw or by his descendants, the Smeedes, who held title during most of the eighteenth century, is a question. At a date, also uncertain, an oblong addition of stone was made at the north side of the two square units and beyond that at some time was a frame lean-to, which latter has since been removed but which is witnessed to in a series of photographs and by an overhang, that remains with nothing beneath it. It goes without saying that the wood-trim of the house is all recent, while the interior has suffered years of decay. The interest attached to the Louw house is that of sentiment for a survival rather than for any architectural value, although it is source-material for economics and history in a survey of social conditions.

House of Johannes Masten
Kingston, New York

The house of Johannes Masten on the south side of Pearl Street, west of Washington Avenue, in the city of Kingston, now owned and occupied by Mrs. John W.

Searing, belongs in a group with the Van Buren and Van Keuren houses of Kingston (plates 97 and 99), all three being examples of recent restoration under the direction of Myron S. Teller. A photograph of the house, made before the process of repair had begun, shows a structure barely weatherproof and in a condition hardly credible in view of the beauty and comfort since established. Johannes Masten, whose name is attached to the house as an early occupant, belonged to a family founded by John Marston, an Englishman, of Flushing, Long Island, before 1644, who married a Dutch wife and whose descendants ranked as Dutch with their Dutch neighbors, by whom the name: Marston, was turned into Masten.

Mynderse House
Saugerties, New York

According to the *History of Saugerties* by Benjamin M. Brink there were in 1763 only eleven houses on the north side of the Esopus Creek within the present corporate bounds of the village of Saugerties. One of the eleven was the Mynderse house, built in 1743 and still standing, which occupies a commanding position on a bluff overlooking the Hudson and the Esopus. The land was purchased in 1712 by Jan Persen, who, by his will dated 1748, gave his farm " where he formerly lived " to his daughter, Vannittee, wife of Myndert Mynderse. While the land thus comes down from Jan Persen, the erection of the house is credited to his son-in-law, Myndert Mynderse, a traditional belief supported by the marks on a stone at the south side of the east door:

M M * (J) M
P M * S M
Juni 18 Ao 1743

A great-great-grandson of Myndert Mynderse, William F. Russell of Saugerties, now owns the house, which is built on the familiar plan of two rooms, with a hall between; a half-story above; and a (later) wing to the south on a lower level.

House of Gerret Nieuwkerk
Town of Hurley, Ulster County, New York

On the Mountain Road along the Esopus, west of the village of Hurley, there are three homesteads of the Nieuwkerk family. One, built in 1769, is a quarter of a mile north of the house of Matthew Ten Eyck (plate 90). Another, built in 1811, is directly across the road from the Ten Eyck house. And a third (undated but early) is two miles southward on a high hill west of the road. The house built in 1811 is still owned and occupied by the Nieuwkerks. The undated house was purchased in 1865 by Patrick McSperit, whose son, Thomas, now owns it.

The house built in 1769 (now owned by William Stuart) is dated by a stone over the kitchen window, marked:

G N K

AD 1 7 6 9

It is attributed to Gerret Nieuwkerk, is an ell in shape and small in size but still contains original panelling across the east wall of the northeast room and blue Biblical tiles around the fireplace. The large ceiling-beams, once open to view, have been enclosed. There is a central hall running north and south, with one room on either side; in the east wing is the kitchen; and in the angle of the house there is a lean-to or summer-kitchen.

Osterhoudt House

Town of Ulster, Ulster County, New York

PLATE 81

From the station on the West Shore Railroad called Lake Katrine " the Neighborhood Road " runs west and then south and then turns east again toward the state road. A mile south of the station, on the west side of the by-way that bears so friendly a designation, stands a " homely " little dwelling, identified with the Osterhoudt family for many generations. An original structure of one room, attic and chimney was enlarged by the addition to the eastward first of one room, then of a hall and a room. The latest portion has a stone in the outer east end marked: W OH * S HB * 1740. No date is known for the middle section of the house. The author of the *History of Saugerties*, the late Benjamin Myer Brink, a careful investigator, believed that the first (west) end was built in 1691. The present owner, William Trueman, thinks that there is a marked stone in the west wall, where a frame lean-to has been added which has made the stone inaccessible. The house has a chimney at each end and between the first and second sections. The dormers are early in design. Some of the original ceiling-beams, black with age, survive, as also some primitive wood-trim. The windows are irregularly placed in early frames. Comparison should be made of the pillars and arches of this porch with those of the Storm-Adriance-Brinckerhoff house (plate 135). The dormers are similar to those on the houses of Wessel Wesselse Ten Broeck (plate 87); of Henry Brink (page 186); of Madame Brett (plate 111); of John Brinckerhoff (plate 114); and of Gulian Verplanck (plate 148).

According to the best local information the branch of the Osterhoudt family which built this house occupied it until 1796, when Peter Osterhoudt (born 1736, died 1821), of another line of descent from the same first ancestor, moved into it. His descendants owned it until comparatively recent years.

The initials on the marked stone in the east end of the house fit the names of William Osterhoudt and Sarah Hasbrouck, who were married in 1737, a date which further supports the inscription on the stone. William Osterhoudt was a descendant of Jan Janszen van Osterhoudt ("from East Wood"), Oosterhoudt being a village near Breda in Brabant. Jan Janszen was at Kingston in 1663. Sarah Hasbrouck was a grandchild of Abraham Hasbrouck, patentee of New Paltz (page 204), and a sister of Jonathan Hasbrouck of Newburgh (plate 76).

Pawling House
Marbletown Road, Ulster County, New York
PLATE 82

Two miles south of Hurley village, Ulster County, on the west side of the state road, is the Pawling house (plate 82). While it is built athwart the boundary line of the towns of Hurley and Marbletown and is often spoken of as the house on the town-line, the occupants have always considered themselves residents of Marbletown.

In 1670 Marbletown was formally laid out by a committee, one of the members of which was Captain Henry Pawling, who settled at Esopus about 1669. Henry Pawling was English by birth and came to America with the British forces which took over New Netherland from the Dutch in 1664. After the transfer of sovereignty he remained in the Province of New York and, by his own marriage in 1676 to Neeltje Roosa of Hurley and by the marriages of his children to members of other Dutch families, his descendants were absorbed into the Dutch community in which they lived as were the Nicolls and Salisburys farther up the Hudson.

Captain Pawling was prominent in public affairs in Ulster for many years and became the owner of a large amount of land, in Dutchess as well as in Ulster. He is supposed to have established a home on the Marbletown road about the same time that the town was laid out and an undated but early record is quoted in the history of the county as stating that Captain Pawling was allowed to build a house on the town-line: " for the convenience of travellers and to make a nearer correspondence between the two towns." At present a milestone at the side of the road before the house is placed directly on the town-line, the porch and south end of the house being in Marbletown and the north end in Hurley.

By 1672 there were fifty-three houses on the site of the village of Marbletown, mostly of logs, and it is to be assumed that the dwelling first erected by Henry Pawling was also a log-house. But that a portion of the stone house now standing was built by him is not only possible but probable and the date of the oldest part of the house is thus put on a sliding estimate of: from 1672 to 1695, in which latter year Captain Pawling died. He left a widow, three sons and four daughters, all of his sons being minors. In a few years his son, Albert (baptized 1685, died 1745), came of age, and he it was who occupied his father's house and maintained his mother.

In 1726 Albert Pawling married Catherine Beekman, the widow of John Rutsen and the mother of four children, by which marriage the house on the town-line was ultimately closely connected with the Rutsen-Hardenbergh house (plate 83); the Kip-Beekman house (plate 125); the Ten Broeck house (plate 88); and with the house of Henry Livingston (plate 128); while Albert Pawling's sister, Anna, was the wife of Tjerck De Witt, whose home is shown in plate 69.

Albert Pawling was a member of the New York Assembly from 1726 to 1745 and held many town offices. He and his wife, Catherine Beekman, had no children, and the Pawling property passed by his will to his nephew, Levi, subject to the life interests in it of his mother and his widow. His mother, Neeltje Roosa Pawling, was well on in years when Albert Pawling made his will and her son left to her his negro, Bess, expressly: " to wait and attend her." Levi Pawling, who became his uncle's heir, became also a man honored by public trusts. He was elected to the Provincial Congress of New York in 1775 and 1776 and to the Senate of the State from 1777 to 1782; he served as colonel of Ulster militia in the Revolution; as judge of the court of common pleas and as trustee and supervisor for Marbletown. Colonel Levi Pawling died in 1782.

About 1850—1860 the house on the town-line was purchased by Cornelius Oliver, whose son, John C. Oliver, inherited it, and whose sister, Mrs. John J. Cole occupied it many years. The present owner is John C. Cole, to whom it was willed by his great-uncle, John C. Oliver. In recent years the house has been called the Pawling-Cole house.

As the Pawling house now stands, it is a long and narrow building, facing east, one and one-half stories in height, the gable-end having a sharply peaked roof-line. The accompanying plate shows the west and south walls of the house where old masonry is still visible. The east wall has been covered with cement and a recent veranda extends across it in part. There are several photographs of the house in existence, of various dates, and a careful study of them and an examination of the house itself reveal seams in the walls and in the roof which indicate that the original house was twice added to.

On the ground-floor the interior of the house now contains a south unit, consisting of a hall (with enclosed staircase) and two rooms (south of the hall). This unit has four walls of thick stone and through the north wall has been cut a passageway with steps leading down to a room on a lower level, which runs the depth of the house. Beyond this middle room is one room at the north end of the house. A modern kitchen-wing extends westward from the north room.

The partition walls of the interior of the house correspond in position to the seams in the roof and in the exterior walls and there can be no doubt that construction took place at three times. The first builder may be assumed to have been Captain Henry Pawling and the biographical facts in connection with Albert and Levi Pawling suggest that they, each, enlarged the house, Albert before 1745 and Levi before 1782. The wood-trim of the interior is unimportant, except in the case of the mantel in the southeast room, which is carved in an Adam design of the 1790's. A few panelled shutters and some early window-glass also still remain and a characteristic lilac-planting shadows the primitive cellar-entrance.

The late Louis Bevier of Marbletown, an authority on the history of the neighborhood, held a tradition that the southern end of the Pawling house was older than the rest of the house. The tradition fits the evidence of the walls and the roof and taken together make it possible to visualize, mentally, the house of Henry Pawling before 1695 as a structure of a hall and two rooms and attic which, because of its steep roof of single pitch, belongs in a group with the house of Pieter Bronck (plate 16) and the Van Antwerp-Mebie house (plate 42). The house of Jean Hasbrouck (plate 75) at New Paltz, built 1712, is akin to the Pawling and Bronck and Van Antwerp houses because of its roof-line, although in other respects it is unlike them.

Rutsen-Hardenbergh House

Town of Rosendale, Ulster County, New York

PLATE 83

The photograph of the Rutsen-Hardenbergh house, from which plate 83 was made, was taken on October 3, 1910, by Clarence J. Elting of Highland, N. Y., and is reproduced through his courtesy. Nine months later (on July 5, 1911) the house was struck by lightning and burned. It stood north of the village of Rosendale, near the abandoned canal in the valley of the Rondout, the site being a part of a large tract of land, lying on both sides of the creek, which was purchased in the seventeenth century by Jacob Rutsen of Kingston. Jacob Rutsen (born 1650, died 1730) was a son of Rutger Jacobsen van Schoenderwoert of Albany (ancestor of the Rutgers and Van Woert families) and settled at Kingston about 1678. He engaged in business and began buying choice parcels of land from the Indians and in his old age was possessed of a large estate.

In 1680 Jacob Rutsen leased to Dirck Keyser nine-hundred and sixty acres along the Rondout on condition that Keyser should build a stone house on the property. It is supposed that that structure of c. 1680 formed a portion of the house that burned in 1911. The locality where the house was built was early called *Roosendaal* (Rose Dale), the origin of the name being uncertain. It occurs in Holland but may have been occasioned locally by the wild roses that grow abundantly in the Rondout valley.

About 1700 Jacob Rutsen is said to have moved from Kingston to *Roosendaal*, leaving his store in Kingston in the care of his son-in-law, Johannes Hardenbergh. Colonel Rutsen died in 1730 and was buried near the house on the Rondout, after

216

having served Ulster County many years as a member of the provincial assembly, judge of the court of common pleas and officer in command of militia.

Colonel Rutsen's daughter, Catherine, married Johannes Hardenbergh, one of the patentees of the Great Hardenbergh Patent, and her son, Johannes Hardenbergh, second (born 1706, died 1786), succeeded to and long occupied the home of his grandfather at *Roosendaal*. Johannes Hardenbergh, the second, like his father and his grandfather, was prominent in the public affairs of Ulster. He was colonel of the first regiment of militia, was a member of assembly and of the first provincial congress and of the state legislature.

Jacob Rutsen Hardenbergh (born about 1736, died 1790), son of Johannes Hardenbergh, the second, entered the ministry of the Reformed Dutch Church and from 1758 to 1781 served that communion in Somerset County, New Jersey. From 1781 to 1786 he was pastor of the three congregations of Marbletown, Rochester and Wawarsing in Ulster and in those years lived with his father in the house at *Roosendaal*. In 1786 Dr. Hardenbergh became the first president of Queens (now Rutgers) College and held the office until his death four years later. For two winters while he was pastor at Somerville, New Jersey, General and Mrs. Washington occupied the house next the domine's and as a result of the friendship then formed *Roosendaal* was visited by Mrs. Washington on June 21, 1783. Mrs. Washington had spent the night at Kingston and was on her way to Newburgh in company with Governor Clinton and his wife and the party, leaving Kingston in the early morning, breakfasted with Dr. Hardenbergh in his home at *Roosendaal*. By tradition, Washington himself was also entertained at *Roosendaal* earlier in the war and still another event in the house was when, on October 16, 1777, Colonel Johannes Hardenbergh, second, was host to General Clinton and his troops on their march to the relief of Kingston.

About 1830 the Hardenbergh land at *Roosendaal* was divided into three lots of two-hundred acres each and sold, the lot on which the house stood being purchased by John Woodmancy. The latter's daughter, Mrs. Thomas Cornell, inherited the property and it was known in late years as the Cornell place.

In shape the Rutsen-Hardenbergh house was a T, facing the north, with a small wing at the east of the main portion. It was undoubtedly a growth, an accumulation of additions and alterations, but it would be idle to attempt to judge from photographs the order in which the different parts were built or to try to determine the dates when the changes were made. Pictures of the house occur in: *Olde Ulster* (5 : 52); LeFevre's *New Paltz* (1 : 462); *Concerning Rosendale* (page 7). Colonel Jacob Rutsen is believed to have occupied the house from 1700 to his death in 1730 and to have enlarged the house in those years. His grandson, Colonel Johannes Hardenbergh, the second, was a man of means and importance, and he may well have made improvements also. Indeed, it is inherently more probable that he built the large front portion of the house about 1730—1750 than that his grandfather did so in his old age. That the main house was on a large scale, contained numerous rooms, many fire-places, handsome panelled woodwork and recesses for beds, enclosed by panelled doors, is the testimony of persons now living who have been in it.

Schoonmaker House
Saugerties, New York
PLATE 84

In the northwest angle formed by the junction of Main and Malden Streets, Saugerties, stands the house shown in plate 84. The erection of the house is ascribed to Samuel Schoonmaker, a member of a numerous family founded at Esopus in 1659 by Hendrick Jochems Schoonmaker. Samuel's son, Egbert Schoonmaker, a captain in the war of the Revolution, inherited this property, and his descendant, Lansing Schoonmaker, is the present owner.

East of the porch, in the front (south) wall of the house, is a stone inscribed: P P S 1727; and in the middle of the rear (north) wall is another, cut with the letters: P S M. The main portion of the house, thus dated, has an east wing that is more primitive in appearance than the larger part, although it may not be any earlier in date. The part marked: 1727 has a modern porch and dormer and the wood-trim and hardware of the interior are early nineteenth century. The floor-plan consists of two rooms, with a space between them, the space having a partition across it which sets off in front a small hall with a staircase.

The detached unit east of the house is an excellent example of the separate outbuildings that were the frequent adjuncts of the eighteenth century houses. This one may have been a summer kitchen or quarters for slaves.

House of Hendrick Smit
Town of Esopus, Ulster County, New York
PLATE 85

The old habitation shown in plate 85 is included in this volume for the benefit of the student of economics and of social conditions in the Hudson valley in the eighteenth century. Architecturally, it can only be recorded as a small rectangle of stone at the north end, with a longer frame addition at the south. It stands on a side road, a short distance east of the Methodist church at Rifton, Rifton being a small community on the east bank of the Wallkill, in a general locality known at an early date as *Swarte Kil* (Black Creek), from the stream that skirts it as a tributary of the Wallkill.

Hendrick Smit, a Hollander, emigrated to New Netherland before 1700. Tradition says that he borrowed the money for his passage and after his arrival worked for some time to repay the loan. He then obtained a life-lease for eighty acres of land in the *Swarte Kil* neighborhood, for which the annual rental was a hen and a rooster. Settling himself on this tract, he built first a log-house, which was succeeded

218

about 1715 by the stone end of the house shown in the plate. In late years a whetstone, marked: 1704, was found imbedded in the wall of the house. Before he died Hendrick Smit had earned and saved enough to buy his eighty acres, for which he received a deed that has never been recorded. His farm has passed from him to the present owner in direct male line, the title alternating from Hendrick Smit to Willem, Willem to Hendrick again, and so on down. There has never been a mortgage on the place and the Willem Smit of the 1770's was a soldier in the war of the Revolution. Surely romance and color are found in modest, out-of-the-way corners, where they might least be looked for! And it should be remembered that the prosaic labors of many a "Hendrick Smit" helped in the aggregate to lay the economic and social foundations of the Republic.

The Tack Inn

Stone Ridge, Ulster County, New York

PLATE 86

From plate 86 an excellent idea can be formed of the kitchen-area of a country inn of the eighteenth century. The photograph from which the plate was reproduced was taken some years ago of the Tack inn at Stone Ridge by Miss Sarah C. Lounsbery and is used here through her courtesy. Since the picture was taken the former tavern has been repaired and added to by the present owner, Mrs. E. C. Chadbourne, who has made of it a noteworthy repository for Americana. The house stands on the north side of the main street of Stone Ridge, opposite the Wynkoop-Lounsbery house (plate 104), and was an inn for some time before the Revolution. The proprietor, Johannes Tack (whose Dutch patronymic is pronounced Tock), was succeeded in 1790 by his widow, Sarah, and it is by her name—"Sally Tock's"—that the house is now called.

The Tack family in Ulster County was founded by Cornelis Tack, who married in 1688 Barbara Metselaer. Their son, Jacobus Tack of Marbletown, married in 1727 Jacomyntje Van der Merken and either Jacobus or his son, Johannes, is supposed to have been the builder of the house at Stone Ridge. The walls are two full stories in height and that fact makes it probable that the date of erection belonged in the life-time of Johannes Tack rather than in his father's period. After the burning of Kingston in 1777 the sessions of the county court of Ulster were held for a time in this inn.

House of Wessel Wesselse Ten Broeck

Kingston, New York

PLATE 87

On the corner of Clinton Avenue and North Front Street in the city of Kingston is a long, low, stone house, commonly called the Senate House. It is owned by the

State of New York and maintained as a memorial to the men and events of the Revolutionary period, forasmuch as the sessions of the first senate of the state were held in it from September 10, 1777, when the legislature was organized, until October 7, 1777, when the members adjourned because of the fall of Fort Montgomery in the Highlands and the resultant excitement up the river. It is, however, with its character as an item of early domestic architecture that these pages are concerned with this house rather than with its aspect as a setting for an historic scene and, for that reason, a photograph of it made in 1871 (obtained through the Pennington Studio of Kingston) is reproduced in plate 87. The photograph was taken while the house was still a home and before a disfiguring addition had been made at the north end.

Wessel Wesselse Ten Broeck (born about 1636, died about 1704) emigrated from Wessen, near Munster in Westphalia, in 1659 to New Netherland, arriving at New Amsterdam in the ship: *Faith*. In New Amsterdam he remained some fifteen years and married there in 1670 Maria Ten Eyck. About 1675 he and his wife removed to Kingston, where his wife died in 1694, and where he married in 1695 Laurentia Kellenaer, twice a widow (she had been the wife of Domine Van Gaasbeek and of Thomas Chambers). After his marriage with Mrs. Chambers, Wessel Wesselse Ten Broeck took up his residence with her on the Manor of Fox Hall, as shown by his will (dated February 14, 1695/6, proved January 6, 1704/5) in which he called himself " of Fox Hall." He was survived by four sons and four daughters, to each of whom he willed a one-eighth interest in his house and ground in Kingston.

Wessel Ten Broeck's son: Wessel, the second (born 1672, died 1744), married in 1694 Jacomyntje Van Gaasbeek, a child of the much married Laurentia Kellenaer and her first husband. Wessel and Jacomyntje Ten Broeck also removed to Fox Hall as on April 27, 1743, " Wessel Ten Broeck of the Manor of Fox Hall " made his will. At the date of his will Wessel, the second, held sole title to property in Kingston to which he referred as: " the house and lot which was my father's dwelling house in Kingston." He had, supposedly, bought out the other heirs and he willed the house " which had been his father's " to his five surviving children in equal shares. In subsequent years the title to it became vested in the line of Sarah Ten Broeck Van Gaasbeek, from whom it was inherited by her cousins, the Westbrooks, and by the Westbrooks was sold to the state.

The reference made to the house in 1743 in the will of Wessel Ten Broeck, the second, as: " the house which was my father's dwelling house in Kingston," fixes the date of its erection as before 1704, when the first Wessel Ten Broeck died, and probably before 1695, when he married Mrs. Chambers and went to live at Fox Hall. Tradition quotes 1676, the year following Wessel's arrival at Kingston, as the date of building but in the absence of any documentary evidence in support

220

of the tradition it would be well to accept a sliding estimate of: from 1676 to 1695, as the period to which it is safe to assign the erection of the house.

The main portion of the Ten Broeck house is one room in depth; in length, along the street, it consists of three rooms and a hall, the hall being placed next east of the west room. The front and end walls of the house are of stone and the rear wall of brick, laid in Flemish bond. A thick wall continues all across the rear of the main house, even where covered by a kitchen-wing. There are no seams in the masonry and the house was presumably built as a unit, except that the continuous thickness of the rear wall indicates that, however early the kitchen-wing may have been, it was an after-thought. Had it been part of the original structure, the interior partition wall would have been comparatively thin.

When Kingston was burned, October 16, 1777, in Vaughan's raid up the Hudson, the roof and interior woodwork of this house were destroyed but the walls left standing. Like most of the other dwellings in Kingston it was soon rebuilt and the present interior should be studied as the workmanship of the post-war period. Also of post-Revolutionary construction are the long dormers, the lines of which are similar to those of the dormers on the Brink house of 1743 (page 186); and those on the Osterhoudt, Brett, Brinckerhoff and Verplanck houses (plates: 81, 111, 114, 148).

The family connections of the occupants of this house reached out widely and place the house in a group with the Ten Broeck houses of Albany and *Roeloff Jansen's Kil* (plates: 13, 38, 39); with the Ten Broeck houses at Flatbush, Ulster County (plates: 88 and 89); with the two Salisbury houses at Catskill (plates: 30 and 31); the Van Vechten at Catskill (plate 53); and the Decker house at Bruynswick (plate 65).

House of Benjamin Ten Broeck
Town of Ulster, Ulster County, New York
PLATE 88

Wessel Wesselse Ten Broeck of Kingston gave to his sons, John and Jacob Ten Broeck, a tract of land lying north and east of the city of Kingston in the locality called Flatbush. The property had a frontage on the river a mile in length and it extended westward into the woods for two miles. The present state road crosses it, north and south, about a mile west of the river. The brothers each received from their father half of this parcel and each on his own portion built a house. Jacob Ten Broeck's house on the north end of the tract is standing but altered. It is near the state road and owned by Howard Lewis.

On the southern portion of Wessel Wesselse Ten Broeck's land his son, John (born 1686, died 1775), built a small stone house, supposedly for a tenant farmer. John Ten Broeck married in 1715 Rachel Roosa (daughter of Hymen Roosa and

221

Anna Margaret Roosevelt) and his estate at Flatbush was inherited by his sons: General Petrus Ten Broeck (born 1720, died 1777), who married the daughter of John Rutsen; and Benjamin (born 1724, died 1793).

Benjamin Ten Broeck married in 1748 Ann Elting and (after her death) in 1751 Catherine Jansen. About the time of his first marriage he went to live at Flatbush and built the house shown in plate 88 (the wing being the early tenant house). When General Petrus Ten Broeck died without issue in 1777 Benjamin inherited his brother's interest in the estate. Ultimately the whole property passed to Benjamin's son, John Ten Broeck (born 1763, died 1838). John Ten Broeck married in 1809 Mary Dumont and their daughter, Marianna (born 1810, died 1896), wife of David H. Smith, was the next owner. Her heirs sold the house when modern industrialism (in the shape of brickyards) crept to the very door and in 1904 the house was torn down.

The accompanying plate was made from a photograph, taken about 1898, and obtained through the courtesy of Miss Nellie A. Smith of Kingston, a granddaughter of Marianna Ten Broeck Smith. The plate records the east façade and south gable and reveals early masonry but the porch and shutters are of the nineteenth century. A Dutch *stoep* with side seats was originally in front of this door. A hall ran through the house from east to west and on either side of it was one large room. In the wing were two small rooms, one facing east and one west. There was a fireplace in each of the large rooms and one in the small northwest room. A flight of stairs, leading to the upper half-story, was at the right of the west entrance and another led down to a basement kitchen. A lane approached the west door from the main road. From the south door of the basement a path ran to well and woodshed and southeast of the house were flower-beds.

The house of Benjamin Ten Broeck was close to the bank of the Hudson and was one of the series of homesteads fired upon by Sir James Wallace's frigates in October, 1777. In front of it was a linden tree of great size, the lower portion of which is visible in the background of the photograph of 1898. When the house was burning, on October 17, 1777, the side of the linden toward the house caught fire and a large hole was burned in the trunk. The tree lived and the trunk grew so as to surround the scar and form an interesting record of the flames of war.

House of Benjamin Ten Broeck

Town of Ulster, Ulster County, New York

PLATE 89

The house of Benjamin Ten Broeck, now owned by Steve Chmura, is on the east side of the river-road, about a mile and a half north of the boundary line of Kingston corporation, and stands back from the road in the midst of an open plain. The plain was probably once thickly wooded, to judge from its name: Flatbush, a hybrid, derived from *Vlacke Bosch* (level forest or flat woods). The recent purchaser of the house has whitewashed the stone walls and painted the exterior woodwork a deep green. On the day when a photograph of it was made for this work the plain around the house was pied with daisies, buttercups and grasses and brilliant sunshine flooded the green and white house and the flowering field. Amidst such surroundings the wife of Steve Chmura,—gentle, placid, Slavic,—sat beneath the shadow of the porch, relaxed in figure as one of Perugino's Madonnas, her youngest clinging to her as the Child by any old-world master clings to the Mother in the painting. Unconsciously these European peasants imparted to their home something impossible to define but which never lingers about the habitations of rural democracy. The artistic quality of their setting fitted them and they fitted it and dirt and poverty were forgotten by the visitor because of the subtle suggestion of race and soil and age-long things.

The house was built by Benjamin Ten Broeck for his farmer about the time that he himself built the house by the river (plate 88). When the latter was fired by the British in 1777 the family of Benjamin Ten Broeck took refuge in the farmhouse while repairs were made to the homestead. The farmhouse was inherited from Benjamin Ten Broeck by his son, Benjamin, the second (born 1770), who occupied it. Mrs. Peter Maraquat, daughter of Benjamin Ten Broeck, the second, next lived in it but finally sold it.

Three units constitute this Ten Broeck house. At the east end is an undated section,—one room, a chimney, large fireplace with crane, a door and a porch; in the center the section as originally built contained two smaller rooms behind one larger one, in which latter was a stairway; in the wall of the middle section is a stone, marked: I F 1751 M F; the third or westerly unit consists of one room with an outer door and a casement window and has a stone in the wall, marked: 1765. The initials on the stone of 1751 are supposed to stand for the name of the farmer who lived in the house when Benjamin Ten Broeck first occupied the homestead by the river.

House of Matthew Ten Eyck
Town of Hurley, Ulster County, New York
PLATE 90

On the west side of the Esopus Creek in the town of Hurley is the so-called Mountain Road, which follows the base of a wooded ridge. Crossing the bridge at Hurley village and continuing westward a junction is made with the Mountain Road and three-quarters of a mile north of the junction stands the house built (in part) in 1750 by Matthew Ten Eyck. The date of the house and name of the builder are fixed by large iron figures on the south wall: 1750, and a stone in the same wall cut with: * 1750 * M * TE *.

As a whole, the house is made up of two parts, perhaps of three. It is difficult to do more than to " guess " what the changes in structure have been but a fair guess to make is that there was first a house, oblong in proportion, with its ridge-pole extending east and west; which house contained two rooms, having a chimney between them. In those two rooms the ceilings and doorways are low and the fireplace openings (one seven feet, the other six) only second in size to the fireplace in the kitchen of the Wynkoop-Lounsbery house at Stone Ridge (plate 104). The openings are faced with flat boards and have no shelves.

Apparently the first addition to this house was early made toward the north, doubling the floor-area. A new roof over the two parts may then have been built, with the ridge running north and south as at present (see: notes regarding the Palen-Platt house, plate 131). At some early date a granary door was cut in the eastward slope of the roof (plate 90) and in recent times a large dormer was added south of the door. On the west side of the house is a kitchen extension, known to be of comparatively late date.

The house as built in 1750 was the work of Matthew Ten Eyck, a great-grandson of Coenradt Ten Eyck of Albany, grandson of Mattys and Jannetje (Roosa) Ten Eyck of Hurley and son of Abraham and Jenneke (Elmendorf) Ten Eyck of Hurley. His mother, Jenneke, was a daughter of Coenradt Elmendorf and Blandina Kierstede, whose house in Kingston is still standing (page 200). Matthew Ten Eyck, baptized in 1728, married in 1752 Cornelia Wynkoop, whose parents lived on the Wynkoop farm on the Mountain Road (plate 103) and whose cousin, another Cornelia Wynkoop, was the wife of Jan Van Deusen of Hurley (plate 98). Matthew Ten Eyck's sister, Blandina, wife of Andries De Witt, lived two miles south of him on the Mountain Road (plate 71) and his daughter, Catherine, married Gerret De Witt, whose house on the Green Kill is shown in plate 70. From this latter marriage is descended Matthew Ten Eyck De Witt, the present owner of the house of 1750.

Among the portraits on the wall of the parlor of the house on the Mountain Road is one of Matthew Ten Eyck, the builder, dated 1733 and painted by Vanderlyn. In 1782 while Matthew Ten Eyck was president of the board of trustees of the town of Hurley it fell to his lot to read the address of welcome from the board to General Washington, when the latter rode through Hurley on his way from Stone Ridge to Kingston. The date was the sixteenth of November and the story is treasured locally that there was a cold rain falling but that notwithstanding the guest of honor sat his horse, bareheaded, in Hurley Street to receive and answer the address.

House of Evert Terwilliger
Town of Gardiner, Ulster County, New York
PLATE 91

Two miles north of Modena on the state road to New Paltz, at a point where the road makes a bend and crosses a tiny stream, is the little old homestead, shown in plate 91. It stands in the midst of locust trees and lilac bushes and its veranda almost overhangs the meadow-run in front of it. The house is one of three stone dwellings built on a tract of twelve-hundred acres south and east of the Paltz patent, which land was purchased in 1715 by Hugo Freer, Sr., and his sons. To Hugo's daughter, Sarah Freer, wife of Evert Terwilliger, some of this land passed and in 1738 her husband built this house.

In the north wall of the house are two marked stones, one cut with: 1738 E T W I, and the other with: 1741 E T W. Stones in the south wall are marked: D F I 1760; and I V W 1787. The initials in the north wall represent Evert Terwilliger and his son, Evert, Jr. (born 1718), and the others are believed to refer to Daniel Freer, Jr., and to Isaac Van Wagenen, near relatives of the occupants of the house. Evert Terwilliger, who built the house, was baptized in 1686 and married Sarah Freer in 1717. He was a son of Jan Everts, who came from Vianen, in Utrecht, in 1663, bearing the patronymic: Van der Willigen (from the willows) or Ter Willigen (near the willows), a name now rendered Terwilliger and its meaning seldom remembered.

Two other stone houses were built on the Freer land that was bought in 1715 which are still standing, one on the state road south of the house of Evert Terwilliger and another back on the farm, out of sight from the road. The house shown in the plate has a hall through the center, with an enclosed staircase; one room south of the hall; two rooms north of it. There is but one chimney (in the south room). The large ceiling-beams are open to view and there is some plain wood-trim.

The house remained in the family of Evert and Sarah Terwilliger until about 1805—1809, when it was sold to Colonel Josiah Hasbrouck of the village of New Paltz. Colonel Hasbrouck owned and had occupied the house of Jean Hasbrouck (plate 75) but at an unfixed date prior to October, 1809, he moved from New Paltz to a farm four miles to the southward on the Modena road. There he occupied the house built by Evert Terwilliger until, in 1814, he moved into a frame house of dignified architecture and proportions which he had built for himself immediately west of the stone house. The stone house and the large white house of 1814 are both still owned by Colonel Hasbrouck's descendants.

Terwilliger Houses

Town of Shawangunk, Ulster County, New York

From the village of Wallkill the road runs almost directly west for two miles and a half to a four-corners on the top of a steep hill. There a rocky cut and a sharp turn make a danger-spot for cars. This steep grade is known locally as Hagaberg, which is a corruption of the name: *Hooghe Bergh* (high hill), given to the whole neighborhood by the Dutch settlers. In the southeast angle formed by the four-corners and around the shoulder of the *Hooghe Bergh* is a Terwilliger house.

Jan Everts Terwilliger, founder of the family, had two sons baptized at Kingston (Petrus, 1704; Isaac, 1716), who, in their young manhood, settled in the neighborhood of the *Hooghe Bergh* in Shawangunk. The house above referred to is built in two parts and the earlier part may be the work of Isaac Terwilliger, born 1716. There is said to be a marked lintelstone, covered now by the roof of the front porch. Isaac Terwilliger's son, Evert I. (a captain in the Revolution), had a daughter or grand-daughter, Margaret, who married in 1839 Morris Cameron. Her grandson, Everett M. Cameron, now owns the house.

The house consists of two rooms in the first part, to which one room was added on a lower level to the north. The appearance of the exterior is modernized by two porches but inside a little early panelling remains.

Proceeding northward from the four-corners on *Hooghe Bergh* and taking the first left turn another Terwilliger house is reached at the end of half a mile. It is on the north side of the road and is rented by Martin Mosher from the owner, Mrs. Blauenstein. The date of its erection is approximated by a brace in the barn, cut with the figures: 1766. A frame addition and a porch hide the small original dwelling of stone, which is interesting rather on account of its location than for architectural or genealogical reasons. It stands on a high plateau, on which in 1663 the Indians had their " New Fort," where they held the prisoners they had taken in their raid upon Kingston. The plateau makes an abrupt descent to the meadow flats along the Shawangunk Kill, the same flats that are in view from the Decker house across the stream (plate 65). In the 1760's, when the Terwilliger house at New Fort was built, the site was an outpost, beyond the settled and civilized parts of Ulster, and tales of the Indian still cling both to the locality and the house.

Unidentified House, 1752

Town of Marbletown, Ulster County, New York

PLATE 92

From the village of High Falls a road runs southward along the west side of the Rondout Creek and on the west side of the road a short distance from the village stands the house shown in plate 92, owned by George Le Fevre and rented to tenants. High up in the peak of the south gable is a triangular stone of smooth surface, on which is an inscription in three lines, reading:

I B V

F K   *   E L

1752

A search of title might disclose the names for which these initials stand but until that is made the ownership of the house from 1752 until 1806 must be left to conjecture. By 1806 the place had been acquired by Benjamin I. and Rachel Hasbrouck, a fact within the knowledge of persons living and witnessed to by a marked stone in the north wall, the smooth surface of which is visible in the photograph immediately to the left of and below the one window. The inscription on it reads:

B I HB * R HB

1806

Benjamin I. Hasbrouck (born 1764), a great-grandson of Jean Hasbrouck of New Paltz (plate 75), married his cousin, Rachel Hasbrouck, and moved into this house south of High Falls. He apparently made some changes in the house about 1806 for the divided and panelled front door, with knocker, and the fan-light above the door are in the designs of that period, and two crescent windows under the eaves in front may also be assigned to it. In each gable is a false window, crescent-shaped, and the opening in the north gable is filled with wood which is carved and painted white. The house is said to have contained originally three rooms (with two bed-recesses) on the main floor but it was altered in the nineteenth century. A narrow central hall is now finished in uninteresting modern trim. North of the hall the front room still holds panelled cupboards and blue tiles. But many tiles, known to have been in the house, have been taken from it as souvenirs. An eighteenth century stone smoke-house stands to the north of the kitchen wing, just beyond the range of the camera.

Unidentified House, called *Feather Farm*

Town of Marbletown, Ulster County, New York

PLATE 93

South of the house illustrated by plate 92, on the opposite side of the same road, is an excellent eighteenth century house, now the property of Harry Pearson. It is built on a bluff that lies in the angle formed by the confluence of the Dover Kill (*Doove Kil* or sluggish stream) with the Rondout and looks eastward toward Sky Top, above Lake Mohonk, where the memorial tower is outlined in the photograph (plate 93) against the sky. It is supposed that the land on which the house stands was in the Brodhead family at an early date and passed to the Schoonmakers in the second quarter of the nineteenth century. Who built the house is not certainly known. In floor-plan the house is similar to that which was built at Kerhonkson in 1762 by Johannes G. Hardenbergh (plate 74). It has three rooms on the main floor and each room has an outer door. The finish is plain but substantial, the large unceiled beams and good iron hardware being well preserved. There is a tradition that in the early nineteenth century, when the road past the farm was the stagecoach route between Kingston and Ellenville, the house was used as an inn and posting-station. Under the name of: *Feather Farm*, the present owner has made of the house an attractive dwelling, preserving and restoring its original features and adding only an east porch and west dormers. The ridge-pole of this house is an instance of the irregularity of the work of the early builder, its slight unevenness of line fitting the general character of the construction of the house.

Unidentified House, 1772

Kripplebush, Ulster County, New York

PLATE 94

The house shown in plate 94 stands at the east end of a hamlet in Ulster County called Kripplebush (*Kreupelbosch* or thicket, copse, low growth). It is in the northeast angle of the junction of two roads, near a small bridge, and is owned and occupied by Millard Van Aken. Mr. Van Aken bought it in late years and no one can be found at Kripplebush who knows by whom the house was built. A lintel-stone over the east doorway (shown in the plate) bears the following long inscription, for which no explanation has been obtained, unless it represents the initials of those who worked on the construction of the house.

E C L C C T C V C
C T M L I V M I C

A stone near the north end of the east wall of the house, midway between the ground and the eaves, is marked: M L 1772.

The house is an example of the dwelling of a farmer in the decade before the Revolution. The masonry is primitive, the woodwork plain, there are no ornamental details but, nevertheless, the little old home with its clambering rose vine possesses a quality of its own that tells a story of the back-country districts a hundred and sixty years ago. Inside, a central hall (with enclosed stairs) runs between two rooms on either hand (of unequal size). A bed-recess in the southwest room projects into the central hall.

Unidentified House, detail

Town of Rochester, Ulster County, New York

PLATE 95

On the *King's Highway* of the eighteenth century, overlooking a forgotten red milestone, and at a point where the old *Highway* pitches down a gravelly hillside from the quiet and seclusion of the height above to the rushing traffic of the state road below, is hidden a little house in the town of Rochester, Ulster County, the beginnings of which nobody knows. Since 1861 it has been the home of Elias Markle, who is now well over ninety years of age. Mr. Markle recalls that before his purchase of it it was owned by Mrs. Jacob De Witt, who sold it to the Snyder family, from whom it came to him. The house stands on a lot of five acres, surrounded by very large tracts that were patented early by the De Witts and the De Puys. The five acres may have belonged to one or the other of those families and the house have been built for a newly married son or daughter, later becoming a tenant-dwelling and finally being sold. That it was built before 1776 there can be no doubt and in 1861 it was unaltered from its original condition. It then consisted of two rooms, with a chimney between, and a half-story above. Mr. Markle raised the roof, built dormers and, with partitions, made two rooms into four. At the present time may still be found in the southeast room large ceiling-beams of white pine, the color now of tobacco or of a seal's fur, their rich hue being the combined result of time and of smoke from the open fire. Each of the original two rooms has an outer door, two primitives, between which it was hard to choose for the accompanying plate. The door selected leads into the northeast room and on a sunny summer morning, when rose- and honeysuckle-vines made play with shadows, when the cottage windows were irridescent in the light and the little flagged path pointed the way to the worn sill, the picture presented was as unspoiled a bit of the eighteenth century as could be wished for.

In design this door should be compared with the doors of the Bevier-Elting, Brink and Wynkoop-Schoonmaker houses, plates 58, 60 and 105.

Van Aken House
Town of Esopus, Ulster County, New York
PLATE 96

The Van Aken homestead shown in plate 96 is in the town of Esopus, Ulster County, a mile south of the village of Port Ewen by the state road and then a half-mile west by a side-road. Modern porches and windows have changed the appearance of the house in late years and the plate was made from a photograph taken about 1870 and kindly loaned by the present owner of the house, the widow of Henry Van Aken. The photograph is important as providing a record of an unaltered primitive farmhouse of the eighteenth century. Like the De Puy house at Soccanissing (plate 68) the Van Aken house helps to prove by its few windows and doors how little light and air the pioneers had within their dwellings. There is no marked stone in this house but family tradition says that the builder was Gideon Van Aken and that the land was purchased under Queen Anne (1702—1714). Peter Van Aken, emigrant from Holland to New Netherland, is said to have settled in what is now the town of Esopus in the latter part of the seventeenth century and to have been the father of sons named: Gideon, Marinus, Peter and John. The house as shown in the photograph was perhaps built in two parts, the first part at the east end with a chimney in the center and a door toward the north. The north door gives entrance to a room in which is still a fireplace having a primitive wood facing. This room

229

has also a door to the west (leading into the supposed addition) in which are bull's eyes. The house contains original beams and some early hardware.

Van Buren House
Kingston, New York
PLATE 97

The house now standing on the southeast corner of Green Street and Maiden Lane in the city of Kingston and owned by Mrs. Harry Gordon is a Van Buren homestead of the eighteenth century which was occupied by members of the Van Buren family until late years. Recently the house was restored for the present owner under the direction of Myron S. Teller of Kingston, a member of the Holland Society possessed of specialized architectural knowledge of the stone houses of Ulster County. The accompanying view of the house (plate 97) is offered as an illustration of the possibilities latent in many old dwellings for the creation of artistic modern homes. The plate should be examined in connection with the picture of the Van Keuren house (plate 99) and the text reference (page 211) to the Masten house.

In October, 1777, the Van Buren house was partly burned in the British raid upon Kingston. It was rebuilt and approximately on original lines, as was disclosed during the work of restoration. The date of its erection is not known. Associated with it is the name of Tobias Van Buren but whether as builder or as occupant is not certainly known.

The Van Buren family of Kingston was founded by Tobias Van Buren, born in 1687 (of Cornelis, of Martin, of Gerret Cornelis Van Buren), who came down from Rensselaerswyck and married at Kingston in 1712 Helena Bogardus. He may have built the house and lived in it or the builder might have been his son or grandson. Tobias Van Buren's marriage to Helena Bogardus allied him to a family connection of many ramifications. Mrs. Van Buren was a great-granddaughter of Domine Everardus Bogardus and Anneke Jans (plate 13). Her aunt (her father's half-sister) was Mrs. Roger Brett of Fishkill (text for plate 111) and her mother (Rachel De Witt, wife of Cornelis Bogardus, 2nd) was a daughter of Tjerck Claessen De Witt (text for plate 69). Helena Bogardus Van Buren was cousin to the countless Bogarduses, Kierstedes, Tellers, Bretts, De Witts, Pawlings and others of the Hudson valley in a wellnigh hopeless genealogical tangle. But the tangle provides many associations for the house of the Van Burens which are of personal interest to those concerned in it.

Van Deusen House
Hurley, Ulster County, New York
PLATE 98

No portion of Ulster County has more of story and tradition attached to it than the short stretch of roadway, a mile and a half west of Kingston corporation, which constitutes the village of Hurley. From 1663 when, as *Nieuw Dorp* (New Village), it was burned by the Indians to the days of the Revolution, when it was the scene of events of interest, Hurley was a Dutch settlement, compact in area and also in community-spirit. Its inhabitants were interrelated genealogically and successive generations adhered closely to the old homes and old customs so that Hurley formed an outstanding instance of Dutch village life in Ulster. Today, it requires the eyes of faith and imagination to visualize pre-Revolutionary Hurley for most of the earlier houses are gone and those remaining are so altered or added to as to have lost much of their distinctive character.

One of the few eighteenth century dwellings now left at Hurley is the Van Deusen house (plate 98), which stands on the north side of the street. Jan Van Deusen of Claverack moved down the river to Ulster and married at Hurley in 1719 Hillegonda Roosa. On February 1, 1743/4, he conveyed this house to his son, Jan, Jr., who had married in 1741 Cornelia Wynkoop. Title to the house passed through the names of Van Deusen, Krom, Ten Eyck and Nash to the present owner, Samuel Gibson, the successive transfers being witnessed to by marked stones in the wall, inscribed: J V D Jr 1744; J G K 1815; A T E 1862; G W N 1906.

In shape this house is an L and (to judge from the absence of seams in the masonry) was built as a unit. A hall runs through the center, on either side of which were, originally, two rooms (the front rooms larger than the rear); in the wing is one room. A frame lean-to fills in the angle of the L between the wing and the main house. Some of the wood-trim and hardware are eighteenth century work but the late Dr. George W. Nash, while he owned the house, put in some finishings which were reproductions of early designs. Unfortunately, he placed iron strap-hinges (reproductions) on the outer side of the front door. In all the houses observed in the field-survey made for this volume, where conditions are unchanged, the hardware is on the inner side. The present owner of the Van Deusen house has a nice understanding of period work in architecture and furniture and the house is destined to be given good care by him.

Historically, the house of Jan Van Deusen is distinguished by the fact that the Committee of Safety of the State of New York held sessions in it. The Committee (which was an executive arm of the newly organized state) met in the Elmendorf house in Kingston (page 200) from October 11 to 15, 1777; in the Oliver house at Marbletown (since torn down) from October 18th for one month; and from November 18 to December 17 in the Van Deusen house at Hurley. On December 17th the members voted to remove from Hurley to Poughkeepsie because the house at Hurley was too cold. The reason given for removal is difficult to understand for there are four chimneys in the Van Deusen house, with fireplace openings. And at Poughkeepsie as elsewhere no heating arrangements other than open fires were known in 1777.

It may be pertinent to note here that the houses at Kingston, Marbletown and Hurley in which the Committee of Safety held its sessions were all of the same type of domestic architecture and it is beyond question that, when the committee moved to Poughkeepsie, they found the same style of dwelling common there.

Van Keuren House
Kingston, New York
PLATE 99

The house shown in plate 99 stands on the southeast corner of Green and John Streets, Kingston, and is known as the house of Gerret Van Keuren. It was built before the Revolution and partly burned on October 16, 1777, as proved by the finding of charred beams when the building was done over in late years by Myron S. Teller for the present owner, Mrs. W. Anderson Carl. That the flames started by the British were in this case soon extinguished is witnessed to by the fact that the beams were but slightly damaged and are still doing duty. This house and its neighbor, the Van Buren home (plate 97), and the Masten (page 211) are noted in this volume in the hope that the kindly treatment given them may lead to the salvage of other old dwellings.

House of Jacob Aertsen Van Wagenen
Town of Rosendale, Ulster County, New York
PLATE 100

The course of the Rondout Creek in Ulster County from Le Fevre Falls to the Hudson is marked in general by bluffs so high as to form a gorge for the passage of the stream. But at a point near the nineteenth century hamlet called Creek Locks the banks flatten out for a short distance and there is low, arable land on both sides of the stream. This secluded spot was known in the eighteenth century as *Wagen Dal* (Wagon Dale) and here on the west bank of the Rondout a house (plate 100) was built by Jacob Aertsen (born 1652, died about 1716), who is said to have come from Wageningen in Gelderland, Holland. It would require research, however, to determine whether Jacob Aertsen derived his patronymic: " Van Wagenen " from the city of Wageningen on the Dutch reaches of the river Rhine or from the occupation of some forbear as a wagoner and, further, to prove what connection there may have been between his family name and that of *Wagen Dal* in Ulster. That connection did exist between him and the city and with the place-name in Ulster is the belief of his descendants.

The house built by Jacob Aertsen at *Wagen Dal* bears in its west wall a stone cut with the figures: 1699. It consists of two structural parts. The first is oblong east and west, faces north, and contains a hall between two rooms; the ceilings are

232

low, the wood-trim plain and primitive. The second part was added at the south at an unknown but early date. The property descended in the direct male line from Jacob Aertsen Van Wagenen to the grandfather of the present owner (Miss Elizabeth Snyder).

Jacob Aertsen married in 1677 Sara, daughter of Evert Pels. Of their fifteen children eleven were named in the will which " Jacob Aertsen of *Wagendal* " made in 1714. For two of his sons stone houses were built at *Wagen Dal*, one to the west and one to the south of the house of 1699, which are standing, but which have modern roofs, porches, windows, etc. East of the house of 1699 is a fourth Van Wagenen home, now out of repair, in the wall of which is a stone marked: 1775 I V W. The photograph of this house (plate 4) shows the *dal* in which the Van Wagenens lived.

Almost directly across the creek is a fifth Van Wagenen house, which carries a stone marked: A V W 1745 I V W, and which is now owned by William J. Van Wagenen, a descendant of the builder.

Originally, a sixth dwelling built by this family stood where, later, the settlement of Creek Locks grew up on the edge of the canal. When this house fell into decay in recent years it contained an iron fireback which Cornelius I. Le Fevre of Rosendale removed and affixed to the outer wall of his own house. The fireback bears the date: 1742, and a representation in ornamental iron-work of the publican and pharisee of St. Luke, 18: 10—14.

From *Wagen Dal* the Van Wagenens spread out in several directions. One branch, that of Jacob Aertsen's son, Evert, settled in Dutchess County and plate 145 shows a house occupied by Evert's descendants. Jacob Aertsen's Dutch Bible, containing family records written by his own hand, is owned by Victor Van Wagenen of Stone Ridge, N. Y.

Vernooy-Bevier House
Town of Wawarsing, Ulster County, New York
PLATE 101

Approaching the village of Wawarsing from the northeast by the state road a visitor finds a farm-lane leading to the left to farm outbuildings near the foot of a hill. The farm is owned by Arthur Hoornbeck and rented to James Smith. Tucked in among the barns is a little dwelling that was built when this neighborhood was the frontier of white civilization in Ulster. Before and during the Revolution another house stood close to it in the shadow of the near-by hill (which is crowned by an ancient burial-ground). Of the two houses, one belonged in 1781 to Peter Vernooy and the other to Cornelius Bevier and both were besieged in the raid made in that year by Tories and Indians on Wawarsing. The raid was the occasion of great violence and much bloodshed, when the householders battled for their lives and this now quiet back-water saw horrible sights. Whether the house now standing was a

Vernooy home or a Bevier is a matter of opinion, lacking positive proof, but the point is of no consequence here for the house serves equally well under either name as an example of plan, materials and workmanship in the period of the pioneer. The accompanying plate, number 101, is from a photograph made in 1906 by Clarence J. Elting of Highland and reproduced through his courtesy. The house (now closed) was then occupied. Inside are two rooms, a central chimney, wide fireplace opening, plain wood-trim, enclosed staircase and an attic. The frame structure to the left is detached from the main building.

Westbrook House

Town of Rochester, Ulster County, New York

PLATE 102

The Westbrook family of Ulster was founded by Jonathan Westbrook, an Englishman, said to have been an officer under Cromwell. He came to New Netherland early and settled in Ulster County, where his descendants merged themselves completely with the Dutch element in the community (like the Nicoll, Salisbury and Pawling families, mentioned in connection with plates 29, 30 and 82). The name of Westbrook was identified ultimately with the ministry of the Reformed Dutch Church and members of the family were prominent in Ulster in military service and as members of the bar.

Settlement in the town of Rochester was made early in the eighteenth century by descendants of Jonathan Westbrook, one branch becoming established on *Peter's Kil*, a tributary of the Rondout Creek, on which they built a grist mill. The accompanying plate, number 102, shows the homestead at the mill-site on *Peter's Kil*, a beautiful rural location. The date of the erection of the house and the name of the builder have not been learned but at the time of the Revolution the house was the home of Lieutenant Dirck Westbrook (of Jonathan, Dirck, Jonathan). In after years his descendants sold to a purchaser named Duryea, whose daughter, the late Mrs. James Lounsbery, inherited it. The place is now held in the estate of Mrs. Lounsbery's husband, whose death followed hers.

The Westbrook house on *Peter's Kil* stands in a bend of a side-road that runs from Accord to Whitfield. The stream makes a drop here (providing the power for the former mill) and the house is shadowed by fine locust trees. In shape the building is an L, facing east, the wing extending westward at the north end. The wing retains its eighteenth century characteristics: the Dutch oven (under the vines); inset door; small windows; and an interesting overhang of the roof. On the main house the roof was raised at a date presumably around 1800—1810 and small oblong openings, called: lie-on-your-stomach windows, were cut in the wood crown that was placed on the stone walls. Probably at the same time the house was given the

234

excellent front door and interior woodwork which it still contains in good order. But because the main door and the porch across the east front are not eighteenth century work the house was photographed from the rear. This old home bears the signs of loving care. It is in perfect repair and its white rail-fence and stone paths, its trees and shrubs and plants, form a setting that tells of a long and comfortable domestic history.

The Wynkoop Farm
Town of Hurley, Ulster County, New York

PLATE 103

Crossing the Esopus by the bridge at Hurley village and proceeding over the flat that borders the creek on the west the cross-road soon joins the Mountain Road. In the southeast angle formed by the two roads stands the Wynkoop house, owned and occupied at present by William A. Warren. The house is made up of an original stone portion with large frame additions. It bears internal evidence and there is family knowledge of the fact that an oblong house, facing south, was first built. To that was added at the northeast in the rear a wing, forming an ell as a whole. Later, the west end of the first portion was torn away (leaving an oblong north and south) and finally at the west was put a large frame extension. The interior of the house still contains original ceiling-beams and early mantels but the exterior has lost its eighteenth century appearance by the additions that have been made to it.

The photograph reproduced in plate 103 was taken to show the location of the Wynkoop house rather than its architecture for the land on which the house stands was purchased about 1667 by the founder of the Wynkoop family of Ulster County. The farm lies along the Esopus on a rich alluvial flat which is famous for productivity and from the first owner, Cornelius Wynkoop (who died about 1676), was inherited in direct male line through Major Johannes Wynkoop, deceased 1730—'33; Derick, born 1698; Colonel Cornelius D., born 1734, deceased 1792; Derick C., born 1763, deceased 1838; George, born 1814; to James D. Wynkoop (born 1843, died 1904), the step-father of the present owner. Thus title to the land was held in one family name for nearly two-hundred and forty years. It is not known which of the Wynkoops built the stone portions of the house but tradition assigns the earliest part to Cornelius the first of the name. Cornelius D. Wynkoop, colonel in 1776 of the third regiment of Ulster militia, certainly lived in the house and there can be small doubt but that his birth in 1734 occurred under its roof. A portrait of Cornelius D. Wynkoop at the age of eight, which was painted on mahogany in 1743, hangs in the dining-room of the house today. There are in the Hudson valley regrettably few homes that have remained in one family from the colonial period and which have been maintained by successive generations in accordance with a continually rising standard of living. Among the few such instances the Wynkoop house should be recorded.

Wynkoop-Lounsbery House
Stone Ridge, Ulster County, New York
PLATE 104

Of all the pre-Revolutionary houses now standing in Ulster County the one at Stone Ridge, known as the Wynkoop-Lounsbery house, reaches the highest degree of architectural development and, of the houses in Ulster that were built before 1776 and since then razed (of which photographs or written records are to be had), the only one which approached it was the Rutsen-Hardenbergh house at Rosendale (plate 83). In size and dignity, in elegance of finish and in a certain sophistication the Wynkoop-Lounsbery house is conspicuous in Ulster County.

The house was built in or before 1772 by Cornelius E. Wynkoop (born 1746, died 1795), was sold about 1800 to one of the Lounsbery family and is now owned and occupied by William Lounsbery. It is two and one-half stories in height with a gambrel roof, two features that are a departure from the architectural type characteristic of Ulster before 1776 (the type consisting of one and one-half stories and a roof of single slant). Although the stone walls are laid up in a crude mixture of lime, sand and cow-hair, the stones are somewhat tooled and the walls have the dressed appearance of trained masonwork. Original panelled shutters, shutter-hooks and windows remain, as well as a handsome entrance-door but the porch, unfortunately, is of the nineteenth century.

On the first floor the room-plan is individual. There is the familiar arrangement of a central hall, with two rooms at each side (one larger, one smaller), but the lines are broken by the projection of a bed-recess from the northwest room into the main hall, which fills the corner at the right of the front door. The staircase rises in the middle of the hall and between the hall and the southwest room is a small additional passage, leading to the kitchen wing.

There is still in the central hall original panelling, now white, but at an early date painted in pink and blue. To the east of the main door, a door into the northeast room contains bull's eyes. The stairs are in three banks of steps (narrow treads, with high rise) between the first and second floors and in a single flight to the attic and both flights are unenclosed. In the northwest room on the first floor the south wall and chimney-breast are panelled, original paint of unusual shades of blue and of mulberry being still visible. The smaller southwest room contains a panelled corner-cupboard and chimney-breast; tiles around the fireplace opening and in the fireplace a wrought iron fireback marked: C W K Nov 5 1772.

On the second floor the northwest room has a handsome panelled chimney-breast and blue fireplace tiles. It was in this room that General Washington was the guest of Major Wynkoop on the night of November 15, 1782. On the other side of the hall, in the northeast room, is a natural curiosity. The bevelled panel

236

across the chimney-front measures thirty-three inches by forty-six and is made from one piece of white pine, its size indicating the growth attained by the tree from which it was cut. In the upper southeast room a granary door, formerly in the east wall, has been closed up, an alteration which can be seen in the photograph above and to the left of the first floor window.

At the rear of this handsome house there is a wing, containing a kitchen and other service rooms, which is so different from the main house that there can be little doubt that it was an early unit, preceding the larger building in date of erection. The stones in the walls are rough and untooled and the structure was apparently all built at one time to serve as a dwelling. Some changes have been made in the floor-plan but the fireplace in the kitchen, eight feet wide and four and a half feet high, testifies to primitive living conditions. In this large opening are two cranes (of which the upright bars are forty-two inches high, horizontal bars forty-one inches, diagonal support thirty-six inches) and formerly there was a Dutch oven on either side of the chimney, projecting from the outer side of the south wall.

Major Cornelius E. Wynkoop, the builder of the house at Stone Ridge, was a great-great-grandson of Cornelius Wynkoop of Hurley, whose home-acres are shown in plate 103. During the Revolution Major Wynkoop was an officer of Ulster Minute Men and a member of the committee for the detection of conspiracies. From his house at Stone Ridge his guest, General Washington, rode on horseback to Kingston on November 16, 1782, to stay with the Major's brother, Colonel Dirck Wynkoop. The latter was distinguished in public service as a deputy to the Provincial Congress of New York, member of the Assembly, and as delegate to the Constitutional Convention of 1788. Colonel Dirck Wynkoop's house on Green Street in Kingston (no longer standing) is shown in *Olde Ulster*, 3: 14.

Wynkoop House

Town of Marbletown, Ulster County, New York

About three miles south of Hurley village on the east side of the state road is a Wynkoop house, now owned by Mrs. Christina Oliver Dixon. It was once the home of a branch of the Van Buren family, and the author of: *Ulster County under the Dutch*, Augustus Van Buren, was born in it. The house was built in or before 1763, to judge from a fireback in the southwest room, marked:

1 7 6 3
A W K

In the northwest room is another fireback, whereon an urn, filled with flowers, is surrounded with the inscription: Nov 5 C W K 1772. This marking duplicates that which is on the fireback in the Wynkoop-Lounsbery house at Stone Ridge (plate 104) and for which duplication no explanation has been found.

Changes in the exterior of this house have destroyed its pictorial quality as an eighteenth century item but the location of it on a high, rocky roadside, with ancient barn and well near by, holds something of interest. The front door has an arched top and is probably of the period of the early Republic. The hall across the center of the front of the house, between two main rooms, extends to only half the depth of the building. Back of it the equivalent floor-area is divided into a narrow passage, running to a rear door, between an enclosed staircase at the south and pantries at the north. An arched doorway is between the front hall and rear passage. This is an unusual floor-plan and the general character of the woodwork is such as to suggest that originally there were three main rooms and that the one in the center was sub-divided at a later date.

Wynkoop-Schoonmaker House, detail

Town of Saugerties, Ulster County, New York

PLATE 105

The primitive door, shown in plate 105, embowered by a climbing yellow rose, is a detail of a house which stands in the town of Saugerties about one mile due west of a station on the West Shore Railroad named Cockburn. The house is on a back road that parallels the base of a mountain-ridge. There is a hazy tradition that the land on which it is built was owned originally by the De Witts or the Brinks. Uncertainty exists as to the name of the builder or the date of erection of the house. The earliest occupant of it positively known was Alida Wynkoop (born 1799), who married Henry Schoonmaker and whose son, Tjerck Schoonmaker (born 1820), inherited it. From Tjerck Schoonmaker and his wife, Sarah De Witt, the property passed to their son, Abram T. Schoonmaker (now of Hudson, New York), and their daughter, the late Mrs. Clinton De Witt. The present owner is Dr. George Bentz.

Alida (Wynkoop) Schoonmaker was a daughter of Henry Wynkoop (born 1769, died 1828) of the town of Saugerties, who was a descendant of Cornelius Wynkoop of Hurley (plate 103). The house under consideration is, however, apparently a mid-eighteenth century structure and it is improbable that Henry Wynkoop, born in 1769, was the builder. Only a thorough search of title would provide a record of the ownership of the land back to 1750 and furnish clues to a more exact history of the house. In plan, the house consists of three rooms on the ground floor and a half story above, the latter reached by an enclosed flight of stairs that rises in the middle room at the left of the main door. There are three chimneys and the opening of the fireplace in the kitchen is especially large and primitive. The wood-trim and hardware are all early. The front porch was an addition (perhaps made soon after 1800).

In its surroundings the house enjoys an artistic setting; a wooded ridge is immediately to the west, there are towering sycamore trees in front, graceful vines cling to the old walls and the road bends abruptly around the northwest corner of the building so closely as nearly to graze the gable-end.

This Dutch door should be compared with those of the Bevier-Elting, Brink and Unidentified houses, shown in plates: 58, 60 and 95. The window in the upper half of the door was undoubtedly cut in the nineteenth century.

PLATE 58
Bevier-Elting House,

Huguenot Street, New Paltz. Dates from the first half of the eighteenth century. Primitive in construction and finish. Has suffered few changes. The plate shows the west door, an excellent unaltered original.

241

PLATE 59

House of Coenradt Bevier,

Napanoch, Ulster County. In the south gable-end may be seen a vertical seam in the masonry which outlines to the left the original stone unit in the southwest angle of the building. To the east of the seam is the first addition. Across the north side from east to west a second addition was made. The roof was raised over all three parts. The house illustrates the principle of growth in building stone houses, as contrasted with that of design.

PLATE 60

West front of the house of Cornelis Lamberts Brink,

town of Saugerties, Ulster County. The south end (at the right of the plate) was built in 1701. The north end was an addition and in recent years was replaced by a frame structure. The inset door is one of the battened divided doors, characteristic of the stone houses of the eighteenth century. The plate was made from a photograph obtained through the courtesy of Mrs. Fremont Davis, a descendant of Cornelis Lamberts Brink and the owner of the house.

PLATE 61

Detail, house of Cornelis Lamberts Brink,

town of Saugerties, Ulster County. Rough stones project from the southwest corner of the house which (by tradition) were used as steps to reach the roof when attacks by Indians were feared and when distant observations were desired. The shutters and strap-hinges recorded by the plate are eighteenth century items.

PLATE 62

Southeast corner of the house of Jacobus Bruyn,

town of Wawarsing, Ulster County. The curved roof-line is individual and illustrates the way in which untrained local workmen sometimes showed instinctive feeling for line and proportion.

PLATE 63

House of Jacobus S. Bruyn,

Kingston, N. Y. Built before the Revolution, partly burned 1777, rebuilt after the war. The gambrel roof dates
from the post-war reconstruction and is one of the few gambrels in Ulster County.

PLATE 64

Bruyn House,

Wallkill, N. Y. An unusual house in Ulster County because built of wood and covered by a gambrel roof. The time of its erection is uncertain. Tradition quotes a pre-Revolutionary date. Architectural details imply 1790-1810.

PLATE 65

Decker House,

town of Shawangunk, Ulster County, from the northwest. Built in four parts that form a T. A Dutch oven in the west wall of the crossbar of the T shows in the plate. According to family tradition the slaves were quartered in the north wing, which forms the standard of the T. The house is interesting in structure and floor-plan and its site is in a neighborhood full of story.

PLATE 66

Decker House,

town of Shawangunk, Ulster County, from the south. The western portion was built first, a small square house typical of the period of the pioneer. The plate shows the suture where the long double house towards the east was added in 1776. As a whole the house has individual character; and its setting, near a stream and bridge, suits it well.

PLATE 67

House of Jacobus De Puy.

A landmark in the town of Rochester, Ulster County. Owned by the builder and his descendants for nearly two-hundred years. Now in decay, but still possessed of many primitive features in masonry, woodwork and hardware.

PLATE 68

De Puy—De Witt House,

town of Wawarsing, Ulster County, as it was in 1906. The plate was made from a photograph taken by Clarence J. Elting of Highland, N. Y., and obtained through his courtesy. The house was a frontier dwelling, subjected to raids by Indians and Tories. It had few doors and windows and affords direct evidence of the hardships experienced by the pioneers in the valley of the Rondout.

PLATE 69

DeWitt House,

Hurley Avenue, Kingston, N. Y. The house stands on land which was acquired by Tjerck DeWitt in the third quarter of the seventeenth century, and which was owned by his descendants for two-hundred years. The structure consists of three parts, the earliest dating (perhaps) to 1670 and the latest to approximately 1790—1800. The hood over the main entrance is in the style of the hoods on the Bronck, Coeymans, Coeymans-Bronck, Van Voorhees and Westervelt houses (plates 16, 18, 19, 144 and 150).

PLATE 70

House of Johannes DeWitt

on the Green Kill, Ulster County. The original (front) part of the house was built in 1736. An extension across the rear was made at an early date at the place where a vertical seam shows in the gable-end next the kitchen-door. The porch, large dormer and the roof (with broad overhang) are nineteenth century work and destroy the original appearance of the house.

PLATE 71

House of Andries DeWitt,

Marbletown, Ulster County, from the southeast. The central portion of the house (between two chimneys) dates from about 1753; the south end was added soon after; the north end has a stone marked: 1800. The east porch is of (approximately) 1800. In the west wall are eighteenth century Dutch doors. A large farm, famous for fertility, went with the house and was owned by the DeWitt family until recent years. During the Revolutionary war the house was a storage-place for military supplies.

PLATE 72

Deyo House,

at *Bonte Koe* on the Wallkill near New Paltz. A homestead in the Deyo family from the early eighteenth century to the late nineteenth.

PLATE 73

DuBois-Kierstede House,

Saugerties, N. Y. The walls of the house were erected in 1727, as witnessed to by a marked stone near the main entrance. Most of the exterior details are of later date. Handsome locust trees give the house a beautiful setting, and the building is in good repair.

PLATE 74

House of Johannes G. Hardenbergh,

town of Wawarsing, Ulster County, built in 1762. Some original features survive as part of the structure; but in the main the building is out of repair and is used only to house farm-tools. In 1777 it was the place of deposit for the public records of the state of New York, of New York City and of Ulster County. Ten wagon-loads of books and papers are said to have been hidden in this remote place.

PLATE 75

House of Jean Hasbrouck,

New Paltz, N. Y., built in 1712 and still possessed of most of its original details. It is maintained as a Memorial House by the Huguenot, Patriotic, Historical and Monumental Society. The roof is its significant architectural feature and should be compared with the roofs shown in plates 16, 42, and 82.

PLATE 76

House of Jonathan Hasbrouck,

Newburgh, N. Y., as sketched in oils about 1834 by Robert W. Weir, professor of drawing at the United States Military Academy. The original painting is owned by Silas Wodell of Millbrook, N. Y., and is reproduced through his courtesy. The house was built in three parts: one before 1747, one in 1750 and one in 1770. From April, 1782, to August, 1783, it was occupied by General Washington as his headquarters.

PLATE 77

House of Thomas Jansen,

town of Shawangunk, Ulster County. It stands at the eastern base of the Shawangunk range with no near neighbors. A stone, marked 1727, is in the wall of the main portion; but the porch and dormers are of the nineteenth
century. The date of the west wing is uncertain. The Jansens and Van Keurens of Ulster descend from a common
ancestor, Mattys Jansen Van Keulen (Van Köln?).

260

PLATE 78

Krom House,

town of Rochester, Ulster County. The low rear wall, the granary door in the gable and the rain-barrel are unaltered examples of details highly characteristic of early houses in Ulster.

PLATE 79

House of Abraham LeFevre,

town of Gardiner, Ulster County. Built about 1740. In outline and proportion and in the character of the masonry the house illustrates an architectural type that was common in Ulster in the eighteenth century.

PLATE 80

The house of Pieter Cornelise Louw

in Frog Alley, Kingston, can lay no claim to beauty. It is worth recording because the eastern (right) half was built by Pieter Cornelise Louw probably between 1665 and 1690 and illustrates seventeenth century masonry. The house shows also the small size and general crudity of the home of an early settler. The western half is supposed to have been added in the eighteenth century by the Smeedes family. Owned from 1783 to 1816 by Benjamin Bogardus and his widow, Rachel, the house is commonly called the Bogardus house.

PLATE 81

The Osterhoudt house

on the Neighborhood Road, town of Ulster, Ulster County, was built in three sections: the first (supposedly) in 1691 and the third in 1740. The windows vary in size and relative position. The dormers and porch are presumably early nineteenth century additions. In line, proportion and setting the house has a simple beauty that holds attention.

PLATE 82

The Pawling house,

Marbletown, Ulster County. Built in three sections. The southern end of the house, here shown, is the oldest part and was built (supposedly) between 1672 and 1695. The walls of this portion are now the most primitive feature of the structure as a whole, which, unfortunately, has lost much of its original appearance by the introduction of modern porch, shutters, windows and other details.

265

PLATE 83

The Rutsen-Hardenbergh house,

Rosendale, Ulster County, was burned in 1911, and plate 83 was made from a photograph taken in 1910 by Clarence J. Elting of Highland, N. Y., and reproduced through his courtesy. It is supposed that a small stone house of the 1680's (probably the rear wing) was added to in the eighteenth century by the erection of the main portion of the dwelling. In size and in interior finish this was one of the largest and handsomest houses in Ulster prior to 1776.

PLATE 84

Schoonmaker House.

Built in 1727 the Schoonmaker house at Saugerties, N. Y., is still, at the end of two-hundred years, owned in the Schoonmaker family. A nineteenth century porch, dormer and windows alter the character of the appearance of the main house; but the east wing and detached outbuilding are unaltered eighteenth century items.

PLATE 85

The house and farm of Hendrick Smit

occupy an obscure location in the town of Esopus, Ulster County. The interest attached to them is chiefly from the viewpoint of economics as the farm of eighty acres was acquired early in the eighteenth century under a lease at an annual rental of a hen and a rooster. Few wells of the type shown in the plate are now left in the Hudson valley.

PLATE 86

At Stone Ridge,

Ulster County, in the eighteenth century Johannes and Sally Tack kept an inn, and the kitchen area of the former tavern is here shown. The plate was made from a photograph obtained through the courtesy of Miss Sarah C. Lounsbery of Stone Ridge, N. Y.

PLATE 87

House of Wessel Wesselse Ten Broeck,

Kingston, N. Y. Built between 1676 and 1695. Occupied for a month in 1777 by the Senate of the State of New York. Partly burned by the British in 1777. Owned by descendants of the builder until late in the nineteenth century. Now owned by the State of New York. The plate was made from a photograph taken in 1871 and obtained from the Pennington Studio, Kingston, N. Y.

PLATE 88

House of Benjamin Ten Broeck,

Flatbush, Ulster County. Built about 1748. Torn down 1904. The plate was made from a photograph taken about 1898 and obtained through the courtesy of Miss Nellie A. Smith of Kingston, N. Y. The house stood near the shore of the Hudson on a tract of land that was owned by the Ten Broeck family from approximately 1704 until 1904. Sir James Wallace's ships fired on the house in 1777. In the nineteenth century the original Dutch *stoep* was replaced by the porch shown in the plate.

271

PLATE 89

House of Benjamin Ten Broeck.

The house shown in plate 89 is on the Ten Broeck land at Flatbush, Ulster County, and was built and owned by Benjamin Ten Broeck. It is in three sections, of which the walls of the second and third are cut with the dates: 1751 and 1765. The first part, undated, is at the east (right) end. In the western portion is an unusual double window. The panelled shutters are of the eighteenth century, the dormer of the nineteenth.

PLATE 90

The house of Matthew Ten Eyck,

town of Hurley, Ulster County. A particularly interesting dwelling; but one which does not lend itself to photography. Structural additions and a large dormer have altered original lines. The plate records the granary door in the east wall as a detail of importance.

273

PLATE 91

House of Evert Terwilliger.

The house built in 1738 by Evert Terwilliger stands on the highway between New Paltz and Modena, Ulster County. In walls and floor-plan it is typical of the time of its erection. Although probably not original, the wood-trim is now old and harmonizes with the house. A stream, locust trees and lilac bushes create a setting artistic in quality.

PLATE 92

Unidentified House, 1752.

Near High Falls, Ulster County, is a house built in 1752 by an unidentified owner. About 1806 a new owner, Benjamin Hasbrouck, put in a new front door with a fan-light and cut crescent-shaped windows under the eaves in the front wall. False windows, crescents in shape, were put in each gable. The porch, dormer and window-glass are changes of still later date. Particularly worthy of note is the curve in the roof-line of the wing. Behind the camera is a stone smokehouse.

PLATE 93

Unidentified House, called Feather Farm.

Very little is known of the history of the house shown in plate 93. It stands on the former stagecoach route between High Falls and Ellenville in Ulster County and looks eastward to Sky Top at Lake Mohonk. The dormers, shutters and window-glass are modern; but walls, floor-plan and interior finish are of the eighteenth century and are similar to those of the house of Johannes G. Hardenbergh (plate 74), built near Kerhonkson in 1762.

PLATE 94

House at Kripplebush,

Ulster County. Crude in masonry, out of repair and yet, withal, possessed of character. A good example of eighteenth century farmhouses in the interior of Ulster. A stone in the east wall is cut: M L 1772.

PLATE 95

Unidentified House, detail.

This door and window overlook the *King's Highway* in the town of Rochester, Ulster County. They are part of a small, undated house, the name of whose builder is forgotten. There could be no more perfect example of the designs and workmanship of the doors and windows of the farmhouses of Ulster in the eighteenth century than the plate affords.

PLATE 96

Van Aken House,

town of Esopus, Ulster County. From a photograph taken about 1870 and obtained through the courtesy of Mrs. Henry Van Aken of Port Ewen, N. Y. In outline and proportion the house was then typical of architecture in Ulster early in the eighteenth century. The small number of windows bears witness to the period of the pioneer.

PLATE 97

House at the corner of Green Street and Maiden Lane,

Kingston, N. Y. Owned in the eighteenth century by the Van Buren family. Partly burned by the British in 1777.
Lately restored.

PLATE 98

Van Deusen House.

On the north side of the street, Hurley, Ulster County, is the Van Deusen house, built about 1744. It is an L in shape, solid in construction and well finished. Many original details survive, some have disappeared and been replaced by modern reproductions. In the fall of 1777 the Committee of Safety of the State of New York held sessions for a month in the house.

PLATE 99

The Van Keuren house

at Green and John Streets, Kingston, was one of the dwellings partly burned by the British in 1777. It has lately been restored, and its shutters, porch-hood and other trim reproduce suitable early designs.

PLATE 100

House of Jacob Aertsen Van Wagenen,

town of Rosendale, Ulster County. One of five stone houses at *Wagen Dal* on the Rondout, all homesteads of the Van Wagenen family. The front portion of the house shown in plate 100 is cut with the date: 1699; the rear is undated but early. A descendant of Jacob Aertsen Van Wagenen owns and occupies the house.

PLATE 101

The small house near Wawarsing,

Ulster County, shown in plate 101, may have been the home in the eighteenth century of the Vernooys or of the Beviers; but in either case it is a survival of the type of dwelling built in the Rondout valley when the valley was the western frontier of the Province of New York. The house was raided in 1781 by Tories and Indians. The plate was made from a photograph taken in 1906 by Clarence J. Elting of Highland, N. Y., which was obtained through his courtesy.

284

PLATE 102

Westbrook House.

The rear wing of the Westbrook house on Peter's Kill, Ulster County, retains much of its original appearance. Under the vines is a Dutch oven, and the doorway, windows and shutters and the overhang of the roof all witness to a well defined type of domestic architecture of the eighteenth century. About 1800 the roof of the main portion was raised on a crown of wood, small windows were cut in the front at the new eaves-line and a new front door was put in. The location of the house is one of true rural beauty.

PLATE 103

The Wynkoop Farm.

West of the village of Hurley at the base of a mountain-ridge lies the farm that Cornelius Wynkoop purchased about 1667 and title to which remained in the name of Wynkoop until 1904. The plate illustrates the relation of the farm-land to the ridge and the sheltered position of the homestead. The house overlooks rich alluvial flats, bordering the Esopus Creek, and the view is bounded at the south by the Shawangunks at Sky Top where the sky-line of the hills is particularly interesting.

PLATE 104

Wynkoop-Lounsbery House.

In size, plan and finish the house built at Stone Ridge about 1772 by Cornelius Wynkoop is conspicuous by comparison with all other houses now standing in Ulster. The roof is one of the few gambrels in the county, the two-story walls were exceptional in 1772, and the floor-plan and wood-trim of the interior show an advanced standard of living. The nineteenth century porch is a regrettably discordant item in an otherwise admirable whole.

287

PLATE 105

The doorway of the Wynkoop-Schoonmaker house,

town of Saugerties, Ulster County, shows a genuinely primitive door-frame and steps. The door of vertical strips, battened on the inner side, bears excellent wrought iron hinges and latch. The glass insert is probably of much later date than the door itself.

WESTCHESTER COUNTY

GARDEN-PATH,
VAN CORTLANDT MANOR HOUSE

WESTCHESTER COUNTY

WHATEVER ELSE may, in the long run, have affected the development of domestic architecture in Westchester County, the primary influences at work before 1776 were the racial make-up of the population and the forms of land-tenure which prevailed.

The county was organized as an administrative unit in 1683 (when all the counties in New York were created by an Act of the Provincial Assembly) but, before then, land had been purchased within the area that subsequently was marked out as the county of Westchester and settlers had arrived to occupy it.

Those portions of Westchester which touch the Connecticut line on the east were taken up by families from New England and the same was true in the county where, at the south, it faces the Sound, except that at New Rochelle there was a notable French community. The Dutch element in Westchester was to be found from the Harlem river, northward, in a narrow strip of territory that extended the length of the county's frontage on the Hudson and which was punctuated by Dutch churches at Fordham, Sleepy Hollow and Cortlandtville. While an occasional Dutch family might have been noted in the northeastern, eastern, central and southeastern parts of Westchester, those neighborhoods were predominantly English in character and only along the western border could any communities be pointed to that were essentially Dutch in feeling. A searcher, looking in Westchester for Dutch homes prior in date to 1776, could therefore hope for reward only in that restricted section and the survey made for this volume has in the main been confined to that.

Land in Westchester was acquired by white men partly by purchases for which Crown patents were obtained and partly in manorial grants. Four small manors (Fordham, 1671; Pelham, 1687; Morrisania, 1697; and Scarsdale, 1701) were south of the center of the county, with their natural outlook toward the Sound and toward New York City. The two large manors, Philipsborough (1693) and the Manor of Cortlandt (1697), occupied the shore-line of Westchester on the Hudson, Philipsborough from Spuyten Duyvil to the Croton river and the Manor of Cortlandt from the Croton northward to the county-line (barring Ryck's Patent, a small parcel at Peekskill), and on those two manors were gathered most of the Dutch residents of the county.

Living conditions on the manors were those of the leasehold system, the system of landlord and tenant. A leaseholder could cultivate a farm, have a comfortable dwelling and enjoy many physical comforts but he could hardly go beyond a certain degree of material prosperity as he could not obtain absolute title to the values he himself created. This fact led, ultimately, to the removal of energetic young men from the farms on the manors to freehold lands elsewhere. In Rockland, Orange and Dutchess Counties many a family name is heard which can be traced to Westchester and it is certain that about 1725—1750 there was a definite outward movement from the manors to those parts of the Hudson valley where greater independence and opportunity could be had.

The leasehold system also acted as a check to a rising standard in housebuilding. The houses that were built on the manors at an early date were of stone, in the style commonly followed by the pioneers in all the river-counties and of which many examples are recorded between these present covers. But of all the stone farmhouses standing on the two great manors in Westchester before the Revolution there are now few left. After diligent search one was found to which few alterations had been made (plate 107) and the reader is asked to accept the one as typical of many.

That the stone houses of Westchester were similar to the stone houses in the other counties is witnessed to by the record of the house of Wolvert Ecker, which Washington Irving remodelled and called: *Sunnyside;* and also by the Martlingh-Van Tassel-Van Houten-Mott house on Broadway, Tarrytown (recently torn down to make room for a new school-building), which is said to have served Irving as a prototype for the house he wrote of in the: *Legend of Sleepy Hollow.* In 1866 Lossing published in: *The Hudson from the Wilderness to the Sea* a sketch of the house of Wolvert Ecker, which shows a stone dwelling of one and one-half stories, with roof of single slant and clapboarded gable. Of the Martlingh house Edgar Mayhew Bacon made a sketch shortly before it was removed, a copy of which drawing is included in his work: *The Chronicles of Tarrytown and Sleepy Hollow.* The drawing records a stone house, square in proportion, with a modern porch and a frame addition, but which in the height of the walls and line of the roof was true to form.

In: *The History of Westchester County,* published in 1886 by J. T. Scharf, there is quoted an unprinted manuscript, written by Mrs. Pierre Van Cortlandt of the manor-house at Croton, which contained an account of the early homes on the manors and in which paper the writer referred to the typical stone houses and stated that there were also some early houses built of brick. Mrs. Van Cortlandt mentioned shingled siding and roofs of double pitch (the gambrel) as coming into use in a later period of construction and she described features of the exteriors and interiors of the houses (such as: *stoeps* and lean-tos; and the large fireplaces, the panelling and wainscoting and the chairboards) which were then to be seen throughout the length of the Hudson valley.

Mrs. Van Cortlandt's testimony is almost as good as that of a camera. She was an accurate observer and had had every opportunity to learn exactly the conditions that once obtained on the manors. It is unfortunate that there is so little now left standing with which to supplement her account pictorially. Of the brick houses and the gambrel roofs of which she tells no trace has been found except in one instance, a brick house at Cortlandtville, built by the Van Cortlandt family in 1773, which originally had a gambrel roof but which later was given wings and piazzas and a different roof and is now, to all appearances, a house of late date. In the absence of complete information it is impossible to judge to what extent the brick houses with gambrels flourished in Westchester in the eighteenth century. They are noted in Rensselaer County before 1750; north of Albany 1750—1760; in Columbia County in the 1760's; in Dutchess in the 1760's and 1770's; but it is open to proof whether or not they were built in Westchester in any number before 1776. The War of the Revolution did away with entails in New York and after the war many manorial farms were purchased in fee simple. At that time improvements in house-building probably occurred and the people of Westchester would naturally have continued to use the architectural style that prevailed immediately before the war for it is an established fact that a considerable time elapsed after the Peace of 1783 before architecture in America was affected by any new influences. The next period of distinct change and development was that of the first quarter of the nineteenth century.

Over against the story of the dwellings of the tenants on the Manor of Philipse-borough and the Manor of Cortlandt must be set the story of the houses on the manors that were occupied by the two manorial families, the Philipses and the Van Cortlandts, and as soon as analysis is made of the latter it is evident that it consists of two parts, one that relates to absentee landlords and one to resident proprietors. The first chapter has to do with the profits of trade with the natives; with the clearing of the forest; the fear of attack by Indians; the building of strong houses and of saw-mills and grist-mills; and the coming of tenants to newly opened farms. In those first years the lords of the two manors had their homes in New York City and they used the substantial stone structures on the manors only occasionally when they came from New York to transact the business connected with their mills and farms.

Frederick Philipse (born 1626, died 1702), first lord of Philipse Manor, had two stone buildings which served him in the manner just outlined. One was on the Neperhan at the present Yonkers; one on the Pocantico at Sleepy Hollow; and both are still standing in the sense that their foundations and walls are in existence. But the two rectangular constructions of stone have been so added to and covered by later additions that their identity is lost completely. At the mouth of the Croton a stone structure owned by Stephanus Van Cortlandt (born 1643, died 1700) is said by tradition to have been built by fur-traders as a dépôt for their goods and to have been taken over by Stephanus Van Cortlandt in 1687 when he bought the land. It was not until many years later that it assumed the form in which it now appears (plate 109).

Of these three buildings the one at Sleepy Hollow continued as a place of transient residence only, the property of an absentee owner, until in 1785 it was purchased by Gerard G. Beekman and became his fixed home. The other two were transformed into important permanent dwellings for resident owners and many changes and alterations were made in them. As they first were built the three stone houses were a development on a larger scale of the general architectural type of the houses on the farms and resembled some of the better stone houses of the upper valley of the Hudson, such as the houses of Ariaantje Coeymans, Francis Salisbury and John Brinckerhoff (plates 18, 30, 114). The house on the Croton is said to have been taken over as a permanent home by Pierre Van Cortlandt of New York City in 1749 and from that day to this it has been a center of family-life with gracious traditions clustered about it. The house on the Neperhan was ultimately so enlarged as to be a veritable mansion (in the popular sense of the word), covering an extensive ground-area; having large rooms, broad halls, imposing stairways and with woodwork carved so elaborately as to be almost overpowering in its effect.

The enlargement and decoration of the Philipse house at Yonkers is attributed to the second lord of Philipse Manor who was married in 1719 and died in 1751. Tradition cites the year 1745 as the date of the changes made by him but for the accuracy of that there is no proof and an exact date is not of special moment. It is obvious that in the second quarter of the eighteenth century wealth and sophistication had reached a point in New York City where a resident there was led to make of his property in the country a great country-seat, at which he lived for a large part of every year, and in which he entertained lavishly and created a social center, famous for luxury and gayety. The mode of life in the house at Yonkers,—where were fifty servants (white and black), a bountiful larder, handsome dress, prominent guests, formal functions,—was at one extreme of the social scale and the farmhouse on the *King's Highway* (plate 107) at the other and the contrast between the two forms an epitome of the life on the manors in the eighteenth century.

The house of Frederick Van Cortlandt (plate 110) at Lower Yonkers (now Van Cortlandt Park), which was built in 1748, is also a reflection of the standards of living created by the wealth of the merchant-class of New York City and it should be bracketed with the Philipse manor-house at Yonkers as a mansion and as the product of the material prosperity of its period. Socially and economically it represented the city rather than the country and architecturally it was an exotic.

In a general way the architectural history of Westchester County is akin to that of Dutchess. Westchester and Dutchess lie south and north of the Highlands, respectively, the mass of the mountains between them, but in terrain they resemble each other and the distribution of the racial elements of the population of the two counties was much the same, with the result that in both the frame houses of the families from New England predominated in certain sections and the stone houses

294

of the Dutch in another. At New Rochelle the French made use of both stone and wood. Little is now left standing there of eighteenth century construction but *New Rochelle Through Seven Generations* (C. H. Augus, 1908), *The French Blood in America* (Lucian J. Fosdick, 1906) and other published works contain pictures of houses of stone and of wood, built with the usual story-and-a-half walls and with roofs of single slant; some houses whitewashed, some shingled and some clap-boarded. In a few instances the rear roof-lines sloped nearly to the ground and in the case of the Guion and Parquot and Pugsley houses and an un-named Huguenot house on the Lester farm there were used shingles with rounded lower end that matched the shingles on the houses of Madam Brett and Henry Livingston and Johannes Coerte Van Voorhees in Dutchess (plates 111, 128 and 144). In a picture of an old house at Peck Slip and Water street, New York, published in Valentine's *Manual for the City of New York for 1858*, opposite page 248, similar shingles are shown.

HOUSES in WESTCHESTER COUNTY

Dutch Church, Philipse Manor
Sleepy Hollow, Westchester County, New York
PLATE 106

At North Tarrytown, on a knoll, where the state road runs down-grade to the bridge over Pocantico Brook in Sleepy Hollow, stands the Dutch church that was built by the first lord of Philipse Manor. A view of this church-building is included in a volume devoted to a record of Dutch homes in the Hudson valley because association with the Reformed Dutch Communion was an essential factor in the life of every Dutch household living between New York and Albany and also because the stone structure at Sleepy Hollow is one of the most distinctly Dutch bits of construction now left in the river-region. The exact date of its erection is uncertain. On the iron church-bell, made in Holland, is the date: 1685; settlers gathered along the Pocantico in the 1680's and the 1690's; a resident domine was called in 1697 for a congregation then in existence and the church-building was certainly put up by order of the first lord of the manor, who died in 1702. So it can safely be attributed to the late seventeenth century.

The photograph reproduced in plate 106 shows the north wall and the east end of the church, which were chosen for illustration for the reason that they are almost the same now as when built. The original entrance to the church was in the middle of the south wall but in 1837 that door was closed and a new one opened in the west end and, at the same time, all the windows were cut down about two feet and given pointed tops. Except for the enlargement of the windows, the exterior of the church as shown in the photograph looks the same as when the first settlers of Philipse Manor worshipped within it. Surmounting the east end of the building is a seventeenth century, wrought iron weather-vane, which is cut with the letters: VF, in a monogram to record the name of the donor, Vreedryck Fylipse (as he signed his name), first lord of Philipse Manor. The interior was altered in 1837, and the building is used now only for special ceremonial occasions, not for regular services.

The congregation of the church at Sleepy Hollow was made up of Dutch families (except for a negligible sprinkling of Huguenots and English) and remained strongly Dutch in feeling so late as 1785, when it revolted vigorously against Domine Van Voorhees, who had the temerity to use the English language at a baptismal service. In the days before the Revolution the congregation presented a striking picture of class distinction in the social life of Philipse Manor. Between the manor-family on the one side and the congregation as a whole on the other there was a line of social cleavage which only disappeared after the Revolution, when the manorial lands were confiscated and sold. It was inevitable that the feudal system, operating in close proximity to freehold land-tenure, should meet with difficulty and for the student of history or of economics there is much that is informing to be learned from the local conditions that are reflected in the story of the Dutch church at Sleepy Hollow.

Dutch Farmhouse, Philipse Manor
Irvington, Westchester County, New York
PLATE 107

The house shown in plate 107 is a perfect example of the Dutch farmhouses that were to be seen on Philipse Manor in the eighteenth century. It is almost the only one of its kind that now remains and it stands a little south of Irvington, on the west side of the state road (Broadway), occupied as the gatehouse of an estate and with modern motor-traffic rushing, roaring past it day and night, in striking contrast to the placidity of its eighteenth century simplicity.

Facing south, the house has a porch across the front and consists in its main portion of two rooms, behind which a lean-to provides further floor-space. The two rooms of the main part were built at different dates. That at the east end has four thick walls of stone and the one toward the west has three frame walls. Evidently the stone unit was one of the early and primitive dwellings on the manor and was the work of a pioneer, who built a substantial shelter of just one room with an attic above it. The attic must have been reached by a ladder for there is no trace of a stairway within the four stone walls. The present half-story is partitioned into three rooms and is reached by an enclosed staircase that rises from the west room. In the north wall of the stone house there is or was a large fireplace (now closed) and there is now a little panelled woodwork on either side of the fireplace, which probably was added when the house was enlarged by the addition of the west room. A clue to the date of the addition is afforded by a stone in the south wall marked:

C

M   S

May 8

1746

The stone house was almost square in its proportions and its roof must have been one of sharply pitched single slant. By the addition of the second room the house assumed lines familiar in the Hudson valley in 1746 and thoroughly typical of that time. In the east wall the original stonework is still open to view. The south wall is stuccoed and the west end is completely clapboarded. Some of the window-

298

sashes are of early date. An unusually good example of an eighteenth century door gives entrance from the porch to the east room, the door being made with broad boards, set vertically, cut across the center and hung by specially large wrought iron hinges (in a pattern common to all the river-counties). The door is set at the inner line of the thick stone wall and over it are two rows of small panes of glass.

Associated with this house are the names of Captain Jan Harmense and Jonathan Odell. Captain Harmense, a son-in-law of Ryck Abrahamsen Lent (one of the patentees of Ryck's Patent that covered the site of Peekskill), was a witness to a baptism in the church at Sleepy Hollow in 1699. He joined the church in 1717, became a member of the consistory and died between 1739 and 1742, in which years his will was made and proved. Captain Harmense left grandchildren (children of his daughter, Grietje, the wife of Herman Montross) but whether any of them succeeded him in his stone house is not clear. By the time the Revolutionary war began the house was occupied by Jonathan Odell and it is assumed that this house is the one referred to when, on August 31, 1776, the Committee of Safety of New York, on its way from Harlem to Fishkill, held a meeting " at the house of Mr. Odell in Philipse's Manor."

Philipse Manor-House, detail

Yonkers, New York

PLATE 108

At the corner of Warburton Avenue and Dock Street in the city of Yonkers is a long, low building of stone and brick which was the manor-house of Philipse Manor in the years before the Revolution and which has a romantic history. The house is now owned by the State of New York and is open to the public as an historical museum, with the American Scenic and Historic Preservation Society occupying it as custodian. In 1912 a member of that society, Edward Hagaman Hall, L. H. D., published an account of the Philipse house which is an admirably accurate monograph and to it the reader is referred for many details that cannot be included in these pages for lack of space. Mr. Hall reviewed the facts in the history of the title to the manor; the documentary references to the manor-house as a building; the genealogical and social history of the Philipse family; the manor-house as the scene of great social events; its setting in the neutral ground between the American and British forces in the Revolution; and, finally, its fate as part of the confiscated estate of a prominent Loyalist.

Briefly to summarize the story of the manor-house it may be said that Frederick Philipse, a rich merchant of New York City, began to buy land along the Hudson above Spuyten Duyvil in 1672 and that in 1693 his several purchases were consolidated and chartered as a manor. Before 1672 other men had begun the work of settlement at the mouth of the Neperhan (the stream that flows through the city of Yonkers), and it only remained for Frederick Philipse to continue their endeavors and to make of the locality an important center, which he did. He operated a mill on the Neperhan and had near it a stone house, which served as a dwelling when he came up from the city to superintend his affairs in the country and which also was held as a place of safety in case of Indian attacks. The year 1682 is often quoted as the date of the erection of this house but the exact date is not really known and it does not really matter; the important point is that during the last quarter of the seventeenth century Frederick Philipse developed the neighborhood at the mouth of the Neperhan on permanent lines, much as Madam Brett opened up the lands of the Rombout Patent in Dutchess at the mouth of the *Vis Kil* in 1708 (page 325).

Frederick Philipse himself lived in New York City (where he had a handsome house at the corner of Whitehall and Stone Streets) and when he died in 1702 he willed his estate at Yonkers to his grandson (the child of his deceased elder son), Frederick Philipse, the second (born 1695, died 1751), who succeeded him as lord of the manor. The second lord came into his property at his majority in 1716, married in 1719 and was the father of ten children (born between 1720 and 1742). He maintained a home in his grandfather's house in New York and was a man prominent in the business, social and political affairs of the province. To him, with his numerous family, is attributed the enlargement of the house at Yonkers from a rectangular stone structure of medium size to an ell-shaped building. The base of the ell, which faces south, is composed of an east and west parlor on the first floor and an east and west bedroom on the second, with a broad hall between each pair of rooms and a wide stairway leading in two square turns from the lower floor to the upper. A thick stone wall separates the hall and the east parlor, and it is supposed that it was the outer east wall of the original house. The east parlor was built on, against the old wall, and a wing was extended northward from the new room so as to form the arm of the ell. In the wing another broad hall (with a handsome stairway) lies between the east parlor and a dining room. Beyond the dining room were kitchen and pantries, the floor-space of which was all thrown into one in the nineteenth century. All the rooms in the manor-house are large and suited to formal, ceremonial living. The roof is a peculiar one. It rises from the eaves to a balustrade and presents from the ground the appearance of a hipped roof with a flat deck but, within the balustrade, is a second upward slope to the ridge-pole and so it may be classed as a gambrel.

At the death of the second lord of the manor in 1751 the house passed to his son, Frederick Philipse (born 1720, died 1786), the third and last lord, who is reputed to have had quiet, literary tastes and to have been especially interested in landscape gardening, so that in his day the grounds around the manor-house were laid out and developed.

Philipse Manor-House was one of the few houses outside of New York City

300

in the Province of New York in the middle of the eighteenth century which were notably large and elegant. Passing by its social and historical importance, its architectural significance is to be considered and, in the last analysis, that significance lies in the fact that the house was a growth, an aggregation of parts. In that respect it is one of a group of houses which illustrate the principle of growth along original native lines, in response to individual needs and circumstances, but which also to some extent reflect an effort to adapt old buildings to new ideas. Some of the other houses in this group are: *Crailo* (page 113); *Klaver Rak* (plate 48); and the Glen-Sanders, Nicoll, Van Vechten, Kip-Beekman and Livingston houses (plates 23, 29, 53, 125 and 128).

In contrast to the above group of houses there stands out another, composed of: *Clermont*, 1730 (page 87); the house of Frederick Van Cortlandt, 1748 (plate 110); *The Pastures*, 1762 (page 97); the Van Rensselaer manor-house, 1765 (page 112); and *Vly House*, before 1767 (plate 21). This second group of houses represents the direct result of the importation of architectural designs. Each house was built as a unit, according to plans decided upon in advance, and none was altered subsequently in any way that changed its primary character. With this second group Philipse Manor-House has in common the fact that it was given elaborate interior trim made from Georgian English designs. A comparison of the east staircase and of the panelling in the east hall of the house at Yonkers with the main staircase and woodwork in the hall of *The Pastures* at Albany will illustrate this point.

As most of the photographs of Philipse Manor-House show the whole building, which inevitably has acquired something of the appearance of a public institution, plate 108 records merely a detail, the south doorway, which is offered as domestic in quality and in keeping with the spirit of this work. The picture was taken under difficulties because of lack of adequate space for the camera.

Philipse Castle

North Tarrytown, New York

The community of North Tarrytown occupies a tract of land which was purchased in 1680 by Frederick Philipse of New York City and which in 1693 was included in the area set up by Crown charter as the Manor of Philipseborough. At an early day Frederick Philipse began to utilize the water-power of Pocantico Brook (which enters the Hudson at North Tarrytown) by building a mill on the stream. Near the mill he erected a stone house and invited settlers to come upon his land. In the 1690's enough Dutch families had gathered within a radius of the mill to constitute a congregation of the Reformed Dutch Church and at an undetermined date the lord of the manor built the stone church shown in plate 106, for their accomodation and benefit.

301

The stone house on the Pocantico (which acquired the name of Philipse Castle) was not used by Frederick Philipse as a permanent home. His mercantile interests in New York were such as to keep him in the city most of the time but the house was a necessity as a place to stay when the business of the manor was to be transacted. When the first lord of the manor died in 1702 he willed the property on the Pocantico to his second son, Adolphus Philipse (born 1665, died 1750), and he, at his death, bequeathed it to his nephew, the second lord. The latter died the following year and the place passed to his son, the third lord, from whom it was confiscated in 1779. In 1785 the Commissioners of Forfeiture sold the property to Gerard G. Beekman. Mr. Beekman died in 1822 and in 1835 his widow (Cornelia Van Cortlandt Beekman) laid out the land adjoining the house in building-lots, a measure which ultimately created a center called Beekmantown (now North Tarrytown). Mrs. Beekman died in 1847 and her heirs continued to hold the house until (1860?). Since then the title has passed through several names, the owner in 1926 being Miss Elsie Janis. As owned and occupied by Miss Janis, the house appears to be solely a modern clapboarded dwelling, painted white, and the travelling public, passing on the state road near by, have no occasion to suspect that it includes within its wood siding a core of stone masonry that dates from before 1700 and which had two-hundred years of independent existence before undergoing eclipse.

The southern end of Miss Janis's house is the portion built by the first lord of Philipse Manor. It was a rectangle of stone nearly square in its proportions and as such stood from before 1700 until about 1785, when Mr. Beekman bought it. Mr. Beekman built an addition toward the north, which made the house an ell in shape and which increased its east wall to a much greater length. In the nineteenth century a frame wing was put on at the south end of the west wall and changes were made in porches and other details; while still a third transformation took place when the building was done over as at present. The author of: *The Chronicles of Tarrytown and Sleepy Hollow*, Edgar Mayhew Bacon, has preserved therein the information that according to his personal observations the walls of the early house were more solidly built than those of the addition toward the north; that in the southwest wall of the cellar were portholes; that the ceilings, doors and mantels in the first part differed from the trim in the part built about 1785; that the front and rear doors of the hall in the first part were divided in halves and finished with heavy transverse bars of oak, bound with iron; and that the inner doors between rooms were made with joiner work characteristic of the Dutch in the seventeenth century.

In 1866 Benson J. Lossing published in: *The Hudson from the Wilderness to the Sea* a sketch of Philipse Castle as he imagined it to have looked before the addition was made to the north, a sketch of which an enlarged copy is shown in: *Sleepy Hollow Church Records*, printed 1901 by the Yonkers Historical and Library Association. In the latter volume there is also a photograph, made from a high point south of the Castle, which affords some confirmation for the sketch. There are also two views of the house on file in the library of the Metropolitan Museum, New York City. One is a woodcut (scrapbook: *Colonial Architecture*, volume 1, page 139), endorsed as from a photograph of 1876, and the other (ibid.: page 334) is a photograph made in 1904; but both show more of the additions and the alterations than they do of the original structure.

One problem the house presents and that is in connection with the roof. Lossing's sketch records a gambrel roof, places the main entrance to the house in the gable-end and would make the central hall parallel with the ridge-pole,—an anomalous arrangement throughout. Furthermore a gambrel on a house built before 1700 is definitely open to suspicion and when that fact is taken in conjunction with the further one that the gambrel was in use in 1785 when the Beekmans bought the Castle it is at least a plausible theory that, as built before 1700, the house had a roof of single slant, sloping north and south, (which would allow for a main door to the south and a north-and-south hall, as in Lossing's sketch), and that when the north wing was added the old roof was removed and a new gambrel placed over all.

The location of Philipse Castle, still attractive, must have been particularly beautiful in its natural state. Pocantico Brook rises on higher ground above and follows a winding course to the river through the valley called Sleepy Hollow and the Castle stands close to the stream. North and east of the house on a slight elevation is the Dutch church (plate 106) of Sleepy Hollow and the *King's Highway* runs north and south between the two. The lesser buildings of a small town now occupy what once was open ground in the immediate vicinity but with the eye of the imagination it is possible to visualize the scenery which tempted the pen of Irving.

An article, entitled: *History of the Domestic Affairs of the Inhabitants of New York, Anterior to the Time of the Revolutionary War*, was published by D. T. Valentine in: *The Manual of the Corporation of the City of New York for 1858*, in which a detailed account is given of the store in New York of Adolphus Philipse and of his house at Sleepy Hollow. Mr. Philipse was one of the largest importers of his day in New York and his three-story warehouse was stocked with grain, hardware, silverware, dry goods and general merchandize. Of his house on the Pocantico the article says:—" Mr. Philipse, whose manor-house at Tarrytown had been erected by his father and was surrounded by an estate of many miles in extent, made this country residence his occasional home, although his mercantile pursuits in the city for the most part required his absence from his estate. Mr. Aartse was the overseer of this establishment. The consequence of the absenteeism of the lord was of course the absence of all the usual appendages of state and social style in manorial life and the manor house was at this period simply the head-quarters of the estate, at which upon stated periods the tenants paid their rents in wheat. The house was situated at the head of a little bay on the river shore, into which emptied the stream which traversed Sleepy hollow. A dam at the head of the bay formed a mill-pond adjacent to the house and a mill, the only one in that vicinity, was the great center of cereal deposit of that district. On the estate were six working-slaves, four aged and infirm, five women, seven boys and a girl; six oxen, twelve cows, twenty-four heifers, thirty sheep, twenty-seven hogs, three stable horses, three horses in the woods, seventeen mares, and colts. In the room of the manor house occupied by Mr. Philipse on his visits the furniture consisted of a backgammon-table, a brass candlestick, a Dutch Bible, and some other books, bed and bedding, a looking-glass, a trunk, six cane chairs, a wig-block, a case with bottles, a pair of handcuffs, and a slate and pencil. The furniture of the other rooms was of an ordinary and plain description."

Van Cortlandt Manor-House
Croton-on-Hudson, New York
PLATE 109

Of the countless travellers who gaze idly through train-windows while engines are exchanged at Harmon on the New York Central and Hudson River Railroad, thirty miles north of the terminal in New York City, how many observe the Van Cortlandt Manor-House on the north side of the Croton river near the highway-bridge and, seeing it, recognize it as one of the important historic landmarks of the Hudson valley?

The Croton enters the Hudson just below the railroad-yards and the point of land that forms the northern boundary of its mouth was a gathering-place of the Indians, a place where they had a village, fisheries and a burial-ground. A generally accepted tradition states that in the seventeenth century white men established a trading-post near this Indian center, in order to deal with the natives in furs, fish and game, and that soon the newcomers began to buy land also. One of the men who became interested in real estate in upper Westchester was Stephanus Van Cortlandt (born 1643, died 1700), a prosperous merchant of New York City, who by 1687 had acquired eighty-five-thousand acres. For his great estate he obtained in 1697 from the English Crown a charter, erecting it into a manor with a court leet and court baron and with provision for the inheritance of the lordship of the manor under the law of primogeniture.

A second tradition, locally endorsed, is that when, about 1687, Stephanus Van Cortlandt took possession of his land along the Croton river there was standing on it a square stone building with a flat roof, which had been the dépôt of the former trading-post and, further, it is believed that the walls of the main part of the present house are the walls of that dépôt. Built of red sandstone, the walls are three feet thick and they are pierced with funnel-shaped openings, similar to the musketry embrasures in the walls of *Crailo* (page 113) and of the DuBois house (page 198).

It is said that at a date not known the flat roof of the fort-like dépôt was replaced by the Van Cortlandts with a roof of single slant and the interior of the structure adapted to occupation as a dwelling. But the house did not become a family home for all the year until 1749 and, in the period between 1687 and 1749, the understanding is that the members of the Van Cortlandt family lived in New York City and used the place on the Croton as a hunting-lodge and as an office at which to conduct business with their tenants.

Stephanus Van Cortlandt died in 1700 and the manor-land was held in common by his heirs until 1734, when a division was made by which his son, Philip (born 1683, died 1746), took title to the portion bordering the north side of the Croton, on which stood the stone house. From Philip Van Cortlandt the house was inherited by his son, Pierre (born 1721, died 1814), who in 1749 married, left New York City, and made the house at Croton his permanent residence. Pierre Van Cortlandt's wife was Joanna Livingston and it is pertinent to interpolate that she was a sister of Henry Livingston of Poughkeepsie and a niece of Henry Beekman of Rhinebeck, whose houses are shown in plates 128 and 125.

Kinship with the Beekmans was undoubtedly the reason which, in 1777, made Rhinebeck a place of refuge for the family of Pierre Van Cortlandt. To his character of country gentleman he had added valuable service in public affairs and, when the Revolution came, he was a member of the second, third and fourth Provincial Congresses and president of the Council of Safety. His house at Croton thus became the object of Tory attacks and, when the lower reaches of the Hudson fell into the hands of the British in 1777, the members of his household were obliged to seek safety in Dutchess County, where they are supposed to have lived in the house shown in plate 125. They returned to Westchester after a time only to find that the manor-house had had hard usage and needed immediate repair. From those repairs, made at the close of the Revolution, dates the panelled woodwork which is now in the four rooms of the main part of the house. Pierre Van Cortlandt continued long in public life, holding office as lieutenant-governor of New York from 1777 to 1795, and he died at the ripe age of ninety-four. About 1810, under his son, Philip (born 1750, died 1831), a wing was added at the northeast rear corner of the manor-house and about 1845 another Pierre Van Cortlandt built a wing at the northwest rear corner. The date of the erection of the broad veranda across the south front of the house (plate 109) is uncertain but in style it suggests the nineteenth century and it is fair to assume that the veranda followed the wing of 1845.

For the purpose of this volume, that is: the collection of data regarding houses built before 1776, it is necessary in considering the manor-house at Croton to forget the two wings and the veranda and to visualize the stone house as it was without those additions. The house was built on sloping ground, a location that afforded opportunity for the large front basement on the lower level, which still contains primitive features. The rear door of the hall on the main floor opens on the upper ground-level and the floor-plan of the first story is the one found in so many houses of the eighteenth century: two larger rooms in front, two smaller at the back and a hall between. For this floor-plan comparison should be made with the Van Rensselaer, Van Deusen, Wynkoop, Brett, Brinckerhoff, De Peyster, Van Wyck and Verplanck houses (plates 50, 98, 104, 111, 114, 115, 146, 147, 148 and 149), and for the entrance with high steps, which presumably preceded the veranda, reference should be had to the Coeymans, Van Wie and DePeyster houses (plates 18, 54 and 115), which were built on two levels and which have doorways high above the ground.

The Van Cortlandt Manor-House is one of that small number of houses now remaining in the Hudson valley which were established as homes before the Revolution and which are not only still occupied by descendants of the original owners but which have been maintained in accordance with rising standards of living. At Croton the best of the past has been retained, the best of each later period incorporated. The house is filled with the treasures of successive generations in furniture, portraits and documents and is instinct with the spirit of hospitality. Could the message of the manor-house but penetrate the consciousness of some modern nomads, the nomads might realize that the easily folded tent is found wanting when weighed in the balance with the things the old homes stand for.

House of Frederick Van Cortlandt

Van Cortlandt Park, New York City

PLATE 110

The house now standing in Van Cortlandt Park, New York City, which is owned by the city and is cared for as custodian by the Society of Colonial Dames, was built in 1748 by Frederick Van Cortlandt (born 1698, died 1749), who was a nephew of the first lord of Van Cortlandt Manor. Although the house is within the corporate limits of the city of New York it is not on Manhattan Island and, being north of Spuyten Duyvil, its site is within the territory surveyed for this volume, for which reason it is listed here; but no detailed description of it is offered in these pages because accounts of its structure and history have already been published and as a public museum it is visited by thousands of people and is well known. The view of the house shown in plate 110 is from the northeast and was chosen as one less familiar than that of the south front, which has often been photographed, and which is seen by all who approach the building from the city.

In a survey of the pre-Revolutionary architecture of the Hudson valley the importance of the house of Frederick Van Cortlandt lies in its size and its elegance of finish as compared with the size and finish of other houses in the same territory in 1748. In those respects it was more closely akin to the best houses in New York

306

City of the same date than to the dwellings up the Hudson and, standing as it did only a short distance from the city, it was perhaps more of a suburban establishment than a rural home. In 1748 the only houses outside of New York comparable to it in size were *Clermont* (page 87) in the then Albany County and Philipse Manor-House in the present city of Yonkers; for it was not until after 1760 that the great houses of Albany were built: *The Pastures* in 1762; the new manor-house of the lord of Rensselaer manor in 1765; and *Vly House* before 1767 (pages 97 and 112; plate 21).

These several handsome dwellings, few in number, scattered in location, ranging in date from about 1730 to 1765, all showed a trend toward the Georgian English style in architecture and had many features in common. They should be studied as a group quite as much as singly. As a group they are historically significant, not primarily for their architecture as such, but because the choice of the style by the owners reflected certain social and economic conditions in the middle of the eighteenth century in the Hudson valley.

PLATE 106

Dutch Reformed Church,

Tarrytown, N. Y. Commonly called the Sleepy Hollow Church. Exact date of erection not known, but conservatively approximated as between 1685 and 1697. The north side and east end (shown in the plate) are the same as when built, except that in 1837 the windows were enlarged. The wrought iron weather-vane, given by the first lord of Philipse Manor (who died in 1702), is cut with the initials of the donor: VF, for *Vreedryck Fylipse* (Frederick Philipse). The iron bell, cast in Holland, bears the date: 1 6 8 5.

PLATE 107

Farmhouse on the former Philipse Manor,

Westchester County. Typical of the average dwelling on the manor in the eighteenth century. In general characteristics it resembles the houses built by the pioneers in Albany, Ulster and Dutchess Counties.

PLATE 108

South entrance, Philipse Manor-House,

Yonkers, N. Y. The Dutch door, with its bevelled panels, leaded light, bull's-eye and panelled jambs, is a hand-some (late eighteenth century?) detail. The roof and pillars of the porch are presumably of later date than the doorway.

PLATE 109

Van Cortlandt Manor-House,

Croton, N. Y. The house consists of a main portion of red sandstone (ascribed to the seventeenth century), a wing at each rear corner and a veranda (which were added in the nineteenth century). The stone portion, built on sloping ground, has a high front basement and should be compared with the Coeymans, Van Wie and DePeyster houses (plates 18, 54 and 115). In height, roof and floor-plan the house is typical of the eighteenth century. The portholes in the walls are similar to those in *Crailo*, Rensselaer, N. Y., and in the DuBois house at New Paltz, N. Y.

PLATE 110

Northeast wing of the house of Frederick Van Cortlandt,

Van Cortlandt Park, New York City. The main part of the house was built in 1748 and was exceptional in size for its day, when the severity of the winter climate of the Hudson valley and the inadequacy of heating facilities discouraged the erection of large houses. It was one of the first local examples of the Georgian type of architecture.

DUTCHESS COUNTY

EIGHTEENTH CENTURY
CASEMENT WINDOWS,
HOUSE OF ABRAHAM DE PEYSTER

DUTCHESS COUNTY

ON A preceding page reference has been made to the speculation in real estate which occurred in the Hudson valley in the last quarter of the seventeenth century. At that time extensive areas were erected into manors, to which feudal privileges were attached, but in addition to the manors there were tracts of wild land that were purchased from the Indians by men prominent in the community and for which Crown patents were issued. As a rule the patentees of the Crown patents made their purchases only to divide up their large holdings into smaller parcels and to sell the latter as homesteads but, in a few instances, they retained title to the land themselves and developed their properties by the system of the lease in fee. For the homesteads deeds in fee simple were given. By a lease in fee a settler, who had paid little or no money to the patentee, took possession of an uncleared parcel, laid out a farm, cultivated the same and paid to the owner a quit-rent in kind ("two fat fowls" or "a bushel of good merchantable wheat", etc.). Leases in fee were made for a term of years or for a life or lives and were subject to renewal. A lease-holder remained in possession of the land so long as he paid the quit-rent and upon failure to pay he might be evicted. The system of the lease in fee was abolished by law early in the nineteenth century and it need hardly be stated that while it was in existence it retarded social and economic progress in some sections.

To the speculative activity in the purchase of vacant lands the opening for settlement of the Dutchess's County (as it was named when created in 1683) was directly due. The territory comprised within the present boundaries of the county is covered by ten Crown patents (granted between 1685 and 1706), with the exception of a strip on the eastern edge, called (from its shape) The Oblong, which was formed in 1731 by the rectification of the boundary-line between New York and Connecticut. There were no manorial grants in Dutchess. One patent (the Rombout) was obtained with the intention of using it in connection with the fur-trade but after some years the owners found it profitable to dispose of the land in farms to incoming settlers. A few patentees adopted the policy of issuing leases in fee but the amount of land so controlled in Dutchess was relatively small. Title to the greater portion of the acreage of the county was conveyed in fee simple and the influence of the independent freeholder became the predominant one and was reflected in the general life and affairs of the people.

It was in the 1680's that white men began to come in on the forested area which

317

constituted the Dutchess's County but the first arrivals were stragglers or squatters, who failed to acquire valid title for the sites they occupied. Severyn Ten Hout and Arien Teunissen are mentioned in 1685 in records pertaining to land now contained in the town of Poughkeepsie. "Peche DeWaal" was living in 1688 (tradition says) at the mouth of the *Vis Kil*. And "Ye Frenchman" was recorded in 1689 on a map of the Rombout Patent as living at the mouth of the Wappingers. Ten Hout removed to Shawangunk, Ulster County. Teunissen disappeared. "Peche DeWaal" (who was probably Pietertje, or little Pieter, the Walloon) may have been identical with "Ye Frenchman", inasmuch as the Walloons spoke French and as confusion could easily have arisen regarding which stream he settled on; but however that was no further mention of "Peche DeWaal" has been found.

The first arrival in the county who remained as a permanent resident seems to have been Pieter Pieterse Lassen and it is not outside the bounds of possibility that the references to "Peche DeWaal" and "Ye Frenchman" really applied to him. Pieter Pieterse Lassen, who sailed from Amsterdam in the ship: *De Vergulde Beever* (The Gilded Beaver) in 1659, went to *Beverwyck* upon his arrival in New Netherland and lived there until about 1681 when he left to establish a new home down the river. He was at Esopus for a short time perhaps and finally, in June, 1688, the patent granted to Colonel Pieter Schuyler of Albany for land in Dutchess mentions as a landmark the house of Pieter immediately south of the mouth of Jan Casper's Kil in the present town of Poughkeepsie. Within recent memory a stone house (such as was built elsewhere in the river-counties before 1700) was still standing on this site and was, supposedly, the house mentioned in the patent. Or, if the house of 1688 were a log-dwelling, the stone house soon followed. A Lassen family burial-ground was near the house and the property was inherited in the Lassen family for several generations.

On the site of the city of Poughkeepsie five Dutchmen were living in June, 1691, as tenants of Robert Sanders and Myndert Harmense Van Den Bogaerdt, who had taken out the Sanders and Harmense Patent in 1686. The five men were: Baltus Barents Van Kleeck, Hendrick Oostrand, Jan Oostrum, Jan Buys and Symen Schouten and they rented land for a while, apparently to try out local conditions. Eventually Buys and Schouten removed to the valley of the *Vis Kil* in southern Dutchess; Oostrand removed to an unknown point; and Oostrum and Van Kleeck stayed at Poughkeepsie. In 1697 Baltus Barents Van Kleeck purchased outright a large farm under the Sanders and Harmense Patent and the deed from the patentees conveyed to him specifically a house and a barn. The house at Poughkeepsie, mentioned in the deed of 1697, is the second permanent dwelling in the county for which documentary evidence is at hand and the story of it is told in detail in connection with plate 142.

The next permanent occupation of home-sites in Dutchess was at *Kipsbergen*, a tract on the shore of the Hudson in the present town of Rhinebeck, for which a patent was obtained in 1688 by Gerret Aertsen Van Wagenen, Arie Roosa, Jan Elton, Hendrick Kip and Jacob Kip, all then residents of Ulster County. There in 1700 Hendrick Kip built a house, which is shown in plate 125. Another, smaller house, near by, bears a stone marked 1708 (page 348), although there is a bare possibility that it was erected just before the house of 1700.

Between 1708 and 1713 five men acquired land at the mouth of the *Vis Kil*, in the portion of the Rombout Patent that fell to the share of Catharine Rombout Brett, and they formed the third small community within the limits of the county. The five were: Casper Prince, Thomas Brasier and Youry (Jeurriaen) Springsteed, of whom little more is known, and Peter Du Bois and Jan Buys, who stayed on as lifelong residents of Dutchess.

The three small groups of pioneers at Poughkeepsie and *Kipsbergen* and *Vis Kil* all clung closely to the shore of the Hudson and penetration of the interior was slow for some years. Among the settlers who arrived in the first quarter-century were Dutchmen, Huguenots and Walloons, as well as Germans from the Palatinate. Their total number was not large however and they all were to be found within easy reach of the river. About 1740 the population of the county began to increase and the several censuses, taken from 1737 to 1771, show that from being in 1737 the seventh county in the province in point of numbers Dutchess had risen in 1746 to fifth place and in 1756 and in 1771 was listed as second only to Albany County (which was much larger in extent). This noteworthy growth was due to immigration into the county from New England, Long Island, New Jersey and Westchester County. From New England large numbers of families pushed westward and occupied the eastern half of Dutchess. The arrivals from Long Island, New Jersey and Westchester were chiefly Dutch and they chose the valleys of the *Vis Kil* and the Wappingers and the Sprout to make homes in.

Thus as a whole the population of the Dutchess's County was a mixed group. Men differing in race and in language lived near each other and they lived on a terrain which enabled them to mingle with comparative ease. Topographically, Dutchess presents a rolling surface with only one mountainous ridge to form a barrier between sections. The one ridge is in the eastern part of the county, running north and south and separating the valley of the Ten Mile River and that of the upper portion of the Croton from the remainder of the county. West of the ridge the streams flow across arable flats, from which rise meadows, upland and woodland and, because it was possible to go from place to place without encountering natural obstacles too difficult to surmount, direct effects are to be seen in the social and economic history of the people. Intermarriages occurred, customs were interchanged and the houses that were built reflect those facts for the several elements in the population are each found living in houses similar to those of the others and it is only

319

in subordinate features that individual architectural contributions can be traced.

In a general way it can be said that the stone houses in Dutchess originated with the settlers who were derived from the continent of Europe and that the frame houses were characteristic of the settlers from New England. But the general statement must be qualified for, while it is true that houses were built of wood by the English in the eastern half of the county, it is also true that a frame house was built at Poughkeepsie in 1713 by Pieter Viele, a Frisian (page 402), and that in southern Dutchess the Dutch erected many frame houses.

For a volume devoted to Dutch houses it thus becomes necessary to determine what neighborhoods in Dutchess had a distinctly Dutch quality and no better gauge exists by which to measure the extent of Dutch influence in a locality than the presence or absence of an organized congregation of the Reformed Dutch Church. Guided by that rule, it appears that before the Revolution there were in the county Dutch churches at Poughkeepsie (1716), *Vis Kil* (1716), Rhinebeck (1730), New Hackensack (1756) and Hopewell (1757); that all those churches were in the western half of the county and that the congregations were drawn from the homes established on the good farm-lands along the streams.

No tradition has been heard in Dutchess of dug-outs. By the time that the first white men arrived (1685—1700) it was possible for them to start out from well established communities, to travel by sloop on the river to the point selected for settlement, to bring supplies with them, to plan to make their journey in the spring or summer and to complete the erection of a first dwelling during warm weather. Almost immediately they built houses of stone and the use of stone in house-building continued in Dutchess until about 1800, although wood and brick both came into prominence in the middle of the eighteenth century and continued after the use of stone came to an end.

The stone houses of Dutchess were the same in general character as those in the other river-counties and numerous examples of them are noted in succeeding pages. They were almost invariably one and one-half stories in height, with roof of single slant. Before the Revolution exceptions to this rule were rare. In shape the stone houses were rectangular and their proportion was usually that of greater length than depth. The finish they contained was severely plain and there was little attempt at decoration.

Houses built of stone are found in a few instances in the eastern half of the county; one, still standing, in the Clove, was built by Nicholas Emigh in 1740; one, near Amenia Union, by Hendrick Winegar in 1761; and one in the town of Milan by the Rau-Rowe family (probably in the 1760's). The Emighs, Winegars and Raus were Germans from the Palatinate and their dwellings are mentioned in this work on Dutch houses to illustrate the fact that the Germans and the Dutch used the same materials and designs. Another item of construction by the Palatines

320

is the house of Gottlieb Martin on the Post Road at Red Hook, which stands in a locality that was settled chiefly by the Palatines and in which vicinity were once many examples of the typical stone house. The neighborhood was one where a German majority and a Dutch minority overlapped and intermingled.

The use of stone by the Dutch in house-building can be traced from the northern end of Dutchess at *Kipsbergen*, Rhinebeck and Red Hook, southward to the *Vis Kil*, in a narrow strip of territory which was bounded at the west by the Hudson and through which ran the course of the *King's Highway*. The church at Hopewell was the most easterly outpost of Dutch settlement but the houses near it were chiefly of wood and the eastward limits of construction in stone were in the valleys of the Wappingers and Sprout Creeks.

In 1713 the house of Pieter Viele at Poughkeepsie presents the first dated instance of frame construction in Dutchess. The house consisted of mud walls (such as are shown in plate 8) and was sided with boards. The latter may have been cut in the saw-mill which, by 1699, Myndert Harmense Van Den Bogaerdt had built at Poughkeepsie. Bartholomeus Hoogeboom, who lived at Poughkeepsie from 1709 to 1730, was a carpenter and he may have found enough to do there to make his trade a good source of revenue in addition to the cultivation of his farm. It is probable however that wood was little used at Poughkeepsie until after the Revolution and that the same was true of the section of the county traversed by the *King's Highway* between Poughkeepsie and Red Hook. Southward from Poughkeepsie houses built of wood began to appear about the middle of the eighteenth century and it is significant that the printed forms for leases that were issued by the Verplanck family for farms on their share of the Rombout Patent contained about 1750 a clause providing that the lessee should erect on his farm either " one framed or stone dwelling house, of at least eighteen foot square, with a lento at one end there-of, with one framed barn, all to be well shingled." The provision for a house either of wood or of stone probably marks the beginning of a more common use of wood in the western part of the county. In the valley of the *Vis Kil* the extensive use of wood in the eighteenth century is attributable in large part to the Dutch families from Long Island who were unfamiliar with stone and accustomed to frame construction. The earliest frame walls were filled with mud or clay, instances of which are the Brewer-Mesier, Southard and Swartwout houses (plates 112, 133, 8). Brick filling for the wall-frames was an advance from primitive conditions as brick had to be imported or manufactured. Examples of brick-filled walls occur at *Lithgow* and in the Storm-Adriance-Brinckerhoff house at Hopewell (plates 122 and 135).

The early frame houses of Dutchess repeated the main features of the stone houses. They were a story and a half in height, had roofs of single slant and the floor-plans exhibited similar arrangements of rooms. Some of the first frame houses were shingled and important examples of that form of siding have survived on the

321

house of Madam Brett at Beacon (plate 111). Similar shingles show in the pictures of the former Livingston and Van Voorhees houses (plates 128 and 144) and shingles (possibly of the same shape) covered the houses of Cornelius and Richard Van Wyck (plate 146 and page 401). Contemporaneously with the shingles and following them were broad clapboards, sometimes laid to meet smoothly, sometimes to lap. The dormer windows on so many of the eighteenth century houses are difficult to date but they belong, presumably, in large part to the post-Revolutionary period, when greater comfort in the half-story began to be asked for. The longer the slope of the dormer the earlier may be the date ascribed to it, those on the house of Madam Brett (plate 111) illustrating the earliest type. Just below the line of the eaves of the story-and-a-half frame houses are often to be seen oblong windows (measuring perhaps twelve by thirty inches). They came into use in the 1790's as an evidence of the increasing desire for light and ventilation and they preceded, by a few years only, the introduction of the two-story frame house in the style that was popular until late in the nineteenth century.

Brick was utilized in Dutchess at a later date than stone and wood because, as has just been stated, it had either to be imported or manufactured. Importation involved transportation from a distant brickyard by sloop on the river to a landing and hauling by wagon from boat to farm and hauling by wagon implied that roads were open from the landing to the interior. Manufacture of brick, at the place where a building was to be erected, required time and it presupposes somewhat settled living conditions in a vicinity; for a pioneer, sheltered in a temporary structure, would hardly incur the delay of manufacturing the material for his permanent dwelling when stone and wood were at hand in plentiful amount. Known instances of the local manufacture of brick are those of the house of Sarah Tobias Newcomb (plate 129) and of the Storm house (plate 134) and local method of manufacture, in one case at least, is revealed in the recorded item that the brick for the house built in 1798 at Clinton Corners by Abel Peters was made by throwing all materials together and having oxen tread the mass to mix it. The incidental use of bricks in small quantities in gables, for chimneys, for facing window-openings and as filling for frame-walls probably occurred before houses were built of brick throughout, as for example in the house of John Brinckerhoff (plate 114) the west gable is filled with red bricks and black bricks are inlaid in the figures: 1 7 3 8.

Brick houses in Dutchess County represent therefore the period that followed that of the pioneer, one in which prosperity reached a point where it was possible for a householder to exercise preference in the material selected for his dwelling. The first house with brick walls that has been learned of in Dutchess is the DePeyster (plate 115) at Beacon, to which the date: 1740, has been ascribed by a local authority. But if error has crept in here, if the house were not built so early as 1740, it still may confidently be assigned to the pre-Revolutionary period. It was some years

322

after 1740 that brick houses were built in Dutchess in any number; then several were put up in close succession to each other. In 1763 Jacob Evertson erected a large brick house (page 342) in the town of Amenia, which was followed by the Glebe House of Christ Church, Poughkeepsie, in 1767 (now standing at 635, Main Street); the Verplanck house (plate 149) in 1768; the house of Dr. Stephen Thorn at New Hackensack in 1772; the DuBois house (page 339) about 1774; the house of Sarah Tobias Newcomb (plate 129) about 1777; and the Duryea house at Fishkill Plains. The last is said by local tradition to have been built at about the same time as its neighbors, the Verplanck and Thorn houses. At the close of the Revolution (that is, about 1783) John Wilkinson built a brick house a mile east of Moore's Mill, which is shown by an oil painting to have been a perfect example of a pre-war type.

Among the nine brick houses just noted there was variety in detail. The De-Peyster, Verplanck and Wilkinson were one and one-half stories high, with gambrel roofs and hence they belong in a group with the Lansing house of 1750; the Muller, 1767; the Ten Broeck, about 1773; and the Van Schaick, before 1762 (plates 27, 28, 39 and 52); except that the rear walls of the DePeyster and Verplanck houses were of rough stone. The Evertson and Newcomb houses of 1763 and (1777?) respectively were similar to the Ten Broeck house of 1762 (plate 38) in that they were two full stories in height and had gambrel roofs. The Thorn house of 1772 had a roof of single slant. The DuBois house on the Wappingers Creek, built about 1774, is perhaps on a smaller scale than the Ten Broeck house of 1762 and its rear wall is of stone but in floor-plan and in its two stories it is the same as the latter. At Poughkeepsie in 1767 the builders of the Glebe House adhered in design to an early style, made familiar in stone and wood (of walls a story and a half high and roof of single slant); in materials they used stone for the rear wall but brick for the front and ends. The Duryea house at Fishkill Plains was originally one and one-half stories (with roof supposedly of single slant) but about 1875 it was enlarged and its general appearance wholly changed.

In the pre-Revolutionary houses that are still standing in Dutchess County there is to be seen some original interior wood-trim, principally in the frame and brick houses. About 1790—1810 many repairs were made to old houses in the course of which original woodwork was torn out; Adam mantels were put in, new doors and shutters, inserts of ornamental patterns in leaded glass above and beside the entrance-doors, larger panes of window-glass, brass door-knobs, and so on. Here and there is left a handsome wrought iron fireback, wrought iron strap-hinges are plentiful and many fine hand-cut ceiling-beams are still doing duty. The strap-hinge that is usually found is the one most frequently seen throughout the river-counties, which has a circular plate at one end and is tipped at the other with a curve resembling the curve of an anchor. In some parts of Dutchess the long, straight, pointed hinge occurs but the examples of the latter pattern are less numerous than those of the former.

The improvements that were made to old houses soon after the war and the new houses built between 1800 and 1830 afford direct evidence of the prosperity of the farms of Dutchess at that time. When land in Dutchess was first sought by white men it was acquired from the Indians without friction. Peaceful relations prevailed between the races and the county was built up in the enjoyment of the advantage derived from an entire absence of violence or warfare. In the time of the pioneers who cut the forests and cleared the farms and opened the roads the houses were as severely plain as, under those conditions, they might naturally be expected to be. But the houses of the second half of the eighteenth century and of the first quarter of the nineteenth show a steadily rising architectural standard. From the pioneer type they advanced to one which showed traces of a more sophisticated social life and a tendency toward that which was decorative, not merely useful. This fact is traceable to favorable economic conditions. Good land, held by intelligent freeholders; easy access to the river; large markets in New York, reached by water-transportation; these and other factors made the farmers the opulent and influential men of the county and their houses reflected the situation. There is still a surprisingly large amount of interesting architectural material left in Dutchess and particularly in the decorative details of 1790—1830 is there much to be recorded and correlated. The era of prosperity for the farms of Dutchess ended in the mid-nineteenth century when western grain and beef came east in large quantities. Then the farms declined and ambitious sons, born under old rooftrees, sought their fortunes in the towns in commerce, manufacturing and the professions. Only a few of the old farms are held now by descendants of the original owners and the houses on them are in all degrees of repair and in all stages of decay.

HOUSES in DUTCHESS COUNTY

House of Madam Brett
Beacon, New York
PLATE 111

The house shown in plate 111 stands at the heart of the city of Beacon, New York, where modern city-growth has crept to its very door but where, when it was built, there was only wild land. It is one of that small number of houses in the valley of the Hudson which have been occupied continuously, since before 1776, by one family-line, and which have been maintained by successive generations in accordance with advancing standards of living. Sentiment, tradition, long and unbroken associations, all combine to endow this particular home with a rich heritage of an intimate, personal sort but they need only be cited in these pages as they have already been sympathetically set forth by Alice Crary Sutcliffe in a monograph entitled: *The Homestead of a Colonial Dame.* For the purposes of the present work consideration must be confined to other aspects of the history of this important landmark.

From the view-point of a study of Dutch houses in the valley of the Hudson and assuming that the occupation of a house by people of Dutch descent creates what may be called a Dutch home, the house of Madam Brett is preponderantly Dutch in character. The builder of the house, Catharine Rombout Brett (born 1687, died 1764), was the child of a Walloon father (François Rombouts) and a Dutch mother (Helena Teller) and the wife of an English husband (Roger Brett) and in her speech used a mixture of Dutch and English (to judge from a letter she wrote in 1749, which appears in the Year Book of the Dutchess County Historical Society for 1921). Her son, Francis Rombout Brett (born 1707, died 1787), who inherited her house, married a Dutch wife, Margaret Van Wyck (notes, plate 146); and her grand-daughter, Hannah Brett (born 1743, died 1825), who was the third occupant, married a Dutch husband, Henry Schenck. Mr. and Mrs. Schenck were succeeded in the house about 1800 by their daughter, Alice (born 1765, died 1845), and her husband, Isaac DePeyster Teller, and since the time of Mr. and Mrs. Teller the house has been known as the *Teller Homestead.* Margaret Teller (born 1808, died 1888) came into sole possession of the *Homestead* after her parents and several unmarried sisters all had died and she, by her marriage to the Reverend Robert Boyd Van Kleeck, a descendant of Baltus Barents Van Kleeck of Poughkeepsie, linked it with the house of the latter, shown in plate 142. From Mrs. Van Kleeck the property passed to her daughter, Mrs. Robert Fulton Crary (Agnes Boyd Van Kleeck), and Mrs. Crary's children now hold it.

325

Architecturally, the house of Madam Brett is an example of a type of dwelling which was characteristic of southern Dutchess in the eighteenth century and, as the population of southern Dutchess was at that time largely Dutch, both in origin and feeling, it is to be supposed that Dutch sanction was given to an architectural norm that was very generally adopted. But before proceeding to analyse the structure of the house of Madam Brett it is necessary to record the story of her personal career in order to relate her dwelling to an historical setting.

François Rombouts, Madam Brett's father, a citizen of Hasselt in the diocese of Liége (which was a portion of the Low Countries occupied by Walloons), migrated in the seventeenth century to New Amsterdam, where he prospered as a merchant and trader and served as mayor of the city. In 1683, in partnership with Gulian Verplanck of New York, he bought eighty-five thousand acres of land in Dutchess County from the Indians, for which purchase in 1685 a Crown patent was issued to him in company with the heirs of Verplanck (who had died) and with Stephanus Van Cortlandt (who had acquired an interest in the partnership). The Rombout Patent (as it always has been known) covered a wilderness and the property was obtained by the patentees for its value in connection with the fur-trade, for which reason no settlement on the land was attempted by them or their heirs for a generation. In 1703 François Rombouts died and on March 15, 1708, a partition of the major portion of the patent was made between the representatives of the three patentees. By the partition, a large tract, bordering the *Vis Kil* (Fish Stream) from the Hudson eastward, fell to the share of Rombout's only surviving child, Catharine, who by then had become the wife of Roger Brett and was living in her father's house on Broadway, New York City.

Upon taking title to her portion of the Rombout Patent, Mrs. Brett seems to have formed at once a decision to develop her inheritance by opening the land for settlement and, as it is with the modern promotion of real estate where capital and personal supervision both are necessary, so it was with Mrs. Brett and her husband. The land-records reveal that they borrowed money on bond and mortgage a number of times, presumably using the funds so obtained for the expenses they incurred, and they ultimately left New York City and made their permanent home in Dutchess County in close touch with their business affairs. Some of their transactions in connection with their real estate are recorded in the Register's Office, New York City, some in the office of the Secretary of State, Albany, and some in the office of the Clerk of Dutchess County and, as a review of the documents in detail would be tedious to the general reader, there is offered here merely the condensed result of a careful editorial study of them. The study was necessary in order to obtain the evidence the records supply regarding the date at which Mr. and Mrs. Brett erected their own dwelling in Dutchess.

It was in March, 1708, that Mrs. Brett received her inheritance and she and her husband maintained their residence in New York City until after April, 1711, up to and including which date the land-records record them as " of " New York City. On May 1, 1713, they were described as " of " Fishkill, Dutchess County, and the deed in which they were mentioned as of Fishkill was given when they sold their house on Broadway, New York, to Thomas George. It thus is obvious that their actual, personal settlement at Fishkill was between April, 1711, and May, 1713, at which latter date, by disposing of their home in New York, they severed connection with the city.

Meanwhile, before changing their residence, they had begun to lay the foundations of a small community in Dutchess. Near the mouth of the *Vis Kil* they built (in 1708—1709?) a grist-mill and a dwelling and set aside three-hundred acres to go with the two buildings. They also, between June, 1708, and April, 1713, sold or rented five farms.

The mill and house and three-hundred acres remained as a property-unit throughout the eighteenth century. In 1709, 1711 and 1729 this security was mortgaged by Mrs. Brett but in 1743 Abraham DePeyster cancelled all liens and bought out Mrs. Brett's equity and the history of the house that now occupies the site will be found in connection with plate 115.

By the coming of five settlers to the vicinity of the mill between 1708 and 1713 Roger and Catharine Brett escaped the first brunt of the hardship of making a clearing in the woods and it can be assumed that in 1708—1711, while retaining their comfortable home in the city, they went up and down the Hudson by sloop, superintending the erection of the mill and of the house adjoining it and also interviewing prospective customers for their lands. The five men, who in the years 1708—1713 actually arrived at the *Vis Kil*, took up about five-hundred acres and they must have cleared and planted their land to some extent before the Bretts came as permanent residents in 1711—1713.

In October, 1714, Roger and Catharine Brett of Fishkill entered into an agreement with Robert Dengee, carpenter, of Hempstead, Long Island, the terms of which were that: " the said Robert Dengee (was) to work justly and faithfully, if it (pleased) God to give him life and health, for the above-said Roger Brett or Catherine, his wife, or either of them or their heirs, for one whole year, upon the condition that upon performance thereof he (was) to have made over to him a hundred acres of land forever." The agreement having been performed by Dengee, the Bretts conveyed to him on June 30, 1716, one-hundred and ten acres and the bonus above the terms of the agreement witnesses eloquently to their good will and the character of Dengee's services.

The employment of a carpenter for a whole year implies that more or less construction was undertaken by the Bretts and, in view of the fact that the house now known as having been their home is a frame house that called for a carpenter,

327

it can hardly be doubted that it was built by Robert Dengee between October, 1714, and June, 1716.

As Roger and Catharine Brett were " of " Fishkill in May, 1713, they presumably lived in the house by the mill until their own house was ready. All the records relating to the mill-property refer consistently to: " the grist-mill, the messuage and three-hundred acres of land," messuage being a legal term (derived from old French) and meaning specifically a dwelling or a dwelling with its curtilage. Of that first " messuage " by the mill nothing is certainly known but the probability is that it was a stone house (like many another built by the pioneers) and it is even possible that a portion of it forms the basement of the present brick house (plate 115).

Up the valley of the *Vis Kil* (adjoining the east end of the three-hundred acres that went with the mill) the Bretts set off about two-hundred acres for their own occupation, on which they built the house shown in plate 111 and which land is now cut in city-streets. In the deeds covering the property the place is called the *Old Farm* but the term does not imply length of tenure; it is one that in the eighteenth century was customarily used in deeds to signify the land which was the homestead of the owner.

In the spring of 1713, just as they took up their residence on the *Vis Kil*, Roger and Catharine Brett placed two large mortgages on their unoccupied lands in Dutchess. The money so obtained was undoubtedly desired for use in making surveys, laying out roads and farms and, perhaps, in erecting a saw-mill, which was greatly needed; but all this enterprise was halted by the death in 17(17?) of Roger Brett. He was drowned in the Hudson between October, 1716, and January, 1718, leaving his wife a widow, with two young sons to care for and on her shoulders the burden of a large amount of real estate that was still in the preliminary stages of development.

The first echo of the tragedy is heard when the interest, due on one of the large mortgages, was not paid. The mortgage was held by George Clarke, Secretary of the Province of New York, and he, as a man of affairs and as a friend to a woman suddenly left alone in a difficult position, at once set about retrieving his own interests and straightening the widow's financial affairs by selling large parcels of land in fee simple. In 1718 two-thousand acres were sold to Dirck Brinckerhoff of Flushing, Long Island, other sales followed and finally matters were placed on a sound basis.

The energy and capability with which the young widow carried out the task that thus fell to her lot won for her the complimentary title of " Madam " Brett, by which she still is spoken of in southern Dutchess. In selling farms, operating a mill and in joining with the men of the community in the establishment of a landing and a store-house on the river-front she acquired a lasting reputation for executive ability and just dealing and " Madam " Brett is credited today with having rendered valuable service to Dutchess County in her character as pioneer and promoter.

The house now standing, which was her home, is a frame structure, longer than broad, a story and a half in height. Whether the main walls are built of mud or brick is not known (both materials are found in interior partitions) but they are sided with notable shingles of red cedar. Similar shingles have been observed in New Jersey, on Long Island, at New Rochelle and at Poughkeepsie but whether they are Dutch or English in origin is not clear. The ridgepole of Madam Brett's house extends beyond the walls of the gable-ends to a degree that forms an unusual projection of the roof (see plate 111), the only other roofs of the kind, noted in this survey, being the one that, in 1823, was placed on the house of Abraham Salisbury at Leeds (page 92) and that which is on *Lithgow* (plate 122). The lines of the corners of the house of Madam Brett (where the walls join) rise from the ground to the eaves in a slight inward slant as if to spread the weight of the walls on a broad base.

The foundations of the house are of field-stone, crudely but solidly laid, and in the cellar, supporting the main floor, are numerous posts that are merely young trees, set up just as they were cut in the forest, the marks of the ax still showing on them. These rough, crooked posts are the most primitive feature now left in the house.

Leading into the cellar from outside is a door, fastened by a hand-made wooden latch that is operated by a string through a hole,—the only instance of the time-honored synonym for hospitality that this survey of the Hudson valley revealed. That the sole example of the latch-string should pertain to a house famed for the welcome it has given to innumerable guests is a happy coincidence!

The plan of the main floor of the house of Madam Brett is the one so often found of a central hall, flanked by two rooms at either side. Originally the staircase at the northwest end of the hall was enclosed. It led to an open half-story and family tradition says that the slaves slept there in early days. Of the rooms on the main floor those toward the south are unusually large in area, those toward the north smaller. The ceilings are low. The south door was at first used as the main entrance (the change to the north door, now used as the front, occurring early in the nineteenth century). In the southeast room (now the dining-room) there is a recess at either side of the chimney, one of which now holds a sideboard while the other is a passageway to an east wing. As niches that were intended for sideboards date from approximately 1795, it is probable that these two spaces were built to hold beds and were so used by the family when the slaves slept in the attic.

In the southwest parlor there is a carved wooden mantel, which dates in design from about 1800 to 1810. Its presence is accounted for by the fact that many changes were made in the house by the Teller family, who took possession about 1800. To them, in the early nineteenth century, may be attributed almost all of the interior wood-trim; the brass doorknobs; the designs in leaded glass over the main doors; the north and south porches and the window shutters. Perhaps, too, the attic was partitioned by them into bedrooms and the long dormer windows cut in the roof.

329

The house of Madam Brett illustrates the axiom that in the case of dwellings long occupied each generation leaves its mark upon the structure. Alterations and additions accumulate with time and the student who has learned characteristic work can, by critical analysis, reconstruct the history of a building. In this instance, traces of the early and middle eighteenth century, of 1810 and of 1910 are all plainly visible and, when the several changes are viewed as a record of the needs and the customs of the people who made them, they form a story of human interest and significance.

Brewer-Mesier House

Wappingers Falls, New York

PLATE 112

In the center of the village of Wappingers Falls, surrounded by a small park, is the Brewer-Mesier house, shown in plate 112. The park lies within the portion of the Rombout Patent which fell to the Verplanck family and is part of a large farm that was purchased in 1741 by Nicholas Brewer. Soon after 1741 Nicholas Brewer built a tiny frame house and, somewhat later, a larger house of thick, mud-filled walls, clapboarded, the two units forming an ell. The smaller house is a complete dwelling in itself, primitive in size and finish. It contains two rooms, a large chimney and fireplace and steep enclosed stairs that lead to a low half-story, lighted by very small windows. The date of the erection of the larger house is not known but it is safe to place it in the middle of the eighteenth century and at as early a day as Nicholas Brewer's finances permitted. Beside his large acreage of farm-land he owned a mill and a dock below the falls of the Wappingers and was a prominent resident of the locality for nearly fifty years, dying in 1787.

As built by Nicholas Brewer the main house lacked the porch and dormers and eaves-trim which it now carries. It was and is a story and a half in height and at the rear the roof slopes nearer to the ground than in front. Across the front are three rooms, with a hall running the depth of the house between the western and middle rooms. Smaller rooms are behind the front ones. An enclosed stairway is at the rear east corner of the hall. Dutch doors are at the ends of the hall. A second entrance-door leads into the front room at the east end of the house. In this southeast corner room is good panelling, with cupboards, all of the style of the mid-century. The southwest corner front room is wainscoted and has a chimney-breast carved with Georgian details. A specially fine Adam mantel, somewhat similar to the mantel in the Pawling house in Ulster County (plate 82) was formerly in the middle front room but has been removed to the house of W. Willis Reese of New Hamburgh, a descendant of Peter Mesier who, on May 1, 1777, bought Nicholas Brewer's homestead.

Peter Mesier (born 1733, died 1805) was a descendant of Pieter Janszen Mesier, a citizen of New Amsterdam in 1658. While the name: Mesier is French or Walloon,

Peter Mesier of Wappingers Falls was more than half Dutch in blood through his mother, Jenneke Wessels, and his grandmother, Elizabeth Couwenhoven. He married in 1764 Catherine Sleght (a descendant of Cornelis Barentsen Sleght of Esopus 1655) and when the troubled days of the Revolution came removed his family from New York City to Wappingers Falls, where he apparently opened a store in his dwelling house. Peter Mesier's political sympathies were with the Crown, and as a Tory, albeit a peaceable one, he was a thorn in the side of the local Whigs. In time of war passion runs high, even in obscure rural communities, and so at Wappingers Falls a lawless element among the Whigs raided Peter Mesier's house on the pretext of disputing the price of the tea he had for sale. On May 19, 20 and 22, 1777, soldiers, other men and farmers' wives attacked the house, breaking open the door, striking the owner, beating his slaves and drinking the wine stored in the cellar. Thus " the Dutchess's County " had a " tea-party " all its own, the story of which is recorded in the minutes of the committee for the detection of conspiracies.

The house remained in the possession of the descendants of Peter Mesier until 1891, when it was conveyed to the village and with the surrounding grounds was set aside in perpetuity as Mesier Park. It is a pity that photography was unknown when this house was first built. Today it stands in the midst of a manufacturing community which has grown up beside the Wappingers Creek, attracted by the water-power. But the factories and many small buildings occupy a location which in its natural state was one of remarkable beauty. The creek comes down from rich arable flats above and drops suddenly over a precipitous ledge to a deep curving rocky gorge, through which it pours itself to the river. Under date of December, 1780, the Marquis de Chastellux, French general officer, en route from Newburgh to Saratoga, said in his diary that he arrived at: " the Fall of Wapping. There I stopped some moments to take in, under different points of view, the charming landscape which that stream forms as much by its cascade, which is rushing and picturesque, as by the groups of trees and of rocks, which united with the saw mills and other mills made a picture most pleasing and agreeable."

House of Derick Brinckerhoff
Town of Fishkill, Dutchess County, New York
PLATE 113

When, in the first quarter of the eighteenth century, Madam Brett offered her lands in Dutchess County for sale in homestead farms, one of the first large purchasers was Dirck Brinckerhoff (born 1667, died 1748) of Flushing, Long Island, who in 1718 bought two-thousand acres lying along the course of the *Vis Kil* from Fishkill village to the Sprout Creek. This tract was taken up and developed by his four sons: Abraham, John, Isaac and Jacob.

Abraham Brinckerhoff (born about 1700, died before 1743), eldest son of Dirck of Flushing, removed from Long Island to Dutchess County in his early manhood and there built a stone house of two rooms, with a chimney between, similar to other known dwellings of pioneers. He died before middle life, leaving a widow (Femmetje, daughter of Joris Remsen Vanderbeck of Long Island) and seven children. His eldest son, Derick (born about 1720—'25, died 1789), married in 1747 Geertje Wyckoff of Flatlands, Long Island, and succeeded to his father's house and lands in Dutchess. Derick Brinckerhoff was a man of energy and initiative. He built a grist-mill on the *Vis Kil*, carried on a store near the mill and prospered. In person he is known to have been tall and heavily built, with dark hair and florid complexion. He kept fine horses and rode in a phaeton, a conveyance which carried two passengers and was driven by a negro coachman. The phaeton was a novelty in its time and has now come to a long home in Henry Ford's collection of vehicles. Derick Brinckerhoff's capacity made him prominent locally in public life and he served the county both in civil and military affairs. From 1768 to 1775 he was a member of the Provincial Assembly; in 1775 a delegate to the first Provincial Congress of New York; and he was a representative in the first, second, third, fifth, seventh, eighth, ninth and tenth sessions (1777—1787) of the Assembly of the newly organized State of New York. During the Revolution he was colonel of a regiment of militia and chairman of the vigilance committee of the town.

At an unknown date before the Revolution Derick Brinckerhoff enlarged the house he had inherited from his father. He extended to the east a frame addition, carried up all the walls to two full stories, clapboarded the whole and put on a gambrel roof (the latter a clear reflection of the fashion of the day). About 1830 the gambrel was removed and a roof of single slant substituted and new wood trim given to the rooms on the first floor. Again, about 1875, the roof of single slant made way for a mansard, which still remains. The house, now owned by the heirs of the late Frank Brinckerhoff (a descendant of the builder), stands about two miles east of Fishkill village on the north side of the road at the hamlet known as Brinckerhoff. It is now completely modern in appearance and the passer-by would never suspect that under the clapboards of the west end are the thick stone walls of the two-room house built by Abraham Brinckerhoff early in the eighteenth century.

At the time of the Revolution the house bore the appearance recorded in a sketch, which is reproduced with acknowledgements from *The Family of Joris Dircksen Brinckerhoff* by T. Van Wyck Brinckerhoff and shown in the accompanying plate. It was then that for many weeks the Marquis de La Fayette was ill in the upper southeast room, where he was an honored guest and well-nursed patient. Immediately west of the house in those days was the Rombout Presbyterian Church, which was used as a hospital for sick soldiers from among the Continental troops stationed at Fishkill. The road in front of Colonel Brinckerhoff's house was a main route of travel between New England and the South so long as the British held the Hudson below the Highlands and all the world and his wife of that day passed back and forth over it.

House of John Brinckerhoff

Town of Fishkill, Dutchess County, New York

PLATE 114

John Brinckerhoff (born 1702, died 1785), son of Dirck Brinckerhoff of Flushing, married in 1725 Jannetje Van Voorhees (whose father built the house in Dutchess shown in plate 144) and moved from Long Island to Dutchess County, where he settled on part of the large tract of land that his father had purchased from Madam Brett. In 1738 he built a house on the high, fertile flat which lies on the west bank of the Sprout Creek near the confluence of the Sprout with the *Vis Kil*, from which location there is a beautiful outlook toward the Clove and the Beacons. There he and his wife lived for half a century, dying in their eighty-third and eighty-eighth years, respectively, after having outlived all of their five children.

Of the children of John and Jannetje Brinckerhoff, their daughter, Aeltje (born 1732, died 1774), married in 1754 Dr. Theodorus Van Wyck. After their marriage Dr. and Mrs. Van Wyck remained under the roof of Mrs. Van Wyck's father in order that her parents should not be left alone. The death in 1774 of Mrs. Van Wyck was followed by that of her husband in 1789 and it was to her son, John Brinckerhoff Van Wyck (born 1762, died 1841), that her father, John Brinckerhoff, in 1785 bequeathed the homestead. From John Brinckerhoff Van Wyck the house passed to his son, Alfred (born 1801, died 1894), who sold it out of the family.

While living in this house, Dr. Theodorus Van Wyck was a delegate from Dutchess to the third Provincial Congress of New York and throughout the Revolution he was prominently and usefully engaged in public services. In the fall of 1778 General Washington made the house his headquarters from time to time. He occupied the parlor-bedroom at the rear of the west side of the house and a homely tradition is current that motherly Mrs. Brinckerhoff saw to it personally that the Commander-in-Chief was warmly tucked up in his bed on the cold autumn nights. Tradition tells too of family worship, led in Low Dutch by John Brinckerhoff, which Washington attended, and an anecdote, handed down, is to the effect that the general, when questioned once by his host as to military affairs, asked for assurance that the enquirer could keep a secret, and upon receiving such assurance replied: So can I.

The house of John Brinckerhoff is on the south side of the main highway between Fishkill and Hopewell, some distance back from the road at the end of a long avenue, which latter is outlined by stone walls and maple trees. Built of stone, a story and a half high, with large attic-space, the front wall of the Brinckerhoff house is now

333

covered with cement and the east gable clapboarded. The west gable is filled with red bricks and contains the date: 1 7 3 8, built in, in black bricks.

Inside, the original floor-plan of the house consisted of a central hall, with a larger front room and a smaller back room on either side. The first staircase was at the left rear of the hall and was enclosed, space for it being taken from the west parlor-bedroom, which was smaller than the parlor to that extent. Of the original interior wood-trim there remains the panelled window-casing in the west parlor-bedroom; two panelled bedroom doors in the second story; and two panelled doors at the rear of the main wall, one of which shut off the former staircase (its space now a pantry), and the other presumably gave entrance to a cellar stairway. The ceilings are high, which was unusual in 1738, when heating facilities were inadequate.

About 1800 a partition was built, dividing the original hall into two parts at a point in line with the depth of the two front rooms. The front portion was then finished with panelled wainscoting, about three feet high, and doors to correspond were given to the southwest parlor. A wood mantel carved in Adam details was placed in the latter room and two handsome carved door-casings matched the mantel. On the east side of the hall the partition was taken down between the rear east room and the hall, while in the front east room a wood mantel was added which bears an Adam design applied in plaster. The present main stairway is of the late nineteenth century.

In the north wall of the house are two windows which are tall and narrow, the panes numbering three in a row and there being three rows in each sash. These windows belong to the first years of the house and none like them were found elsewhere during the survey made for this volume. All other windows in the house are of the nineteenth century. In the west front room the fireplace contains a particularly fine wrought-iron fireback, the center of which is occupied by the spirited figure of an angel, carrying a staff or crook, and flanked by conventionalized flowers and human figures.

The decorations given the house in the period of 1800 must have been the work of John Brinckerhoff Van Wyck and probably date from the time of his second marriage, which occurred about 1798. He married in 1790 Gertrude Brinckerhoff, whose mother (Sarah Brett) was a granddaughter of Madam Brett of the house shown in plate III. Gertrude Brinckerhoff Van Wyck died about 1791 and her husband married secondly Susan Schenck, a daughter of Paul and Joanna (Livingston) Schenck of Poughkeepsie. Paul Schenck lived in 1774 in the house at the Upper Landing, Poughkeepsie (page 373), and about 1800 he occupied a dwelling which is still standing at 319—321, Main Street, Poughkeepsie, but which has been converted into stores.

By the residence in it of Susan Schenck (the bride in whose honor it was supposedly redecorated), the house of John Brinckerhoff is linked not only with the houses just mentioned but with the house of her grandfather, Henry Livingston, at Poughkeepsie (plate 128) and with the home of her sister, Joanna, wife of Matthew Mesier of Wappingers Falls (plate 112). Dr. Theodorus Van Wyck, son-in-law of John Brinckerhoff, was brought up in the Van Wyck homestead listed at page 398, and his sister, Mary, wife of Zephaniah Platt, lived in the house on the Wappingers Creek shown in plate 131. And so it follows that the occupants of all these houses knew each other well and the houses form a group with associations and reminiscences in common.

In 1926 the house built by John Brinckerhoff was purchased by Teodar Wiitala of New York City, representing a group of Finnish-Americans who will use the house and the farm as a cooperative colony.

House of John Delamater

Troutbeck, Amenia, New York

During the great exodus from France of the Huguenots Claude le Maistre (as he signed his name) of Richebourg, Artois, took refuge in Amsterdam, whence he migrated to New Netherland. He was first at Flatbush, then by 1666 of Harlem, where he died about 1683. His son, Jacobus, moved to Ulster County and Jacobus's son, Isaac, to Dutchess and Isaac's son, who went by the name of "John Delamater", married in 1752 a Dutch wife, Maria Kip, and they in 1761 built a house in the town of Amenia that is still standing. The house has walls of frame, one and one-half stories high, clapboarded; its east gable-end is filled with red bricks and, inlaid, there are black bricks recording: J M D 1 7 6 1. The house is on land that now forms a part of the estate called: *Troutbeck*, the property of J. E. Spingarn, and the owner gives it sympathetic care.

House of Abraham DePeyster

Town of Fishkill, Dutchess County, New York

PLATE 115

On a preceding page the story has been told in detail (in connection with plate 111) of how Catharine Rombout Brett, one of the heirs to the Rombout Patent in Dutchess, built a gristmill and a house about 1708—1709 near the mouth of the *Vis Kil* and set aside three-hundred acres of land to go with the two buildings. The house shown in plate 115 stands on the north side of the *Vis Kil*, not far from the original mill-site and on land which was part of the mill-farm but it is not the original dwelling on the property. The house which Madam Brett built about 1708—1709 is assumed to have been one of the stone structures typical of the period of the pioneer and it presumably was occupied by her and her husband until their own house (plate 111) was ready for them.

335

The date of the erection of the present brick and stone house on or near the site of the first dwelling is not certainly known. Madam Brett retained title to the mill-farm until 1743 but in 1709, 1711 and 1729 she mortgaged the property and the three mortgages all remained in force until, in 1743, Abraham DePeyster of New York City bought out her equity and paid off all the liens. The third mortgage on the mill-farm was held by Isaac DePeyster of New York, whose wife, Maria Van Baal, was Madam Brett's half-sister and whose son, Abraham, bought the property. It has been said that Madam Brett built the house for her brother-in-law but the statement seems improbable. In 1729, when he became third mortgagee, Isaac DePeyster was a man of sixty-seven years and little likely to wish to remove from the city to the country while, in the years during which he was one of the three mortgagees, Madam Brett was carrying a heavy burden in other mortgaged real estate and was in no position to engage in building an expensive house.

A monograph, entitled: *Historical Sketches of the Town of Fishkill,* published in 1866 by T. Van Wyck Brinckerhoff, states that in the wall of the house on the mill-farm was cut the date: 1 7 4 0, which mark cannot now be found. Assuming that the search recently made for the inscription was not sufficiently thorough and that it is still in existence, there remains a possibility that it was misread in 1866, or that a typographical error occurred in Mr. Brinckerhoff's book for all the known facts in the history of the mill-farm point to the erection of the second house after 1743.

Abraham DePeyster, Madam Brett's step-nephew (born 1701, died 1775), was a prosperous merchant in New York City and able to build and own a handsome country home for occasional use if he cared to do so. When he took title to the mill-farm in 1743 the deed mentioned three-hundred acres of land, the mill and one house but in 1792, when his heirs sold the property they conveyed the land, the mill and two houses. The plan and finish of the house are such as to remove the building from the period of the pioneers and to place it later, at a time when greater luxury was known. On the face of the facts therefore and in the absence of positive proof, the reasonable assumption is that the house was the work of Abraham DePeyster in the middle of the eighteenth century.

At his death in 1775 Mr. DePeyster left neither wife nor children and he willed to a brother and a sister a life-interest in all his real estate, directing that after their deaths his property should go to his great-nephews, Oliver Teller and Isaac DePeyster Teller (sons of Isaac Teller of Fishkill). When the latter two received their inheritance, Isaac DePeyster Teller bought his brother Oliver's share, married Alice Schenck and established himself on the mill-farm. Soon, however, he sold the place and he and his wife removed to the house of Madam Brett (page 325) which had been the girlhood home of Mrs. Teller. For much of the nineteenth century the brick and stone house on the mill-farm was owned and occupied by the Newlin family and it is still spoken of as the Newlin homestead although held now in the

Ramsdell estate. It is rented to Italian and Slavic tenants and as a railroad has been built immediately behind it and a factory in front of it the domestic and rural aspects of its surroundings have been sadly changed. Originally, its location was one of much natural beauty.

The house on the mill-farm stands on sloping ground and faces south. The front and rear walls are of stone, very thick; the front wall is faced with brick; the east and west walls are built of brick. The roof is a gambrel. The main floor rests upon a high stone foundation which affords a large basement. Within the basement is a hall, running north and south between two south rooms and two north cellars. The southeast room contains a fireplace and Dutch oven (both of great size), the oven projecting from the exterior of the east wall of the house but enclosed in a modern lean-to. The southwest room has also a fireplace and the two rooms may at first have served as kitchen and dining-room, respectively. In each of these basement rooms are two sets of casement windows, over which bricks are laid in an ornamental arch; each window is in two parts; each part has six panes of glass in two vertical rows of three; and the wood shutters are panelled (vignette, page 315). Similar casements and brickwork occur in the house of Pieter Bronck (plate 16) and casements without brick decoration are in the stone wall of the house of Benjamin Ten Broeck in Ulster (plate 89).

The main floor of the house of Abraham DePeyster has a wide hall through the center and two rooms at either side, the front rooms larger, the back ones smaller. The ceilings are ten feet, two inches in height. The front entrance is very high above the ground (as in the case of the Coeymans, Van Wie and Van Cortlandt houses, plates 18, 54, 109) and the design of the first flight of steps can only be conjectural as the steps long ago disappeared. A photograph of the porch that did duty in the middle of the nineteenth century is owned by William E. Verplanck of Beacon, N. Y. The original front door (panelled, tall and heavy, with long iron hinges and divided horizontally) was removed in late years to the house of Mrs. Louis A. Gillet of Beacon and a modern door now swings in a narrow modern frame that is set into the former wide opening. At the north end of the main hall a door opens on the level of the ground and a mill-stone forms the door-step. The north door is broad, cut across the center, is panelled and is hung by very large wrought iron hinges.

In the four rooms on the main floor are eight windows (four south and four north) finished with deep panelled seats. Two windows in the west wall of different size and shape were cut at a later date. All the woodwork of this floor is a unit in design and particularly good. The whole east wall of the southeast room is panelled and it is probable that the west walls of the two west rooms were at first also completely decorated with carved wood but the cutting of the two late west windows altered one side of each west chimney. Panelling remains in the west rooms across the chimneys and in one wall-space in each room. The bevelled panel in the center

337

of the chimney-breast in the southwest room, made from one piece of wood, measures forty-eight inches by thirty-seven. The hall-doors of the four main rooms and the Dutch door at the rear of the hall repeat the design of the panelling of the cupboard-doors in the main rooms and an arch that spans the middle of the hall carries out details that occur in the southeast room. The latter is slightly more elaborate in finish than the southwest room and was undoubtedly the best parlor of the house. From the central hall a staircase rises (with two square turns) to a half-story, in which under the gambrel roof are four bedrooms. On the first landing of the staircase is a deep window-seat and window-sashes with old panes of glass.

That the occupants of this house in the eighteenth century were subjected to some strenuous experiences is indicated by a paragraph in a newspaper of July 12, 1765, which reads: " We hear from the Fishkills that for a week or two past a tiger or panther has been seen in the woods in that neighborhood, not far from Mr. DePeyster's house. It had killed several dogs; torn a cow, so that she died the same day, and carried off the calf; it likewise carried off a colt about a week old. Eight men with their guns went in search of it and started it at a distance; it fled with great swiftness and has not since been seen at the Fishkills."

House of John DeWitt
Town of Clinton, Dutchess County, New York
PLATE 116

At the western boundary-line of the town of Clinton, Dutchess County, two main roads intersect and south of the intersection a small stream takes a drop in its course. Extra traffic occurs at a road-crossing and power is provided by a waterfall, two advantages which were seized upon here by John DeWitt (born 1752, died 1808). He, in 1773 or 1774, built for himself and his bride, Catherine Van Vliet (daughter of Dirck and Helena Van Vliet), the frame house on the high stone foundation (plate 116) which stands in the southwest angle of the roads and in 1775 he built a mill across the road on the stream. A few years later John DeWitt made a large addition to his dwelling, which now forms the main portion of the house, lying across the north end of the first or southern wing. A wing to the east of the main part was put on by John LeRoy in 1855.

For twenty-seven years John DeWitt operated his mill and created an important center of trade at the four corners. During this period he was prominent in all community affairs, serving as an officer in the War of the Revolution, as sheriff of Dutchess County and as a member of assembly. He was a delegate to the Convention of the State of New York, held in the court-house at Poughkeepsie in 1788 and voted in favor of the ratification of the Federal Constitution.

In this home of John DeWitt was born in 1780 his son, Peter, who, early in the nineteenth century, established a law-office at 45, Cedar Street, New York City. After a few years Peter DeWitt removed his office to 88, Nassau Street, where the law-practise he established is still conducted by his descendants. Peter DeWitt's successors in the firm he founded have been: his sons, Edward and Cornelius J. DeWitt; his grandsons, George G., William G. and Theodore DeWitt; and his great-grandson, Edward DeWitt.

From the point of view of family sentiment the house of John DeWitt should be linked in thought with the house (plate 69) of his grandfather, Tjerck DeWitt, on Hurley Avenue, Kingston. Tjerck DeWitt's son, Petrus DeWitt (born 1722, died 1790), left Kingston in young manhood and settled in Dutchess, where he married Rachel Radcliffe and where his son, John, was born. In 1751 Petrus DeWitt bought land in lot number three of the Pawling Patent and built a house on the site of the present residence of the Dinsmore family, north of Staatsburgh, which he named: *Wittemount*. This he sold in 1783 to Brockholst Livingston and removed to a site south of Staatsburgh, where he built a house on the east side of the post road and called the place: *Rockdale*. Both *Wittemount* and *Rockdale* have long since disappeared.

DuBois Farm on the Wappingers Creek
Town of Poughkeepsie, Dutchess County, New York

In 1730 Matthew DuBois (born 1679) of Ulster County, a son of Louis DuBois the patentee of New Paltz, bought some thirteen-hundred acres of land on the west side of the Wappingers Creek in Poughkeepsie Precinct, Dutchess County, the tract extending along the creek from (approximately) the vicinity of the dam at Titusville to a point below Red Oaks Mill. Matthew DuBois was a man of mature years at the time he made this purchase and he removed from Ulster to his extensive holdings in Dutchess accompanied by his wife, Sarah Van Keuren, and several of his sons and daughters. He died in Dutchess between March 2, 1748, when he made his will, and June 7, 1748, when the tax-list of Poughkeepsie bears the entry: Mattys Du Bois widow.

At the time that Matthew DuBois settled beside the Wappingers a road ran from the village of Poughkeepsie into the interior of the county, crossing that portion of the DuBois property which Matthew had taken as his homestead farm. That road was the equivalent of the road that now runs from Poughkeepsie to New Hackensack but its actual course in the eighteenth century was not exactly the same as the course of the modern concrete highway. Both old and new courses were laid out to approach the Wappingers from the west over a wooded ridge, which the Dutch called *Hanebergh* (Rooster Hill), and which nineteenth century neighbors referred to as Hornyback. From the foot of the ridge the early course ran in a straight line eastward (close to where the house of A. B. Gray now stands) to a bridge over the creek. The bridge, of which some timbers and masonry are still imbedded in the bank, was known about 1739 as LeRoy's Bridge as it led to the house of Simeon and Blandina LeRoy on the east side of the creek. At the spot where is now the Gray house a fork in the old road led southward and continued over what is at present a leafy, retired lane. A portion of that old fork is now the shaded avenue approaching the Gray house from the concrete road.

On the stretch of level ground between the ridge and the Wappingers, bisected as described by one of the principal roads of the county, Matthew DuBois created his homestead-farm about 1730. Three houses were built on the farm, two of stone and one of brick and stone combined. The stone houses stood in the shelter of *Hanebergh*, close to the east foot of the hill, one on either side of the road, and portions of their foundations, embowered in old lilac bushes, still may be found to identify their sites. The house of brick and stone is the house still standing, owned and occupied by Mr. Gray.

Matthew DuBois's homestead-farm was owned from 1773 to 1791 by his great-grandson, Lewis DuBois (born 1744, died 1824), who served at Quebec as a captain in the third regiment of the Continental Line. The owner in 1792—1793 was Henry G. Livingston, who gave the place the name of: *Ann's Field* (presumably in honor of his wife, Ann Nutter). In 1793 James Greenleaf bought *Ann's Field*, renamed it: *Green Vale*, and rented it to Duncan Ingraham. *Green Vale* (as it still is called) was owned in 1813—1818 by Abraham Adriance (member of the senate and assembly of New York), and later by the Varick family. The present owner is A. B. Gray.

Matthew DuBois doubtless lived in one of the two stone houses at the eastern base of *Hanebergh* which have now disappeared. The house occupied by Mr. Gray was presumably erected about 1774 by Lewis DuBois. It consists of brick walls at the front and the gable-ends, with a thick stone wall at the rear, all of which are two full stories in height. The original roof may have been a single slant or a gambrel but a mansard has long done duty in its place. The porch, windows and shutters all are modern. On the first floor, where there is a central hall between two rooms, the rooms have been modernized in finish. In the hall is eighteenth century wainscoting and the original staircase. In each of the two upper rooms one wall is completely panelled, that in the east room being particularly noteworthy. In floor-plan and in its two full stories the house of Lewis DuBois duplicates the Ten Broeck *Bouwerij* of 1762 (plate 38).

By the marriage of Matthew DuBois's daughter, Catharina, to Madam Brett's son, Robert; and by the marriage of his son, Eleazer, to a daughter of Johannes Coerte Van Voorhees, the DuBois farm on the Wappingers was linked with the Brett and Van Voorhees houses at Fishkill (plates 111 and 144). Matthew DuBois's son, Hezekiah, built the house at Saugerties shown in plate 73; his nephew, Daniel, built the house of 1705 on Huguenot Street, New Paltz (page 198), and other family relationships brought the Van Kleeck and Van Der Burgh houses (plate 142 and page 387) into a group with the farm of Matthew DuBois.

House of Peter DuBois

Town of Wappinger, Dutchess County, New York

Peter DuBois (born 1674, died 1738), a son of Jacques DuBois and a nephew of Louis, the patentee of New Paltz, came to Dutchess County before June, 1713, at which date he is referred to in the recital in a deed as in possession of a parcel of land in Madam Brett's share of the Rombout Patent. Another deed discloses that he held one-hundred and nine acres and an island at the mouth of the *Vis Kil* as a life-tenant. At the mouth of the stream he apparently remained until about 1729, in which year he received a deed from Gulian Verplanck for four-hundred and fifty-six acres lying on the Sprout Creek. West of the Sprout in the present town of Wappinger, he built a stone house a short distance south of the house of John Montross (page 370), which is now owned by one of his descendants, Mrs. Charles H. White. The house stands at a four-corners (formed by the intersection of roads from Hopewell and New Hackensack) but it has been altered by frame additions and its age is not obvious. The stone house is believed to have been built in two parts, the north part first and then a southerly extension. In late years, in tearing down the north part a stone was found in the original outer south wall marked: HH 1732 IM. The stone was saved and placed in the west wall of the second stone unit, next to the main entrance. The initials have not been interpreted but the figures are evidence for the date of the erection of the older portion of the house. Peter DuBois's gravestone is in the yard of the Dutch church at Fishkill and many of his descendants still live in Dutchess. He was a first cousin of Matthew DuBois of the Wappingers Creek, town of Poughkeepsie.

Duryea House

Town of East Fishkill, Dutchess County, New York

A mile northward from the four corners called Fishkill Plains is a house, now held in the estate of the late Duryea Remsen Robinson, which is known to have been the home of Abraham Duryea who died in 1802. The land on which the house stands was a part of the Rombout Patent and fell to the Verplancks. Philip Verplanck sold this particular farm in 1748. In 1771 Stephen Duryea bought it, only to sell it three years later to Abraham Duryea, since when it has remained in the tenure of a succession of kinsfolk.

Structurally, the house bears witness to many changes. The north and east walls are of stone, very thick, to the height of a story and a half. The south and west walls and the upper parts of all four are of brick. Possibly the stone house

341

of a pioneer-settler of 1748 was altered by Abraham Duryea in the 1770's and his dwelling entirely made over later by his descendants. A neighborhood tradition is current that the Duryea, Verplanck and Thorn houses (which stand within a short distance of each other) were built at nearly the same time and, as the Verplanck and Thorn houses (plate 149 and page 323) are known to have been built in 1768 and 1772, the tradition fits in with the purchase of this property by Stephen and Abraham Duryea in 1771 and 1774, respectively, either of whom might have improved the house on the farm at a time when brick was in vogue locally. Originally one and one-half stories in height, the house was built over into two full stories in the middle of the nineteenth century and many changes made in porches, dormers, windows and shutters. A hall runs through the center but the rooms west of it have been thrown into one and the house in general, inside and out, has been modernized.

The Duryeas of Dutchess were descended from Jost Durié, a Huguenot, who fled to Mannheim and from there came to Long Island but the line of the family that spread to Dutchess was so intermarried with Van Wycks, Remsens, Boerums and other Dutch neighbors that no Duryea thought of himself as of French extraction.

House of Jacob Evertson

Formerly in the Town of Amenia, Dutchess County, New York

Jacob Evertson (born 1734, died 1807), a native of New Jersey, removed to Dutchess County about 1760 and purchased some seventeen-hundred acres in the Great Nine Partners Patent. He was a grandson of Nicholas Evertson, who came from Holland to New Netherland in the seventeenth century, and of Margaret Van Baal Evertson, who, through her mother, Helena Teller, had a wide circle of kinship in the Hudson valley. Jacob Evertson married in 1761 Margaret, daughter of George Bloom, and in 1763 built a brick house in the town of Amenia about a mile south of the locality called: The City. He occupied the house until about 1795, when he moved to Pleasant Valley, where he died in 1807 and was buried in the yard of the Presbyterian church. While living in the house in Amenia he represented Dutchess County in the second Provincial Congress of New York that met in 1775—1776.

The brick house built by Jacob Evertson in 1763 was torn down about 1880 by J. W. Putnam, from whose daughter, Mrs. H. B. Conklin, particulars about the house have been obtained. It was two full stories in height, with a gambrel roof; across the front were two files of windows, with a Dutch door in the center and a small porch; a hall ran through the house from front to back on both floors; a straight staircase rose from the first floor hall; there were two rooms on each side of each hall; all the finishings were plain and the house lacked wainscoting, panelling, carved mantels, &c. It was built on a large scale, the bricks were of superior quality and the walls so thick as to form deep window spaces.

It is to be regretted that no old photograph of this house has been found for, in general structural design and in materials, it is a significant item for 1763 in the story of architecture in Dutchess County. It was evidently similar in height, in roof and in the use of brick to the house of Sarah Tobias Newcomb (plate 129) built some fifteen years later in the town of Pleasant Valley.

House at the Farmers' Landing

Town of Wappinger, Dutchess County, New York

PLATE 117

The land on the south side of the mouth of the Wappingers Creek was covered by the Rombout Patent and it fell to the share of the Verplanck family when the patent was divided. William Verplanck (born 1693, died 1745) received in 1722, under the patent, lands along the Sprout Creek (about five miles back from the river), where he settled and built a house (page 401) and a mill. With the growth of the business of his mill an outlet for its product was necessary and so in 1741 and 1742 the county records of roads tell of the opening or the improvement of a highway leading from the mill of William Verplanck, through *Middel Bosch* (i. e. Middle Grove, now called: Middle Bush), to a landing at the mouth of the Wappingers. The terminus soon came to be known as: the Farmers' Landing, and the highway as: the Farmers' Landing Road, and road and landing served the residents of New Hackensack, Sprout Creek, Swartwoutville and Hopewell all through the eighteenth century.

The landing was inherited from William Verplanck by his nephew, Philip, and then by the latter's son, William Beekman Verplanck, and while business was conducted there by the members of this family the stone house near the dock was undoubtedly the dwelling of their resident representative or agent. William B. Verplanck sold the dock, storehouse and dwelling before 1800 and for a few years Abraham Lent and Peter Waldron of Dutchess County and Nicholas Cruger of New York City held joint interests in it. But with the rise of New Hamburgh as a shipping point in the first quarter of the nineteenth century competition drove the Farmers' Landing out of existence as a commercial feature of the river-front. Only the picturesque dwelling (now on the estate of Mrs. Henry Pierrepont Perry) is left as a reminder of a once important center of trade and transportation.

The main portion of the house (there is a wing of later date) consists of two rooms (each with an outer door) and two chimneys. The rooms contain some primitive wood-trim.

House of Johannes A. Fort

Town of Poughkeepsie, Dutchess County, New York

PLATE 118

The house on the east side of the state road (the former *King's Highway*), about four miles south of the city of Poughkeepsie and now owned by Frank Dickerson, was known years ago as the Fort homestead. The land it stands on was sold in 1759 by Christopher Van Bommel to Johannes Abraham Fort (" late of Ulster County ") and the house was built either by the Van Bommel family between 1742 and 1759 or by Johannes A. Fort about 1760. The walls are of stone, the west front being faced with brick and the gable filled with the same. While the dormers and the porch are recent the interior still contains early wood-trim. The original floor-plan consisted of two rooms on either side of the central hall but the two on the north are now thrown into one. A pane in one of the windows of the dining-room is cut: Jane Fort 1778, and another pane bears the inscription: Henry Dawkins, engraver.

The Fort family was established in upper Albany County by 1700, where the name occurs as: Laford, La Fort, Fort and VanderVort. Johannes Fort, born at Niscayuna, drifted down to Kingston and married there in 1749 Rebecca Ostrander. He it was who in 1759 removed to this farm of three-hundred acres in the precinct of Poughkeepsie. Johannes Fort's son, Abraham (born 1750, died 1822), who was locally prominent in the War of the Revolution, succeeded his father in the house. And it was Major Abraham Fort's wife, Jane, daughter of Peter Monfort of Sprout Creek (page 355), who cut her name on the window-pane.

On the hillside across the road from the house is a family burying ground, where Major Fort and his wife are buried.

House of John Frear

Town of Poughkeepsie, Dutchess County, New York

PLATE 119

Three miles south from the court house at Poughkeepsie, on the east side of the former *King's Highway* in the eighteenth century was the farm of John Frear, colonel of a local regiment of militia in the Revolutionary War. John Frear (born about 1725—1730, died 1809) was descended from Hugo Frear, patentee of New Paltz, in the line of Hugo, the second, and the latter's son, Simeon. Simeon Frear married in 1720 Maritje Van Bommel and removed from New Paltz to Poughkeepsie. John Frear, of the fourth generation, married at Poughkeepsie in 1752 Maria Van Kleeck (of Baltus, of Barent, of Baltus Barents Van Kleeck) and in 1755 bought the farm referred to. In 1798 he advertised this property for sale in the columns

344

of the *Poughkeepsie Journal* and stated that the dwelling on the farm was a stone house of six rooms. The house now on the farm (plate 119) consists of both stone and wood and it can only be surmised that part of the original stone structure was torn down and new construction in wood substituted. The workmanship, whether in wood or stone, is all crude. All wall-spaces are uneven and the beams are old and large; but modern windows, shutters and dormers replace original details.

While Colonel John Frear occupied this house his first cousins, the Lows, were living at New Paltz in the house that still stands at the northeast corner of Huguenot Street; his first cousins, the Terwilligers, were in the house (plate 91) on the road from New Paltz to Modena; and his wife's cousin, Baltus P. Van Kleeck (born 1725, died 1794) was the occupant of the Van Kleeck homestead (plate 142) at Poughkeepsie. Other near cousins of Mrs. Frear were at the same time in the Van Wagenen house (plate 145) and in the unidentified house at Poughkeepsie (plate 140).

House on the Garrison Farm

Town of Clinton, Dutchess County, New York

PLATE 120

In 1741 Joost Garrison (then of Westchester County) and Francis Van Dyke and Adolph Banker bought in partnership seven-hundred acres of land in Dutchess County which in 1743 they partitioned between them. Garrison (who was a son of Jonas and Cornelia De Groot Garrison of Tappan) received by the partition about two-hundred and twelve acres, on which he settled. The east (right) end of the house shown in plate 120 was built on the farm of Joost Garrison as a tenant-house. About 1837 the west end was added. While the enlarged house is of so late a date in completion it belongs in design to the period before the Revolution and is really a good illustration of the type of frame house that was built in Dutchess in the eighteenth century. It stands on the north side of the road, west of the hamlet of Pleasant Plains and is now owned by Mrs. H. Reed Hawley and her sister, Mrs. Robert J. Knox.

House of Benjamin Hasbrouck

Town of East Fishkill, Dutchess County, New York

PLATE 121

Between Stormville and Gayhead, on the south side of the state road, is a stone house owned by Jeremiah Fowler and rented to negro tenants. In the rear or west wall of the house is a stone marked: B H 1755, the initials being those of the builder,

345

Benjamin Hasbrouck, who moved from Ulster County to southern Dutchess before 1737, in which year he married Jannetje De Long. The house is a bit of Ulster County, transplanted; for Benjamin Hasbrouck built for himself a dwelling as nearly like those he had known in his youth as he could make it except that it is almost square and its proportions are unusual. The finish of the interior is rigidly plain. A large room in the southwest corner takes the greater part of the floor-area. This room opens into an oblong chamber in the northwest corner of the house. Across the east side are two small connecting rooms and an entry. The entry contains an enclosed staircase and has a doorway, opening to the east. The original door here was a typical one; panelled, divided across the center and hung on heavy iron hinges. A wing on the south side of the house has recently been torn down but may not have been part of the original house. In the west wall a former door has been made into a window.

House of David Johnstone, called *Lithgow*
Town of Washington, Dutchess County, New York

PLATE 122

When Dutchess County was first opening for settlement a group of men, prominent in the Province of New York and possessed of capital, bought the greater part of the northern end of the county as a speculation in real estate. The patent which they obtained for their purchase was known as the Great Nine Partners Patent. One of the nine partners was David Jamison, who had come from Linlithgow, Scotland, to New York, where he served the province as secretary of state, attorney-general, &c. Jamison's rights under the Great Nine Partners Patent were inherited by his daughter, Elizabeth Jamison, who in 1717 married John Johnstone of New Jersey. David Johnstone (born 1724, died 1809), son of John and Elizabeth Jamison Johnstone, was a well-known resident of New York City and he it was who about 1758 built a country home in Dutchess County on lands which he had inherited through his mother from his grandfather. The house stands on the east side of the state road between Millbrook and Amenia. David Johnstone named the property: *Lithgow*, in honor of his grandfather's home in Scotland and the name extended itself ultimately from the gentleman's seat to a hamlet that grew up a mile south of it. In 1813, after David Johnstone's death, *Lithgow* was sold to Isaac Smith (formerly of Long Island), whose great-grandson, Isaac Smith Wheaton now owns it.

In ownership *Lithgow* has no connection with the Dutch. But in architecture competent professional opinion considers it one of the best bits of pre-Revolutionary construction now to be seen in the Hudson valley and one of the best surviving examples of the Dutch spirit in design. As contrasted with the severity and rigidity found in houses in New England, *Lithgow* exhibits the more mellow and expansive

346

character usually credited to the Dutch in their manner of living. Always having been maintained as a gracious and dignified private home, it has escaped exploitation and this volume is fortunate in including a record of it as an illuminating item in the general architectural history of the region of the Hudson.

The house David Johnstone built consists of frame walls, filled with brick and faced with broad clapboards (see: notes on *Cherry Hill*, 1768, plate 50). It is one and one-half stories high, with an unusual gambrel roof of triple pitch. The roof extends beyond the wall of the gable-end in the same way as does the roof of Abraham Salisbury's house at Leeds (page 92) and as that on Madam Brett's house at Beacon (plate 111). A central hall has a Dutch door at either end. At the south is an inset porch (plate 122), the ends of which are enclosed on the same principal of construction as in the Van Vliet house (plate 143). An open porch runs across the whole width of the north façade, which was used as the front of the house at first when the road-course was nearer by. On the north front are two large drawing-rooms, one on each side of the hall, finished with chair-rail and fine mantels. The southern half of the first floor is partitioned in such a way as to make two secondary halls, one with a staircase; a large dining-room on the east side; and, on the west, master's offices. Beside the triple pitch of the roof a notable feature of the house is the height of the ceilings of the rooms on the main floor, the walls of which rise to twelve feet. There are five finished rooms in the second or half-story, generous in floor-area, but subject in the height of the ceilings to the lines of the gambrel roof. In 1910 a large wing was added to the house at the east in harmony, architecturally, with the old structure. Surrounding the house are remarkable locust trees and a garden, which was a very early planting, adjoins the south lawn. The lovely old place is infused as a whole with the beauty of simplicity and refinement; and discriminating occupation for six generations has made it a rare haven in these later years.

The King's Highway

Dutchess County, New York

PLATES 123 and 124

The two small stone houses shown in plates 123 and 124 stand on the west side of the state road south of the village of Rhinebeck and are owned by Maunsell S. Crosby. Who built them is not known, nor is the year of their erection recorded and little can be gathered about their occupants. But in their anonymity and in their undoubted character as survivals of the eighteenth century they furnish excellent illustrations of the type of house that dotted the *King's Highway* all along its course in Dutchess in the pre-Revolutionary period.

In 1703 the legislature of New York passed an act for the better laying out and regulating of a post road from King's Bridge to Albany. At that date there were in all Dutchess County but a few houses; there is knowledge of two at *Kipsbergen*, of three or four at Poughkeepsie, of one at the mouth of Jan Casper's Kil, but none at Fishkill. The county was a wilderness and travel to or from it was almost entirely by water, in preference to the use of the Indian trail as a bridle-path. In 1712 a recorded deed mentions a wagon-path at Poughkeepsie where the state road now runs and slowly thereafter a road came into existence, along which was a succession of just such houses as those here shown.

Many of the stone houses on or near the *King's Highway* are known now only on early maps or by references to them in deeds. Others have vanished within the memory of living persons. Of the latter group members of the Roosevelt family recall the one on the east side of the road, just north of the boundary between the towns of Hyde Park and Poughkeepsie, which was John Pride's tavern in the Revolution and in which the Marquis de Chastellux spent a night when on his journeyings. The late William H. Van Benschoten of Knoxville, Tennessee, lived as a boy in a stone house on the east side of the road, opposite the present entrance to the estate of Frederick R. Newbold, and his description of it identifies it accurately as one of this established type. Just south of this last mentioned house (and opposite the property which was the home of the late Mrs. John F. Winslow) was another, now gone, in which was a stone marked: 1787, and a photograph of which (taken in late years when it was uninhabitable) is in the collection of the late Frank Van Kleeck of Poughkeepsie.

A house still standing and belonging in the class with the two illustrated is on *Steen Valetje*, the estate of Lyman Delano at Barrytown, and another (enlarged by a brick addition) is at *Speck zyn kil* in the town if Poughkeepsie, owned by Edward E. Perkins.

Kipsbergen, Dutchess County, New York
PLATES 125 and 126

In 1686 five Dutchmen, living in Ulster County, bought from the Indians a tract of woodland on the east shore of the Hudson, opposite the mouth of the Rondout Creek. A Crown patent for the land was obtained in 1688 but no settlement on it is known of with certainty until 1700.

The land was acquired in two parcels and one patent confirmed title for the two. The boundary between the two parcels was a stream, which enters the Hudson to the north of the present station of the New York Central and Hudson River Railroad at Rhinecliff. South of the stream the land was bought by three partners: Gerret Aertsen (Van Wagenen), Arie Roosa and Jan Elton. North of it the patentee was Hendrick Kip of Kingston, whose brother, Jacob Kip, became his partner in this enterprise and partitioned the land with him in 1702.

The name: *Kipsbergen*, derived from Hendrick and Jacob Kip, was extended

348

to include the property of Aertsen, Roosa and Elton and serves now as a reminder of the fact that the Dutch were the first settlers in the vicinity of Rhinebeck, although they were outnumbered in a few years by the many Germans from the Palatinate who were settled by Henry Beekman on the flats farther back from the river.

Through the land of Hendrick and Jacob Kip ran the Sepasco Trail of the Indian, eastward from the Hudson, the course of which trail is now the highway to the village of Rhinebeck.

Near the place where the Sepasco Trail left the river one of the Kip brothers built a two-room stone house, one and one-half stories high, of which house the west and north walls are now standing, but which has been so enlarged by frame additions that nothing pictorial remains. At the north end of the west wall, on the line of the original first story, are cut the letters: H K, which make it almost certain that Hendrick Kip built the house. Beside the front door are cut the figures: 1708, which have been accepted usually as the date of erection. The house is known, however, to have been occupied by Jacob Kip, who lived in it many years and who gave it to his son, Roeloff Kip. In the small cove before the house Jacob Kip had the terminus of a canoe-ferry to Kingston, which ferry he operated before 1721 and for which his son, Abraham, obtained a charter in 1752. The apparent discrepancy as to the builder, the age and the occupancy of this house is explainable on the theory that Hendrick Kip was the first to leave Kingston and make settlement on the tract of woodland on the east side of the river; that he built this house just before 1700; and that Jacob Kip took possession of the house on his arrival soon after.

It is suggested that Hendrick Kip may have built the small house just before 1700 because he built another dwelling (plate 125), southward from the one by the cove, which stood on the east side of the road to Rhinecliff and which bore in its wall a stone marked: Ao 1700 HK AK. The initials are those of Hendrick Kip and of his wife, Annatje Jans Van Putten, and it is understood that they occupied this house (a typical story-and-a-half stone structure) until 1726 when Hendrick Kip exchanged the house with Henry Beekman, the second, for certain lands owned by the latter.

Henry Beekman, the second (born 1688, died 1776), was a widower with one child when he acquired this house. His first wife, Janet Livingston, died in 1724 and he married soon after Gertrude Van Cortlandt (daughter of Stephanus Van Cortlandt and Gertrude Schuyler) and he and his second wife made the house at *Kipsbergen* their home for many years. Colonel Beekman died " at his seat in Dutchess County " in the first days of the Revolutionary War (January 3, 1776) and his wife a year or two later and the title to the house passed to Colonel Beekman's only child (the daughter of his first wife), Margaret Beekman (born 1724, died 1800), who in 1742 had married Robert Livingston and gone to live at *Clermont* (page 87). On October 20, 1779, Mrs. Livingston conveyed her father's house to her son, Henry Beekman Livingston (born 1750, died 1831), a distinguished officer in the

War of the Revolution and who long occupied the old home. From Colonel Henry B. Livingston the house was inherited by his daughter, Miss Margaret B. Livingston, who sold it to Andrew J. Heermance and as the Heermance house it was known in the second half of the nineteenth century. Between the time when Colonel Henry Beekman died and the time when his grandson, Colonel Livingston, had finished his military services in the Revolution and taken up residence at *Kipsbergen* it is supposed that the house was a haven for Pierre Van Cortlandt of Croton and his family. The household of the manor-house (plate 109) at Croton were forced to leave Westchester County at the approach of the British up the Hudson and they are known to have sought safety near Rhinebeck in Dutchess. As Pierre Van Cortlandt was a nephew of Colonel Beekman's widow and his wife a niece of Colonel Beekman (recently deceased), what more natural than that the Beekman home should be their place of refuge?

No tradition has been learned as to when or by whom the house built by Hendrick Kip in 1700 was enlarged. As it finally appeared, it consisted of three parts: a southern unit of stone (the original house); a northern unit of stone; and a link of brick between the two. As the earliest construction in brick in Dutchess that has been dated belongs in the third quarter of the eighteenth century and as the end of the period of stone is approximated as about 1800, it is suggested as probable that the two additions made to the house of Hendrick Kip were either the work of Colonel Henry Beekman between 1750 and 1776 or of his grandson, Colonel Henry B. Livingston, between 1783 and 1800. As the plate reveals, roofs, porches, windows and shutters all were changed in the nineteenth century.

Successive occupation by the Kips, Beekmans, Van Cortlandts and Livingstons links this house at *Kipsbergen* with the Kip, Pawling, Rutsen-Hardenbergh, Van Cortlandt and Livingston houses, shown in plates 127, 82, 83, 109, and 128.

A third house at *Kipsbergen* stands at the point where the road from Rhinebeck to Rhinecliff forks; one turn is to the south and passes the ruins of the house of 1700; the fork to the west is the Sepasco Trail, which continues to the river and leads to the house of Jacob Kip. The third house (plate 126) was the home of Jacob Kip's son, Abraham. The western end of it was built first, as is shown by the projection of a large exterior chimney into the hall of the east portion. The two parts are on two levels, the westerly one consisting of two rooms, the easterly of a hall and two rooms. The ceilings are low and some of the large beams are unenclosed but most of the eighteenth century details have been replaced with later finishings. The house was used by Abraham Kip as an inn. It was on a main line of travel east and west and the business of the ferry and of the adjacent wharf (long known, locally, as the Long Dock) contributed to its value as a location for a house of entertainment.

The house of Abraham Kip at the fork of the road and a large estate surrounding it are still owned by the Kip family. The estate bears the name: *Ankony*, in memory of its original Indian owner.

House of Hendrick Kip

Town of Fishkill, Dutchess County, New York

PLATE 127

West of the village of Fishkill on the south side of the road to the river is a long low stone house, painted red, that fits into the landscape as if it properly belonged there. Fifty years ago old residents at Fishkill held a tradition that the builder of this house was James Hussey, a tradition confirmed by the fact that James Hussey's purchase of the land on which the house stands is on record as having been made in 1720. On May 13th of that year Madam Brett deeded to Hussey one-hundred acres, with house, barn, outhouses, etc., but reserving such timber as was suitable for her own sawmill. After 1736 the name of James Hussey disappears from the tax-lists. Ten years later, in 1746, the name of Hendrick Kip is entered as a tax-payer and he, supposedly, acquired then the Hussey farm although no deed is to be found.

The little red house that nestles so confidingly into its setting consists of a hall, with one room to the west and three to the east (one larger and two smaller) and has a kitchen-wing (of about 1860) to the south. At the rear is a door that is one of the best examples to be found of a primitive eighteenth century divided door, with bull's eyes in the upper half. The front doorway is early nineteenth century in design; the porch is modern; the interior has lost its eighteenth century details. It is highly probable that the east end of the house (two small rooms, with a door to the south and having one chimney) constituted the primitive dwelling of James Hussey (1720—1737) and that Hendrick Kip added toward the west two rooms and a hall. In the north front wall, about in line with the chimney, is a stone, marked: 1753, and immediately to the east of the front porch is another stone, cut with: H K 1 7 5 3.

Hendrick Kip was born in Kingston in 1688, spent part of his boyhood in the house of his father at *Kipsbergen* (plate 125) and married in 1715 Jacomyntje Nieuwkerk. Where he and his wife lived between 1715 and 1747 (when they settled at Fishkill) is not known. They had but one child, a daughter, Jannetje, born 1716, of whom her father recorded in Dutch in his Bible: " 1727, March 23rd, Is my daughter, Jannetje Kip, slept in the Lord in the morning at the breaking of the day." The Bible (printed in 1714) contains the further entry of the death of Hendrick Kip, himself, on November 29, 1754, so he enjoyed the occupation of his home at Fishkill for a short time only.

By his will Hendrick Kip left his estate to his wife, during widowhood. After her death or re-marriage he bequeathed it to her nephew, Cornelius Nieuwkerk. In less than a year after Hendrick Kip's death (that is: before October, 1755) his widow married Captain Peter DuBois of Fishkill and she outlived her nephew, Cornelius Nieuwkerk, who died in 1763—1764.

Tradition says that after the death of Cornelius Nieuwkerk the house of Hendrick Kip was occupied by Johannes Swart and that during the Revolution it was for a time headquarters for Baron von Steuben. The land records of Dutchess County show that in 1792 the place was owned by Evert Wynkoop Swart (who came to Dutchess from Ulster) and from him to Mrs. J. B. Davol, the present owner, the chain of title is complete. The tradition regarding von Steuben is derived through several independent channels and is inherently probable, for the house is on a road which was a main thoroughfare between New England and the South, while the British held New York City, and officers, troops, the Hessian prisoners, civil officials and private citizens all passed this way.

House of Henry Livingston
Formerly in the Town of Poughkeepsie, Dutchess County, New York
PLATE 128

Henry Livingston (born 1714, died 1799), son of Gilbert and Cornelia (Beekman) Livingston of Kingston, established himself at Poughkeepsie when he was twenty-five years old. An old account-book shows that from November, 1737, to April, 1738, he paid board to Francis Filkin, which means that for six months he lived in the Van Kleeck house (plate 142), as Francis Filkin had married Peter Van Kleeck's widow and he and his wife occupied Peter's house from their marriage in 1733 until they removed to New York in 1746.

A map of the east shore of the Hudson from Mine Point to Crum Elbow made in 1738 by Henry Livingston, himself, records his own residence in 1738 on the site occupied by the house shown in plate 128. Evidently, after a winter spent in the Van Kleeck house, he began with warm weather the practise of his profession, that of surveying, and moved from the village a mile or so to the south on the river-front in a house by himself. That house was, supposedly, a portion of the small wing in the fore-ground of the plate. Who built the primitive structure, taken over in 1738 by Henry Livingston, is a question. Evert Van Wagenen owned the land from 1712 to 1725 and he may have been the builder. John Concklin of Westchester County was a settler in the immediate vicinity between 1725 and 1729 and he may have erected the house. In 1738, when Livingston occupied the site, Concklin (as shown by the map) lived a little south of him. From 1738 to 1742 Henry Livingston probably rented the house but in 1741—1742 he married the daughter of his neighbor, John Concklin, and on December 2, 1742, bought the house from his father-in-law.

The photograph shown in plate 128, taken in 1886 by Henry Booth of Poughkeepsie and reproduced through his courtesy, tells a long story of the evolution of the primitive shelter of the pioneer into a comfortable home by means of a succession of additions. This house, torn down in 1910, stood on land now owned by the Phoenix

Horseshoe Company of Poughkeepsie and an analysis, not only of the plate but of other extant views of the house, shows that an original small structure of rough stones (the common type of the early eighteenth century) was raised in height, perhaps increased in depth and later joined to a larger new unit, which in turn was given a third story as an after-thought and a north-west rear wing, while in the nineteenth century a veranda was built across the whole front.

A sketch of Henry Livingston's house, attributed to the pencil of Henry Livingston, Jr., was published in May, 1791, in the *New York Magazine and Literary Repository* and presents a dwelling consisting of two main parts, one larger and one smaller, the larger part being two full stories in height and covered by a hipped roof. A photograph of the house made by Mr. Booth in 1886 from the west contains details that tend to confirm the record of the sketch as to the hipped roof.

When Henry Livingston died in 1799 his executors advertised his " mansion " and farm of eighty acres to be sold at auction:—the " mansion " was fifty yards from the river; " not new," but " still good and commodious "; it contained " eight rooms, two passages, a pantry, a large kitchen and a servants' bedroom "; the " terrene in front " was " shaded with aged locusts "; there were a large garden and three-hundred peach-trees, five- or six-hundred apple-trees and five-hundred locust trees.

Henry Livingston had need of a commodious dwelling for he and his wife, Susanna, were the parents of four sons and six daughters, born between 1742 and 1767, in which years he presumably built the two-story unit sketched by his son in 1791. It was in those years that Henry Livingston was in his prime and a useful member of the community. To the development of his farm he added ceaseless activity as a surveyor in all parts of Dutchess County and from 1737 to 1789 he held office as clerk of Dutchess County. His habits were methodical and the county owes him an incalculable debt for his careful, legible entry of records in libers and by files.

While Henry Livingston's ancestry in the male line was Scotch, he and his family were so merged with the Dutch element in the community as to be indistinguishable therefrom and the fact that the Reverend John Henry Livingston, so long prominent in the ministry of the Reformed Dutch Church and as president of Rutgers College, was born in this, his father's, house, invests the house with interest for the Reformed Communion.

Although it may be considered that the house of Henry Livingston was a conglomeration of lines, illustrating no defined type of architecture, it is to be observed that such an aggregation of additions and alterations is an example of the manner in which many old homes have undergone change and in that way it is a record of a principle and a key to an understanding of one phase of architectural history in the Hudson valley. The house remained in the Livingston family until 1870. In 1910, when torn down by the Phoenix Horseshoe Company, Edmund Platt

353

recorded in the columns of the *Poughkeepsie Daily Eagle* (May 17 and May 19) that the removal of the shingles showed the walls of the house to be of stone and very thick. The shingles (which can best be seen in a close-up photograph at page thirty-five of the Year Book of the Dutchess County Historical Society for 1919) were similar in size and shape to those which are doing duty today on the house of Madam Brett (plate 111) and which formerly were on the Van Voorhees house (plate 144). The shingles ante-dated the Revolution because one of them bore the mark of a ball fired by Vaughan's raiders in 1777, which struck the house just west of the front door. Mr. Platt noted that some of the original hipped roof remained in 1910 under the roof last built. He also described a fireplace in the living room eight feet and a half wide and stated that the partition walls were frames filled in with sand and clay, mixed with straw. The frames were fastened with long hand-wrought spikes, curved at the larger end.

Through the marriages of Henry Livingston's ten children this homestead came to have many affiliations. Its connection with other houses included a tie with the Platt house (plate 131); the Mesier house (plate 112); and the house of John Brincker-hoff (plate 114). Garret Storm of Upper Hopewell (page 376) was a cousin of Henry Livingston's wife. Henry Livingston's sister married Pierre Van Cortlandt of Westchester County (plate 109) and his uncle, Henry Beekman, lived at *Kipsbergen* (plate 125).

House of Henry Livingston, Jr.

Formerly in the Town of Poughkeepsie, Dutchess County, New York

On the west side of the *King's Highway*, two miles south of the court-house at Poughkeepsie, is *Locust Grove*, a property owned and named originally by Henry Livingston, Jr. (born 1748, died 1828), a son of Henry Livingston whose house is shown in plate 128. Near the entrance-gate at *Locust Grove* is the seventy-ninth milestone from New York City. The house built on the place by Henry Livingston, Jr., about the time of his marriage (1774) stood until well into the nineteenth century and was one of the stone houses typical of the eighteenth, longer than broad, one and one-half stories high.

Particular interest attaches to this house not simply because Henry Livingston, Jr., was a gallant officer of the third regiment of the Continental Line under General Montgomery in Canada but because it was here that he is said to have written the well-known verses entitled: *A Visit from St. Nicholas,* and which begin with the line: " 'Twas the Night before Christmas." That composition, so widely popular, is ascribed to the pen of Henry Livingston, Jr., by the unanimous consent of his descendants, whose belief has much to warrant it. The question of the authorship of the verses (usually attributed to Clement Moore) has been discussed in literary reviews and is merely cited here. An illustrated article, descriptive of the house of

354

Henry Livingston, Jr., his public services, his artistic productions, etc., may be found at pages 30—46, of the Year Book of the Dutchess County Historical Society for 1919.

The house of Henry Livingston, Jr., was ultimately torn down and the house now standing on an adjacent site and owned by Mrs. William Hopkins Young was built by Samuel F. B. Morse in the middle of the nineteenth century.

House of Peter Monfort

Formerly in the Town of Wappinger, Dutchess County, New York

In the second quarter of the eighteenth century there was a noticeable migration from Long Island to Dutchess County, when the sons of long established Dutch families bought large acreages in Dutchess under the sound title of the Rombout Patent. One of those young Dutchmen was Peter Monfort of Flatlands (born 1711, died 1791), who purchased from the Verplancks about 1735 a farm on the Sprout Creek. On his farm Peter built a stone house, which stood until burned at a comparatively late date and the ruins of which are still in evidence on the cross road south of Stringham's Mill.

Peter Monfort's house was one and one-half stories high, with shingled roof and gables. It consisted of a main structure with a wing, or lean-to, at the east end. There were three rooms across the south front and three smaller ones at the rear and some of the rooms are remembered to have contained good wall-panelling and cupboards. The east and middle front rooms each had an entrance-door and the east room, which was the best parlor, was kept closed, being opened only for weddings and funerals, in accordance with the customs of the Dutch on Long Island.

Of the Monfort family on Sprout Creek, Jane (born 1757, died 1823) married Major Abraham Fort, whose house is shown in plate 118, and Magdalena Monfort (born 1762, died 1830) married Cornelius R. Van Wyck, whose house appears in plate 147.

House of Sarah Tobias Newcomb

Town of Pleasant Valley, Dutchess County, New York

PLATE 129

The house on the south side of the state road between Pleasant Valley and Washington Hollow, known as the Newcomb house, was built about 1777 by Sarah Tobias Newcomb while her husband, Zacheus Newcomb (born 1724—1725, died about 1790), was away from home in military service. Mrs. Newcomb's father, Christian Tobias, belonged to a family settled on Long Island, the origin of which is undetermined, but which could have been either Dutch or English in descent. The Newcomb ancestry was solely English. Genealogically, therefore, the connection

355

of Mrs. Newcomb's house with the Dutch is tenuous. Architecturally, the house is Georgian English in style and, at first thought, would seem to have no place in a record of Dutch homes. It is, never-the-less, a specific instance of a trend in house-building, evident in the Hudson valley before the Revolution, a trend which Dutch families emphasized in such houses as: *The Pastures* at Albany, built in 1762 by Philip Schuyler (page 97); in the second Van Rensselaer manor-house of 1765 (page 112); and in *Vly House* (plate 21), built before 1767 by Hendrick Cuyler. The house of Frederick Van Cortlandt in 1748 (plate 110) is an early and outstanding example of the Georgian school, while in Dutchess County a more modest instance of it occurred in the house built in 1763 by Jacob Evertson (page 342).

Sarah Tobias Newcomb was a forerunner of the capable, modern woman of business for she not only superintended the erection of her house in the absence of her husband but directed the manufacture of the bricks used in it. The pond now adjacent to the house was created by the flooding of the pit dug for the clay with which the bricks were made. The walls of the house are laid in Flemish bond and are twenty inches thick. The house is two full stories in height, topped by a gambrel roof. Iron wall-anchors in the west wall are in a shape reversible as the letters: Z and N, and are supposed to have been intended for " Zacheus Newcomb." On the south front the porch (plate 129) is a recent reproduction of the one formerly there. The entrance-door is original. A central hall and four rooms constitute the floor-plan. The rooms contain excellent original wood-trim, good mantels, blue tiles, deep window seats, corner cupboards.

The present owner of the house, Mrs. J. Adams Brown (Flora Newcomb), is a descendant of the builder.

Old Hundred
New Hackensack, New York
PLATE 130

At New Hackensack in Dutchess County there is a little house the builder of which is not known with certainty and the occupants of which have not been Dutch but which is such a pocket-edition of a characteristic type of Dutch domestic design that it is a desirable inclusion in this record of homes in Dutchess.

The land it is built on lies within the Rombout Patent and from 1734 to 1754 changed ownership several times. From 1754 to 1760 Joseph Horton held the title and from 1760 to 1795 John Cooke. The Reverend William Seward, a Yale graduate from Connecticut, bought it in 1795 and the property remained in his family until late years. Either Joseph Horton or John Cooke was, presumably, the builder of the house, which in the Seward family was known as: *Old Hundred*. It is now owned by John Hinners and occupied by a tenant. The old landmark was rescued from a state of decay by Mr. Hinners who, in repairing it, preserved its original features.

It stands on a bend of the road and overlooks a stream (tributary to the Wappingers Creek) on which the eighteenth century owners of the house had a grist-mill. Northwest of the house is a handsome brick house, built about 1840 (by a son of the Reverend William Seward of *Old Hundred*), which was known as *Seward Place* in the nineteenth century and is now the home of the owner of *Old Hundred*.

Old Hundred is built of frame walls, filled in with a mixture of reddish clay and long hair. The front (south) wall is faced with bricks (laid in English bond) and the sides and rear are clapboarded. The roof is a gambrel, its long slope curving out over a modern veranda which replaces an original. Throughout the structure are found handmade wooden pins and iron nails, HL hinges and the strap-hinges of characteristic eighteenth century pattern; the ceiling-beams are large, handcut and irregular in size. The floor-plan consists of a hall at the southwest angle of the house, from which opens to the east a large front room; across the rear extends one room. To the east is a small wing, having two rooms on the groundfloor. A good open staircase (with two turns) leads from the front hall to the upper story (where are four finished rooms) and an enclosed staircase rises from the back room. A Dutch door opening into the front hall bears the marks of the knocker and latches that were on it originally. The doors of the front room are panelled, in handwork; those of the four upper rooms are battened. The east wall of the main room is covered with bevelled panels and the fireplace framed by a shallow cornice. Blue Biblical tiles are known to have been around this fireplace in former years. The fireplace in the north room is also surrounded by a simple facing, is flanked by panelled cupboards and the chimney-breast is panelled. In the rear room of the wing is a large detached cupboard of eighteenth century workmanship and style.

Palen-Platt House

Town of Poughkeepsie, Dutchess County, New York

PLATE 131

On the beautiful flats along the Wappingers Creek, north of Manchester Bridge, lies a farm that Madam Brett conveyed in 1735 to Gysbert Peelen of Kingston. The purchaser (whose name was later Anglicized to Gilbert Palen) is assumed to have been one of the descendants of Brandt Peelen from Nykerk, Gelderland, Holland, who occupied the farm called: *Welys Burgh*, on Castle Island (below Albany) in the colony of Rensselaerswyck, about 1639. Gysbert Peelen married at Kingston in 1712 Hilletje Van Vliet and later, when Madam Brett offered land for sale in Dutchess under the title of the Rombout Patent, he and his wife removed to the farm on the Wappingers.

There Peelen built himself a house, which is mentioned in the county records in 1748 in connection with a description of the road near it. The road is said in the record to have run from the bridge over the Wappingers " at the house of Gysbert Peelen ", along the lane from the bridge to the foot of the hill and so on to a junction with the Filkintown road. The same road-course exists today and the house now standing on the farm bears the same relation to the creek and the bridge, the road and the hill that the above description indicates.

Gysbert Peelen's will, written in Dutch, was dated March 17, 1755. By it he gave all of his real estate to his three sons: Andries, Benjamin and Henry. A clause in the will provided that his beloved wife, Hilletje, should reside in his rear building, called: *de Winkel* (the shop or store), as long as she remained his widow, *de Winkel* to be equipped with certain furnishings and the three sons to take care of a milch-cow for their mother, summer and winter.

In 1762 the sons of Gysbert Peelen sold this property to Zephaniah Platt and there is a clear record of title from that date to the present owner, Frank De Garmo. Zephaniah Platt owned and occupied the place until 1798, when he removed to Plattsburgh on Lake Champlain. During the Revolutionary War, while living in this house, Colonel Platt, beside rendering military service, was a delegate from Dutchess to the Provincial Congress of New York in 1775, 1776, 1777; a member of the Council of Safety, 1777; and of the State Senate from 1777 to 1783; while in 1788 he was a delegate to the State Constitutional Convention at Poughkeepsie. His wife, Mary Van Wyck, was a daughter of Theodorus Van Wyck of Wiccopee (page 398); Mrs. Platt's brother, Dr. Theodorus Van Wyck, lived in the house of his father-in-law, John Brinckerhoff (plate 114); and Colonel and Mrs. Platt's son, Jonas (born 1769), went out from the house on the Wappingers Creek to marry Helen Livingston, brought up in the house (plate 128) of her father, Henry Livingston, at Poughkeepsie.

The house on the Wappingers Creek has no marked stone. A near neighbor, Peter R. Sleight, told Silas De Garmo in 1854 that the house at that time was one-hundred and twenty-five years old,—provided the statement made to him by his father, Colonel James Sleight (born 1752, died 1825), was accurate. This estimate would date the house from 1729. As Gysbert Peelen bought the farm in 1735 and had a house on it in 1748 it is probable that he built a dwelling soon after he took possession of the land.

As it now stands, the house is unmistakeably the sum of several additions and alterations. A careful examination of it leads to the belief that Gysbert Peelen built a stone house of two rooms, facing east and having a cellar under the south room only. The walls of this unit are two feet thick and of primitive masonry and it is a fair guess that over the two rooms was a half-story or attic under a roof of single slant. Against the west wall of this house an addition was later made, consisting of a broad hall, with north and south doors and two rooms west of the hall, thus creating a house with the typical floor-plan of a central hall and two rooms at either

358

side. Over this enlarged dwelling was placed a gambrel roof (plate 131); the front of the house was established toward the south and the east and west gables were filled with brick, laid in English bond. Toward the south the roof-line sloped out over a porch that ran the width of the front. Such an alteration of the direction of the ridge-pole of a house possibly occurred also in the house of Matthew Ten Eyck (plate 90) in Ulster.

While there is no proof for the statement that Zephaniah Platt enlarged the house when he bought the farm in 1762, there can be little doubt but that such was the fact. In 1874 Silas De Garmo removed the long porch from the south front, substituted the one now there and added the cornice at the roof-line and some dormer windows. The plate illustrates the stone- and brick-work of the walls, the gambrel roof, two early windows in the rear wall and hints at the wonderful trees which surround the house and the view of the meadow-flat along the creek.

Inside the house some excellent wainscoting, Dutch doors and an early staircase have survived. In the older (east) part the one chimney has fireplaces opening on a slant across the corner of each room. In the southeast room the opening measures seven feet and is framed in a wood-facing of simple design. The cellar below the southeast room bears evidence of having been used formerly as a kitchen.

Parsonage of the Reformed Dutch Church

Formerly at Poughkeepsie, New York

In September, 1731, the Reverend Cornelius Van Schie arrived in the Province of New York from Holland and came directly to Dutchess County to meet the members of the congregations of the Dutch Reformed Churches of Poughkeepsie and Fishkill, whom he was to serve jointly as pastor. On October 4th representatives of the two congregations met and voted to buy six acres of land, to build a house, make a garden and plant an orchard, the site for such a parsonage to be chosen by the domine. Mr. Van Schie elected to live at Poughkeepsie and accordingly the churches bought a lot which, in modern terminology, was bounded north by Main Street and east by Little Washington Street.

Mr. Van Schie removed to Albany in 1733 and in 1734 a call was sent to Holland for another minister. The call described the parsonage as: " a new and suitable residence, 45 feet long and 27 broad, having three rooms and a study upstairs, a large cellar under the house, and a well with good water, a garden, and an orchard planted with one-hundred trees."

Eleven years passed before, in 1745, the Reverend Benjamin Meenema came over to succeed Mr. Van Schie and in the interval between 1734 and 1745 the parsonage at Poughkeepsie was rented to John Constable. The call that was sent to Holland in 1745 offered to the Reverend Mr. Meenema: " a free and very comfortable

359

dwelling house, long 45 and broad 27 English feet, containing besides the hallway, two rooms, a basement kitchen and a study, also a well of good water, a garden and an orchard of a half-morgen planted with good apple-trees and situated next to the house. The house, well, garden-fence and orchard will at proper times be kept and repaired. Free firewood, enough for summer and winter, will at proper times be delivered at his house by the members of Poughkeepsie. Further shall his Reverence at his arrival here be furnished with a good stable-horse, as his service among us requires. But after this horse will have served out, his Reverence shall have to provide his own. There-above shall he receive at Fishkill and wherever his service among us calls him free lodgings and free livelihood."

The Reverend Benjamin Meenema occupied the parsonage at Poughkeepsie from 1745 until his death in 1756 (he was buried in the yard of the Dutch church at Fishkill), and following him the Reverend Jacobus Van Neste lived in it from 1758 until he, also, died in 1761 and was buried in the churchyard at Fishkill.

From approximately 1760 to 1772 the congregations at Poughkeepsie and Fishkill shared in the general disturbance that prevailed in the Dutch Reformed Communion over the question of the validity of ordination in America as compared with ordination in Holland, the former upheld by the Coetus party and the latter by the Conferentie, and as a result two ministers served the two parties: the Reverend Henricus Schoonmaker, 1763—1774, and the Reverend Isaac Rysdyk from about 1765 to about 1772. Apparently Mr. Schoonmaker lived in the parsonage. Mr. Rysdyk may have had residence at New Hackensack, of which church he was pastor 1766—1790 and in the yard of which is his grave.

After the settlement in 1772 of the question regarding ordination the congregations at Poughkeepsie and Fishkill each called their own pastor and the church at Poughkeepsie was served by: the Reverend Stephen Van Voorhees, 1773—1776; the Reverend Solomon Freligh, 1777—1780; the Reverend John Henry Livingston, 1781—1783; and the Reverend Andrew Gray, 1790—1793.

In the pastorate of the Reverend Mr. Gray the stone parsonage was torn down and a frame house built on nearly the same site. The frame house was succeeded in 1844 by one of brick. The third parsonage stood until 1920 and when, in that year, it was razed a marked stone was uncovered in the foundation at the west end of the south wall. The marks on the stone were:

J VBG D SLR HVK 1732
MVK 1792

A second stone, below the first, was cut with the letters: HVK BVK. Inasmuch as the first stone was built in with the letters upside down it is a fair inference that it was taken from the parsonage of 1732, incorporated in the foundation of the frame house of 1792 and again incorporated in the house of 1844. The initials undoubtedly refer to elders or deacons or members of a building committee. The monogram: VK, stands for Van Kleeck. Possibly Jacobus Van Den Bogaerdt (out of whose farm the site was purchased) was represented and SLR might have meant Simeon LeRoy.

House of John Pawling

Formerly in the Town of Hyde Park, Dutchess County, New York

PLATE 132

The house shown in plate 132 stood formerly north of the village of Staatsburgh on the east side of the *King's Highway* near the head of the long grade called Clay Hill. It was built in 1761 by John Pawling and burned down about 1899. Shortly before it burned a photograph was taken of it, a copy of which is owned by Starr Institute, Rhinebeck, and which, through the courtesy of the Institute, is here reproduced.

John Pawling, builder of the house (born 1732, died 1819), was a son of Henry Pawling (who married, in 1713, Jacomyntje Kunst) and a grandson of Captain Henry Pawling and his wife, Neeltje Roosa, whose house in Ulster County is shown in plate 82. After the death of Captain Henry Pawling his widow and children in 1696 obtained a patent for lands in Dutchess which he had purchased from the Indians. By a series of quit-claim deeds John Pawling took up a portion of this patent in his early manhood and built his house thereon. In the front wall of the house, between the two windows that are over the porch, was a stone, marked: JP NP July 4 1761. The initials stood for John Pawling and Neeltje, his wife, who was also his first cousin. Mrs. John Pawling was a daughter of Thomas and Mary (Pawling) Van Keuren and a granddaughter of Henry Pawling, the original purchaser of the land. To the south of their house John and Neeltje Pawling's near neighbor was their cousin, Petrus De Witt, who through his mother was also a grandson of Captain Henry Pawling.

Of John Pawling's house little can be said accurately in detail. The photograph records its appearance about 1899, when the porch was obviously modern. The dormers and wooden extension are known to date from 1870. The main portion of the building was an oblong, facing west; but there was a wing at the north-east, creating an ell-shaped whole, which the photograph does not show. On the east wall of the wing was a large Dutch oven of stone. The heavy exposed ceiling-beams remained until a recent date in the rooms of the first story but whether the floor-plan of the late nineteenth century was the floor-plan of 1761 cannot now be known. Only a careful examination of the masonry could have determined whether the house was built originally in two full stories or in one and a half. In 1761 two stories were not usual and when there is found a house of that height which is supposed to ante-date the Revolution the question always arises: was the roof raised at some

361

later date? If John Pawling built his house in 1761 two stories high, he built a dwelling handsome for the day but, as the house is now gone and close scrutiny of its structure impossible, it is unsafe to use it as a basis for general observations and conclusions.

House of Walton Roosevelt

Town of Hyde Park, Dutchess County, New York

About three miles south of the village of Hyde Park on the east side of the state road (once the *King's Highway*) there stands a frame house of the pre-Revolutionary period. Because of alterations made to it in late years it has lost its pictorial quality but, in its first estate, the house bore close resemblance to the Southard homestead (plate 133) at Fishkill, which was built at very nearly the same date. The exterior lines of the two houses were characteristic of frame construction in Dutchess in the eighteenth century and their floor-plans were much the same. The house in the town of Hyde Park is built on stone foundations, two feet thick and roughly laid, and it rests on sloping ground, which latter fact afforded opportunity for a large basement. The basement was divided into two parts: a kitchen at the west and cellar at the east. From the cellar steps rose to the main floor, which consisted of four rooms: two larger ones across the south front and two smaller ones across the north rear. In a small space between the two rear rooms a boxed-in staircase led to a half-story above and access was also had to the steps down to the cellar. The house is oblong in proportion, faces south, with its west gable to the state road and is sided with modern clapboards. Originally there was a large chimney at each end of the house and fireplaces opened into the front rooms. In one fireplace there was a fireback of wrought iron which now is on the ground, outside the house. The fireback is decorated around the rim with a semi-circle of rosettes and inscribed within the semi-circle with the figures: 1 7 6 3, which indicate the erection of the house at approximately that time. The property is now owned by St. Andrew's Novitiate of the Jesuit Order and the interior of the house has recently been rebuilt as a barrack for laborers employed on the farm.

The land on which the house stands is a portion of water-lot number two of the Great Nine Partners Patent, which in the first division of the patent fell to the share of Colonel Henry Filkin of Flatbush, Long Island. From Colonel Filkin water-lot number two passed about 1737 to his daughter, Antie, and her husband, Frans Hegeman. The record of title is not clear between the tenure of the Hegemans and that of Walter Livingston of Columbia County, who acquired the property in later years. In 1738 Frans and Antie Hegeman sold three-hundred acres in water-lot two to Johannes Marshall, which parcel probably included the site of the house. The executors of Johannes Marshall's will disposed of part of his holding in 1772, and it is a fair " guess " that the house of 1763 was his home in the last years of his life. In some way, unknown, the place passed to Walter Livingston, a non-resident (who probably held it for rent as an investment), and in 1803 the executors of his will sold it. Since 1803 it has been owned by: Jacob Bush, 1803—1814; Zephaniah Pells, 1814—1820; James Roosevelt, 1820—1833; and Michael Hyser, 1833—1835. In 1835 John Reade Stuyvesant bought it and occupied the house until, later, he built a new one on the west side of the road where, now, the large buildings of the Novitiate have been erected. The whole estate (called *Edgewood*) remained in the Stuyvesant family until sold to the Order in late years. While the house was owned by James Roosevelt (1820—1833), it was occupied by his son, Walton Roosevelt (born 1795, died 1836), and as it is still known more or less by the latter's name it is so listed here.

Schenck House
Town of Wappinger, Dutchess County, New York

On the west side of the road that runs south from New Hackensack to Swartwoutville stands a house that was owned in the eighteenth century by the Schencks, was inherited later by the Ackermans and is now the property of A. D. Adams. It is midway between two road-crossings known as Myers' Corners and as White's Corners. On a stone smoke-house near the dwelling is cut the date: 1773, which perhaps approximates the date of the erection of the house.

In a general way the house suggests the house of Cornelius Van Wyck (plate 146) but it is on a smaller scale. An early west wing was torn down in recent years. The main portion of the house, still standing, consists of a frame structure, one and one-half stories high, with a roof of single slant and a porch at the front and at the rear. The floor-plan gives three smaller rooms across the rear, with two rooms and a hall at the front. The stairs in the hall are boxed in. The southeast parlor has some panelled woodwork. In the southwest parlor is a wood mantel and in the fireplace an iron fireback. A representation of the Virgin and Child fills the center of the fireback and a fan-pattern the corners of it. Original doors on the first floor carry some good iron hardware, including butterfly-hinges and strap-hinges. A unique feature of the house is a wine-closet in the cellar. A stone arch, such as is shown in plate 5, is closed off by panelled doors and made into an ornamental place of storage.

The land on which this house stands was owned in the eighteenth century by Abraham Schenck, a descendant of the Long Island family of that name, who died in 1800 and willed the life-use of the farm to his uncle, Roeloff Schenck. The latter died in 1803—1804 and the farm passed to John Ackerman (the husband of Roeloff Schenck's niece, Sarah Schenck), from whom it was inherited by his son, Schenck Ackerman. John Ackerman's first wife, Dorothy Monfort, was one of the family of Peter Monfort (page 355), whose acreage was east of the Schenck land on the Sprout Creek.

In 1926 a copper coin, marked: Britannia 1730 Georgius II Rex, was turned up in the soil near this house by the present owner of the property.

Three Houses of Johannes Schurrie

Formerly near New Hackensack, New York

About 1740 Johannes Schurrie removed from Hackensack, New Jersey, to New Hackensack, New York. He purchased land (which in after years was divided into what were known as the Diddell and Rowe and Wicks farms) and built three stone houses, one for himself and two for married daughters.

The earliest of Johannes Schurrie's three houses stood east of the hamlet of New Hackensack on the north side of the road. It was torn down in 1861 and a frame house placed on its site. The frame house was built and occupied by the Rowe family and is familiar to motorists as the house which is reached from the highway by a small foot-bridge that spans a roadside stream. When the old house was razed a stone, marked: 1744, was saved from it and put in the wall of the cellar of the frame house. At the same time a pencil sketch was made of the original house by James E. Hicks of New Hackensack which records it as having been a typical stone house of 1744. It was one and one-half stories high; the rear roof-line sloped almost to the ground (like the house of Teunis Van Benschoten, near by); the front roof-line extended over a long front veranda; the roof and gable-ends were shingled; there were two end-chimneys; the ground-level sloped and there was a basement at the front of the house.

A stone house built by Johannes Schurrie stood east of the railroad track at Diddell's station on the north side of the road and was followed by a frame house, now standing on or near the site of the first and owned by Jacob Diddell. A stone from the first house, marked: 17(48) is in the foundation of the frame house.

The third (undated) stone house built by Johannes Schurrie stood until 1909 east of the house of 1744 on the south side of the road. A photograph of it, too faded to reproduce well, shows it as rectangular, oblong, with a roof of single slant and having modern wood-trim.

The name Schurrie is found in old records in several phonetic spellings: Sjeere, Jurry, Yerry, and may perhaps have been derived from the Dutch baptismal name: Jurriaen, transmitted as a surname.

Johannes Schurrie died in 1784 in his seventy-fifth year and his wife, Johanna, daughter of Thomas Outwater (sometime of New Jersey), in 1771 in her sixty-seventh year. Their gravestones are in the yard of the Dutch church at New Hackensack.

House of Zebulon Southard
Town of Fishkill, Dutchess County, New York

PLATE 133

West of the village of Fishkill, on the north side of the road to the river, there stands a house (plate 133) which is an excellent example of the Dutch spirit in house-building. While the structure is rectangular and its actual dimensions small, it strikes the note of home in its general architectural character; its lines are easy, not stiff, and its proportions create an impression of a generous and comfortable manner of living.

The builder of the house, Zebulon Southard, a captain in a Dutchess regiment in the Revolution, bore an English name; but he married in 1763 a Dutch wife, Jennetje Van Voorhees (whose mother was a Van Benschoten and whose grandfather, Johannes Coerte Van Voorhees, built the house at Fishkill shown in plate 144); his son, Zebulon Southard, Jr. (born 1777, died 1854), who inherited the house, married Catherine Van Voorhees; and his grandson, Sylvester Southard (to whom the house next passed), married Sarah Storm. Thus the fact that the house was built by a man of English descent is offset by the circumstances that he built, in a community that was preponderantly Dutch in make-up, a house which shows the Dutch influence in architecture and which was presided over by housewives of Dutch descent for nearly a century and a half. Zebulon Southard bought the land on which the house stands (a farm of over two-hundred acres originally) in 1766 and his great-grand-daughter sold the place in 1903 to her aunt, Elizabeth B. Storm, who in 1909 conveyed it to the present owner, Dr. George E. Maurer.

As this farm was purchased in May, 1766, by Zebulon Southard from Francis Brett (who had inherited the land from Madam Brett, but who did not live upon it) the erection of the house may be credited to that year with reasonable assurance. Structurally, it consists of thick, hard walls, made of a lath framework that is filled with a mixture of clay and straw and cornstalks and then clapboarded. It contains two rooms on the main floor (with modern additions at the rear), a large half-story above and a basement below. The basement was made possible by the sloping ground-level and the east end apparently was used as the first kitchen. In it is a built-in oven at one side of a large fireplace; there are large, hand-cut ceiling-beams and great eighteenth century doors and wrought iron strap-hinges. On the main floor each room has a divided Dutch door opening on the long front porch, doors which are battened and carry original iron hardware. A steep enclosed stairway in the southwest corner leads to the half-story. There were at first two open fireplaces, one at each end of the house, but the one in the west room has been closed. In the east room there is panelling across the chimney-breast and side wall but, super-imposed on the chimney-breast, is a mantel of wood, of a later date than the panelling.

365

Between the Southard house at Fishkill and a house on the *King's Highway* in the town of Hyde Park (listed at page 362 as the house of Walton Roosevelt) there was great similarity in style before the house in Hyde Park suffered alterations. Both houses were built in the 1760's, with much the same exterior lines, and should be studied together as evidence of a type of frame house that was familiar in Dutchess County at that time.

Stone Houses of Dutchess County

The period in which there was a general use of stone for house-building in Dutchess County may be loosely approximated as from 1700 to 1775. Of the houses built of stone by Dutch families a number are listed in this volume but there are a few, still standing, which have only slight connection with the Dutch and yet which are grouped here under one caption because it is desirable to place them on record. They are part of the architectural history of the county and knowledge of them is fast fading out of the popular mind. These houses, salvaged from oblivion, are given below.

Houses near Barnegat

The Dutch name: *Barnegat,* which a literal translation renders as " firehole ", was applied in the eighteenth century to a locality in the town of Poughkeepsie on the shore of the Hudson where for many years the calcining of limestone was a prosperous industry. Ruins of several of the stone kilns are still in evidence in the vicinity of the present station of the New York Central and Hudson River Railroad called Camelot.

About half a mile north of the railroad station on the east side of a narrow road that runs close to the bank of the Hudson is an eighteenth century stone house, with nineteenth century wood-trim, and the whole badly out of repair. The house was owned from 1837 to 1860 first by George Vanderbilt and then by his widow, and the place is known by old residents as the Vanderbilt farm. Before the Revolution the occupant was Hendrick Wiltsie, who leased the land from the owner and whose son, another Hendrick, took title to it in 1819.

North of the Wiltsie-Vanderbilt house and on the west side of the road is a second stone house, now in a condition of much decay and altered in details from its original state. No tradition has been learned of its pre-Revolutionary occupation. At the close of the war Caleb Bishop of Mount Pleasant, Westchester County, leased it and operated lime-kilns near by and in 1834 his descendants bought the property, retaining title until 1883.

In 1774 Abraham Lott, treasurer of the Province of New York, made a voyage up the Hudson from New York to Albany and return and kept a diary of his trip.

366

The diary records on June 23rd on his sail down the river that he reached: " the place called *Barnegat* or the Lime Kilns; went ashore at the House of Hendrick Wilse, who lives on a farm of Mr. Ray of New York; he was born at Flushing on Long Island and has lived 37 years on the place at 12 Bushels of Wheat per Annum; he made us Welcome and offered us some cucumbers for which however paid him 1/7. We also took Some Cool Spring Water on Board from his Spring and he went with us to take a Drink of Punch."

Mr. Lott's statement that the farm leased by Hendrick Wiltsie was owned in 1774 by Mr. Ray of New York was incorrect. He probably became confused in his recollection of what was told him while on shore at *Barnegat* for the records in the office of the clerk of Dutchess County show that the farm owned by Mr. Ray was the one where, later, Caleb Bishop lived.

A large purchase of land was made in the vicinity of *Barnegat* at an early date by Robert Sanders of Albany, out of which his widow, Elsie, and son, Thomas, on May 10, 1712, conveyed two farms,—one to his son, Barent Sanders of Albany, and another to his son-in-law, Richard Ray of New York City.

Of the two farms the first remained in the possession of the heirs of Barent Sanders until 1819. It was leased to Hendrick Wiltsie in 1737 (according to Mr. Lott's diary) and in 1819 Sanders Van Rensselaer sold it to Hendrick Wiltsie's son (or grandson) of the same name.

The other farm was owned by Richard Ray and his descendants (Rays of New York and Lansings of Albany) from 1712 to 1834; was leased late in the eighteenth century by Caleb Bishop; conveyed in 1834 to him (or his son of the same name) and sold in 1883 to Charles Whitehead.

Robert Sanders of Albany, to whom the land at *Barnegat* belonged originally, was the founder of the family connected with the Glen-Sanders house (plate 23) and Sanders Van Rensselaer was of the family at *Cherry Hill*, Albany (plate 50).

Farther north on the same road as the houses of Hendrick Wiltsie and Caleb Bishop is a stone house, known as a Westervelt home. It is painted yellow, has modern wood-trim and is in repair. Whether it was built by a Westervelt or merely occupied at some time by that family is uncertain.

Club House, Country Club
Beacon, New York

One of the small stone houses of the eighteenth century forms (with modern additions and alterations) the club-house of the country club at Beacon-on-Hudson. It stands on land which was conveyed in 1730 by Philip Verplanck to Johannes Coerte Van Voorhees and was built, presumably, by some member of the Van Voorhees family for occupation either by the owner or by a tenant.

367

Cooper-Shook House

On a cross road that runs from the state road to White's Corners in the town of Wappinger is a house owned now by Frank B. Shook. At first glance the house looks like a unit in construction but examination of it shows that one roof covers two parts. The east end was an early stone house, with very thick walls, to which the west end was added. Who built the stone house is not known. It was owned and occupied by Obadiah Cooper (born 1749, died 1807), who married Maria Van Benschoten and whose sons and daughters also married into Dutch families. Entrance to the stone house is had through an admirable Dutch door on which is eighteenth century iron hardware but in the interior of the house may changes have been made.

House of Moses De Graeff

The hamlet of Manchester Bridge on the east side of the Wappingers Creek in the town of La Grange is a growth of the early nineteenth century. Before 1800 there was no bridge over the creek at this point and no road approaching the creek from the west. In the eighteenth century a road came from the east to the stream and forked abruptly to the north and to the south to reach Palen's bridge and Le Roy's bridge, respectively. At the fork, Moses De Graeff (born 1724, died 1800) took up a farm (about 1750?) and built a stone house near the junction of the roads. Close to the house was a small water-course (tributary to the Wappingers) on which he built a mill, damming the stream to create a mill-pond. Ultimately the stone house disappeared and on an adjacent site was built the frame dwelling that is still standing. The frame house was probably built about 1790—1810 but no exact dates have been procured for either of the two structures. Moses DeGraeff was a great-grandson of Jean le Comte, a Huguenot, who was at Harlem in 1674 and whose only child, Moses le Comte, settled at Esopus. Dutch neighbors at Esopus translated le Comte's name into its Dutch equivalent: DeGraeff, by which designation all but a few of his descendants have been known. The family spread from Ulster to Dutchess, where it once was numerous. Moses De Graeff, whose house is here listed, married his second cousin, Antoinette Van Kleeck, a great-granddaughter of Baltus Barents Van Kleeck (plate 142).

House of Jacob Griffin

On the east side of the Sprout Creek, north of the bridge at Swartwoutville, a stone house of the eighteenth century is standing now but almost entirely disguised by nineteenth century additions of wood. It was occupied during the Revolution by Colonel Jacob Griffin and was the meeting-place of the committee which in 1775 canvassed Dutchess County to secure signatures to the Articles of Association put

368

forth by the Provincial Congress of New York. At that time it obtained the name of *The Rendezvous*, by which it continued to be known. A picture of the house is presented at page 121 of: *The Van Wyck Family*. Colonel Griffin's daughters married into the Van Wyck, DuBois and Adriance families and, after the colonel's death in 1800, his house was purchased by Colonel Aaron Stockholm for the latter's daughter. It is now owned by David Eifert of Yonkers, New York.

In 1775 *The Rendezvous* was one of the stone houses that were a familiar sight at the time in all the river-counties; it was oblong in proportion, had a hall through the center with two rooms to the north and two to the south, was one and one-half stories high and had a roof of single slant. The walls of the original house are now covered with stucco, which is ruled to simulate ashlar (a form of siding which was current in the early nineteenth century and another instance of which is noted on page 88 in connection with *Clermont*). On the roof of the original house are three early dormers, two on the east slope and one on the west. When a wing was built toward the west in recent years the roof of it was placed over part of the west slope of the first roof and the west dormer enclosed by it in such a manner that from the attic of the wing the dormer is still visible. The house bears traces of a general activity in repair and improvement in the early nineteenth century, probably after the property was newly purchased by Colonel Stockholm. The front door may be ascribed to that time and also a mantel in the southeast room, which must have been the main living-room of the house as it was the one to receive new trim. In the northeast room there still remain two panelled wall-cupboards, one on either side of the chimney, and the chimney-breast is known to have been panelled originally across its width. It is flanked now by pilasters and topped by a cornice and the whole north wall was once a unit in design. It can hardly be questioned that in 1775 the southeast room was similarly finished. In the cellar a stone arch (such as is shown in plate 5) supports the north chimney but the cellar was probably used as the first kitchen of the house for, at the south end, is a very large fireplace. The doors in the cellar have good iron hardware and there is almost a grove of locust posts supporting the floor of the main story. The posts are crooked young trees that were not stripped of their bark when cut, the bark being plainly visible under a coat of whitewash.

Low-Van Der Burgh-Smith-Myers House

The house-lot now known as 103, Market Street, Poughkeepsie, was sold from out the farm of Jacobus Van Den Bogaerdt in 1733 to Henry Filkin and between 1733 and 1751 a stone house was built on it that stood until the middle of the nineteenth century. A deed, dated 1751, refers to the house as standing and another, dated 1811, mentions "the old stone house" on the lot but which of the owners of the lot between 1733 and 1751 built the house the record of title does not show.

In succession the owners of the land prior to 1751 (any one of whom might have been the builder) were Henry Filkin, William Low, Samuel M. Cohen, Moses B. Franks and Jacob Franks. Of those men only William Low was certainly a resident of Poughkeepsie and the probability therefore is that it was he who built the house during his tenure of the lot from 1739 to 1742. The property was purchased in 1757 by William Van Der Burgh, who owned it until he died; it then belonged to Captain Samuel Smith and his heirs for a quarter-century and from 1811 to 1858 was owned by the Myers family. The record that three Hebrews of New York City owned this house from 1742 to 1751 is the first instance so far noted of any connection of their race with Dutchess County. Samuel M. Cohen bought the place at a sheriff's sale in 1742 and he and the Franks presumably held it as non-resident owners.

House of John Montross

In the Monfort family of the town of Wappinger, Dutchess County, there is a tradition that a certain John Montross of Long Island made a journey to Dutchess to inspect lands for purchase, having with him his son. The latter, who was sick, expressed admiration for the lovely lowlands along the Sprout Creek and a wish to be buried there when he died and so in 1728 John Montross obtained a deed from the Verplancks for three-hundred acres on the Sprout and on that farm may be seen today the house he built and also the family burial-ground in the orchard, where his son's unmarked grave is supposed to be.

The stones forming the thick walls of the Montross house are laid up in clay. The exterior of the house has been given a modern roof, dormers, porch, etc., and nothing pictorial remains. Within the main part of the dwelling there is a central hall with one room at either side. The hall is wainscoted; the staircase is early; and one parlor has a carved mantel; originally the cellar had a fireplace and was used as a kitchen. To the east is a frame wing (a complete unit in itself and of more primitive finish than the main portion), which consists of a small entry (with enclosed stairs), two rooms and a kitchen lean-to. The main room of the wing has a large fireplace-opening and plain but characteristic woodwork.

In 1774 the executors of the will of John Montross sold his house and farm and since then the title has passed through the names of Jackson, Scofield, Teller and Brown to the present owner, Christian Vorndran. By the will of John Montross the portion of his farm which " then was for a Christian burial ground " was to " be and remain for that purpose forever."

House of Bartholomew Noxon

The house now known as 81, Market Street, Poughkeepsie, was built in 1741 by Bartholomew Noxon. Bartholomew Noxon (born 1703, died 1785) was a son of Thomas Noxon, a Scotchman, who settled before 1700 in Ulster County and in later years removed to New York City to serve as headmaster of Trinity School. The first mention of the name of Bartholomew Noxon on the tax-lists of Poughkeepsie occurs in 1731 and about that date he probably removed from Ulster and took up residence in Dutchess. He continued as a tax-payer at Poughkeepsie from 1731 to 1753. Then from 1754 to 1770 he lived in Beekman Precinct, paying taxes there, returning to Poughkeepsie in 1771 and continuing there until his death. From 1756 to 1770 the Poughkeepsie tax-lists carry the entry: " Bartholomew Noxon's House " (a form which was used when a property-owner was non-resident), and the entry fits in with other records which show his presence in Beekman at that time.

Fifty years ago there was a tradition current that number 81, Market Street, Poughkeepsie, was occupied in the eighteenth century by a Swede, Von Beck, as an inn and the tradition may account for the use to which the house was put while the owner was on his farm in Beekman. Poughkeepsie was the half-way point between New York and Albany and a natural stopping place for travellers on the *King's Highway*. It was the county-seat and the scene of periodical court sessions and of the meetings of the board of supervisors so that transients in the village needed places of public entertainment.

In 1785 Bartholomew Noxon's house was inherited by his son, Dr. Robert Noxon (born 1750, died 1833), who occupied it until he died. Dr. Robert Noxon was one of the prominent early physicians of Dutchess. The land that went with his house extended east from Market to Academy Street and after his death Noxon Street was cut through the property. After 1833 title to the house changed often. In 1858 the German Lutheran congregation acquired it and held religious services in the house until 1863. The present owner, Dr. H. L. B. Ryder, remodelled the building into apartments in 1922.

The original house was built of stone with a roof of single slant. Before the middle of the nineteenth century it was two full stories high but whether it was built in that way in 1741 it is now too late to determine with certainty. The date of erection is learned from a stone in the east wall marked:

E

B   N

1741

for Bartholomew and Elizabeth Noxon. The stone is at the north end of the rear wall of the house about where the eaves-line would have come on a house a story and a half high. It was retained in its position and carefully protected when the house was done over in 1922. At page thirty-three of *The Eagle's History of Poughkeepsie* by Edmund Platt is a photograph of the east wall or rear of the Noxon house, taken in 1904, and the location of the marked stone is behind the branches of a tree, near a second story window. In the middle of the nineteenth century the front (west) wall of stone was taken out and a brick wall substituted and the roof of single slant replaced by a mansard. In 1922 many other structural changes were made so that it is impossible now to be sure what the original height of the house was. If it were two full stories in 1741 it must be noted as a very unusual dwelling for that day.

House of Abram Sleght

Cornelis Barentsen Sleght, who came from Woerden, South Holland, before 1655, was one of the first settlers at Kingston, New York, where he founded a family. His great-grandson, Abram Sleght, married at Kingston Ariaantje Elmendorf and in the second quarter of the eighteenth century removed from Ulster County to the town of La Grange in Dutchess. There, east of the Wappingers Creek and about a mile north of Manchester Bridge, he bought a farm and built a stone house which was undoubtedly a house of the style common at that time (one and one-half stories, with roof of single slant). In that house in 1753 his son, Jacobus Sleght (or Sleight, as later generations spelled the name), was born. Jacobus Sleght, in 1798 (two years before his father's death), replaced the original house on the farm with a large, two-story, stone dwelling that is still standing and occupied by David Barnes Sleight. By the marriage of Jacobus Sleght to Elsie DeRiemer, a descendant of Isaac DeRiemer (one of the early mayors of New York City), the story of this stone house near the Wappingers becomes linked with that of families well known in New York (DeForest, Wesselse, Roosevelt) and, locally, it has many affiliations. In late years the marriage of Miss Sara Sleight to Frank Van Kleeck of Poughkeepsie tied together the Sleight homestead and the house of Baltus Barents Van Kleeck at Poughkeepsie (plate 142).

The transition in 1798 from the first and smaller house on the Sleight farm to a larger dwelling is significant architecturally, as it reflects the change that occurred in Dutchess around 1800 from houses a story and a half in height to those of two full stories.

House of Joseph Thurston

The road which connects the mill-site on the Sprout Creek near Fishkill Plains with the mouth of the Wappingers Creek was an important route of travel from approximately 1740 to 1815. Title to the lands it crosses is derived from the Rombout Patent through the Verplanck family and enough substantial settlers had, by 1740, taken up farms in the neighborhood to necessitate the opening of an accepted county-road in 1741. In 1750 Joseph Thurston bought about two-hundred acres on the new road and, presumably soon after that date, built the stone house that is still standing a short distance east of Myers' Corners. He died in 1782 and in 1815 his children sold the house to the Scofield family; the latter sold it in 1841 to Obadiah

372

Van Voorhees and his descendants conveyed it in 1921 to the present owner, Elias S. De Garmo. The walls of the house have been stuccoed but the original rough stones, untooled, can be seen in places. In size and plan the house is one of the type that prevailed in 1750 and is chiefly noteworthy now for the survival of a characteristic planting of locust trees about it. Its setting is particularly attractive. East of the house is a stone smoke-house (out of repair) and to the north are weather-beaten barns, with wrought-iron hardware, and probably of the same age as the house.

House at the Upper Landing, Poughkeepsie

The first mill-site developed at Poughkeepsie was on the *Val Kil* (Fallkill) where the stream enters the Hudson between the present plant of the Central Hudson Gas and Electric Company and the yard of the C. N. Arnold Lumber Company. Following a winding course from the bridge at Mill Street to the bridge at North Water Street (which course was called by the Indians *Pondanickrien* or the Crooked Place) the *Val Kil* flows in a succession of cascades, passing under the tracks of the New York Central and Hudson River Railroad at the north end of the station at Poughkeepsie. The Crooked Place lies within the boundaries of a tract of wilderness patented in 1686 to Robert Sanders and Myndert Harmense Van Den Bogaerdt of Albany, which tract included the major portion of the land on which the city of Poughkeepsie is built and out of which in 1710 Myndert Harmense Van Den Bogaerdt sold a large parcel to Leonard Lewis of New York City.

Leonard Lewis (born 1667, died 1730) was a son of Thomas Lewis (who came to New York from Belfast, Ireland); his wife, Elizabeth Hardenbergh, whom he married in New York in 1688 and who accompanied him to Poughkeepsie, was one of the Hardenbergh family of Ulster County and their eleven children, who were prominent residents of Poughkeepsie, were the cousins of the Hardenberghs who lived at *Roosen Daal* in the house shown in plate 83. Leonard Lewis and his wife's brother, Johannes Hardenbergh, were two of the seven patentees of the Great Hardenbergh Patent in Ulster, which covered most of the Catskill range of mountains.

From approximately 1710 until his death in 1730 Leonard Lewis lived at Poughkeepsie and in those twenty years served as colonel of militia, member of assembly (1713—1726), county-treasurer, judge of the court of common pleas, &c. As soon as possible after his arrival at Poughkeepsie he built a mill on the *Val Kil*, the site of which is believed to have been on the north side of the stream, beside the waterfall which now is bounded east by the railroad tracks and west by North Water Street. The road to the mill is mentioned in early deeds as " the mill-road " and later became Mill Street. North and west of his mill Colonel Lewis built his dwelling, the first mention of which is in 1717, when a meeting of the freeholders of the county was held " near it." The mill and the house are shown on the map of the river-

373

front in the Long Reach which Henry Livingston drew in 1738 (notes: plate 128).

By his will Colonel Lewis bequeathed his property to his eleven children, subject to its life-use by his widow. In 1740 Mrs. Lewis leased it to Anthony Yelverton, who then began to buy out from the heirs their rights in the title. By 1755 he had acquired ten one-eleventh undivided shares and those ten shares were conveyed several times between 1755 and 1772. What disposition was made of the remaining one-eleventh, held by Leonard Lewis, Jr. (born 1707, died 1757—'59), the land records do not show but after 1772 the deeds for the property convey a sole interest in it.

Between 1755 and 1800 the business-center at the mouth of the *Val Kil* steadily increased in importance but, with two exceptions, the owners were non-residents of Poughkeepsie and must have been represented by a manager or agent to conduct the mill and supervise the dock. The several owners were: Anthony Yelverton of Poughkeepsie 1755; Colonel Martin Hoffman of Red Hook 1755—1759; Clear Everett of Poughkeepsie 1759—1764; Nathaniel Seaman of Long Island 1764—1766; George Sands, Samuel and Maurice Smith of Long Island 1766—1768; Henry Sands of Long Island 1768; Henry, George and Richard Sands of Long Island 1768—1772; John Schenck, Jr., of New Jersey and Poughkeepsie 1772—1777; John Schenck, Jr., and Paul Schenck of Poughkeepsie 1777—1778; Robert Livingston of the Manor 1778; Walter Livingston of *Teviotdale* 1778—1796; and Robert L. Livingston of *Clermont* 1796—1800. Out of this long list those known to have been resident owners were Clear Everett and John and Paul Schenck. The presence of Paul Schenck in 1774 is referred to in the diary of Abraham Lott when the latter came down the Hudson in a sailboat and on June 23rd stopped: " opposite the old landing at Poughkeepsie, where we sent on shore at about 6 o'clock P. M. and got some milk of Mr. Paul Schenck."

Henry Livingston's map of 1738 shows one mill and one dwelling at the mouth of the *Val Kil* but growth apparently began under Colonel Martin Hoffman. The issue of the *Poughkeepsie Eagle* for March 3, 1849, reports that on February 24, 1849, the mill on the *Val Kil* burned down, in which connection an old resident stated that the mill was built in 1755 and raised on the day of Braddock's defeat; the raising was not completed until the second day and help for it had to be obtained from Fishkill and Rhinebeck. " There was then nothing but a log-bridge over the creek and a foot-path leading from the mill to the Lower Landing. On the second day after the raising of the mill was finished a sham fight was had in canoes in the bay formed by the Caul Rock and Slange Klip, there being then no docks." Although there was no dock at the mouth of the *Val Kil* in 1755 Mr. Lott referred in 1774 to " the old landing" and it is quite probable that Colonel Hoffman (who was an enterprising investor in real estate in Dutchess) began a development that grew steadily out of the needs of the situation.

A dwelling-house northwest of the mill appears on maps of 1738, 1770 and

374

1798 and an old house is now still standing which occupies apparently the same location. The house on North Water Street, Poughkeepsie, was the home of the Hoffman brothers, Martin, Isaac and Robert, who bought it in 1800 of Robert L. Livingston; and also of Howland R. Sherman and Charles N. Arnold, who were prominent residents of Poughkeepsie in the nineteenth century. It is built of stone on a ground level sloping from north to south under the shadow of *Slange Klip* (Snake Cliff), the promontory on which rests the eastern end of the Poughkeepsie bridge. The foundations are old and all the walls thick. In places the stones of the rear and end walls are rough but so much paint has been applied to them that the original character of the masonry cannot be clearly seen. The north wall has suffered few changes; it has an inset doorway and its appearance as a whole is definitely that of eighteenth century work. The south front has been faced with brick (laid in Flemish bond) and the roof of the house has been raised, somewhat after the manner of that of the Westbrook house, plate 102, a wooden crown resting on the stone walls. Inside, the house at the Upper Landing was completely altered in the nineteenth century, nothing of its earlier days can be seen there; and outside nothing now remains that is pictorial. It is possible that in the foundations and the walls something survives of the house built by Colonel Leonard Lewis before 1717. Also, it is possible that the house stands on the site of Colonel Lewis' dwelling and that it was built to replace a first house at about the time that Colonel Martin Hoffman built a new mill. It cannot be questioned seriously that in some form the house existed before the Revolution. The occupation of it in the 1770's by Paul Schenck (born 1741, died 1817) links it with the house of Henry Livingston (plate 128) as Paul Schenck married in 1776 Henry Livingston's daughter, Joanna. Mr. Schenck's brother, Henry (born 1743, died 1799), married in 1763 a granddaughter of Madam Brett and later lived in the Brett house at Fishkill (plate 111).

The Upper Landing at Poughkeepsie, with its mill, dwelling, storehouse and dock, was long a typical Hudson river settlement. It was a center where the farmers of Dutchess brought their grain to be ground and where they shipped grain and general farm-produce by sloops on the river to New York. The landing prospered so long as the river remained the sole key to transportation. After 1824 the farms of Dutchess waned in value because of the construction of the Erie Canal, which introduced competition with the West, and after 1850 when the Hudson River Railroad was opened all economic conditions changed. Thus the Upper Landing became at last only a memory but a memory that still is significant to a few old residents of Poughkeepsie.

Van Den Bogaerdt-leComte-Myers House

An original map, made in 1796 by Henry Livingston, Jr., and now owned by the Adriance Memorial Library, Poughkeepsie, records a farm the title to which was held successively by Myndert Harmense Van Den Bogaerdt, Baudouin le Comte and Nathan Myers, and on the map, at the location which now is the northeast corner of Mill and Bridge Streets, Poughkeepsie, is the entry: "Old Myers House." That same year (1796) Nathan Myers advertised his property in the *Poughkeepsie Journal* as for sale and described " the stone house where the subscriber lives " as having " two large rooms on the lower floor." This primitive dwelling, " old " in 1796 (and which disappeared in the nineteenth century), is supposed to have been the home either of Myndert Harmense Van Den Bogaerdt, who died about 1711, or of his widow and heirs. Myndert Harmense was one of the patentees of the Sanders and Harmense Patent that covered a large portion of the site of the city of Poughkeepsie. He settled on this farm about 1692 and presumably built a temporary dwelling while clearing and planting his land. The location of this, his permanent home, is recorded here because he was a Dutchman and one of the half-dozen pioneers who first occupied the site of Poughkeepsie.

The Farm of Garret Storm
Town of East Fishkill, Dutchess County, New York
PLATE 134

East of the Hopewell Dutch church there is a neighborhood, known locally as Upper Hopewell, which was settled in the second quarter of the eighteenth century by the Storms from Westchester County and the Adriances and Brinckerhoffs from Long Island. It is a stretch of well watered rolling country, on which those families developed rich farms. The families were large in numbers, intermarried frequently, and the titles to the farms remained for generations among kinsfolk. A thoroughly Dutch rural community grew up, thrifty and prosperous, domestic and religious, with the Hopewell Dutch church its center, socially and ecclesiastically.

The Storms of Sleepy Hollow (Tarrytown), Westchester County, descended from Dirck Storm and Maria Pieters Monfort, his wife, of the Mayoralty of Bosch, Holland, who came to New Netherland in the ship *Fox* in 1662. Their grandson, Thomas Storm (born 1697, died 1769) of Sleepy Hollow, bought largely from Madam Brett of her lands in the Rombout Patent in the vicinity of Upper Hopewell and Stormville and three of his sons (Garret, Goris and Isaac) removed from Westchester to Dutchess.

Garret Storm (born 1722, died 1801) built his homestead midway between Upper Hopewell and Stormville on the east and north side of the *Vis Kil*. From his house there was no extended view but the house stood in one of those intimate situations which are peculiarly lovely. The site is in a bend of the road where the ground slopes to the *Vis Kil* and the stream winds it course along road and hill through a small copse to the open meadow beyond.

376

Not peaceful always was the scene however. For on the house of Garret Storm in the days of the Revolution Tories made a raid and hung the master of the house in his own attic, leaving him to die. One of his many slaves crept up, unobserved, and released her master, who lived to make a will twenty years later in which he left a legacy to: " my good and faithful maid, Eype Schouten," and directed his executors to support Eype during her natural life. A burying ground for the slaves is on this farm, south of the road and west of the bridge, and there, presumably, faithful Eype was one day laid to rest.

Nothing is known of the architecture of the house built and occupied on this farm by Garret Storm before the Revolution but no record of Dutch homes in Dutchess County would be complete without mention of the farms and families at Upper Hopewell and for the purpose of identifying the site and preserving the tradition attached to it the story of Garret Storm's dwelling is set down here.

By his will, dated 1797, proved 1802, Garret Storm bequeathed to his son, John, " the farm whereon I now live, with all houses, barns etc." Colonel John Storm (born 1765, died 1835) married Susanna Brinckerhoff and in the 1790's occupied his father's farm. Before 1802 he tore down the house built by his father and erected the one which now stands on the site. Were this volume devoted to descriptions of houses of the early Republic the house of Colonel John Storm would provide excellent subject matter. By tradition the bricks of which it is built (laid in Flemish bond) were made on the farm. It sits well, on a natural terrace. Through a Dutch door entrance is had to a hall, spanned by a central arch and having a stairway with two landings at the extreme end. There are four rooms on each floor, several of which contain carved mantels. Over the doors some casings are carved in fan-pattern. The ceilings are high and the floor spaces generous. The front porch is of the period of the 1830's. If correctly restored this house could be a home of beauty and dignity. It remained in the Storm family until late in the nineteenth century, was purchased in recent years by Edwin S. Hooley of New York City and is occupied now by the farmer in the employ of the owner.

Storm-Adriance-Brinckerhoff House

Town of East Fishkill, Dutchess County, New York

PLATE 135

Garret Storm of Upper Hopewell (notes, plate 134) gave to his son, Thomas (born 1749, died 1833), a large farm about the time that the latter came of age. The farm lies somewhat north of Garret Storm's homestead and faces on the road which leads from Hopewell Dutch church through the Clove to Connecticut. Over this road during the period of the Revolution there was much travel back and forth between New England and the South and so it happened that many of those who passed this way stopped at the house of Thomas Storm for hospitality over night, the guests ranging from Washington, himself, down to the unnamed private citizen. It is related in regard to Washington's visit that in the morning, when he came out of the house word having gone abroad of his presence, a group of nearby residents had gathered on the little green before the door and stood bareheaded to greet the commander-in-chief, only to be told by him to put on their hats, for he was a man like all other men.

Thomas Storm occupied the house shown in plate 135 from about 1771 (when he married) to 1785 and in those years was prominent locally as adjutant and captain in the second regiment of Dutchess militia; as a member of the vigilance committee; and, from 1781 to 1784, as a member of the state assembly. At the close of the Revolution he removed to New York City, which he represented in the legislature from 1798 to 1803 (being twice speaker of the assembly) and where he ran for election as lieutenant-governor. His granddaughter, Glorvina Storm, wife of Samual Verplanck Hoffman, was the mother of the Reverend E. A Hoffman, sometime Dean of the General Theological Seminary of the Episcopal Church.

In 1785 John Adriance (born 1753, died 1794), whose wife, Engeltje, was Thomas Storm's sister, bought the farm. Nine years later he died and in 1795 the executors of his will sold the property to George Brinckerhoff (born 1726, died 1797) of Newtown, Long Island, who removed from Long Island and established in Dutchess a home for himself and his family. His descendant, Mrs. Ernest Clapp of Hawthorne, N. Y., now owns the house and farm. Mrs. Clapp's father, the late T. Van Wyck Brinckerhoff, who long occupied this home, did much to conserve local historical data in his monograph on Fishkill and in a genealogy of the Brinckerhoff family.

The Storm-Adriance-Brinckerhoff house is built of frame, brick-filled and clapboarded, in two sections. The west end (to the left in plate 135) is the older of the two and consists of a main portion with a kitchen wing. A Dutch oven still protrudes from the west wall of the wing. In the main portion is a large front room that was known in the Brinckerhoff family by the Dutch name: *portaal* (vestibule, entrance, forehouse, etc.). Presumably the two long windows it now contains were at first a door and an ordinary window for the room adjoining has one window, cut down, and an ancient Dutch door with eighteenth century hardware.

The east end of the house may safely be attributed to Thomas Storm about the time of his marriage (1771). This easterly unit contains a hall, running from front to rear, two rooms east of the hall and a half-story above. The hall is wainscoted. The chimney-breasts in the two rooms on the first floor are done in typical Georgian designs. The absence should be noted of the small windows at the eaves-line (popularly known as lie-on-your-stomach windows), which came into use in the 1790's.

It is hardly necessary to point out that the small porch on the east part and the

378

posts and arches of the veranda on the old house are nineteenth century work, as are also the dormers, the slatted blinds and French windows. The porch and the veranda recall the design of the woodwork on the Osterhoudt house (plate 81) in Ulster and the general appearance of the whole dwelling is similar to that of the Van Wyck homestead at Woodbury, Long Island, as pictured at page sixty-eight of *The Van Wyck Family*.

A tradition held by the Brinckerhoffs in the nineteenth century was to the effect that military prisoners had been confined in this house during the Revolution and the tradition received confirmation when, about 1880, the flooring was renovated and a trap-door to the cellar was uncovered in the southeast corner of the old part of the house. Under the trap-door were a knapsack, cap and pocketbook. It is to be supposed that the prisoners were men held by Captain Storm when he was a member of the vigilance committee.

This homestead at Upper Hopewell is rich in the background it has of ample living in prosperous Dutch comfort, with numerous slaves and horses, a generous table and enjoyable social life. The family ties of its occupants reached out in many directions. Near by was the house of Captain Thomas Storm's father. Captain Storm's wife, Elizabeth, daughter of the Reverend Chauncey Graham (pastor of the Rombout Presbyterian Church), was a granddaughter on her mother's side of Theodorus Van Wyck of Wiccopee and the intermarriages of the Storms, Brinckerhoffs, Van Wycks, Bretts and others were such that relationship can be traced between almost all of the people who lived in the houses at Fishkill shown in plates: 8, 111, 113, 114, 134, 144, 146, 147 and 149.

Three Stoutenburgh Houses

Formerly at Hyde Park-on-Hudson, New York

On the site of the present village of Hyde Park-on-Hudson three stone houses were built in the eighteenth century by members of the Stoutenburgh family which were torn down in the nineteenth. No photographs of them have survived and the account of them here given is based partly upon the investigations made thirty or forty years ago by the late Edward Braman and Dr. James L. Prichard (accurate research-workers) of Hyde Park and partly upon the testimony of elderly residents of Hyde Park who are still living.

Hyde Park as a village dates from 1791, in which year the farm of Luke Stoutenburgh (born 1736, died 1789) was surveyed and streets and house-lots laid out. Before 1791 large farms occupied the whole site of the village and its immediate vicinity. The area indicated lies in the ninth water-lot of the Great Nine Partners Patent, the greater part of which lot was acquired before 1742 by Jacobus Stoutenburgh (born 1696, died 1772). He, about 1742, removed from Philipseburgh,

Westchester County, to Dutchess, bringing with him his wife, Margaret Teller (whom he married in 1717), and a numerous family of sons and daughters. When he took up his property in Dutchess the land was uncleared. The *King's Highway*, a rough artery of traffic, probably hardly more than wheel-tracks through the woods, crossed it north and south on the flat above the river-level and tradition says that on the east side of the road, at the south end of the present village, a log-house was built for the accomodation of the workers, employed by the owner to clear the tract.

For himself, Jacobus Stoutenburgh built a stone house on the west side of the *King's Highway*, athwart the course of the present Parker Avenue. Parker Avenue runs at right angles to the highway and in 1925, when pipes were laid in the street, the excavations that were made uncovered the foundations of the former house, which extended from the south gutter to the inner side of the north sidewalk. The house was built, presumably, soon after 1742 and it stood until about 1864. In its last days it was a ruin but the report has been handed down that it contained, originally, rooms of good size, handsomely panelled. Portraits of Jacobus Stoutenburgh and his wife, Margaret Teller, painted in oil on wood panels, are now owned by Miss Caroline T. Wells of Rhinebeck, New York. Miss Wells descends from Jacobus and his wife in the line of their daughter, Margaret Stoutenburgh, who married her cousin, John Teller, and lived in the house shown in plate 139. The dress of the subjects of the paintings, as recorded in the portraits, was elegant and in accordance with the tradition of a well built, well finished house. The house is said to have been inherited by Jacobus Stoutenburgh, the second (who married, in 1764, his cousin, Josina Teller), and to have passed to his son, Luke I. Stoutenburgh (born 1779). In the absence of direct evidence as to its structural plan it can only be said that the total silence regarding it goes to show that it was one of the typical stone houses of the 1740's,—rectangular, longer than broad, a story and a half in height.

To Tobias Stoutenburgh (colonel of the fourth regiment of Dutchess militia in the Revolution) his father, Jacobus, gave a farm on the river-front. There Tobias built a stone house on a site south of the present station of the New York Central and Hudson River Railroad at Hyde Park. The house was occupied about 1800 by Tobias Stoutenburgh's son-in-law, Richard De Cantillon, who had a dock and sloops and did a prosperous carrying business not only on the Hudson but to the West Indies. The house was torn down about 1860. A woodcut of it, at page two-hundred and eighteen of the *History of Dutchess County* that was published in 1877 by Philip H. Smith, was based upon an old drawing and shows a house a story and a half in height with a roof-line that sloped close to the ground at the rear (as in the Krom house in Ulster County, shown in plate 78).

Luke Stoutenburgh, above referred to, married in 1762 his cousin, Rachel Teller, and received from his father, Jacobus, the farm that in 1791 was mapped for development as a village. His house stood directly across the line of the present Market

380

Street, Hyde Park, at the point where a gate now leads into the grounds belonging to Edward Wales. From the *King's Highway* (now the main street of the village) a private lane or avenue led west in the eighteenth century to Luke Stoutenburgh's dwelling, the course of which avenue later became Market Street. The drive was lined on either side by a row of cherry-trees, some of which still survive, which planting was similar to one at *The Flatts* at Watervliet (see: notes on plate 33). The house of Luke Stoutenburgh stood until about 1872 and persons now living who clearly remember it describe it as a stone structure, one and one-half stories high; with a roof of single pitch; small windows close to the eaves (probably dating from about 1800); a hall through the center, with a Dutch door at either end; and having a chimney in the south gable. From the descriptions the house ran true to the general architectural form of the 1760's. It was one of Vaughan's many targets in 1777 and several of the balls fired on it by his fleet are preserved.

House of William Stoutenburgh

Town of Hyde Park, Dutchess County, New York

PLATE 136

William Stoutenburgh (born 1722), son of Jacobus and Margaret Teller Stoutenburgh, was given by his father a farm east of the present Hyde Park village, on which he built a stone house which is still standing. The house is at East Park, south of the four-corners, on the west side of the road and is now owned and occupied by Edward Brower.

As shown in plate 136 the house is one of the typical stone dwellings of its day and the houses of William Stoutenburgh's father, Jacobus, and brother, Luke, which were torn down in the nineteenth century, were undoubtedly of the same general plan and appearance as this. On the south side of the front door of William Stoutenburgh's house a stone is cut with the figures: 1 7 5 0, and a stone north of the door is marked: 1 7 6 5. The second date may, perhaps, refer to an addition at the right rear corner that is replaced by a modern frame wing.

As built, the house had a central hall with Dutch door, the boxed-in staircase being at the northwest or back right hand corner of the hall. A partition now divides the hall and the location of the stairs is changed. North of the hall is one room and at the south are two living-rooms and a dark pantry. There is no wood-trim of importance. Traditions of a definite sort associate the slaves with the cellar, where they are said to have slept and cooked.

William Stoutenburgh married in 1753 Maria Van Vleck and they brought up a large family in this home.

381

(Bergh?)-Stoutenburgh-Teller House

Hyde Park-on-Hudson, New York

PLATE 137

The stone house (plate 137) on the east side of the state road, opposite the present northern entrance to the estate of Mrs. Archibald Rogers at Hyde Park-on-Hudson, is believed to stand on a tract of one-hundred acres which was sold between 1780 and 1788 by John Bergh to Jacobus Stoutenburgh, the second. By a deed of 1803 four of the heirs of Jacobus Stoutenburgh, the second (three sons and a daughter), conveyed to a fifth heir, their sister, Margaret, seventy-five acres that included the site of this house. Margaret Stoutenburgh and her husband, John Teller, sold the property in 1835 to William W. Woodworth and he in 1855 to Ann Kip Miller. Mrs. Rogers now owns it. Further clues to the history of the house are found in the record of the title to the land and are briefly submitted here.

The northern boundary-line of the Rogers property at Hyde Park approximates the boundary between water-lots eight and nine of the Great Nine Partners Patent. The greater part of water-lot eight was purchased before the Revolution by Christian Bergh, who lived a few miles to the north near Staatsburgh and who established his son, John, and son-in-law, Martin Dop, on farms in water-lot eight. The map of the post-road, made in 1778—1780 by Robert Erskine, military engineer, records two houses where, now, two houses stand, one at the location of the house shown in plate 137 and the other farther south on the east side of the road.

The stone house to the southward (now painted yellow) is near the southern entrance to the grounds of Mrs. Rogers. It was occupied by Martin Dop until, in 1776, the Committee for the Detection of Conspiracies sent him to a prison for Tories at Exeter, New Hampshire. In April, 1777, Christian Bergh, himself, was under suspicion as a Tory and the same committee ordered him into confinement in his own home. These experiences evidently told upon the old man for he died in 1780 and his lands in water-lot eight went to his son, John, who, meanwhile, had supposedly been living in the northerly one of the two houses shown on Erskine's map.

In 1785 John Bergh mortgaged the major portion of water-lot eight. The mortgage was foreclosed in 1788 and the property sold at auction by the sheriff and in this sale by the sheriff lies the germ of the local tradition that the farm occupied once by Martin Dop was confiscated. Jonathan Hasbrouck of Kingston bought the property at the auction and he, in 1791, conveyed it to James I. and John L. Stoutenburgh. It is now owned by Mrs. Rogers.

The sale at auction did not include, however, all of the original Bergh land. By the recital of title in a deed of 1788 John Bergh is known to have sold one-hundred acres in water-lot eight to Jacobus Stoutenburgh, the second, at some time between

1780 and 1788 and it is on this parcel that the house shown in plate 137 is supposed to be built.

Of the two stone houses now standing on the Bergh land in water-lot eight, the one to the south is inferior in finish and is altered in appearance by a modern veranda.

The house to the north (plate 137) is well built. In materials, in gambrel roof-line, in floor-plan and wood-trim it belongs to the pre-Revolutionary period. But the masonry of the walls (which are built of tooled stones, smoothly laid) suggests the 1780's or 1790's as the actual date of construction. It may have been built by Christian Bergh for his son, John, prior to 1776. Or it may have been built by Jacobus Stoutenburgh to replace a house that John Bergh had occupied on the same site. In any case it is an illustration of a pre-Revolutionary style even if actually built after the war.

Inside, the house contains a central hall, with one room at either side. Originally there were two rooms to the south but the partition has been removed. The mantels, wood-trim and staircase are all simple and good.

First House of Jacobus Swartwout

Swartwoutville, Dutchess County, New York

PLATE 8

In Friesland in the Low Countries, long, long ago, there was a tract known as: *het Zwarte Woud* (the Black Wood). Adopted as a surname by a family living there, *Zwarte Woud* was borne to New Netherland in the seventeenth century in a corrupt, evolved form by Roeloff Swartwout, who was one of the early arrivals at Esopus. Roeloff Swartwout's great-grandson, Jacobus Swartwout, born at Wiccopee, Dutchess County, in 1734, married in 1760 Aeltje Brinckerhoff and settled on a farm on the Sprout Creek. His land lay where two roads form a V. From the northeast comes the main county-road between Hopewell and the Hudson. From the northwest a road from New Hackensack joins the Hopewell road. Jacobus Swartwout's property was on both sides of the New Hackensack road, west and south of the Sprout, and the V-shaped road-junction came to be known as Swartwoutville, a designation that once was significant to many ears but which is now well nigh forgotten. In the days of the Revolution Swartwoutville was a center of activity for the residents of southern Dutchess. Across the creek from the farm of Jacobus Swartwout was the dwelling of Colonel Jacob Griffin (page 368), where the county committee made its reports in 1775 on the lists of signers and non-signers of the Articles of Association, and the home of Jacobus Swartwout, himself, was the scene of much of interest because of his association with men and affairs.

Jacobus Swartwout's public career began in 1759 when he was captain of a

383

company under Amherst at Ticonderoga and Crown Point. In 1775 he was commissioned colonel of a regiment of minute men in Dutchess and was in active service around New York City and in the Highlands in 1776—1777. From 1780 to 1794 he held a commission as brigadier-general in command of the militia of Dutchess County. He was a member of the New York assembly 1777—1783 and of the state senate 1784—1795 and in 1788 was a delegate from Dutchess to the state constitutional convention in Poughkeepsie, where he voted against the ratification of the Federal Constitution. During the Revolution Baron von Steuben is said (by tradition) to have had his quarters for a time in the house of General Swartwout and Washington was entertained in 1778 a mile to the southward in the house of Mrs. Swartwout's uncle, John Brinckerhoff (plate 114).

The first of two houses built at Swartwoutville by Jacobus Swartwout, which presumably dates from about the time of his marriage (1760), is standing but in ruins. Its skeleton is shown in plate 8 to illustrate the manner in which early frame walls were laid up in mud and sided either with shingles or clapboards. The house was one and one-half stories high, with a roof of single slant and contained four rooms (two larger, on the south front; and two, smaller, at the north rear). To the east was a wing, in which was a large kitchen. The fine Dutch barns that belonged with the old home are also standing, eastward from the dwelling, possessed of their eighteenth century iron hardware, but open to the weather. Evidently the southwest room of the house was the best parlor for the west wall had a handsomely panelled chimney-breast and beautiful panelled cupboards at either side of the chimney (the interior of the cupboards carved in shell-pattern). Only a little less elaborate was the panelling of the east wall of the southeast room and of the northeast room, in which latter the fireplace opened on a slant across the corner of the room. Enclosed stairs rose from the southwest corner of the southeast room, next to a door, which opened on a small porch. A door opened on the porch from the southwest room also and the remnant of a porch-hood shows in the plate.

In March, 1924, the carved wood-trim was removed from the house and it is now owned by Geraldyn L. Redmond of Brookville, Long Island, Alexander Kiam of New York City and Mrs. E. E. Walters of Poughkeepsie, N. Y. Shortly after the panelling was taken out, the siding and doors and windows, beams, etc., were also taken, leaving a pathetic wreck that a stranger, passing by, would never suspect had once been a colonial home of the better class.

According to a faded and unrecorded deed this house was sold by General Swartwout in 17(89?), at which time he probably moved into a new house up the road (plate 138). The title passed from him to the three Dutch Churches of Fishkill, Hopewell and New Hackensack and the old deed is now in the custody of the Fishkill church. From 1791 to 1804 the house, with eight acres attached to it, was occupied by the Reverend Nicholas Van Vranken, pastor of the united congregations; and

384

from 1805 to 1810 by the Reverend George Barculo, pastor of New Hackensack and Hopewell. In 1812 the churches advertised the parsonage for sale and General Swartwout bought it back, ultimately bequeathing it by will to his son, Jacobus I. Swartwout (born 1770, died 1846). Jacobus I. Swartwout occupied the house with his wife, Ann Seward of New Hackensack (notes: plate 130), and brought up in it his wife's nephew, Seward Barculo (born 1808; son of the Reverend George Barculo), who from 1847 to 1853 was an able justice of the Supreme Court of New York. In the 1840's the house was rented to the parents of John Lorimer Worden, then a lad, later an admiral of the United States Navy.

Second House of Jacobus Swartwout

Swartwoutville, Dutchess County, New York

PLATE 138

The house shown in plate 138, now owned by Mrs. O. C. Pinckney, stands close to the Sprout Creek. It dates in construction from approximately 1789 and is recorded here not because it is a good example of the type of house built in Dutchess County in the period from 1783 to 1800 but because of the man who built it and the neighborhood in which it stands.

General Jacobus Swartwout, of ancestry purely Dutch, whose public services are outlined in connection with the account of his first house, made Swartwoutville a distinct locality and a definitely Dutch portion of the county and it is but the climax to his story to include his second dwelling. He lived in his second house from about the time he sold his first (1789?), until his death in 1827 and in 1824, when he was ninety years old, he journeyed from this house to Poughkeepsie to be present at the reception given to the Marquis de La Fayette and to sit at La Fayette's right hand at breakfast. From him this house passed to his daughter, Aeltje, wife of John A. Sleight, and it remained in the possession of the Sleight family until the 1850's.

The second Swartwout house is one of the frame structures characteristic in Dutchess County of the years immediately subsequent to the Revolutionary War. Like the former stone houses, the frame dwellings were one and one-half stories in height but they did not at first have small, oblong windows under the eaves. Such windows came into use just before and after 1800. The eaves-windows now cut in the Swartwout house were made by the present owner. The porch found today on the south front of General Swartwout's house is in the style of 1830 and perhaps was added by Mrs. Sleight with a sum of money which in 1827 was given her by her father's will and which the will specified should be used in repairing and improving the house. The doorway that gives entrance to the hall probably dates from the construction of the porch. The floor-plan is original and unchanged, consisting of

385

four main rooms, a central hall and a kitchen wing. The stairway is a duplicate of the one in the house of Cornelius Van Wyck (plate 146), which is ascribed to the period between 1790 and 1810. The kitchen door is eighteenth century. Two parlor mantels are in designs of the early nineteenth century.

House of John Teller
Town of Clinton, Dutchess County, New York
PLATE 139

John Teller (born 1741), a great-grandson of William Teller, who founded the Teller family of the Hudson valley, married in 1764 his first cousin, Margaret Stoutenburgh, a daughter of Jacobus and Margaret (Teller) Stoutenburgh (notes: Three Stoutenburgh Houses, page 379). At the time of their marriage John and Margaret Teller built the house shown in plate 139, which stands near Bull's Head in the town of Clinton and is owned by Harry Husted. It is a stone house (stuccoed), one and one-half stories high, and contains a central hall and two rooms on the main floor. On the landing of the stairway (which rises at the rear of the hall) is a beam, built in against the wall and cut in a peculiar shape. Tradition names it the "witch beam", to keep witches away, but provides no further explanation. This house has suffered much from lack of care and has lost most of its original finishings. By sentiment it is associated with the farmhouse at Rensselaer, New York (plate 26), owned by William and Jacob Van Benschoten Teller, who were grandsons of the builders of this Dutchess County home. Through the builders of this house their descendant, Miss Caroline T. Wells of Rhinebeck, New York, inherited and now owns portraits of Jacobus Stoutenburgh and his wife, Margaret Teller, painted in oils on panels and of life-size.

Unidentified House
Town of Poughkeepsie, Dutchess County, New York
PLATE 140

The little house, shown in plate 140, owned by Peter Powell, stands immediately south of the tract which was long known at Poughkeepsie as the Hudson River Driving Park. The records in the office of the county clerk for land in this vicinity are deficient and confusing because some deeds were not recorded and some of those on file are obscure in the descriptions they contain. As nearly as can be determined the site of the house was owned by Jan De Graeff, who died in 1734. Jan De Graeff's son, Moses, married Antje Kip; and Jan's daughter, Jannetje, married Lawrence Van Kleeck, Jr. Apparently Barent Kip, who was a brother of Moses De Graeff's wife, owned the land from 1753 to 1760 and Lawrence Van Kleeck, Jr., from 1761 to 176(8?). Either Kip or Van Kleeck might have built the house, and in the tangle of family-relationships may lie the clue to the title. At some date subsequent to the tenure of Lawrence Van Kleeck, Jr., Jacobus Frear seems to have owned the place. He died in 1795 and ultimately his son, Jacobus, is found selling the property in 1833. From 1833 to the present owner there is a clear chain of title.

House of Teunis Van Benschoten

Formerly at New Hackensack, New York

Teunis Van Benschoten (born 1706, died 1788) bought land in 1734 in the town of Wappinger, Dutchess County (then a part of Rombout Precinct). The land was immediately west of what is now the hamlet of New Hackensack and lay along a small stream which courses westward into the Wappingers Creek. About a half-mile west of the present post-office at New Hackensack Teunis Van Benschoten built his house and south of the house, on the stream, near the present bridge, he erected a grist-mill. The house and the grist-mill both are gone but descriptions of the house were preserved and record it as built of stone, a story and a half in height. The roof sloped at the rear nearly to the ground (see: Krom House, Ulster County, plate 78 and house of Tobias Stoutenburgh, Dutchess County, page 380); a hall ran through the center of the first floor, on which were two rooms, with a kitchen in the rear; a stairway led to bedrooms in the half-story; oak timbers were used in construction; there were open ceiling-beams and the fireplaces were large. A modern brick house occupies the site of Teunis Van Benschoten's dwelling but a barn and smoke-house of early date are still standing.

Teunis Van Benschoten married in 1737 Antje Sleght and their sons: Matthew (born 1742, died 1825) and Jacob (born 1750, died 1830), inherited the homestead. The two brothers, bachelors, occupied the old farm and were widely known in Dutchess as men of capital who invested their money on bond and mortgage throughout the county. They each had several namesakes among their many great-nephews: Matthew Van Benschoten Ackerman, Matthew Van Benschoten Schryver, Matthew Van Benschoten Brinckerhoff, Matthew Van Benschoten Fowler, Jacob Van Benschoten Conklin, Jacob Van Benschoten Teller (1), Jacob Van Benschoten Teller (2), Jacob Van Benschoten Stoutenburgh and Jacob Van Benschoten Van Voorhees; and the bachelor uncles left their property largely to the members of this unique group of kinsmen.

House of James Van Der Burgh

Formerly in the Town of Beekman, Dutchess County, New York

About a quarter of a mile northeast of the village of Poughquag, Dutchess County, New York, stood until 1860 a house which was built before the Revolution by Colonel James Van Der Burgh. A woodcut of this house appears in the *History of Dutchess County*, published in 1877 by Philip H. Smith, which was based upon a pencil-sketch then owned by the Van Der Burgh family. In the possession of Mrs. Tristram Coffin of New York City there is now a painting made from a sketch that is known to have been drawn by Benson J. Lossing. As the woodcut and the painting are apparently derived from one source it is safe to assume that the ever active hand of Mr. Lossing preserved a record of a dwelling of which there is now no other information to be had.

Architecturally, the house of Colonel Van Der Burgh, as shown by the sketch, was of a familiar type. It was rectangular in form, oblong in proportion; a frame structure, one and one-half stories in height, with a roof of single slant, a high stone basement, a chimney in each gable, dormers resembling those of the Brett house (plate 111) and porch similar to that of the Verplanck house (plate 148). Interest attaches to the house more because it was the home of a Revolutionary leader than for any architectural considerations.

James Van Der Burgh (born 1729, died 1794) was a son of Henry Van Der Burgh, whose house in the town of Poughkeepsie stood at the *Rust Plaets*, very nearly on the site of the present house of John Van Benschoten. He removed in young manhood from the town of Poughkeepsie to the town of Beekman and there, during the Revolution, served as colonel of the fifth regiment of Dutchess militia. In 1776 he represented the county in the Provincial Congress of New York. James Van Der Burgh was married in 1753 to his first wife, Margaret Noxon (a marriage which linked his house at Poughquag to that of his father-in-law, Bartholomew Noxon, at Poughkeepsie, which latter house is discussed on page 370), and in 1767 to his second wife, Helena Clark. His eighteen children (born 1754—1793) grew up in the house at Poughquag and he and his wives and a number of his family are buried in a family burial ground on the hillside opposite where his house stood.

In May, 1781, General Washington made a journey from his headquarters at New Windsor, Orange County, New York, to Weathersfield, Connecticut, for an interview with " the French General," and his diary and accounts record that going and coming, on May 18th and May 25th, he dined at Colonel Van Der Burgh's house. It is traditional that Tories fired upon the house once when Colonel Van Der Burgh was at home sick, thinking a ball might strike his person, but that their purpose failed of accomplishment.

House of Matthew Van Keuren
Town of Poughkeepsie, Dutchess County, New York
PLATE 141

Four miles south of the city of Poughkeepsie a small stream, called by the Dutch: *Speck zyn kil*, enters the Hudson. The land at the north side of the mouth of the stream was purchased in 1729 by Captain Tjerck Van Keuren, blacksmith, of Kingston, whose deed conveyed to him mill-rights on the stream and the privilege of taking from other lands of the patentee timber and stone with which to build a dwelling-house and a mill. Later, Captain Van Keuren bought the land on the south side of the *kil* and both parcels he bequeathed by will in 1742 to his son, Matthew Van Keuren, who was then occupying the property.

The house built (presumably) between 1729 and 1742 by Matthew Van Keuren is now standing on the north side of *Speck zyn kil*. The exterior has been altered by the raising of the roof and by modern shingles and porches and only the stone walls of the first story bespeak the period of erection. The photograph taken of the house (plate 141) illustrates its relation to the river, which forms a grey background beyond the foliage. Inside the house much remains of primitive wood-trim. There is a central hall, with enclosed stairs, one room to the north and two to the south. A basement-kitchen retains original ceiling-beams and only in 1925 was a large Dutch oven torn down from the outer south wall of the kitchen.

The mill, which Matthew Van Keuren built at about the same time as the dwelling, stood on the north bank of the stream and was burned by British soldiers in October, 1777. On its foundations now stands the so-called olive oil building of the plant of R. U. Delapenha and Company.

In addition to his mill Matthew Van Keuren established a ferry to the opposite shore of the Hudson, which was a neighborhood convenience for many years. South of his house there was also a forge, at which (according to a respected local tradition) were made some of the links included in the chain that was stretched across the Hudson at Fort Montgomery in 1776.

In January, 1777, Matthew Van Keuren sold all his property at *Speck zyn kil* to Theophilus Anthony, formerly of New York City, then of Dutchess County. Whether the links for the chain were forged by Van Keuren or by Anthony (as tradition relates) depends upon when Anthony left New York. A reference to him in June, 1776, when he was appointed an executor of the will of his brother-in-law, Henry Brevoort of New York City, would imply that his removal was not until after that date.

When in October, 1777, Sir James Wallace's boats went up the Hudson, some of the soldiers they carried were sent on shore to raid the group of buildings at *Speck zyn kil*. The Anthony family took shelter in the woods but Dina, the family nurse, born in Africa, remained in the basement-kitchen, where she had just finished a large baking of bread. The soldiers fired the mill but Dina bribed them with the fresh bread to spare the house. Dina lived to be emancipated by the state act of 1827, when she left the old home for a while. Like many other elderly slaves she returned to the master's house, died there and was buried in the family burial ground.

Tjerck Van Keuren of Kingston (born 1682, died 1742), who in 1729, bought

389

the land at the mouth of *Speck zyn kil* and settled his son, Matthew, on it, was a son of Mattys and Tjaatje (De Witt) Van Keuren. His mother, Tjaatje, was a daughter of Tjerck Claessen De Witt (notes: plate 69) and, when a child of four, was taken captive by the Indians in their attack on Kingston in 1663, was carried to New Fort (page 189 and page 226) and there rescued by Captain Kregier. Tjerck Van Keuren's sister, Sarah (born 1678), married Matthew DuBois and accompanied her husband to the Du Bois farm on the Wappingers Creek (page 339) in 1730. Tjerck's wife, Maria Ten Eyck, was aunt to Blandina Ten Eyck De Witt and to Matthew Ten Eyck whose homes are shown in plates 71 and 90. His daughter, Rachel Van Keuren (born 1722), was the first wife of Dirck Van Vliet (text: plate 143) of the town of Clinton, Dutchess County; his niece, Mrs. John Pawling (Neeltje Van Keuren), lived at Staatsburgh (plate 132) and his cousin, John De Witt, at De Witt's Mill in Dutchess (plate 116). Thus the Van Keuren property at *Speck zyn kil* was a unit in a group of colonial homes that were bound together by the complicated family ties of their occupants.

House of Baltus Barents Van Kleeck

Formerly at Poughkeepsie, New York

PLATE 142

In 1686 Robert Sanders and Myndert Harmense Van Den Bogaerdt of Albany obtained a Crown patent for a stretch of wilderness in the Dutchess's County, which was then newly outlined on paper. Their purchase covered most of the site of the present city of Poughkeepsie and by 1691 they had four or five tenants on the land. One of that number was Baltus Barents Van Kleeck (whose sister, Elsie, was the wife of Robert Sanders) and in 1697 Van Kleeck bought a large homestead farm of Sanders and Harmense, the deed for which conveyed a house and barn with the land.

Five years later, in 1702, Baltus Barents built a house, which presumably was placed immediately in front of the house he purchased in 1697, the whole forming a main house with a rear wing. This dwelling stood at the approximate site of the present 224—228 Mill Street and was inherited in the Van Kleeck family in direct male line (from Baltus Barents by Peter B.; Baltus P.; Peter B.) down to Margaret Van Kleeck (born 1790, died 1839), who married John Guy Vassar and whose son, Matthew Vassar, Jr., tore it down in 1835 to permit the widening of Mill Street. Mr. Vassar saved the lintel-stone, which is now owned by Baltus Barentszen Van Kleeck of Poughkeepsie (of the ninth generation of the family), through whose courtesy a photograph of the stone is shown elsewhere in this volume (plate 6).

A few weeks before Mr. Vassar razed the house Benson J. Lossing made a sketch of it (that being before the days of photography) and published the drawing in 1838 in *The Family Magazine*, volume six, page two-hundred and forty. Subsequently, on three occasions, Mr. Lossing referred in print to the Van Kleeck house: in 1860 in *The Field-Book of the Revolution* (volume one, page three-hundred and eighty-three); in 1866 in *The Hudson* (page one-hundred and eighty-nine); and in 1867 in *Vassar College and Its Founder* (pages twenty to twenty-two). Each of these text-references is accompanied by a picture of the house from the pencil of Mr. Lossing but no two of the pictures are alike. They agree in essentials but one is a near-by view, one distant; one has foliage, one has snow; one is by daylight and one at night. Gratitude is due Mr. Lossing, despite these variations, for preserving a record of the house which makes it possible to classify it at once, architecturally, with the typical stone houses of the Hudson valley of the late seventeenth and early eighteenth centuries.

In all of his written descriptions Mr. Lossing stated that the Van Kleeck house was solidly built of rough field stones, with portholes in the gable-ends. His sketches all show a rectangular building, one and one-half stories in height, with a roof of single slant, a chimney in either gable, apparently two rooms across the north front of the house and a door opening into the west room. The depth of the house suggests four rooms on the main floor. The wing in the rear was on the same general plan, but on a smaller scale. The fact that the wing was a primitive unit in itself supports the theory that it was built before 1697. The accompanying illustration is from the sketch of 1835 as published in *The Family Magazine* and on which all the other sketches were based.

In the eighteenth century the Van Kleeck house was a tavern, in the sense that the occasional traveller could obtain shelter in it. It stood on the *King's Highway*, and whatever traffic there was passed the door. The accounts of the board of supervisors of the county frequently show payments made for the " victualing " of the members of the board in this house at the time of their semi-annual gatherings in the court-house and from 1777 to 1783, when Poughkeepsie was the capital of the state of New York, many men prominent in public life were guests under its roof. It has been proven by the late Reverend A. P. Van Giesen, sometime pastor of the Dutch Church, Poughkeepsie, that the convention of the state of New York which, on July 26, 1788, ratified the Constitution of the United States, met in the court-house at Poughkeepsie and not in the Van Kleeck house (as had sometimes been said) and it may be assumed that the sessions of the senate and assembly of the state were also held in the court-house, rather than in the small dwelling. But the Van Kleeck homestead was used, without much doubt, as a meeting place for committees and as a place where many civil and military officials of the Revolutionary period were housed.

In its connection with the affairs of the Revolution it is informing to contrast this house with the buildings at Hurley and Kingston in Ulster County which were used by the leaders of the New York militia and by civil officials of the state.

In all three places,—Hurley, Kingston and Poughkeepsie,—the houses were similar in material and plan, being rectangular structures of rough stone, varying slightly in size only, a fact which argues for a general similarity in the average living conditions in the three villages.

Van Kleeck-Hay House

547, Main street, Poughkeepsie, New York

At 547, Main Street, Poughkeepsie, is a stone house owned by the State of New York and occupied by the Daughters of the American Revolution as a chapter-house. Many statements have been made in print about the history of this house which it has been necessary to modify or qualify in the light of documentary evidence recovered since 1920. A discussion of the ownership and occupation of the house was published in the Year Book of the Dutchess County Historical Society for 1922 and for 1925 which, briefly summarized, shows that the house was built about 1765 by Hugh Van Kleeck (of Ahasuerus, of Barent, of Baltus Barents); was sold by him in 1780 to Colonel Udny Hay, Purchasing Agent for the State of New York; was partly burned in 1782—1783 and rebuilt in 1783 by Colonel Hay.

Structural features of the house indicate that it was originally oblong in proportion, one and one-half stories high, and that Colonel Hay altered it into its present form by increasing the depth, so as to make it more nearly square, and by carrying the walls up to two full stories. The labor of rebuilding in 1783 was performed by artificers of the Continental Army, sent from Newburgh to Poughkeepsie by General Washington, a fact attested not only by the official permit issued by the commander-in-chief but by tradition. Peter P. Van Kleeck (born 1757, died 1851; a first cousin to Hugh Van Kleeck), who was married three times, told his son by his third wife, Andrew J. Van Kleeck (born 1829), that he watched the continental soldiers work on the house. This statement was repeated by Andrew J. Van Kleeck to his daughter, Miss Mary J. Van Kleeck of the town of La Grange, Dutchess County, who quoted it to the present writer.

The house at Poughkeepsie is held by the State and the Daughters of the American Revolution as a memorial to George Clinton, the first governor of New York (who lived in Poughkeepsie from 1778 to 1783), and it contains a collection of furniture and documents open to the public.

The original floor-plan of the house consisted, presumably, of a central hall and four rooms, two larger in front, two smaller in the rear. As rebuilt by Colonel Hay after the fire, the two smaller rooms were enlarged. In the nineteenth century the two rooms west of the hall were made into one; marble mantels were added at most of the fireplaces and French windows were cut. In restoring the house the state and the chapter have removed the marble mantels and substituted mantels of wood. The mantel, carved in Adam design, which is now at the southwest chimney-place on the main floor was saved from the house of Henry Livingston (plate 128), when that was torn down in 1910. The stairway now in the house probably dates from 1783 and is an easy, graceful flight. The front porch is a recent reproduction of an early nineteenth century design. In the front wall of the house is a broken stone, cut with the letters: VK, and evidently incorporated in 1783 in the reconstruction of the house of 1765.

In 1777, for a few months, Kingston was the seat of the government of the newly-organized state of New York, a fact which the British raid of October, 1777, and the burning of the village has fixed firmly in the popular memory. For five years (1778—1783) Poughkeepsie was the seat of the state government; it was the residence of the governor; the senate and assembly held their sessions there and state committees their meetings; while civil and military officers came and went on public business. But as a rule the man in the street has forgotten all this and his forgetfulness is partly due to the fact that the city of Poughkeepsie has been built over and has only sites to point to, not buildings. It is fortunate therefore that a house that has definite associations connected with the Revolution has been saved and made to serve as a memorial to important men and events.

House of Cornelius Van Vliet
Formerly in the Town of Clinton, Dutchess County, New York
PLATE 143

Of the Van Vliet family, derived from the Province of Utrecht in Holland and settled in Kingston, New York, in the seventeenth century, a branch was founded in Dutchess County in the second quarter of the eighteenth century by Dirck Van Vliet, who purchased land in the Great Nine Partners Patent in what is now the town of Clinton. He built a house for himself which was replaced by another on the same site in 1783 by his son, Cornelius Van Vliet, and which in turn was succeeded in the second half of the nineteenth century by the dwelling, now owned and occupied by Dirck's descendant, George S. Van Vliet. Through the courtesy of the latter a photograph made many years ago of the house built in 1783 by Cornelius Van Vliet is reproduced in plate 143.

While the house here shown was not built before the War of the Revolution it illustrates a type of dwelling of which there were instances in the period before the war. It is essentially pre-war architecture and of a particularly rural character, and the picture serves as a record of the type.

Dirck Van Vliet, who built the first house on the site, married in 1741 Rachel Van Keuren, daughter of Tjerck Van Keuren of Kingston and sister of Matthew Van Keuren who lived at *Speck zyn kil* in Dutchess (plate 141). Cornelius Van Vliet (born 1760, died 1848), son of Dirck (by his second wife, Helena Weaver) and builder of the house shown in plate 143, married (first) Helena Garrison, daughter of Joost and Magdalena (Van Dyck) Garrison, and plate 120 records a house owned by her father.

House of Johannes Van Wormer Van Vliet
Town of Fishkill, Dutchess County, New York

On the road that runs southward from Tioronda toward Breakneck Point and on land owned by the Aldridge Brick and Land Company there is a stone house of the type characteristic of the eighteenth century. The house is badly out of repair and, when visited, was occupied by tenants (from the Ghetto) whose mode of living was such as to make a real inspection of it impossible. It can be said however that it is a house a story and a half in height, with roof of single slant, thick walls, a central hall, two rooms each side of the hall; and that it has a little early wood-trim remaining.

The house occupies a site that was part of a farm on the Philipse Patent and it was presumably the home of a leaseholding tenant prior to the Revolution. During the Revolution the Philipse Patent was confiscated, and on June 20, 1783, the Commissioners of Forfeiture sold this farm to Judith Cromwell, then " in possession and occupation " of it and who may have been the former leaseholder. The widowed Judith Cromwell gave the place to her son, Benjamin, in 1793 and he sold it in 1801 to Johannes Van Wormer Van Vliet (born 1770, died 1847) and he and his son, John (born 1803, died 1897), occupied the house for much of the nineteenth century. Johannes Van Wormer Van Vliet was a great-grandson of Gerret Adrians Van Vliet (born 1649, died 1723), who moved from Esopus to Fishkill before 1714, when his name was included in the first census of Dutchess.

House of Johannes Coerte Van Voorhees
Formerly in the town of Fishkill, Dutchess County, New York
PLATE 144

Johannes Coerte Van Voorhees (born 1682, died 1757) of Flatlands, Long Island (a descendant of Steven Coerte Van Voorhees from the Province of Drenthe, Holland), bought of Philip Verplanck nearly three-thousand acres in Dutchess County in 1730, on which lands he settled and built the house shown in plate 144. At the time of the erection of this house there were but a few dwellings near it. Its location, described in terms of a later date, was one mile north of Fishkill Landing (now Beacon) on the river road, where it was standing in 1874 a few rods north of the residence of William Henry Van Voorhees. Since 1874 it has been razed.

The house consisted of one story with an open garret above, a cellar-kitchen beneath and a lean-to at the rear. Its two front doors were in keeping with an arrangement characteristic of the houses of the Dutch on Long Island, where Johannes

394

Coerte Van Voorhees grew up. The house of Peter Monfort of Sprout Creek, Dutchess County (page 355), also had two front doors and Peter Monfort, like Johannes Coerte Van Voorhees, came to Dutchess from Flatlands. The walls of the Van Voorhees house were covered with shingles, similar in shape to the shingles still to be seen on the house of Madam Brett (plate 111) and also similar to those on the house of Henry Livingston at Poughkeepsie (plate 128).

The Van Voorhees homestead was one of the dwellings fired upon by Vaughan in his raid up the Hudson in 1777. At the approach of the British fleet the members of the family then living in the house took refuge in the interior of Dutchess with the exception of the master of the house and one slave, Nanna. The latter remained and stayed in the cellar while the firing lasted. Nanna lived to tell stories of this time to Henry DuBois Bailey, who incorporated her reminiscences in his historical sketches of Fishkill.

The accompanying plate is reproduced with acknowledgements from a sketch in: *Ancestry of Major William Roe Van Voorhees* by Elias W. Van Voorhees, privately printed 1881.

House of Evert Van Wagenen

Town of Pleasant Valley, Dutchess County, New York

PLATE 145

About a mile south of Netherwood on the road to the village of Pleasant Valley is a building now used as a barn but which was altered for that purpose from its original domestic character as shown in plate 145. The land it is built on is part of a large purchase made in the Great Nine Partners Patent by Jan DeGraeff (Jean leComte) of Poughkeepsie. Jan DeGraeff died in 1734 and in 1739 the executors of his will conveyed to his daughter, Hester, and her husband, Nicholas Van Wagenen, two-hundred acres in Nine Partners on which the latter spent most of their married life and which tract was inherited by their sons, Nicholas and Gerret. To the original two-hundred acres an addition was made in 1767, when the executors and heirs of Jan DeGraeff conveyed one-hundred and six acres to Nicholas Van Wagenen. Nicholas, by his will (made in 1769 and proved in 1772), bequeathed the farm of one-hundred and six acres to his eldest son, Evert (born 1740), whose descendants in direct male line owned and occupied it until 1923. Evert Van Wagenen's grandson, Benjamin (born 1783), told his family that the house on the farm was built by Evert. If so, it dates from about 1767 but its crude construction suggests an earlier erection. Title to the land remained in the estate of Jan DeGraeff until 1767 and the deed to Nicholas Van Wagenen conveyed a house with the farm. Perhaps it was a tenant-house originally. The old photograph (plate 145), obtained through the courtesy of Harry T. Briggs of Poughkeepsie, shows a dwelling of two rooms and a half-story, each room having an entrance-door. In each gable is a chimney. The walls, still standing, are two feet thick.

Nicholas Van Wagenen (born 1713, died 1772), who married Hester DeGraeff, was a grandson of Jacob Aertsen Van Wagenen, whose house in Ulster County is shown in plate 100 and Nicholas's wife was a first cousin of Moses DeGraeff, whose house is listed at page 368.

House of Cornelius Van Wyck

Town of Fishkill, Dutchess County, New York

PLATE 146

The village of Fishkill in southern Dutchess occupies a small plateau on the north side of the *Vis Kil*. South of the stream is a broad low flat, extending from the stream to the base of the mountains, and on the flat in 1733 Cornelius Van Wyck of Hempstead, Long Island (born 1694, died 1761), purchased from Madam Brett some nine-hundred acres of land. Cornelius Van Wyck moved from Hempstead to this uncleared tract about 1735 and, by degrees, laid out and planted a farm, built a homestead and developed a valuable property out of what was a rough wilderness when he took possession. The *King's Highway* was in 1735 little more than a bridle-path or cart-track through the woods at this point but it ran athwart his land and, east of the road, a mile south of the site of the present village of Fishkill, he built a house that is still standing (plate 146) and in good condition.

The house consists of two units, a larger main portion and a smaller east wing, and there can be little doubt but that the wing was built first as the temporary home of the pioneer and that the larger unit was built afterward, when living conditions were less strenuous. It is not known of what materials the walls of the wing consist but the interior finish is primitive; there is a massive early stone chimney and large fireplace (now closed) in the one large room; and the panelled door leading from the larger room to the smaller one at the back is similar in design to the doors in the house of John Brinckerhoff (plate 114), which are assumed to date from the erection of that house in 1738.

The larger portion of the house of Cornelius Van Wyck is built of a brick-filled frame. Originally the exterior was covered with shingles, a fact to be noted in connection with the shingles on the Brett, Livingston and Van Voorhees houses (plates 111, 128, 144); the floor-plan was that of a wide central hall, with two rooms at each side (those to the south larger than those to the north); and on the east wall of the larger east room there still remains panelling in the style of the middle of the eighteenth century. The height of the ceilings in this house is notable, as was the case with those in the house built in 1738 by John Brinckerhoff (plate 114).

When Cornelius Van Wyck made his will in 1757 he provided for his wife,

Hannah (Thorne) Van Wyck (born 1700, died 1771), the use of "the large west room" in his dwelling-house with the "adjoining little room," with furniture, "a chair and chairhorse," and a "negro wench," which reference in 1757 to the large west room pushes the construction of the main house back of that date.

After Cornelius Van Wyck's death in 1761 his house passed to his son, Cornelius Van Wyck, Jr. (born 1732, died 1767), who had married in 1752 Aeltje Brinckerhoff and with whom his mother, Hannah, made her home after 1761. Cornelius Van Wyck, Jr., died in 1767 and his mother in 1771 and there was an interval when the property was held for minor heirs. Ultimately, the farm was divided between two sons of Cornelius, Jr.: Isaac (born 1755, died 1811) and Cornelius C. (born 1763, died 1832). Isaac received the original dwelling and Cornelius C. built about 1790 a new house, closely resembling the first one, which still stands a short distance north of the first.

Isaac Van Wyck is reported by family tradition to have "liked style." He owned a large yellow coach, which carried a negro coachman and footman, and when he was a member of the legislature in 1794, 1796, 1810 and 1811 he made his journeys to and from the sessions in this imposing conveyance. To him therefore can safely be attributed the decorations given the homestead which unmistakably belong to the period between 1790 and 1810. The changes then made in the house were numerous and included a new mantel in the large west room (carved in Adam design); a new and graceful stairway, which is a duplicate of the stairway in the house (plate 138) built by General Jacobus Swartwout about 1790; new doors at the front and rear of the hall; a leaded design above the doors; new window-glass and shutters and exterior cornices; clapboards in place of shingles and perhaps also the present south porch. In late years other changes have been made but they are obvious when the house is visited and need not be listed.

From Isaac Van Wyck the property passed to his son, Isaac I. (born 1792, died 1862), and then to his grandson, Sidney E. Van Wyck, who died unmarried. It is now owned by Miss S. J. Hustis, who bought from the heirs of Sidney E. Van Wyck, so since 1733 the title has been held in but two family names.

Aside from its primary character as an important early home, the house of Cornelius Van Wyck has much of general interest attached to it in fact and in fiction. In actual fact Continental officers used the house as an headquarters as they came and went in the vicinity of Fishkill during the Revolutionary War; soldiers of the Continental troops camped on the farm, north of the house; and part of the lumber from the barracks of the soldiers is said to be incorporated in the house built about 1790 by Cornelius C. Van Wyck. Army rubbish has frequently been ploughed up from the site of the camp. In fiction the Van Wyck house is the scene of the action in James Fenimore Cooper's novel: *The Spy*, where it is called the Wharton house.

By the marriage of Cornelius Van Wyck's daughter, Margaret, to Francis Rom-

397

bout Brett (Madam Brett's son) and that of his grandson, Isaac, to Sarah Brett (a daughter of Madam Brett's son, Robert) the Van Wyck homestead and the Brett house (plate 111) were closely drawn together. Family ties also link the Van Wyck house with the house of John Brinckerhoff (plate 114) and with the several Van Wyck homes referred to on succeeding pages.

House of Theodorus Van Wyck

Town of East Fishkill, Dutchess County, New York

At the base of the Fishkill mountains in the town of East Fishkill there is an arable flat called Fishkill Hook, a name which is a hybrid form of *Vis Kil Hoeck* (Fish Creek Corner). This descriptive term arises from the fact that the flat is bounded by the creek at the north and by the mountains at the south and puts in at a "corner" between the hills that resembles a bay or a cove in a shore-line. On the broad open flat is the hamlet of Wiccopee (formerly Johnsville) and east of Wiccopee, south of the highway, stands part of a house that was built in the middle of the eighteenth century by Theodorus Van Wyck.

Theodorus Van Wyck of Hempstead, Long Island (born 1697, died 1776), a brother of Cornelius Van Wyck who settled near the village of Fishkill, bought nine-hundred acres near Wiccopee in 1736 and soon after settled his family on his purchase. At the time of his arrival in Dutchess his land was uncleared and he undoubtedly housed his family at first in a temporary structure. His permanent dwelling, erected at the earliest practicable date, perhaps in the 1740's, was one of the frame houses characteristic of the mid-eighteenth century in southern Dutchess. It was one and one-half stories in height, with a roof of single slant; had two chimneys and, through the center, a hall; it faced south and there was a wing at the west end. In 1870 James Van Wyck carried up the walls to two full stories. As the house now stands the foundations and the walls of the first story are understood to be those of the first house and the wing also is believed to be original but the general appearance of the house now is that of a nineteenth century structure. It is, however, desirable to record here its existence and location, altered though it is, for reasons other than architectural.

The builder of the house, Theodorus Van Wyck, was the father of twelve children, of whom seven lived to maturity, and who, before the War of the Revolution, went out from the home at Wiccopee to become influental heads of families themselves. A son, Dr. Theodorus Van Wyck, Jr., is accounted for in connection with the house of his father-in-law, John Brinckerhoff (plate 114). A daughter, Mary (Mrs. Platt), lived in the house on the Wappingers Creek (plate 131). Another, Aeltje, was the wife of Colonel John Bailey of Poughkeepsie, the mother of Theodorus Bailey (a Senator of the United States) and the mother-in-law of James Kent (Chancellor

398

of the State of New York). Elizabeth Van Wyck married the Reverend Chauncey Graham (Yale, 1747), pastor of the Rombout Presbyterian Church, while Margaret and Letitia married Gores and Isaac Adriance of Upper Hopewell and mothered many descendants.

Just before the tide of war swept into southern Dutchess Theodorus Van Wyck died but not until he had served as a delegate from the county to the second Provincial Congress in New York City. Shortly after his death, an arrangement was made with his widow and heirs by John Jay of Westchester County for the removal of Mr. Jay's family from Westchester to Dutchess for safety, in view of the occupation of New York City by the British, and from 1776 to 1781 the house at Wiccopee was a haven for Mr. Jay's elderly parents, his children and his brother. The house remained in the Van Wyck family until recent years and is now owned by a farmer named Ericson. A short distance north and east of it and nearer the highway is a house built about 1800 by Abraham Van Wyck, a grandson of Theodorus, which is a fine example of the work of the early Republic and which is still occupied by descendants of the builder.

House of Cornelius R. Van Wyck
Town of East Fishkill, Dutchess County, New York
PLATE 147

Richard Van Wyck (born 1729, died 1810), son of Cornelius Van Wyck whose house is shown in plate 146, married in 1749 Barbara Van Voorhees (whose grandfather's house is shown in plate 144) and moved from the homestead farm (south of the village of Fishkill, on the *King's Highway*) to a point six miles to the northeast, where, now, is the railroad-town of Hopewell Junction. On the main county road that runs from Hopewell to the river Richard Van Wyck built a house that was a copy of his father's on a reduced scale. A photograph of it occurs at page seventy-four of *The Van Wyck Family* which, although an indistinct print, records it as having been one of the houses of a story and a half, familiar in the eighteenth century, and the text of the family history refers to the fact that the late clapboards were preceded by shingles (as was the case with the house of Cornelius Van Wyck). In the nineteenth century the walls of the house of Richard Van Wyck were raised to two full stories and other changes made so that while the house still stands it is not typical of the eighteenth century in its present appearance and it is possible only to note what its original structural lines were.

Major Richard Van Wyck owned many broad acres in the vicinity of the present Hopewell Junction and out of his estate he set off a farm for his son, Cornelius R. Van Wyck (born 1753, died 1820), whose house is shown in plate 147. The house stands a scant half-mile westward from that of Major Richard Van Wyck, on the north side of the road to the river.

Cornelius R. Van Wyck, a captain in the Revolution, was twice married: first, in 1777, to Anna Duryea; and second, in 1792, to Magdalena Monfort (a daughter of Peter Monfort of the Sprout Creek, page 354). Although by tradition his house was built just at the close of the Revolution and may thus be dated as of approximately 1785, it is on lines typical of the pre-war period. It is a story and a half in height with a gambrel roof. On the first floor are four rooms and a central hall. The staircase is enclosed in the mid-eighteenth century manner. The front door and doorframe, the back door, door in kitchen-wing and a chimney-breast in the rear east room are all mid-eighteenth century in design, as is also much of the hardware. The panelled shutters are original and probably the window-sashes but a porch and dormer of the nineteenth century mar the south front. Behind the house are original frame outbuildings and stone smokehouse and to the east, a little way up the road, is the family burial-ground of the Van Wycks, enclosed by a stone wall.

From Captain Cornelius R. Van Wyck his house was inherited by his son, Peter Monfort Van Wyck (born 1795, died 1854), who married in 1826 Eliza M. Storm, and it passed from him to his unmarried son and daughter, who died in 1905 and 1911, respectively. The present owner is Miss Esther Mulford. Captain Cornelius R. Van Wyck's second son, Richard C. (born 1783, died 1857), purchased in 1827 the house on the Sprout Creek that is shown in plate 149.

House of Gulian Verplanck, called *Mount Gulian*

Town of Fishkill, Dutchess County, New York

PLATE 148

At an uncertain date, between 1730 and 1750, Gulian Verplanck built a house near the shore of the Hudson in Rombout Precinct, Dutchess County, on land inherited by him from his grandfather, Gulian Verplanck, one of the the grantees of the Rombout Patent in 1685. The house is now owned by William E. Verplanck, a descendant of the grantee of 1685 and of the builder of the house. *Mount Gulian*, as the house is called, consists of two parts. The second part dates from 1804, when a wing was built to the north to accommodate a large family. The eighteenth century portion of the house has thick stone walls, stuccoed; a gambrel roof; early dormers and clapboarded gable. The floor-plan is the usual one of a central hall with two rooms at each side and the interior still retains some early trim. The house is approached by a long avenue and faces a circular drive, set with trees of great age and beauty. To the south and overlooking Newburgh Bay is a garden in which many a rare old plant blooms in profusion.

Interest attaches to *Mount Gulian* for the long ownership of the land by one family (from 1685 to today), for the house as an architectural type of the eighteenth century and for the furniture, portraits and documents, accumulated in it in the

400

course of the generations of occupation. The present owner of *Mount Gulian* has rendered valuable community-service in the conservation of the historical materials inherited by him and there are now few places in the Hudson valley where there is so vivid a tradition of the period of the Indian or so accurate a knowledge of land-grants and local history. Of general public moment is the fact that Baron von Steuben had his quarters at *Mount Gulian* for a time during the Revolution and that, at the close of the war, the officers of the Continental Army organized in the house the Society of the Cincinnati. A bronze tablet on the east front, placed by the Society of Colonial Dames, commemorates the latter event.

Verplanck-Van Wyck House

Town of East Fishkill, Dutchess County, New York

PLATE 149

About 1722 Gulian (William) Verplanck, one of the heirs to the Rombout Patent, inherited under the patent land along the Sprout Creek. On that land he settled, at the point where the main county-road that runs from Poughkeepsie to Hopewell crosses the Sprout. North of the road he built a dwelling, south of the road a mill, both on the west bank of the stream. The foundation of the house remains, supporting recent walls, and the third or fourth mill-building now occupies the original millsite.

Before his death in 1745 Gulian Verplanck had made his mill such a center for the farmers who lived in a wide radius around it that there was need to open a road from the mill to the river and to establish a landing on the shore of the Hudson for the shipment of produce. The road ran from Sprout Creek, through what is now Myers' Corners to *Middel Bosch* (now called Middlebush) and so on to the south side of the mouth of the Wappingers Creek, which lay within the Verplancks' share of the Rombout Patent. There a dock, storehouse, dwelling-house and small buildings were built (notes, plate 117) and named the Farmers' Landing, the road from the mill being known throughout the eighteenth century as the Farmers' Landing Road.

From the death of Gulian Verplanck until after the majority of his nephew, Philip Verplanck, Jr., in 1757, the mill and the landing were run, supposedly, by agents but in his early manhood Philip Verplanck Jr. (son of Philip and Gertrude Van Cortlandt Verplanck of Van Cortlandt Manor), went into residence on the Sprout Creek and conducted the business of the mill. In 1764 he married Aefje, daughter of Gerard Beekman, and in 1768 built the house shown in plate 149 on the east side of the creek. The house was inherited by his son, William Beekman Verplanck, whose heirs sold it in 1827 to Richard C. Van Wyck (see: notes on plate 147). Colonel Van Wyck's great-granddaughter, Susan Varick Van Wyck, wife of

Edward B. Stringham, now owns and occupies it, and the mill is known as String-ham's Mill.

This house is one of the most delightful survivals of the eighteenth century now left in Dutchess. No historic event is known of in connection with it. No tales of famous guests are told of it. It is simply a well preserved example of a gentleman's home in the pre-Revolutionary period and, as such, is possessed of definite interest.

The Verplanck-Van Wyck house is built of brick, laid in Flemish bond, except for the rear wall, which is of rough stone. In the west gable black bricks outline the date: 1768, in figures two feet high. The house is one and one-half stories, with a gambrel roof; the roof is surrounded by a balustrade which should be compared in date with the balustrades of *Vly House* and *Cherry Hill* (plates 21 and 50) and of *The Pastures* of Philip Schuyler (page 97). Early dormers, front and rear, have (all but one) been cut down in late years to make it possible to look out of them from the second story rooms, which action made for comfort, but had unfortunate effect, architecturally, upon the front façade. The front porch is mid-nineteenth century. The photograph of the house, shown in plate 149, was made from the west to record the roof-line, the distinctive feature of the structure.

The main entrance of the Verplanck-Van Wyck house is noteworthy. A panelled and divided door, hung on iron strap-hinges, has a large brass knocker and two large bull's eyes, oval in shape and set aslant. The door-frame is carved in Georgian detail. The doorway leads into a central hall, wainscoted, having a carved arch across the center and an enclosed staircase at the right rear. West of the hall one large room has been made out of the original three (one at the front and two at the rear); east of it the original two rooms are unchanged. Only one of the original mantels of wood (that in the rear east room) remains.

House of Pieter Viele

Formerly at Poughkeepsie, New York

A little way beyond the northern boundary line of the city of Poughkeepsie, on the west side of the *King's Highway* and about opposite the present north gate of St. Francis' Hospital, there stood until 1918 (when it burned down) a house which was built in 1713 by Pieter Viele. The site of the house is part of a large tract that was purchased in 1706 by Pieter Viele of Albany County from Myndert Harmense Van Den Bogaerdt. Viele married Anna Van Den Bogaerdt (a daughter of Myndert Harmense), and their son, Myndert Viele, and his descendants occupied the house until after the Revolution.

In construction, the house of Pieter Viele was distinctly that of a pioneer's dwelling. The walls were made of a framework of staves, filled with mud, and were two feet thick; they were sided with broad boards and fastened by large iron nails

402

with flat heads. That the house was built in 1713 is learned from a marked stone (plate 7) in its foundation, which was saved when the house burned by the last owner, Mrs. J. A. Tolland, and by her presented to the Poughkeepsie chapter of the Daughters of the American Revolution.

The Viele house consisted of two rooms, with a hall between them, a half-story above and a chimney in each gable-end. There was a kitchen-wing at the west, in which was a stone and brick fireplace (containing a crane); the opening of the fireplace was very wide and a Dutch oven projected from the exterior west wall. Oak floor-boards in the house were ten inches in width. A frame wing was at some late date added to the north end of the house.

Westervelt House
Town of Poughkeepsie, Dutchess County, New York
PLATE 150

Kasparus Westervelt, baptized at Hackensack, New Jersey, in 1694, bought in 1744 a large tract of land in Poughkeepsie Precinct, Dutchess County, New York, to which he removed with his family. Members of his family ultimately built several houses on their lands in Poughkeepsie, the one shown in plate 150 being understood to be the first and the dwelling of Kasparus, himself. The house therefore dates presumably from soon after 1744, when the land was purchased, and remains today, uncompromisingly severe in appearance, a witness to living conditions in Dutchess as experienced by many of the Dutch families that migrated from New Jersey and Long Island in the 1740's. It is to be noted that Kasparus Westervelt abandoned the type of roof with which he was familiar in northern New Jersey (in which a shallow curved line extends beyond the eaves) for the straight roof common in early Ulster and Dutchess. His house (now the property of Richard Milbank) stands on the south side of the Speckenkill Road in the town of Poughkeepsie. The central hall has one room either side of it, with very plain wood-trim. The porch-hood is eighteenth century (in design at least) and so also is the inset doorway. At the rear is a modern frame wing.

PLATE III

House of Madam Brett,

(now called the Teller Homestead), Beacon, N. Y. One of the landmarks of southern Dutchess. The walls are said to date from the first quarter of the eighteenth century. The shingles are notable and, if not as old as the walls, are still of early date. Roof, dormers, porch and windows are all probably of the first years of the nineteenth century. Tradition, sentiment and long occupation by one family-line invest the house with particular interest.

PLATE 112

The Brewer-Mesier house,

Wappingers Falls, N. Y. Built by Nicholas Brewer, but for a century the home of the Mesier family. The village of Wappingers Falls now holds it and the grounds surrounding it as: Mesier Park. The house retains original structural lines and many early interior details. It illustrates the way in which a large house was sometimes added to a smaller one, as does also the Conyn-Van Rensselaer house, plate 20. In this case the primitive rear wing probably dates from the 1740's and the front portion from the 1750's or 1760's. The slate roof is recent and the exterior wood-trim was added in the nineteenth century. In 1777 the house was the scene of a " teaparty ", when the war-price of tea was the occasion for disputes and violence.

406

PLATE 113

House of Derick Brinckerhoff,

Brinckerhoff, N. Y., as it was in the 1770's and until about 1830. Although standing, the house is now covered by a Mansard roof and has been shorn of the west wing. As a dwelling with a gambrel roof the house was characteristic of the third quarter of the eighteenth century in Dutchess. The plate is reproduced with acknowledgements from a sketch in: *The Family of Joris Dircksen Brinckerhoff* by T. Van Wyck Brinckerhoff. During the weeks of a serious illness the Marquis de La Fayette was a guest in this house. His host, Derick Brinckerhoff, was colonel of a county regiment and a member of the New York assembly.

PLATE 114

House of John Brinckerhoff.

In the west gable of the house of John Brinckerhoff, near Swartwoutville, Dutchess County, black bricks, inlaid among the red, outline the figures: 1 7 3 8. The house illustrates a transition in domestic architecture: its stone walls reflect the houses of the first settlers; but in the height of its ceilings and in its wood trim it shows the progres and development of the mid-eighteenth century. For materials, size and floor-plan it should be compared with the Van Cortlandt manor house at Croton (plate 109), as the latter was when occupied about 1749 by Pierre Van Cortlandt. While the Continental Army was centered at Fishkill, Washington was John Brinckerhoff's guest in this house for some time.

PLATE 115

House of Abraham DePeyster,

Beacon, N. Y. The house occupies a site on the north side of the *Vis Kil,* near the junction of the stream with the Hudson, which is one of much natural beauty, but which in recent years has been marred by a factory, a railroad and brickyard. The gambrel roof on the house points to the third quarter of the eighteenth century in Dutchess, and the brick used for gable-ends and to face the front wall witness to the same period. The front and rear walls are of stone, the material characteristic of the first half of the eighteenth century. Comparison of the relation of the front door to the ground should be made with the entrances to the Coeymans, Van Wie and Van Cortlandt houses (plates 18, 54 and 109).

PLATE 116

House of John De Witt.

The rear (south) wing of the De Witt homestead in the town of Clinton, Dutchess County, was built about 1773 by John De Witt, who a few years later added the larger house toward the north, of which a portion, only, shows in the plate. Across the road from this house stands the mill that John De Witt erected at the same time as his dwelling, and the house and mill, together, at a four-corners, were long an important center in Dutchess County. In 1788 John De Witt was a delegate to the constitutional convention of the state of New York, held at Pough-keepsie, in which he voted in favor of the ratification of the Constitution of the United States.

PLATE 117

House at the Farmers' Landing.

This eighteenth century stone house in the town of Wappinger, Dutchess County, stands close to the shore of the Hudson (which shows at the left of the plate). It is a survival of a group of buildings which, with a dock, constituted the Farmers' Landing from approximately 1750 to 1810. The floor-plan of the house (two rooms, each having an outer door) is characteristic of its period, and the details of doors, windows, and interior finish all are primitive.

PLATE 118

House of Johannes A. Fort.

By the addition of dormers, porch and a south wing, the Fort house, town of Poughkeepsie, Dutchess County, has lost the general appearance it had when erected. But in structural lines, in materials and in many minor details it well illustrates eighteenth century design and work.

PLATE 119

House of John Frear,

town of Poughkeepsie, Dutchess County. Built about 1755 of stone. Later crude, mud-filled frame walls replaced part of the original stone-work (as happened also to the Brink house in Ulster County, page 186). The veranda, dormers and slatted blinds date from the nineteenth century. John Frear, who first owned the house, was colonel of the Poughkeepsie regiment of militia in the War of the Revolution.

PLATE 120

House on the Garrison Farm.

The Dutch oven in the east end of the house on the Garrison farm, town of Clinton, Dutchess County, is a particularly good survival. Three typical fences are recorded in the plate: one of boards, one of pickets and a stone wall with rails. The surroundings of this modest farmhouse are such as were characteristic of the countryside in its primitive days.

PLATE 121

House of Benjamin Hasbrouck,

town of East Fishkill, Dutchess County. Built in 1753 and plain in finish, it has escaped modern improvements and still possesses primitive features.

PLATE 122

House of David Johnstone,

called *Lithgow,* town of Washington, Dutchess County. Built about 1758 and a notably handsome house for its time and location. The triple pitch of the roof is exceptional. In the height of the ceilings of the first floor rooms and in floor-plan and wood-trim *Lithgow* reflects the sophisticated standard of living of the city-bred man who built it, and for more than a century and a half it has been continuously maintained upon the same high plane. *Lithgow* is one of the outstanding survivals of the Hudson valley.

416

PLATE 123

In the eighteenth century the course of the *King's Highway* in Dutchess County was marked by small dwellings built of stone. The house shown above, an example of the type, stands on the west side of the road in the town of Rhinebeck.

PLATE 124

As a companion to plate 123, plate 124 illustrates the farmhouses which stood along the *King's Highway* in Dutchess before the Revolution. This house also is on the west side of the road in the town of Rhinebeck.

PLATE 125

House at Kipsbergen.

The southern (right) end of the house here shown was built in 1701 by Hendrick Kip at *Kipsbergen*, Dutchess County. The central and northern portions were additions, made probably in the eighteenth century, while roofs, doors, windows and shutters were alterations of still later date. In recent years the house was burned, and only ruined walls are now standing. The plate was made from a photograph obtained through the courtesy of Mrs. Theodore de Laporte of Rhinebeck, N. Y. The property is variously known as the Kip and Beekman and Heermance house.

PLATE 126

The house of Abraham Kip at Kipsbergen,

town of Rhinebeck, Dutchess County, was built in two parts, the eastern (right) end being an addition to an original small structure. It stands near the Hudson (to be seen at the left of the plate) and was used in the eighteenth century as a tavern. In front of the house the road is a bit of the Sepasco Trail of the Indians, leading east to the present village of Rhinebeck and west to the site of the former Long Dock (which was a prosperous shipping center for many years).

420

PLATE 127

House of Hendrick Kip,

town of Fishkill, Dutchess County. It is possible that the walls of the east (left) end represent the house of James Hussey, who owned the farm 1720—1736. The main part of the house (with a porch in the center) was built in 1753 by Hendrick Kip. During the Revolution Baron von Steuben is said by tradition to have occupied the house for a time. The front door is of the early nineteenth century.

PLATE 128

House of Henry Livingston,

town of Poughkeepsie, Dutchess County. A valuable illustration of the principle of growth as opposed to that of design in house-building. The east (right) end was built before 1738; the main portion in the middle of the eighteenth century; in the nineteenth century additions and alterations were numerous. In 1910 the house was torn down. The plate was made from a photograph taken in 1886 by Henry Booth of Poughkeepsie, N. Y., and obtained through his courtesy.

422

PLATE 129

The Newcomb house,

town of Pleasant Valley, Dutchess County, was built about 1777, is owned and occupied by a descendant of the builder, and its original features are maintained with care. The front façade, two stories high with double file of windows, is Georgian in style and reflects an architectural trend evident in the Hudson valley in the third quarter of the eighteenth century. Its gambrel roof relates the house to the dwellings built by Dutch families in Albany County at the same period.

PLATE 130

The house called Old Hundred,

which is at New Hackensack, Dutchess County, has had no connection with the Dutch in ownership; but in design it shows Dutch influence. Inside, it still contains many original details of interest.

PLATE 131

The Palen-Platt house,

town of Poughkeepsie, Dutchess County, was built in two parts: the first by Gysbert Peelen about 1735 and the second by Zephaniah Platt (probably in the 1760's). The plate records the northwest corner of the part built by Colonel Platt. The masonry, the windows, the shutters, the lilac bush all convey a suggestion of the atmosphere of an eighteenth century house. Surrounded by old trees, the house overlooks the meadow-flats along the Wappingers Creek.

PLATE 132

House of John Pawling.

Built in 1761 and burned about 1899 the house of John Pawling, here shown, stood on the *King's Highway* in the town of Hyde Park, Dutchess County. The builder was a grandson of Henry Pawling of Ulster County, whose house in shown in plate 82. Plate 132 was made from a photograph obtained through the courtesy of Starr Institute, Rhinebeck, New York.

PLATE 133

The Southard house,

town of Fishkill, Dutchess County, is a well-known landmark in southern Dutchess. It was built about 1766, retains many original features, and in general character reflects the spirit of Dutch construction.

427

PLATE 134

The brick house,

built about 1800 by John Storm in the town of East Fishkill, Dutchess County, is an example of the work of the period of the Early Republic. It is introduced here in order to record the site of the house that was built in the middle of the eighteenth century by John Storm's father. The latter, Garret Storm, was one of the first settlers in the neighborhood of Stormville and the ancestor of a prominent and influential Dutch family.

PLATE 135

Storm-Adriance-Brinckerhoff House.

This house at Upper Hopewell, town of East Fishkill, Dutchess County, was the home during the Revolution of Captain Thomas Storm. The large east end was probably built about 1771, the center and small wing still earlier. Since 1795 the property has been held in the Brinckerhoff family. As a neighborhood, Hopewell was almost wholly Dutch in settlement, and the Storm, Adriance and Brinckerhoff families were numerous and influential.

429

PLATE 136

House of William Stoutenburgh.

In materials, measurements and plan the house of William Stoutenburgh at East Park, town of Hyde Park, Dutchess County, built in 1750, is typical of the stone houses of that day. It has lost, unfortunately, its original door and porch and shutters and other details of finish.

PLATE 137

The house at Hyde Park,

Dutchess County, shown in the plate, was built either by the Berghs or the Stoutenburghs at a date not certainly known. Gambrel roofs were in use in Dutchess just before the Revolution; but in the masonry of its walls there is a hint that this house was built at a post-war date, although in pre-war style.

431

PLATE 138

Second House of Jacobus Swartwout.

The house erected about 1789 by Jacobus Swartwout at Swartwoutville, Dutchess County, is one of the characteristic frame dwellings, a story and a half in height, which were built in Dutchess before and after the Revolution. The porch, windows and blinds are of the nineteenth century; but several interior details are excellent early items. The meadow-flat (bordering the course of the Sprout Creek) and the stone wall adjacent to the house create a setting reminiscent of the farm-homes of the eighteenth century.

PLATE 139

The house of John Teller,

in the town of Clinton, Dutchess County, was built about 1764, when the owner married Margaret Stoutenburgh. Its stone walls have been covered with stucco, not much remains of original wood-trim, and the place is now in decay. But it was once the home of people prominent in the community and widely connected by kinship throughout the Hudson valley.

PLATE 140

Unidentified House.

Near the boundary-line of the corporation of the city of Poughkeepsie is this house, the erection of which is tentatively credited either to Barent Kip, between 1753 and 1760, or to Lawrence Van Kleeck, Jr., between 1761 and 1768. Although the porch is nineteenth century and the window-panes recent, the house is essentially a primitive.

PLATE 141

House of Matthew Van Keuren.

Only the stone walls of the first story of this house can be credited to Matthew Van Keuren between 1729 and 1742; but this particular spot on the bank of the Hudson is the site of a mill, a forge and a ferry which, with the house, were raided by the British in 1777. Although the roof has been raised and the upper part of the house re-sided, the interior retains much of its original appearance.

PLATE 142

House of Baltus Barents Van Kleeck,

one of the first settlers of Poughkeepsie, N. Y. The house was built in 1702 and torn down in 1835. Just before the building was razed a sketch was made of it by Benson J. Lossing. The sketch was published in 1838 in the *Family Magazine*, from which it is here reproduced with acknowledgements. All other extant pictures of the house are based on this one. During the five years that Poughkeepsie was the capital of the state of New York the Van Kleeck house was used as a tavern. As a place of meeting for men in public life it should be compared with the Ten Broeck house at Kingston and the Van Deusen house at Hurley (plates 87 and 98).

436

PLATE 143

House of Cornelius Van Vliet,

town of Clinton, Dutchess County. Built 1783. Torn down 1875. The plate was made from a photograph obtained through the courtesy of George S. Van Vliet of Pleasant Plains, N. Y. It provides a record of a house which, although of post-Revolutionary construction, was in a design characteristic of Dutchess County in the period before the war.

437

PLATE 144

House of Johannes Coerte Van Voorhees.

In its frame-construction and its two front doors the house of Johannes Coerte Van Voorhees, formerly in the town of Fishkill, Dutchess County, reflected the owner's early association with Long Island. The porch-hood and side seats relate it to the Bronck, Coeymans, Coeymans-Bronck, DeWitt and Westervelt houses (plates 16, 18, 19, 69 and 150). The shingles that cover it are like those on the Brett and Livingston houses (plate 111 and 128.) The plate reproduces with acknowledgements a drawing in: *Ancestry of Major William Roe Van Voorhees,* published 1881 by Elias W. Van Voorhees.

438

PLATE 145

The Van Wagenen homestead

in the town of Clinton, Dutchess County, is still standing, but built over as a barn, and the plate here shown was
made from a photograph, obtained through the courtesy of Harry T. Briggs of Poughkeepsie, N. Y., which was
taken before the alteration was made. The house was one of the typical stone houses of the eighteenth century
in the Hudson river valley; with thick walls, one and one-half stories high, and windows of irregular size and
location. The two front doors link this stone house with that at the Farmers' Landing in the town of Wappinger,
Dutchess County (plate 117).

PLATE 146

The Van Wyck house

at Fishkill, N. Y., was the home of one family for about one-hundred and seventy-five years. The east wing was probably built earlier than the main portion. Several successive periods of design are illustrated by the interior and exterior wood-trim. During the Revolution the house was used by Continental officers and J. Fenimore Cooper made it the scene of his novel: *The Spy.*

PLATE 147

The house of Cornelius R. Van Wyck,

town of East Fishkill, Dutchess County, is an excellent example of the type of house, one and one-half stories in height, with gambrel roof, that was popular in the second half of the eighteenth century. Its wood-trim and hardware, as well as its structural lines, are in designs of the pre-Revolutionary period; but it is probable that the actual erection of the house occurred just after the war closed.

441

PLATE 148

The Verplanck house,

Beacon, N. Y., consists of two distinct parts: a southern unit, supposed to date from the 1740's, and a two-story wing at the north built in 1804. The older part is of stone, stuccoed, with clapboarded gable, and the gambrel roof that covers it must have been one of the first instances of that style of roof in Dutchess County. The dormers have particularly good lines, and the house retains many early details. Baron Von Steuben had quarters in it for a time, during the Revolution, and in the northwest room of the earlier part the Society of the Cincinnati was organized.

442

PLATE 149

The Verplanck-Van Wyck house,

town of East Fishkill, Dutchess County, stands close to the east bank of the Sprout Creek. The builder, Philip Verplanck, placed the date: 1768, in black bricks in this gable-end. From 1768 to 1827 the house was owned in the Verplanck family and from 1827 to the present in that of Van Wyck. It has lost some of its original details; but its brick walls, in good proportions, its gambrel roof and its roof-balustrade give it lasting distinction.

PLATE 150

The Westervelt house

in the town of Poughkeepsie, Dutchess County, has little beauty to recommend it; but in its masonry, its inset door and its crude window-frames it tells a plain story of pioneer construction. The porch-hood is in the same design as the hoods shown in plates 16, 18, 19, 69 and 144.

INDEX

445

KEY TO MAP-NUMBERS

Houses Located in Albany, Schenectady, Rensselaer, Greene and Columbia Counties

Houses Located in Ulster County

Houses Located in Westchester County

Houses Located in Dutchess County

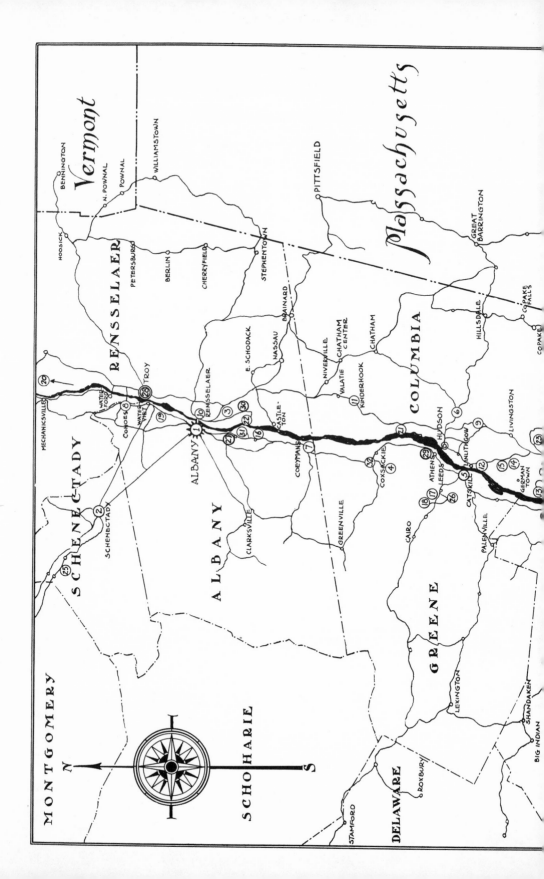

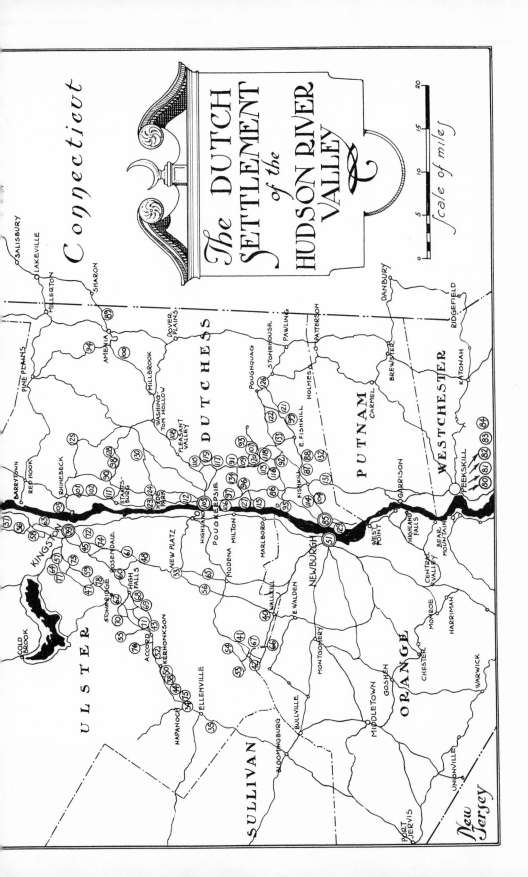